2250

YALE HISTORICAL PUBLICATIONS, MISCELLANY, 108

MILLENARIAN REBELLION IN CHINA

The Eight Trigrams Uprising of 1813

SUSAN NAQUIN

New Haven and London, Yale University Press
1976

Published under the direction of the Department
of History of Yale University with assistance
from the income of the Frederick John Kingsbury
Memorial Fund.

Library of Congress catalog card number: 75–18180
International standard book number: 0–300–01893–2

Designed by John O.C. McCrillis
and set in Baskerville type.
Printed in the United States of America by
The Murray Printing Company, Westford, Massachusetts.

Published in Great Britain, Europe, Africa, and Asia
(except Japan) by Yale University Press, Ltd., London.
Distributed in Latin America by Kaiman & Polon, Inc.,
New York City; in Australia and New Zealand by Book & Film
Services, Artarmon, N.S.W., Australia; in Japan by John
Weatherhill, Inc., Tokyo.

For my parents, Howard and Mary Naquin

Contents

Maps

Acknowledgments

IT has been my very good fortune to have had Jonathan Spence as my teacher and adviser. This work has greatly benefited from his assistance, shrewd insights, and good judgment; his continuing enthusiasm for the Eight Trigrams has given me encouragement and much pleasure. He also taught me to care that this book be a good story and tried to show me how to make it one.

I should also like to express my appreciation to others who read in full or in part the Ph.D. dissertation on which this book is based and helped me improve it: Beatrice S. Bartlett, Hilary J. Beattie, Chuang Chi-fa, Roger V. DesForges, Joseph Fletcher, Daniel L. Overmyer, Frederic Wakeman, Jr., Arthur F. Wright, and Judy Metro of Yale University Press. Antony Marr and Hideo Kaneko of the East Asian Collection at Yale University and George E. Potter of the Harvard-Yenching Library have been very helpful for many years.

Daniel L. Overmyer, whose interest in White Lotus religion long antedates my own, has generously given me much valuable assistance, and it has been a pleasure to share his enthusiasm for the subject. I should also like to thank other friends in Taiwan who taught me about Chinese popular religion and showed it to me live and in action. I am particularly indebted to Parker Po-fei Huang of Yale University, who with much expertise and patience helped me understand Ch'ing texts, especially those dealing with religious practices, ideas, and symbolism.

The Ch'ing dynasty archives in the National Palace Museum in the Republic of China were invaluable to this study. I am most grateful to the director of the museum, Dr. Chiang Fu-ts'ung, and to the staff of the Books and Documents Department for allowing me access to these materials and for all their kind assistance. It was Beatrice S. Bartlett who first called the 1813 palace attack to my attention, and her knowledge of and assistance with the Chia-ch'ing period materials in the National Palace Museum made my work there infinitely simpler and more pleasurable. I also wish to thank the American Association of University Women and the Yale Concilium on International and Area Studies for the financial support that made it possible for me to go to Taiwan and use these archives.

To my family and friends who have been wondering what in the world I have been doing all these years, it is a pleasure to say *voilà*.

S.N.

New Haven, Connecticut
May 1975

Millenarian Rebellion in China

Introduction

IN the autumn of 1813 religious sects calling themselves the Eight Trigrams planned a rebellion that involved simultaneous uprisings in several cities of north China, including Peking. The members of these sects were converts to a three-hundred-year-old millenarian religion whose central deity was known as the Eternal and Venerable Mother. The rebellion, sect leaders promised, was destined to bring about the fall of the reigning Ch'ing dynasty and the inauguration of a new era of "endless blessings." The uprisings took place as planned but were imperfectly coordinated. An attempt to seize the Forbidden City in Peking was quickly thwarted, and government troops were immediately dispatched to restore order in the provinces. The rebels were eventually besieged in a single city in northern Honan province, and after three months of fighting, the city was taken and the rebellion of the Eight Trigrams brought to an end.

This rebellion has been known to historians under a variety of names, and the confusion reflects the fact that it has been studied only in a peripheral way. Although unusually rich primary source material is available, there is no monograph on this subject in Chinese, Japanese, or a Western language.[1] Peasant movements and popular religion in China have not always been favored subjects for research, and in recent writings the 1813 uprising has been overshadowed by the major rebellions of the mid-nineteenth century (those of the Taiping, the Nien, and the Muslims) that had palpable effects on the imperial order and the course of modern Chinese history. Furthermore, these events of 1813 have been caught in the no-man's-land of the late middle Ch'ing, too early for "modern" Chinese history (usually considered to begin in 1840) and too late for "early" Ch'ing history (which presently extends to the late 1700s). Nevertheless, the Eight Trigrams rebellion was the last uprising in north China that posed a real threat to the government in the period prior to the Opium War (1840) and the subsequent penetration of the Western world into China. It occurred at a time when China was allegedly in decline, its armies incompetent, its officials corrupt, and its coffers empty; yet these rebels were suppressed by the Ch'ing government with apparent speed and efficiency. Sufficiently well-organized and long-lived to have shaken the emperor and required several months to put down and yet small enough to have remained close to its original organization and intentions, this rebellion provides an excellent opportunity to study the phenomenon of the traditional peasant rebellion in China.

It is perhaps even more important that the Eight Trigrams uprising was typical of those regular outbursts of peasant protest that occurred in north China during the Ch'ing dynasty (1644–1911) and that were expressed through the organization of a religious sect and a millenarian ideology. The phenomenon of the religiously inspired peasant rebellion, although common in China during the Ch'ing, has been neglected by Western historians. A multiplicity of names for rebel and religious groups appearing again and again in the historical record has obscured the nature of this millenarian religion. Religious sects have been lumped together with criminal gangs of many sorts and collectively described as "secret societies" and dissenters from the established order. Some historians have postulated a geographic difference between such organizations, but the debate over the possible distinctions between those in the north of China and those in the south has continued without being clearly resolved and without further illuminating the problem.[2] Seeing similarities among the northern, seemingly more religious, secret societies, some historians have maintained that they were in fact all part of one long-lived cleverly camouflaged cabal called the "White Lotus Society."[3] A connection between the religious groups and the rebellions in which they were sometimes involved was perceived but not understood.

It is my contention that a careful study of this "White Lotus Society" reveals not a mysterious monolithic organization but small scattered groups of believers whose common religion had been transmitted since the sixteenth century through long and loose chains of teachers and disciples. Followers of this religion, normally concerned with private devotions, also anticipated a period of great cataclysms when they would cast aside their ordinary lives and, following the deity sent to lead them, join together and rise up to usher in a new and perfect world in which all people found salvation through their faith and their faith alone. Practitioners of this discretely transmitted heretical religion could, when their leaders predicted that the millennium was imminent, be literally transformed into openly defiant rebels against the state and the established order. It was this millennial message perpetuated through a normally diffuse but potentially cohesive organization that made believer and rebel merely different phases of the same salvational process.

The Eight Trigrams rebellion of 1813 was one of many uprisings undertaken by these sects during their long history. Through this one example it is possible to see how scattered believers in a common religion were drawn together organizationally and persuaded to risk their lives and fortunes to bring about this heaven on earth. Furthermore, the ideas and organization of this rebellion can provide a yardstick with which later uprisings, influenced by modern Western civilization, can be compared and their new or traditional ingredients clarified and appreciated. These comparisons should affect our understanding of the Boxer uprising of 1900, which was generated by this White Lotus religion; of the Taiping rebellion (1850–65), which was not; and of the Chinese Communists, whose relation to this millenarian tradition has not yet been studied.

The suppression of the Eight Trigrams was deemed of sufficient importance by the Ch'ing government to warrant the assemblage and publication of all essential official documents relating to the rebellion. This eight-volume collection and the many other more detailed documents preserved in the archives of the National Palace Museum in Taiwan provide an enormous wealth of information about these religious sects, their short-lived uprising, and particularly the rebels and would-be rebels themselves. For the most part, government documents describe rebellion through the eyes of its official enemies; the near monopoly on record-keeping by the ruling class assured that all rebellions were so filtered and refined for future generations. The Eight Trigrams uprising is an especially exciting event to study because within the official account are many colloquial descriptions of the rebellion by the men who planned and organized it.

It was standard procedure for Ch'ing officials at all levels to interrogate prisoners before sentencing them and to report these interrogations in writing to their superiors. This policy was implemented with special diligence and at the highest levels in the case of the 1813 rebellion because the reigning Chia-ch'ing Emperor (1796–1820) felt the attack on the Forbidden City to have been an affront to him personally, and because the existence of this dangerous group so near the throne was considered intolerable. Captured rebels were questioned in detail about the nature and extent of their involvement in a religious sect and in the rebellion, and arrests and interrogations continued for at least five years. More than four hundred such confessions have survived, and though they are not always reliable on minor points,[4] they contain a wealth of the kind of information and detail that has been unavailable for the history of most popular uprisings in China.

This study is divided into four parts and begins with an examination of the millenarian religion which during the Ch'ing dynasty inspired periodic rebellions such as that of the Eight Trigrams. Parts Two, Three, and Four focus on the 1813 uprising itself and describe the original Eight Trigram sects and their reorganization under dynamic leadership, the transformation of these believers into rebels against the state, and finally their unsuccessful attempt to defeat government armies in battle.

PART ONE

Inspiration: The Organization and Ideology of White Lotus Sects

IN 1813 members of certain previously uncoordinated and non-violent religious sects, convinced by prophecies contained in their religious literature, anticipated the imminent destruction of existing society and its replacement by a better world and joined together to bring about this change. Nearly eighty thousand people lost their lives in this unsuccessful attempt to destroy the Ch'ing government. While the great majority of rebel supporters could hint at the intensity of their discontent only by giving their lives, the others, the sect members who were both the leaders and the nucleus of the movement, could and did articulate their goals and aspirations. It was their visions of an apocalypse and utopia that gave birth to the rebellion and inspiration to those who died in its cause. Moreover, it was these several thousand sect members who planned the uprisings ahead of time, despite the watchful eye of the Ch'ing government, and then rallied more than one hundred thousand people to their cause. Arranging for uprisings in a dozen cities in three provinces was not an easy or haphazard undertaking, nor was assembling thousands of men to fight a government army a simple matter of ringing a gong and gathering a crowd. Such a rebellion might seem a prairie fire, struck by a single spark and burning everything in sight, but it was not. Finding, recruiting, and mobilizing men for an enterprise of this size and risk involved quietly creating and activating extensive but selective personal networks. Not everyone was interested, useful, trustworthy, or even available for this kind of endeavor. It was the institution of the religious sect that provided the organizational vehicle for initiating and sustaining this rebellion. In order to understand the Eight Trigrams rebellion, it is therefore necessary to examine first the organizational system and millennial vision that produced it.

The religion that inspired the Eight Trigrams uprising had its own beliefs and practices, literature, ritual, and organization. During the Ming and Ch'ing dynasties this religion was branded as heterodoxy and prohibited by law. In consequence, its ideas and practices were transmitted in simple fashion on an individual basis with little reliance on public institutions such as temples or clergy. The religion thus manifested itself as short-lived groups consisting of a senior teacher and all his pupils and their pupils. Each group would have its own name, would gather occasionally for small meetings in a private home, and might persist for one or more generations in any

7

one place. After the death of its senior teacher, a group often fragmented into smaller branches, some of which might take a different name. Not only were these groups separated in time and place from one another and often different in their specific practices, but they tried deliberately to be so. Each teacher sought to isolate and pass on the true system and set of practices that would bring salvation. Nevertheless, all drew on a common tradition, subscribed to a common core of beliefs, and based their teachings on scriptures particular to this religion.

Believers called this religion their *chiao* 教, "teaching." They also used this same word *chiao* to refer to the organization through which that teaching was perpetuated. Because of a regrettable lack of alternatives I have translated the organizational usage of the term *chiao* as "sect." In choosing a single name for this admittedly diverse popular religious teaching, I have—with even greater reluctance—followed traditional historians and called it the White Lotus religion.[1] There was, however, no single "White Lotus Society." There was only a diverse White Lotus religious teaching that found expression in sects calling themselves by a wide variety of names. The following section explains this matter more fully.

Most, perhaps all, of the elements of the White Lotus tradition existed prior to the Ch'ing dynasty and were deeply rooted in China's past. This fact and the occasional use of the name White Lotus by both religious and rebellious groups since the Sung dynasty[2] have obscured the relatively late genesis of this sectarian religion. In fact, the various components do not appear to have crystallized into this distinctive religious tradition until the middle of the sixteenth century. It was during this period that the first references to the central deity of this religion, the Eternal and Venerable Mother, appear in the historical record, and most sect literature handed down to believers for centuries afterward dates from the late sixteenth century.[3] Many sects place their own founding in the late Ming period, and it is at this time that frequent reports of sect activity of this type are recorded by historians.[4]

Although it is not clear how or why this religion took shape, its ideas and practices are somewhat more accessible. Little research has been done on this subject, however, and such information as does exist is widely scattered and of very uneven quality. What follows in Part One is therefore only a patchwork with many of the pieces still missing. I have relied primarily on information found in Ch'ing documents for the years 1812 through 1820 (by the Chinese calendar

Chia-ch'ing 17 through 25) and supplemented this with material from the religious literature of these sects dating from the 1830s (some of which has been preserved),[5] and to a lesser extent with primary and secondary source material on nineteenth- and twentieth-century sects.

COSMOLOGY AND HISTORY

The central deity of these sects was a powerful mother goddess who, though she became an object of sectarian worship in the sixteenth century, had antecedents in Chinese popular religion from earliest times. By the first century B.C. a deity known as *Hsi-wang-mu* 西王母 (Mother Ruler of the West) had already become associated with millennial expectations.[6] White Lotus sects of the Ming and Ch'ing dynasties called her *Wu-sheng lao-mu* 無生老母, Eternal (literally, without birth or beyond rebirth) Venerable Mother. She was also known as *Wu-sheng fu-mu* 無生父母 (which I have rendered as Eternal Progenitor) or, more rarely, *Wu-sheng fo-mu* 無生佛母 (Eternal Buddha Mother).[7] Since the late nineteenth century she has been called by a variety of other names, including *Yao-ch'ih chin-mu* 瑤池金母 (Golden Mother of the Jade Pool), *Wang-mu niang-niang* 王母娘娘 (Empress Mother Ruler), and *Lao-sheng-mu* 老聖母 (Venerable Sagely Mother).[8]

The story of the Eternal Mother was to be found in the literature of her sects. There she was described as the progenitor of mankind: she had given birth to a son and daughter who had married and were in turn the ancestors of all men. She had sent mankind, her children, to the "Eastern world" to live on earth. To the Eternal Mother's great distress, her children soon "indulged in vanity and lost their original nature."[9] "All living beings were confused and lost in the red dust world; they had fallen and knew not how to return to their origin." The Eternal Mother, seeing her offspring in this state, was filled with sorrow. "[She] weeps as she thinks of her children. She has sent them many messages and letters [urging them] to return home and to stop devoting themselves solely to avarice in the sea of bitterness. [She calls them] to return to the Pure Land, to come back to Mount Ling, so that mother and children can meet again and sit together on the golden lotus."[10]

Sectarian literature combined this image of an aged mother, longing and weeping for her lost children, with a romantic vision of a

splendid paradise where both could be reunited. The Eternal
Mother wanted her children to return to their "primordial native
land," their "original home in the world of true emptiness" (*chen-
k'ung chia-hsiang* 真空家鄉), the spiritual paradise that mankind had
once left and where their mother still resided. On one level this
Original Home was the place where one's ancestors had lived and
where one's roots were, symbolizing for all believers what the ances-
tral village meant to every Chinese family. On another level, this
home meant the womb from which all were expelled at birth. "When
he ascends to the eternal realm," stated one scripture, "the child
sees his dear mother. When he enters the mother's womb, . . . he
eternally returns to peace and security." "When the child meets his
mother," said another, "he confirms that he is unborn (*wu-sheng* 無生)
and will not again turn in the wheel of transmigration." The Original
Home was a nirvana: "in contrast to a life of uncertainty and aimless
wandering, full of unending suffering, if one is able to ascend to the
Primordial Native Land, then for him, birth and death forever cease."
As a spiritual paradise, this Original Home in the World of True
Emptiness symbolized safety and security, stability, comfort, and
consummate dependence. It was also a splendid and luxurious place,
a paradise that incorporated many of the features of the Pure Land,
or Western Paradise, of popular Chinese Buddhism. The Eternal
Mother was said to live in a beautiful palace there, with "seven-
treasure pools and eight-virtue streams. The ground is made of yellow
gold, and bordered with golden ropes. There are buildings, terraces,
halls, and pavilions of great variety."[11]

Having described this paradise to which the Eternal Mother
longed to bring her children, the literature of these sects goes on to
explain how the Eternal Mother would, to this end, intervene in
human history. She would send down to earth gods and buddhas
who would teach a new system of values by means of which men
could find salvation and thus "come home." Because mankind was
"steeped in wickedness" the Eternal Mother had been compelled to
make repeated efforts to open this road to salvation. She had first
sent down the Lamp-lighting Buddha (*Jan-teng fo* 燃燈佛) to save the
world; then she had sent down the Sakyamuni Buddha *(Shih-chia fo*
釋迦佛) to try again. Each had been able to save some of her children,
but most of mankind remained lost. Therefore, the Eternal Mother
had promised that she would send down yet another god to lead men
to salvation, the Buddha Maitreya (*Mi-le fo* 彌勒佛).

It is one of the salient characteristics of this religion that believers expected the arrival of each of these Buddhas to coincide with the termination of three great periods of history. Each of these eras was termed a "kalpa" (*chieh* 劫 or *chieh-shu* 劫數). In traditional Buddhist thought, history was divided into great kalpa periods, each lasting hundreds of thousands of years. Each period was marked by a steady degeneration, and toward the end of each kalpa, Buddhist teachings would appear, prevail at first, and then be gradually undermined. At the end of a kalpa a cosmic holocaust would destroy the world and a new period would begin.[12] White Lotus sects had absorbed and adapted this view. They asserted that there would be only three kalpas, each "governed" by the Buddha sent by the Eternal Mother. Each kalpa would last a specified length of time (considerably foreshortened from the Indian original) and would be associated with a certain teaching. At the end of each period, those "children" who had been saved would be greeted by a Dragon Flower Assembly (*lung-hua hui* 龍華會) held in the Eternal Mother's palace and attended by all the gods and immortals.[13] One sect member described the scheme as follows:

> The first [period] was that of Lamp-lighting Buddha who was in charge of the world for 108,000 years; he sat on a five-leafed azure lotus throne. The name [for the teaching during this period] was the Azure Sun Assembly (*ch'ing-yang hui* 青陽會) or the Ch'ing-yang sect (*chiao* 教). When the period of Lamp-lighting Buddha's responsibility was over, it was Sakyamuni Buddha who became responsible for the world. He sits on a seven-leafed red lotus platform. The name is the Hung-yang (Red Sun) Assembly, or the Hung-yang sect. When the period of Sakyamuni Buddha's responsibility is over, it is Maitreya Buddha who will be responsible for the world. He will sit on a nine-leafed white lotus platform. The name will be Pai-yang (White Sun) Assembly or Pai-yang sect.[14]

A great many religious books were used by sect members, and they provided elaboration of this iconography and variations in detail. According to one, the length of the kalpas was specified as 108,000, 27,000, and 97,200 years respectively.[15] One scripture stated that each kalpa would be characterized by a different time system (perhaps related to cosmic changes). In the first, the Ch'ing-yang era, there were six hour-periods (that is, twelve hours) in each day,[16] fifteen days in each month, and only six months in a year. In the present, Hung-yang, period, there are twelve hour-periods (twenty-four hours) in a day, thirty days in a month, and twelve months in a year. During the coming Pai-yang era, there will be eighteen hour-periods (thirty-six hours) in a day, forty-five days in a month, and eighteen months in a year.[17]

The end of one kalpa would be characterized, sect members believed, by great disorder caused by both human wickedness and natural disasters. At such a time, "The Three Powers [Heaven, Earth, and Man] will not be in harmony. When Heaven is not in harmony, the stars and planets will roll about chaotically. When Earth is not in harmony, the five grains will not grow. When Man is not in harmony, the people will be in great distress."[18] These calamities would be sent down by the Eternal Mother as a punishment to mankind for refusing salvation and for allowing the "true way" to disappear once more.[19]

Some sects believed that each "turn of the kalpa" (yun-chieh 運劫) would be accomplished with its own distinctive type of calamity. For example, one group believed that there was flood after the first kalpa, fire after the second, and wind after the third.[20] All sect members believed that at the end of the present kalpa, there would again be an apocalypse, and the literature is full of descriptions of the horrors to come:

> When Maitreya comes to rule the universe, there will be chaos for seventy-seven days. The sun and the moon will alter their courses, and the climate will change.

> At that time the four elements, earth, water, fire, and wind would all shake at the same time so that not only the people would suffer death, but also the gods would have no place to live on earth.[21]

One group awaited widespread death caused by the "Old Tiger Epidemic," and another claimed that "a great calamity was about to descend, a wind of destruction was about to sweep the world from the sky."[22] Rebels in 1796 expected that "for an entire day and night, a black wind (黑風) will rise up and blow, killing countless people, leaving mountains of white bones and oceans of blood." In 1813 the Eight Trigram rebels, heirs to this tradition and its visions of apocalypse, predicted that "the great Pai-yang kalpa would arrive and cut away [the past] with a black wind for seven days and seven nights."[23]

These were terrifying prophecies of catastrophe and destruction, especially for nonbelievers, who were told that the Eternal Mother would mercilessly use this apocalypse to punish them. For her followers, however, the Eternal Mother promised protection and safety in the midst of chaos. One believer explained: "In the future those who are not in our assembly will meet with the disasters accompanying the arrival of the kalpa"; another told a friend more bluntly, "In this sect there are lots of good benefits. If you join the sect, you live. If you don't, you die. Wait until the 15th of this month [when the kalpa was expected to arrive] and you will understand."[24]

Most sects of the Ch'ing period believed themselves to be living in the second kalpa, and they anticipated the arrival of the third and last Pai-yang era.[25] They believed that as the kalpa ended, the Eternal Mother would send down into the world Maitreya Buddha, who, armed with the correct teaching (*chiao*), would save all believers by showing them how to survive the apocalypse and return to their Original Home. Since it was through belief in the correct and true teaching that one could be saved, the central concern of all believers was to determine the nature of this teaching and to follow it. Different teachers and different interpretations, all based on these same traditions and texts, produced a variety of teachings, a variety of sects. Each sect group claimed that its own practices and predictions were more correct than the others and assured its members that theirs was the true path to salvation. Always bearing in mind the death and destruction that awaited those who did not follow the Eternal Mother, each sect tried to propagate its own "excellent system for rescuing the scattered and lost" and to convert all nonbelievers, so that their teachings could be established as the foundation for all ordered human activity.[26]

Anticipating the day when their teachings would prevail, Ch'ing dynasty White Lotus sects saw the coming Pai-yang era as a millennium. The calamities accompanying the end of the second kalpa would eliminate nonbelievers and only the followers of the Eternal Mother would remain alive. Some sect members expressed this romantic and utopian vision in the form of a metaphor, asserting that when the kalpa catastrophes occurred all believers would go to a place called Yun-ch'eng 雲城 (Cloud City) where they would live and be protected:

> Yun-ch'eng is a general term we use because looking at it from afar, it seems to be a cloud; looking at it from up close, it appears to be a city. This place is very wide and broad. It reaches as

far as the Yellow River in the south, to Yen in the north, to the Eastern Sea in the east, and to the mountains in the west. In it there are several ten thousand people. All are in the sect.[27]

In more concrete terms, the turning of the kalpa meant the elimination of existing society and the coming to power of the followers of the Eternal Mother. Sect members hoped for wealth and power and prestige in a world where "everyone was in the sect." Their teachings, the true moral order, would be the basis for all relationships between men and between heaven and earth and man, so that the "harmony of all things would be achieved." In such a utopia, "heaven and earth will be in harmony. Among men there will be neither youth nor old age, neither birth nor death. There will be no distinctions between men and women. This then is the Great Way of Long Life in which all will live for eighty-one thousand years. When the time destined by Heaven has been fulfilled, this new universe will be established."[28]

This was the view of history transmitted by these sects, the key to understanding events of the past, present, and future with which their literature and tradition provided them. They believed that they truly understood what was happening in the world, and they felt this knowledge to be a privilege and a responsibility. Sect members waited with impatience for the time when the Eternal Mother would signal the turn of the kalpa when they, with her protection, would survive the calamities and greet the millennium. In consequence of this, a major focus of their religious literature and of the sect leaders who interpreted it was on the problem of determining exactly when the crucial time would come. Two events always accompanied the end of the kalpa, great calamities and the appearance of the Buddha sent by the Eternal Mother; believers therefore looked constantly for signs that these might be occurring.

In bad times—periods of great wars, droughts, famines, or epidemics—members of White Lotus sects would ask themselves whether this meant that the turn in the kalpa was about to come. Of course the converse was equally true, and if a sect teacher announced the kalpa was ending at a time when life was relatively good, his followers might be skeptical. "If you want to rebel, you must wait a few more years," one sect member counseled another. "How can you do it during such a peaceful time? You all are too early."[29] If, however, there had been a series of natural disasters, believers might then begin looking for the Buddha promised by the Eternal Mother. At such a time, a man teaching a new set of religious practices and claiming to be Maitreya reincarnated might, if he were persuasive, gain a large following.

There are no indications that this Maitreya incarnate would have any special identifying characteristics other than a generally "extraordinary" appearance.[30] Nor is it easy to find any precise indications as to what sect members expected him to do. Was he to be the founder of a sect, bringing the correct teaching to the world? Or would he merely assist or inspire a prominent teacher, giving the Eternal Mother's sanction to the other man's teachings and joining with him to usher in the new era? It is possible that each sect answered these questions differently; nevertheless, although Maitreya might not be recognized by appearance or even actions, he might possibly be identified by his surname. It appears that there were certain names traditionally favored, by others as well as by members of White Lotus sects, as the surnames of great rulers or gods reborn. These names were Li, Liu, Chu, Chang, and Wang.

The surname Li 李, often called by the names of the component elements of the written character itself, Mu-tzu 木子 or Shih-pa-tzu 十八子, was the surname of the ruling family of the T'ang dynasty (618–907). More important, it was the traditional surname of Lao-tzu, who had since the Han period become a messianic figure to some popular religious sects, a god who would be reborn on earth to save mankind.[31] Liu 劉 (also called Mao-chin 卯金 or Mao-chin-tao 卯金刀) was the surname of the Han dynasty (206 B.C.–220 A.D.) ruling house and after this formative period became a natural surname for would-be rulers. To the Eight Trigrams of 1813, Liu was also both the surname used by Maitreya in a previous incarnation and the name of a prominent family of sect teachers.[32] Chu 朱 (also called Niu-pa 牛八) was the surname of the Ming (1368–1644) ruling family whose restoration was the frequent goal of many rebellions during the Ch'ing period.[33]

Chang 張 (called also Kung-ch'ang 弓長) was the surname of Chang Chüeh and Chang Tao-ling, leaders of the Yellow Turban millenarian rebels at the end of the Han. The charisma of this surname was perpetuated through the title of Heavenly Master (t'ien-shih 天師) held by the Chang family of Taoist masters in Kiangsi province since that time. One sect scripture told the story of the Patriarch Kung-ch'ang to whom the Eternal Mother transmitted the law.[34] The surname Wang 王, although it has the meaning of "king," was not generally considered an especially imperial or holy name

except within the White Lotus tradition. There it became identified
with a family of sect practitioners from a small village in northern
Chihli province. This Wang family had transmitted sect teachings
since the sixteenth century and over time their network of pupils
became very extended. The preeminence of this family was asserted
and published in religious books written about them. This literature
predicted that "Maitreya Buddha will appear in the family of the
sect patriarch named Wang from Stone-buddha village."[35]

If a leader claiming to be Maitreya had made himself known
during a period of some distress, the problem still remained for
believers to determine exactly when the great cosmic catastrophes
would descend. It was usually a sect leader (who may or may not
have claimed to be Maitreya himself) who made this determination
according to sect literature. White Lotus scriptures, written in poetic,
sometimes abstruse language, were full of phrases and passages that
could be interpreted and reinterpreted. Some scriptures named
certain years, designating them by the sixty-year stems-and-branches
system, as the time of the arrival of the new kalpa. Of these, the first
year of the sixty-year cycle, the *chia-tzu* 甲子 year, had long been
considered a likely and auspicious time for such a beginning. One
sect text stated:

> In the *chia-tzu* year, a holy one will be sent down, and on the 3d
> day of the 3d month during the noon hour-period will be born
> as a member of the Mu-tzu [Li] family. During the third *chia*
> year after that [i.e., thirty years later], all men of talent will go
> to the Yu and Yen [Peking] area for there will be great calami-
> ties.[36]

Another scripture quoted the Eternal Mother as saying:

> During the final period in the *chia-tzu* year,
> the end of the kalpa will approach.
> In the *hsin-ssu* year there will still be no harvests,
> and the people will die of starvation.
> In the *kuei-wei* year, caught in the conjunction of the three
>   afflictions, epidemics will spread.[37]

A year specified by both its stem and branch name would occur only
once every sixty years. Other predictions, such as "the catastrophes
of the *hsu* and *hai* years,"[38] specified only the branch name, and years
fulfilling these prophecies would recur every twelve years. The variety
of different predictions using this year system gave a sect leader

considerable flexibility and, like fortune-tellers of all sorts in China, sect masters manipulated these cyclical characters and used them to prove conjunction between current events and the prophecies set forth in sect scriptures.

Within the year, certain days (such as the 3d day of the 3d month, mentioned above) would be specified for the start of the new kalpa, the birthday of Maitreya, and so forth. One sect predicting the coming millennium for the year 1814 had calculated the first day of the kalpa in terms of the first day of spring, traditionally referred to as "when the dragon lifts his head" (that is, when the ice breaks). They figured that "traditionally the 2d day of the 2d month was considered the dragon's head, and the 29th day of the 2d month was considered the dragon's tail; therefore they had chosen [2/29 as] their date by selecting the time when the manifestation of the dragon would be complete."[39] Any *chia-tzu* day (for the days of the year were also so numbered) would be considered auspicious, and as we shall see below the 15th day of the 8th month also appears to have been a frequently favored day.[40]

Once a sect leader could point to a reincarnated Maitreya and to the signs of escalating catastrophe and could predict a date on which the new kalpa would begin, he and his followers did not simply sit back and wait for the millennium to arrive. Their certain knowledge of this imminent apocalypse drove them to convert and save as many people as possible. As the terrible day approached, they distributed special charms, identifying signs (banners, clothing, headgear, for example), and other protective devices which, leaders assured their followers, would save all believers in the Eternal Mother from harm. Even more important, sect members believed it their responsibility to "respond to the kalpa" (*ying chieh* 應刼) by mobilizing their sects and, as the agents of the Eternal Mother and the avant-garde of the millennium, to speed the destruction of the existing order and its replacement by a better system. Sect members called this "making known the Way" (*ming-tao* 明道)[41] and in this response to the kalpa were transformed from secret believers into openly and publicly committed followers of the Eternal Mother.

In order to transform religious sects into revolutionary organizations, a higher level framework was necessary, one in which many dispersed and separate sects could be incorporated and coordinated. Such frameworks were often simple, even crude, borrowings from White Lotus tradition or popular religion in general. For example, one sect found a phrase in a scripture that said "the twenty-eight

constellations will not come into world the until the *ping-hsu* year";
they used this to pull together many different sects whose different
leaders were designated the "twenty-eight constellations (*hsiu* 宿)."[42]
A more common practice was to combine eight or nine groups on an
equal basis by naming each one after either the eight trigrams
(*pa-kua* 八卦) or the nine mansions (*chiu-kung* 九宮). The eight trigrams
were symbols representing the eight possible combinations of three
solid (representing *yang*) or broken (representing *yin*) lines. These
eight trigrams themselves could be combined in sets of six lines to
form the sixty-four hexagrams on which the *I Ching,* or *The Book of
Changes*—a perennial source of symbolism—was based. The nine
mansions were astrological divisions of the sky which, like the eight
trigrams, had become associated in popular religion—the White
Lotus tradition in particular—with an array of colors, gods, directions of the compass, elements, numbers, animals, and symbols and
objects of all sorts.[43]

SECT SCRIPTURES

Although many sect ideas and practices were transmitted orally,
it was through the written word that the story of the Eternal Mother
and the three kalpas was safely passed down within these White
Lotus sects for nearly four hundred years. The preceding summary
of this cosmology and history describes only the most basic tenets of
sect ideology and does not suggest the great variety of legends and
stories and elaborations on basic themes that filled these scriptures—
books that are called in Chinese *ching* 經 (sutras or classics) or *pao-
chüan* 寶卷 (precious volumes).

In addition to the accounts of the Eternal Mother, of the birth of
mankind, and of the three Buddhas and three kalpas, many of these
scriptures told the story of how a particular sect was founded. They
described the birth of the sect patriarch and told how he communi-
cated with the Eternal Mother [44] and was sent by her to bring the
true teaching to the world so that those who believed and followed
it could be saved. Said one book: "On the 15th day of the 1st month
of the *chia-wu* year of the Wan-li reign [1594], the most honored
P'iao Kao Venerable Patriarch, while living on the Great Tiger
Mountain, opened wide a new means of salvation to save the multitude of the lost."[45] There were many such stories, and the following,
condensed from a much longer passage serves as another example:

The divine Buddha, the Holy One, will enter the world and be born among those of the Eastern world. The place where he will come down and be born is on the central plain, south of Yen, in San-yuan-li: Ta-pao village. He will be called Kung-ch'ang. . . . The Eternal Mother told Kung-ch'ang, "Come in person and receive the Law. Mother will transmit to you this very day the ten steps to self-perfection." . . . The Venerable Mother then instructed Patriarch Kung-ch'ang to go to the east to find the scriptures [and] Kung-ch'ang went to the region of Stone-buddha village to get the true scriptures. . . . [She] told Kung-ch'ang about the coming kalpa calamities and Kung-ch'ang said, "In this kalpa, how can we be saved?" The Eternal Mother said, "I will give you magic charms to save people."[46]

In addition to these pseudohistorical accounts, sect literature contained a variety of other tales of the Eternal Mother, often interwoven with traditional myths and legends. In one such story, for example, "Buddha converted the brothers Pao-chung and Pao-hsiao, their mother, and their wives. While they were on their way to Hsiang-shan to fulfill their vows, they met the Eternal Mother on a wagon drawn by a white ox. She asked them to ride in her wagon to the Cave of Immortal Water at the Heavenly River to see the Thousand-armed and Thousand-eyed Buddha."[47] These stories not only helped to establish the Eternal Mother as a legitimate actor in mythological dramas, but provided sect members with a convenient proselytizing device.

Sung Chin-yao and the others often assembled [and] . . . listened to [their teacher] Ku Liang tell stories about buddhas and immortals. . . . When Ku Liang sat and talked, they didn't close the gate, and so people would come to listen and see what was happening. Their fellow villagers [here named] . . . often came and listened and in that way became familiar [with the sect].[48]

The storytelling atmosphere was emphasized by the language of some of these scriptures, which was similar to that of Chinese folk plays and popular songs. Sometimes, perhaps in imitation of sutra readings, a simple drumbeat or gong would be provided to give rhythm to the reading or recitation of a scripture.[49]

Not all sect literature contained stories. Some preserved instead abstruse technical information used by sect leaders. There were books containing pictures of *fu* 符, charms that were part character and part drawing, and the uses to which they were designed. A *fu* would be copied from the book onto a piece of paper and then burned. The ashes would be immersed in water or tea and then drunk by a person who was ill; this would effect a cure. Other books contained *chou* 咒, incantations. These would be recited and, like charms, had a beneficial, protective, or healing effect. While many charms and incantations could be transmitted orally, these books served as reference manuals for those who needed them.[50] Like the "inside story" which the sect scriptures related, the books of magic spells and formulas were repositories for the "secrets" disclosed by the Eternal Mother to her followers. Because of the great power of the Eternal Mother, these charms and incantations had more than ordinary efficacy: "If you burned and drank [a certain charm], it would enable you to enlighten your mind and realize the Buddha-nature within you," said one sect teacher; moreover, with it "you could avoid the calamities of fire, flood, and the sword."[51]

Most of the scriptures used by White Lotus sects during the Ch'ing were written and first printed at the end of the sixteenth century. Since that time, these scriptures had been carefully preserved and reprinted, or copied and recopied by hand.[52] The Ch'ing government had a firm policy of confiscating all heretical (*hsieh* 邪) books, declaring them to be "full of wild and irregular talk with rebellious passages that make one's hair stand on end."[53] Whenever a sect teacher was arrested, his house was searched and all suspicious literature was seized and then destroyed. Books were sometimes even destroyed by owners who were afraid of being caught with incriminating evidence.[54] Therefore, despite the dangers involved in ownership of the books themselves or their printing blocks, constant efforts and frequent copying and reprinting were a necessity if a steady supply of sect scriptures was to be maintained.[55] These books looked much like the Buddhist sutras after which they were modeled. According to the district magistrate Huang Yü-p'ien, who confiscated many of these scriptures in the 1830s, "they were printed in large type, bound with brocade covers, with pictures of buddhas on the first and last pages." They usually consisted of only one volume, although some were two or even three volumes in length.[56]

Because of their scarcity, illegality, and importance to sect doctrine, these scriptures were treated with great respect. They contained the Eternal Mother's keys to understanding history and truth and were believed to have great value and power. The author of one book encouraged the reader, saying, "If this book be in anyone's family, then those who fully understand its meaning will not be exposed to any adversities or obstacles; their door will be guarded by the Holy Ones. . . . All who are unwearied in the study of this book will ascend bodily to the Purple Cloud [where Immortals live]."[57] Sect leaders with prophetic power (or aspirations) would use these books to prove the accuracy of their predictions and their understanding. A few lines quoted from a scripture could achieve wide currency and provide proof of the consonance between sect plans and the heavenly order.[58]

These religious scriptures did not circulate freely among all members of White Lotus sects. On the contrary, as treasures they were almost always the exclusive property of sect leaders. The evidence further suggests that many of these books were owned by a relatively small number of leaders, those men and women who had transmitted sect ideas within their families for many generations. There was a general tendency for power within these sects to gravitate to and remain in the hands of hereditary leaders; by virtue of their long experience and large network of pupils, some families who had passed on sect teachings since the sixteenth century acquired great prestige and authority and came to constitute an informal hereditary elite among believers.

One of the most striking examples of such a family is the Wang family of Stone-buddha village (Shih-fo-k'ou 石佛口) in Luan district in northeastern Chihli province. In the Wan-li reign of the Ming dynasty (1573–1619) a man named Wang Sen 王森 had founded and propagated an Incense Smelling (Wen-hsiang 聞香) sect. His son succeeded him as sect master and in 1622 predicted the collapse of the dynasty and organized a rebellion. The rebels were defeated by Ming armies within three months, but the Wang family was not eliminated. They continued to transmit their teaching, which was known by a variety of other names, and family members became hereditary sect masters. The rebellion had probably been generated by a prophecy in their scriptures—which date from the late Ming— stating that when Maitreya Buddha comes down to earth, he will be born in Stone-buddha village as a member of the Wang family. Despite the failure of this first rebellion (and perhaps because of the attempt), the scriptures reinforced the family's position as acknowledged authorities on sect practices and as potential leaders of the "great undertaking" (ta-shih 大事), a traditional euphemism for rebellion. They were active in proselytizing, and as members of the family or their pupils changed residences, their network of followers spread throughout the north China plain and into Hupei and Kiangsu. Copies of their scriptures multiplied as the network grew, and those without books would commit to memory the important passages. This family was periodically investigated and arrests were made, but they and their particular scriptures survived for at least two hundred years, into the Tao-kuang reign (1821–50).[59]

This Wang family was only one of many families of this informal hereditary elite. Members of a family named Kao 郜 were leaders of a Li Trigram sect in Honan that will be discussed in some detail at the end of Part One. There was, as another example, a Mrs. Liu Kung (that is, 劉龔氏, Mrs. Liu née Kung) who was arrested in 1816. Her son admitted that their sect and sect literature had originated with "his paternal grandmother twelve generations back, Grandmother Mi (米奶奶), who had lived during the Wan-li era of the Ming. . . . She had been the sect master and people called her Patriarch Mi. In their family this sect had been passed down through the women."[60] In addition to those families who could trace their leadership in a sect back to the sixteenth century, there were many more families with somewhat less impressive pedigrees who passed down a sect teaching for several generations and possessed their own religious books, and who constituted a lower echelon within this White Lotus elite. The teaching transmitted in Peking in 1813 by a Mrs. Kao Chang, for example, could be traced back four generations within her own family. She was the acknowledged sect master and possessed at least thirty-five volumes of religious literature. During those four generations, the sect had grown and spread through four branches and two other provinces.[61]

At any point in time there were many sect leaders with varying pedigrees, but more authority and a greater number of religious books were concentrated in the hands of those with the longer claims to leadership. At the same time, this literature and authority was being diffused outward as these leaders propagated the religion and converted followers. A teacher might give a religious book to one of his pupils who was not a member of the family or might allow him to make a copy. "I went to [my teacher's] house. He took out two books which he told me were true scriptures spoken by Buddha. He gave me one volume, but he told me I should make a handwritten copy of the other one."[62] A limited number of books and this system of transmission tended to restrict possession of scriptures to people who were in a legitimate line of descent of teachers and who thus had credentials as sect leaders. In a way sect members had made a virtue of necessity, for this system helped protect them from charlatans and other irresponsible persons who were interested only in utilizing the potentially inflammable (and illegal) sect ideology to their own ends.

It was possible however for a leader to gain access to sect literature and its legitimizing power even if he did not inherit it from a relative or teacher. Lin Ch'ing 林清, one of the two major leaders of the 1813 rebellion, did not join a White Lotus sect until he was thirty-seven years old. He took over local leadership of his sect after the death of the previous leader, forced those pupils and relatives of the old teacher who disapproved to form a splinter sect, and inherited no books. He added to his knowledge of sect doctrine by visiting and talking with the leaders of separate sects in villages nearby. He was apparently able to master sect history and cosmology in this way, because within three years his predictions about the coming kalpa and arrival of Maitreya (Lin Ch'ing himself) were sufficiently convincing to enable him to begin organizing a rebellion. It was not until after such planning had begun that one of Lin Ch'ing's pupils presented him with a religious scripture. We do not know where this book came from though it had been used by White Lotus rebels fifteen years before and was one of those transmitted by the Wang family of Stone-buddha village. It was entitled "A Comprehensive Manual for Responding to the Kalpas of the Three Buddhas" (*San-fo ying-chieh t'ung-kuan t'ung-shu* 三佛應劫統觀通書), and with it Lin Ch'ing determined the date of the uprising and the new hierarchy that would prevail during the coming era. This is a good example of how these religious books might slowly come into the hands of those who needed and could use them.[63]

The majority of sect members were evidently illiterate, a fact that bolstered the power of those leaders able to read and explain sect scriptures but that also limited the production of miscellaneous writing that might serve the historian. Fortunately Ch'ing sources do suggest what some of these other kinds of written material might have included. When one sect leader died, his son asked a literate friend to write up for him a handbill (*ch'uan-tan* 傳單) that could be sent to others in the sect to announce the death.[64] Another sect member named Wang Ying-chieh possessed two certificates (*chih-chao* 執照) made of yellow cloth on which were written a few lines (probably from a sect scripture) about the Eternal Mother and her palace in the Original Home. Wang claimed that these were for burial with his mother to guide her spirit after death (presumably to guarantee her entry into the Eternal Mother's paradise).[65] When leaders of a Ta-sheng 大乘 (Greater Vehicle) sect that had already been dispersed after a government investigation the previous year decided to reassemble, they made up placards (*pang-wen* 榜文) "which could be used as a call to action for the members of the assembly," and at the top stamped in vermilion ink a homemade seal. These were distributed to members, but it was not long before a copy came to the attention of the government.[66] Obviously, the danger of these "heretical" materials falling into the hands of the authorities discouraged their production.

On the other hand, there was one kind of written record kept by a great many sects—that is, lists of the names of their members. These "books for the names of pupils recruited" were usually called *pu* 簿, and they would consist in their simplest form of names only. In some cases, donations made by believers were also recorded there. A sect head with a large following might have many volumes full of thousands of names and making and keeping these lists could be a full-time job. Many sects undertook to compile registers of names when they anticipated the arrival of the new kalpa and wanted records of those believers who would survive. Prior to the Eight Trigrams rebellion in 1813, sect groups that had not previously done so were asked to register their members so that rewards could be distributed later. One group had no members with sufficient education and had to ask the local schoolmaster (a degree-holder) to write down the names dictated to him. Another group, not knowing how to make up such lists and wanting to be inconspicuous, copied the *pao-chia* registration placards (which listed households and the names of their members) with which they were already familiar. Sect name lists were of obvious value to the government, despite their relatively innocuous appearance, and the need to call on the literate elite for assistance was a source of great danger. In the case described above, the local schoolmaster went directly to the district magistrate to report the sect members' activities.[67] It is no wonder that sect members normally kept few records, for it was their general lack of incriminating written materials and religious paraphernalia that protected them from government scrutiny and allowed them to survive despite their illegality for hundreds of years.

THE EIGHT-CHARACTER MANTRA

During the Chia-ch'ing reign converts to White Lotus sects were taught a protective incantation consisting of eight characters; many believers also received instruction in certain special therapeutic techniques, the most common of which were yogic meditation, massage for curing illness, and beneficial fighting exercises. Instruction in preventive medicine and the curing of illness was of course by no means limited to these sects—far from it—but from the very large body of such "arts" diffused throughout Chinese society, certain techniques had, together with the eight-character mantra, become part of the teachings of many White Lotus groups.

The basic chant taught to sect members in the early nineteenth century consisted of the eight characters *chen-k'ung chia-hsiang wu-sheng fu-mu* 真空家鄉無生父母, "Eternal Progenitor in Our Original Home in the World of True Emptiness." During the early Chia-ch'ing reign these characters had replaced a very similar chant that had ended with another name for their mother deity, *Wu-sheng lao-mu* 無生老母,[68] the Eternal Venerable Mother. Some sects in the Chia-ch'ing period treated these eight characters as part of a longer chant:

> Respect the Buddhist law,
> Eternal Progenitor
> In Our Original Home in the World of True Emptiness,
> Now the Buddha-to-come,
> Our patriarch, will soon be here.[69]

The basic eight-character mantra (*chou-yü* 咒語 or *ke-chueh* 歌訣) was formally referred to as the "Eight Character True Sutra" (*pa-tzu chen-ching* 八字真經) or the "Wordless True Sutra" (*wu-tzu chen-ching* 無字真經) or sometimes simply the eight-character "true words" (*chen-yen* 真言). Given to a new member by his teacher, this mantra was a secret known only to believers, a magic formula that was the exclusive property of sect members and the basic source of the "good benefits" offered to converts. These eight characters could be quickly memorized by even the most uneducated or simpleminded; thus membership in a sect was not restricted to people with learning or great intelligence. Realizing that knowledge of the chant indicated true membership in a sect, the Ch'ing government used this as a criterion for assigning punishments.[70]

The mere recitation of this formula, like the mantras of Tibetan tantric Buddhism, had the magical power to "encourage good things and protect against bad ones."[71] When a convert learned the eight characters from his teacher, he was usually given instructions about when and where and how to recite, and thus benefit from, this chant. The nature of this ritual recitation ranged from the elaborate to the very simple. In some sects (or for more sophisticated believers?) there was a formal ritual to be performed three times a day. In the morning, one faced east, bowed to greet the rising sun, and recited the chant twenty-seven times. At noon, one faced south, again bowed to the sun, and recited the eight characters fifty-four times. And in the evening, one faced west, bowed to bid farewell to the setting sun, and recited the chant eighty-one times. During the recitation the believer sat cross-legged like a monk, with eyes closed and arms clasped to the chest.[72] This ritual of kneeling or bowing (*kuei* 跪) and "facing and performing ritual obeisance to the sun" (*ch'ao li t'ai-yang* 朝禮太陽) was a way of paying tribute to the power of *yang* 陽, the positive force in the world.[73]

In keeping with the general pattern of great flexibility in sect practices, this ritual could be, and often was, simplified. Sect members could merely face in the appropriate direction without kotowing, or could simply "face the heavens." The chant did not have to be recited a specific number of times. Some believers were instructed to perform the ritual only in the morning. Others were told merely to "recite" or "silently intone" these eight characters "often" or "every so often" without any accompanying ritual. Sometimes incense was burned as part of the ceremony.[74]

Most members explained the purpose of this ritual rather simply, saying that the chant "was very efficacious and could bring good benefits (*hao-ch'u* 好處)." One sect leader, trying to convert a friend of his, elaborated: "I will teach you a system by means of which you can encourage good fortune and avoid bad fortune and be saved from poverty." Others claimed the eight characters provided protection against illness and disease: "If you were sick and recited it you would become well"; "He said that if I recited this chant often then all my illnesses would be cured."[75] The recitation of the mantra, in its more elaborate forms, was part of an act of meditation: "To recite these words several times would enable you to circulate your breath"; "[My teacher] taught me to sit and meditate and silently intone them [the eight characters]."[76] Many converts were taught to meditate as part of learning the chant. A close look at this meditation affords a better understanding of the benefits that were believed to be derived from recitation of this mantra.

This meditation was a type of internal exercise—of a kind known in China since at least the fourth century B.C.—designed to move and circulate one's vital breath (*ch'i* 氣) throughout the body. The effects were believed to be therapeutic, bringing good health and long life.

> "[His teacher] declared that if after a long time one could meditate effectively (*kung-shen* 功深), one could have long life and not die. . . . When a member of the first and highest rank completed his study, he would attain the Tao and become an immortal. When a member of the second rank had completed his study, he could conquer illness and lengthen his life span. A member of the third rank could [at least] avoid difficulties and survive calamities.[77]

To meditate, one usually sat cross-legged, with eyes closed and arms folded, in a pose like a Buddhist monk; this was called *ta-tso* 打坐. By concentrating, one could then guide and move his vital breath within his body (*yun-ch'i* 運氣). If successful, one would go into a type of trance (*tso-kung* 坐功). In this meditation, eyes, ears, mouth, and nose were considered the "four gates," and there was a chant with the lines, "to encourage the ruler, the four gates must all be tightly closed." Thus, in order to control and circulate your *ch'i*, your internal energy, "you first brought your hands toward your face and touched and closed your eyes. A breath of air from your lungs and abdomen was sent down and circulated. Then it was expelled through the nose."[78] The circumstances under which this meditation was carried on varied with each sect. Many combined it with the recitation of the eight-character chant and the morning, noon, and evening rituals to the sun. One sect insisted that it be done in private and never in the presence of nonbelievers, otherwise "there would be no benefits." Other sect members assembled to meditate together, or did so oblivious to the presence of outsiders. In general such sessions do not appear to have lasted more than a few hours at the most.[79]

If one meditated successfully, a trancelike state could ultimately be achieved and even used to other purposes. One government official wrote: "Hsing Shih-k'uei was very good at circulating his breath. When we tried to interrogate him, he just closed his eyes and held his breath for a while. His complexion became that of a dead man and it was impossible to get any confession from him."[80] If one was successful in achieving a trance, this was interpreted to mean that one's soul was going up to the heavens to pay its respects to the Eternal Mother. One sect scripture described this as a ten-step process, beginning with "taking up the shining [*ch'i*] from the bottom of the sea" and concluding with "going out through the K'un-lun mountains [meaning the top of the head]" and going up to the heavenly palace there to be with the Eternal Mother and "never come down to earth again."[81] The teacher of a Huang-yang 黄洋 (Yellow Ocean) sect in Chihli in the 1810s taught his pupils to recite several long chants. One was:

> . . . As you breathe out and in
> the heavenly gate opens.
> Your soul [*yuan-shen* 元神] manifests itself
> and goes up to heaven to bow respectfully
> to the Eternal Progenitor.

Another was:

> As there are eight trigrams in heaven
> and eight rivers on earth,
> so there are eight houses in your body.
> If you meditate and enter into a trance,
> your white breath will rise up to heaven.
> It will go to the Imperial Heaven
> to Our Original Home in the World of True Emptiness.
> There it will bow respectfully to the Eternal Progenitor
> and by means of this, prepare for a time to come.[82]

This yogic meditation was believed to result in a variety of benefits. According to the beliefs of one sect, the soul will be able to become a buddha if at the time of death it leaves the body by passing through the "dark pass" (*hsuan-kuan* 玄關). The dark pass refers to the place between the eyebrows, and this group believed that one type of meditation would teach the soul the location of this dark pass so that it would be able to find the way more easily at death.[83] Another sect member claimed that through meditation he became able to predict the future: "He was able to meditate and circulate his breath, to make his spirit leave his body and to know about future events."[84] One sect referred to this mediation and recitation of the eight-character chant as "learning the right way" (*hsueh-hao* 學好) and so reaching the Tao. The whole process was sometimes called "meditating successfully and learning the right way" (*tso-kung hsueh-hao*). Others called it "circulating one's breath and nourishing one's nature" (*yun-ch'i yang-hsing* 運氣養性).[85]

Although recitation of the eight characters was rather easy, this type of yogic meditation, if done properly, was far more difficult and was only learned and practiced by those willing to invest the time and the energy. Converts who learned first just to recite the eight characters might later, if they so desired, be taught how to meditate. There were those who learned how to meditate and later gave it up. Liu Wen-t'ung said, "I recited the eight characters often but got no benefits. The meditation made me depressed, and so my mother forbid me to do it any more." T'ang Ssu-chiu "had trouble breathing through his nose, and so he found it difficult to do the meditation."[86] Because the art of meditation could be learned at many different levels, a student could begin with a very simple intoning of the magical formula and progress as far as he wished through gradually more difficult and time-consuming rituals, perhaps ultimately learning to go into trances for long periods of time.

Meditation was only one form of "skill" or *kung-fu* 工夫[87] transmitted through these White Lotus sects. A different skill taught in some sects was a system of massage for curing illness. This massage, *an-mo* 按摩, was also called *t'ui-na* 推拏 or *an-na* 按拏,[88] terms that suggest the pulling and pushing motions involved. One sect transmitted a system of applying pressure at the body's "caves and roads" (*hsueh-tao* 穴道), certain nerve centers and channels also used by acupuncturists for curing and by Chinese boxers for striking paralyzing blows.[89] No system of massage is described in the source material in any detail, and the following reference is typical:

> [One day] Sung Shang-chung invited me and Kao Chu to have some wine with him. Kao Chu wasn't feeling very well. Sung Shang-chung massaged his body a little, and Kao Chu was better. Sung Shang-chung said he was in a group called the Jung-hua Assembly. It was for "learning the right way." He urged us to join, and we said we would. He taught us the eight characters, "Eternal Progenitor in Our Original Home in the World of True Emptiness." He also said he would teach Kao Chu how to do massage in order to cure illnesses.[90]

A great many sect teachers were healers of some sort who recruited pupils and converts by persuading their patients to join the sect. The techniques they used are not specified except for the system of massage, but a wide variety of diseases and injuries were treated.[91] Religion and medicine were very closely connected in traditional China—as in all folk societies—and expertise in one field was assumed to mean expertise in the other.[92]

Healing might precede or follow conversion. In some cases the healer would tell the patient that in order to be cured he had first to join the sect. Sometimes the healer extended this requirement to other members of the patient's family, telling them that "because the cure was difficult, they . . . should first take [the healer] as their teacher and join the sect." In most cases, however, it was the grateful patient, now cured, who (perhaps together with relatives who had been impressed by the cure) kotowed to his "doctor," became his pupil and joined the sect. In many instances, the teacher then shared with his former patient the "secrets" of the sect, and might teach him how to make and recite healing charms or how to do massage. The healer's skill in curing illness was transformed into authority on religious matters as well, and the doctor–patient relationship only strengthened the sect teacher–pupil bond.[93]

Another skill transmitted within these sects was that of "boxing" or "boxing and fencing" (ch'üan-kun 拳棍, ch'üan-pang 拳棒). These exercises, performed bare-handed or with a stick, were designed to be at once useful for self-defense and beneficial for one's health and therefore one's spirit.

Chin-chung-chao 金鐘罩, Armor of the Golden Bell, was one method of fighting transmitted to sect members. A man named Chang Lo-chiao studied it, and his teacher told him that after learning Chin-chung-chao, he need not fear anyone trying to attack him with a knife. He evidently meant that this system could confer physical invulnerability, for later Chang Lo-chiao practiced by stabbing himself in the shoulder and in the ribs. He found that indeed he was not hurt and only a white scar appeared in the places he had stabbed. Another fighter in this school made a similar claim: "He couldn't be injured by the stab of a knife or the jab of a sword."[94]

A student of Chin-chung-chao could learn more than a system of fighting; he could learn, if he were interested, a set of chants and formulas for charms that cured illness. Liu Yü-lung was given a book by his teacher in the Armor of the Golden Bell entitled "Chang Lin-ts'un's Sacred Manual of Mystical Practices" (Chang Lin-ts'un fang-shan shen-ts'e 張林存放山神冊), which contained lists of formulas used to heal illnesses and convert followers.[95] A pupil of Liu's describes his cure:

> I had an ulcer on my back. I heard that Liu Yü-lung could effect cures. He used incense and drew for a while with it on the ulcer [writing a charm there] and also spit on it, saying that it would now get better. Then he said that he knew another good spell which he could teach me which would make everything

be however I wanted it to be. He recited the eight characters "Eternal Progenitor in Our Original Home in the World of True Emptiness" and taught them to me.[96]

Chang Lo-chiao, the Chin-chung-chao boxer mentioned above, was also a healer. Being illiterate, however, he had only memorized a few of the chants: "When he is curing someone, he merely recites what he remembers and gets someone else to write it down."[97]

The Armor of the Golden Bell was by no means the only school of fighting taught by sect members. One kind in which there were eight prescribed steps was called Eight Trigrams boxing (*pa-kua ch'üan* 八卦拳). Others were called Yin-yang 陰陽 boxing, Mei-hua 梅花 (Plum Flower) boxing, Pa-fan 八番 (Eight Times) boxing, and I-ho 義和 (Righteous harmony) boxing—the latter being made famous by the Boxers in 1900.[98] These exercises were believed to act as preventive medicine by aiding digestion and circulation, and by keeping the body supple and fit. They could also be used for fighting, and contests between practitioners of different schools at fairs and markets were not uncommon. There were probably other schools of boxing associated with the White Lotus tradition; certainly there were other forms of Chinese boxing that were *not* associated with these sects. But a sect member who instructed his pupils in fighting (like those who taught healing or meditation) offered them a permanent relationship, stronger than the usual one between boxing teachers and pupils because it was not dependent on relative fighting skills. Students of the Armor of the Golden Bell, as we have seen, were also given access to the sect "secrets"—special incantations for healing, the beneficial eight-character chant, and the protection of the sect should the kalpa calamities arrive.

SECT MEMBERSHIP

The eight-character mantra and the various arts described above were perpetuated through a chain of teachers and pupils stretching from the sixteenth into the twentieth century. To join a White Lotus sect meant becoming a part of this chain by being the pupil of someone already in a sect.

During the Ch'ing dynasty sect members could not appeal openly for new members, and the healing skills possessed by many—yoga, massage, or boxing—became in essence advertisements and avenues of access to the sects. Many new members joined a sect for the ex-

plicit purpose of learning either to fight or to cure illnesses. Such
conversions tended to follow very similar patterns:

> I became ill and Wang Ta of T'i-shang village cured me. So
> he told me to take him as my teacher and join the Jung-hua
> Assembly. He also taught me to recite the eight characters,
> "Eternal Progenitor in Our Original Home in the World of
> True Emptiness." He said that if I recited this spell often then
> all my illnesses would be cured.[99]

One sect member who performed a great many cures stated that he
would not let patients whom he had helped present him with gifts
(as was usual); instead he urged them to become his pupils and join
the sect.[100] The gratitude a person normally feels toward the one
who has saved him from pain or death was thus channeled into the
pupil–teacher bond and strengthened it. The tie was even stronger
when the doctor not only cured his patient but then taught him how
to do cures himself, thus sharing his power as well as his secrets.

For men who were interested in fighting techniques, it was normal
for a pupil to study with a master for a period of time and to consider
the latter his teacher. If two men fought, by chance or in a public
match, and one man clearly bested the other, the loser was expected
to acknowledge the other's superiority and ask to receive instruction.
Learning the boxing techniques of a White Lotus sect was no
different: "A man from my district . . . sponsored me to go to
Te district and compete with Sung Yueh-lung. Sung Yueh-lung
couldn't surpass me, so he and his son . . . both took me as their
teacher and they joined [my] Li Trigram sect."[101]

Boxing and curing skills were an important drawing card for
White Lotus sects. Healers and fighters traveled about the countryside, the former looking for patients, the latter competing at market
fairs and providing an occasion for gambling. People of different
backgrounds and different villages with common interests or a common problem could meet, and a sect would spread along the random
lines that such a network would create.

Many, perhaps most, sect members did not have this kind of
"professional" interest in the sect, but rather joined in order to
benefit from the efficacy of the powerful eight-character chant and
its meditative techniques. The existence of the chant was not adver-
tised, and this kind of conversion therefore proceeded along the lines
of preexisting relationships. Parents instructed their children; friends
and neighbors told one another. Pien Erh, for example, moved to a

certain village and found a job working for Li Shih-te. Subsequently, at age twenty-eight, "he took Li Shih-te and his wife as adopted parents, and then followed them, and joined their sect. Li Shih-te taught him to recite the Wordless True Sutra." A stone-worker named Su Chien-te stated: "I happened to go to Hou-hsin village to the house of Yang Lao to make a stone mortar for him. Yang Lao invited me to join their assembly; he said there would be good benefits, so I agreed to do so."[102] In some cases, explicitly material benefits were offered to potential converts, or at least given to them later. One sect member testified:

> I have known Chang Ssu-hu-tzu . . . for a long time. He makes his living by controlling who is granted the right to plant Banner lands. In 1811 Chang Ssu-hu-tzu and I were going to market and talking along the way. He mentioned that he was in the White Lotus sect. He told me that if I joined his sect, he would give me some Banner land to rent, and he'd do so at a lower rate. Since I didn't even have the money to pay the rent on such land, I said I didn't want to join. But then he said that if I wanted to join the White Lotus sect, he would let me go along with him later when the harvest was in to collect rents from the tenants on the Banner lands, and he would let me help carry the rent payments. He said he would pay me 10 cash for each *mou*'s worth of rent which I carried. I agreed. After I joined the sect, Chang Ssu-hu-tzu taught me to burn incense three times a day facing the heavens.[103]

Initiation into a sect took the form of a very brief and uncompli- cated ceremony that could be performed nearly anywhere or any- time. The minimal ritual was simple: the pupil knelt and kotowed to his teacher and the teacher recited and taught him the eight- character chant. "He told me to kneel down, and then he transmitted to me the eight characters, 'Eternal Progenitor in Our Original Home in the World of True Emptiness.' He told me to recite them every so often."[104] More elaborate ceremonies did, however, take place. Incense, whose smoke rising into the sky established communi- cation between men and gods, was considered a desirable part of the ceremony. In one sect, the pupil would light and hold the stick of burning incense as he knelt; in another, it was held by the teacher. In one case the ceremony was performed in front of an image of a buddha.[105]

Other chants might be recited by the teacher during the initiation and learned then or later by the pupil. Members of one Chia-ch'ing-period sect described in detail their more elaborate ceremony, in which the teacher first burned incense and knelt in front. The pupil who was learning the chant knelt behind him. Then they both recited:

> Our faith is on high.
> The three Buddhas guide us upward.
> We, your pupils, are here below.
> We are converted to our faith,
> converted to the Buddhas,
> converted to the law,
> converted to our teacher.
> We are converted to these three treasures.
> If we, your pupils, do not respect the Buddhas' law,
> or if we divulge this Way of the Immortals,
> may our flesh be reduced to congealed blood.
> We will never go against this teaching.
> If we should go against this teaching
> may a thunderbolt strike us dead.

After both had finished reciting this, then the teacher alone recited:

> I am a teacher and a sponsor,
> I do not teach a heretical sect.
> If I should transmit any heretical teaching
> or if I should use tricks to get people's money for myself,
> then may a thunderbolt strike me dead.[106]

The swearing of an oath—a common way to bind a compact from earliest times—was not infrequently part of the initiation ritual, even when the ceremony was less elaborate. One woman told how "first they told me to burn incense and then to swear that if I let it [the sect teaching] be known, then Heaven should strike me with a thunderbolt. So I swore and [my teacher] taught me the eight characters."[107] Another related that "his teacher . . . instructed him to kotow and to swear to be his pupil. He received his teacher's warning: if he broke the fast of vegetarianism [practiced by that sect] or violated any of the other abstentions, his body would turn into pus and blood."[108]

An initial contribution of money was expected from new members in some sects. In return the new member might receive a receipt (*piao* 表) that he could burn and so "register" the contribution with the Eternal Mother.[109] (The financial dimension of sect organization will be discussed in greater detail below.) In general, initiation rituals were flexible and varied, and each sect and each teacher could introduce innovations at will—within the limits of what was safe. The leader of the 1813 Eight Trigrams, Lin Ch'ing, had been given a vermilion scroll with a seal at the top, dragons along the sides, and an efficacious charm (*fu* 符) drawn in the center, and he considered putting this to use in initiating new pupils. He wanted to have each pupil kotow to the scroll as well as to their teacher. Eventually, however, he rejected the idea, feeling that the scroll with its blatantly imperial pretentions might attract too much attention.[110] Considerations of secrecy and flexibility encouraged simplicity and brevity.

Some sects physically marked new members. "His teacher put his hand on a place on the back of his head, recited a spell, and wrote a charm which was then burned and put in water for him to drink. After that, a sore appeared in that place and then a half-moon scar where no hair would grow." Less magical methods were used to the same effect: a small area of hair under the queue was burned off with moxa, or a strand of hair in the queue was simply cut off. [111] This mark was considered a "secret identifying sign" and as such was used to a limited degree (possibly very limited) by some participants in the 1813 rebellion. This kind of mark had the advantage of being verifiable but not readily visible and was considerably less drastic than the queue-cutting or hair-growing adopted by some rebels.

There is also evidence that some White Lotus sects, at least in the Chia-ch'ing period, used secret hand signals as identifying gestures. One man stated that his teacher had told him about some of these hand signals, but the only ones he remembered were that "the Li Trigram hand signal was to point the thumb straight up; the K'an Trigram sect signal was to extend one's hands and make the character for the number ten with one's fingers." Some rebels were told that "if you meet a comrade whom you don't know, you clap your hands as a secret sign." Another described a different procedure: "Whenever two people from the sect ran into one another, they put out their two fingers and rotated them until they pointed upward. This was given the name *chien-chueh* (劍訣)."[112] Ch'ing sects did not usually have physical tokens of membership because of the danger, and so these identifying gestures were a far safer form of proof.[113]

The teacher–pupil relationships thus created constituted the links in the chain that held these sects together. This bond was a strong and respected one in China. It was an important relationship among members of the elite, cementing friendships between those who had studied and been examined on the Confucian classics. Among non-elite it usually played a lesser role, except perhaps between masters and apprentices. Thus, the White Lotus sects made it possible for ordinary people to attain the respected status of teacher and to be treated with deference, respect, and obedience by others. And yet it was not difficult to become such a teacher; the information was available to all on a variety of levels and one could simply study and master sect doctrine and practices to a minimal degree.

Just as joining a sect was a personal and individual choice, so each believer was free to "leave the sect" (*ch'u chiao* 出教) any time he wished. Severing the teacher–pupil relationship was even simpler than establishing it. Yen Hsing "changed his mind [about the sect] and because he saw that their activities had no benefit, he had no further contact with the men in the sect."[114] Short of terminating this contact, an individual could simply reduce his participation in sect affairs by degrees. Because of the relative ease of leaving, those whose commitment was more shallow, especially those who were looking for quick benefits, were more likely to drift away when they became disappointed with the lack of results. Such people were often men who had never taken the trouble to convert followers of their own, and their leaving meant no serious loss of manpower. On the contrary, it was in the interest of all White Lotus followers to discourage the marginally interested from remaining and so increase their collective security. One scripture circulating in the late nineteenth century stated this view rather well:

> But as to such persons as are not changed and are not true disciples, it would be better to let the fire of the incense die out than entrust to them our rules of abstinence or communicate to them those doctrines which tell what gods and men practice and which are not to be transmitted to men of a low grade. Let there be mercy, diligence, anxious care, and extreme strictness in propagating our religion.[115]

Like most missionaries, sect members had to balance the desire for converts against the undesirability (and in their case the danger) of attracting those who could not be fully trusted to appreciate the value of the sect teachings.

Government investigations into sect activities or the suppression of a sect-led uprising could drive many, including people with a deeper commitment, to take the step of severing relations.

On account of the legal proceedings [involving the sect] I was
afraid and asked Yang Erh to strike my name off the list of those
in the sect . . . . [He told me] if you are not going to be in the
assembly, then you should explain to Lin Ch'ing [the sect
head]. . . . [So I went to see him] and said that I didn't want
to be in the assembly. Lin Ch'ing and [another man] were
standing in the courtyard and they really cursed me and we had
a big argument. I never went there again.[116]

At the time when the Eight Trigrams uprising was being suppressed
in 1813, some members of unaffiliated sects in the Tientsin area
formally broke the vegetarian regimens practiced by their group and
left the sect.[117] The government recognized such a renunciation.
Indeed it tried to make it easy for sect members to declare publicly
that they had left their sects: people were invited to go to their local
officials and swear oaths or bonds (chü-chieh 具結) to this effect. Sun
P'eng, for example, went to the district offices and swore that he had
repented and left the Ta-sheng sect; he did not, however, go so far as
to destroy his religious literature until later when he learned of a new
government investigation and feared that even his public renunciation was not enough.[118]

A sect member could have only one teacher at a time, but it was
possible for a person to have a number of teachers in sequence. For
example, if a man moved and lost contact with his teacher, or if he
left one sect and then joined another, or if his teacher died, he could
take a second teacher. Men who specialized in the fighting skills of
the White Lotus tradition appear to have been more likely to study
with many different people. Consider Chang Lo-chiao:

In 1782 he followed his elder sister's husband's elder brother
Wang Yueh-heng (who is now dead) and learned boxing and
fencing, plus curing illness by massage. In 1793 he followed
Chang Huai-chin . . . and learned the Armor of the Golden
Bell. Then he went around to various places doing boxing and
taking pupils for profit. In 1800 he then followed Wang Hsien-
chün . . . and practiced the Li Trigram sect, reciting the True
Emptiness chant. Later, since Wang was always wanting money
from him, he practiced it no more.[119]

There were some people who went from sect to sect, joining first
one and then another, always searching for the "best" system. Ma
Sheng-chang, for example, first joined the Jung-hua Assembly, then

a few years later an acquaintance persuaded him that another sect was "doctrinally more profound," and so Ma became his friend's pupil instead. A year later, members of the Jung-hua Assembly, came and tried to persuade Ma Sheng-chang to rejoin their group, but Ma resisted and explained, "I had already taken several teachers and I didn't want to be a member of their sect again." These veteran seekers were both desirable and undesirable converts. They were familiar with and serious about sect matters on the one hand, but they were always looking out for more efficacious charms, more persuasive ideas, more "beneficial" practices, and so could not be counted on for their faithfulness.[120]

There were no restrictions as to who could join a White Lotus sect, and one teacher's claim that "it didn't matter if [your pupils] were men or women, young or old" is fully confirmed by the evidence available about sects in the Chia-ch'ing period. Sect members ranged widely in age, from as young as sixteen to as old as "over eighty" and all ages in between.[121] Similarly, "any person male or female could transmit and practice a sect," and despite the Ch'ing government's greater interest in male members—who were after all the ones who became active rebels—it is clear that many women became followers of White Lotus teachings. Unfortunately, the fact that the government tended not to prosecute women for the crime of belonging to a heretical sect means that the full extent of female participation in sect activities is not revealed in the sources.[122] We do know, and shall discuss in more detail below, that women did act as teachers and sect leaders.

It is difficult to generalize about the class or occupational background of Chia-ch'ing-period sect members. The most striking fact is the wide variety of occupations and great range of social classes represented. Sect members included Chinese and Manchu, the destitute and the well-to-do, country folk and city dwellers. There were members of the Manchu nobility, military officials of low and medium ranks, holders of the lowest degree in the system of military examinations, clerks and runners in the district yamens, and ordinary citizens of all kinds. Information on more than two hundred people who belonged to a sect in the Peking area in the 1810s yields the following occupational breakdown: 4 percent were ranked office- or title-holders;[123] 14 percent had low-status positions in service to the government;[124] 19 percent derived at least part of their income from doing hired agricultural labor;[125] 19 percent derived income from the land;[126] 32 percent very probably were also supported by agriculture;[127] and 12 percent made their living from a variety of crafts and services (these included peddlers and sellers of windowpanes, beancurd, firewood, paper, fruit, vegetables, chickens, and ducks; household servants, weavers, cart drivers, stone masons, a brick-factory worker, cook, waiter, bow-maker, theater owner, and the proprietor of a teashop).[128] Practically the only thing that all of these individuals had in common was the fact that none enjoyed the prestige of a degree obtained through the civil service examinations based on the Confucian classics.

INTERNAL ORGANIZATION

It was not a person's occupation or social class that determined his place in a White Lotus sect. In order to see how power within a sect was structured, let us begin by looking, as an illustration, at the organization of the Jung-hua Assembly. A sect teacher named Ku Liang had begun teaching this sect in the area of Sung-chia village just southwest of Peking in about 1796. A dozen years later, the sect had grown to include at least seventy members who lived in that and adjacent villages. Ku Liang was regarded by all as Sect Master (*chiao-chu* 教主). There were no active connections with Ku Liang's teacher, whoever he was, and for all intents and purposes, Ku Liang was the head of the sect. These seventy-odd sect members, men and women of all ages, were pupils under Ku Liang, either directly or through his pupils' pupils or their pupils. Formally, teachers were called "preceptors" (*ch'ien-jen* 前人) and pupils "receptors" (*hou-jen* 後人).[129] The structure of this sect as diagramed from available information might resemble figure 1. Most sect organizations would look something like this, but obviously an infinite variety of structures could be created within the framework of only one teacher for each pupil and any number of pupils for each teacher.

The person who was generationally senior within an area, as Ku Liang was in the above case, was referred to familiarly as a "sect head" (*chiao-t'ou* 教頭 or *chiao-shou* 教首). Those leaders who could claim direct transmission from a sect founder (called a patriarch or *tsu* 祖), and who often backed up this claim to authority with religious literature, were called "sect masters" (*chiao-chu* 教主). The term "master" (*chu* 主) was used by White Lotus sect members to indicate one with considerable expertise and authority. The usual term for "teacher" was *shih* 師 (or *shih-fu* 師傅) and for "pupil"

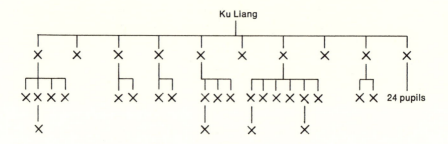

Fig. 1

t'u-ti 徒弟, both phrases in ordinary usage. Some teachers were respectfully addressed by their pupils as "sir" (*yeh* 爺). Several of the sects that later made up the Eight Trigrams employed the term "manager" (*tang-chia* 當家) to designate some sect leaders.[130] With the possible exception of the term "master," all these titles were in common usage and did not represent esoteric language.[131]

While this sect organization was well suited to secrecy, I have seen no indication that members felt it necessary to conceal the identity of the sect head. On the contrary, it was considered desirable for all members of a sect to be formally presented to their sect leader and to kotow to him "while he remained standing and received this courtesy."[132]

Within each sect there was some awareness of generational levels, called *pei* 輩 or *ts'eng* 層. Most believers knew the line of teachers between themselves and the sect leader, and could usually name these men or women. Hsing Shih-k'uei, for example, could name the nine preceding generations of teachers in his sect. A pupil was expected to treat all those in that direct line "above" him as teachers, to kotow in greeting them, and to accept their authority in sect matters.[133] The structure of these sects was fundamentally hierarchical, and fellow believers, even pupils of the same teacher, did not refer to one another as "brothers." This is in sharp contrast with the Triads and other "secret societies" of south China.[134]

Relations between teachers and pupils in White Lotus sects were not, however, bound by the same requirements of hierarchy prevalent in Ch'ing society as a whole. There the superior–inferior relationship of a teacher to his pupil paralleled other unequal relations, elder to younger, men to women. In Chinese society in general, an older man seldom treated a young man (much less a young woman) as his teacher, and it was rare for any man to have cause to study with or learn professionally from a woman of any age. These pervasive but informal rules did not apply to White Lotus sects, although certainly their influence was felt. In these sects, the respected skills of healing or fighting and the protective secret of the eight-character chant could be learned by sect members of all ages and both sexes, any one of whom could teach it to anyone else, and was actively encouraged to do so. It was possible and not uncommon for a pupil to be older than his or her teacher. Of the members for whom all the relevant information is available (again based on the Peking area sects), nearly 16 percent had teachers who were younger than they.[135] For the women on whom information is available, 76 percent had men as their teachers, and 24 percent had female teachers. Of women teachers, half had women as their pupils, half had men.[136] Such flexibility as compared with normal practice was an attractive feature of White Lotus sects for those individuals, women in particular, who wished to escape from the restrictions imposed on them by the hierarchical nature of their society.

Just as women or younger people could be teachers to anyone they converted, so there were no formal restrictions on who might be treated as a sect head. Whoever was the first believer in a village and who began to teach the sect there would be considered the leader. A younger man who wanted to build up a following of his own could do so by moving or traveling to new places. Itinerant healers converted pupils in the villages and towns through which they passed.

Custom as well as bound feet circumscribed the movements of most women; nevertheless, they could and did act as sect leaders. Mrs. Liu Kung was considered a sect master; moreover she had inherited this position of authority from her great grandmother eleven generations past who was herself the founder and patriarch of their Dragon (*lung* 龍) school sect, in which the teachings and responsibility were transmitted through the women of the family.[137]

The words used for leaders in these sects could be applied equally to men or women. The commander of the government forces sent to suppress the 1813 Eight Trigram rebels commented on the role of women: "With these bandits who practice a sect, it was in many instances the women who taught the men. . . . The women are cunning and dangerous (*yin hsien* 陰險) and this heterodoxy leads to rebellion. . . . Moreover, [in battle] our forces have so far killed more than one woman."[138]

Most Ch'ing White Lotus sects did not have firm rules for determining succession to the position of sect head. There was, as we have indicated, a bias in favor of hereditary succession, and if a son (or daughter) could command the respect of his father's pupils, he could inherit his authority. This was especially probable in families in which the sect had been practiced for generations and in which there was sect literature to be inherited, although the line of transmission was not necessarily from father to son. "Wang Fa-hsien's ancestors had transmitted the Pai-yang Assembly. . . . He had learned the sect from his older cousin Wang Hsuan. . . . After Wang Hsuan died, Wang Fa-hsien became the senior member of the assembly."[139]

A problem arose more readily when a sect leader died (or was arrested) without leaving a natural successor. His pupils would then jockey for power, and anyone who could command the respect of the group by a combination of personality, mastery of sect ideas and practices, and size of personal following, would be acknowledged as the new leader. In several cases described in greater detail in Part Two, this acknowledgment took ritual form, and all those in the sect not previously pupils under the new leader would kotow to him and "submit to his authority." Those who did not wish to do so could, however, simply take their pupils and withdraw. Because of the natural tendency for these sects to fragment if crucial links in the chain were broken, many "succession crises" were probably ignored, and instead the sect was allowed to divide into its component units at the next generational level down. It was also possible for a pupil to reject his sect leader and transfer his allegiance to another man; we shall see instances of this below.

Changes in leadership were frequently accompanied by changes in sect name. The multitude of sect names has been a problem for historians; some assume that one group would change its name as the result of government persecutions and others assert that each name means a different group.[140] My investigations indicate that a group of believers could and did change its name, but it did so not in response to persecution but on its own initiative and in order to reflect new organizational arrangements. The evidence indicates that pupils who acknowledged a common sect master at any one point in time referred to their group by the same name. This name could be very short-lived; it might be changed if the sect leader died, or if he himself later acknowledged a higher teacher and became part of his following. Relationships between sects were generally amiable, and these mergings and branchings took place more or less continually.[141] If a pupil moved away and converted his own followers in another village, he might be treated by them as a sect leader, even though he distantly deferred to his own teacher as a higher authority. Such a branch group might keep the same name, might take an entirely new name, or might call itself by a double (or triple) name combining both old and new. Sect members appear to have been very comfortable with this plethora of names and used a variety of ways to express the relationship between branches and their trunk sect, including such names as the "Venerable Prince school of the Li Trigram sect, also called the Righteous Harmony school,"[142] or the "Eastern Section of the Chen Trigram sect, also known as the Dragon Flower Assembly."[143]

The Eight Trigram rebels themselves used a series of names. Originally the rebels belonged to small isolated sects, each of which had its own name. These were pulled together organizationally and redivided into eight groups, each of which was called by one of the eight trigrams and which were known collectively as the Eight Trigrams sect. When it was time for the new kalpa to arrive, the sect members declared the establishment of the T'ien-li 天理 (Heavenly Doctrine) Assembly.[144] All these changes occurred within the space of three years and were the results of affirmative decisions by sect leaders, in no way related to any government action. The changes were, however, related to organizational shifts, and each new name signaled a realignment of the teacher–pupil chains along which believers were organized.

The terminology used by sect members to describe these various sect groups appears to have been more precise than is usually assumed. As we have seen, the term *chiao* 教 is used in one sense to mean the teachings of the White Lotus religion and in another to refer to the organizational structure through which these teachings were transmitted, a usage I have translated as "sect." The term *hui* 會 does not have either of these meanings but refers to a group of believers who are actively meeting and practicing the religion as a

congregation; I have translated it as "assembly."[145] Branches
founded by pupils of a certain teacher were sometimes called *chih* 枝,
but more often *men* 門, "school." Thus it was possible for a sect
member to tell a government official that in his religion, there were
thirty-six *chiao* (sects with their own teachings and teachers) and
seventy-two *men* (branch schools of those sects).[146] In the Chia-ch'ing
period, some members of White Lotus sects referred to themselves as
"believers," *tsai-li* 在理 (literally, "living according to doctrine").[147]

The way in which sects were formed, grew, and related to one
another can perhaps be best illustrated with a concrete example.
Let us look at what happened to a sect called the Yuan-tun sect
(圓頓 Completed and Sudden Enlightenment), which at the end of
the seventeenth century was being practiced by a resident of Peking
named Kao Pa-kang 高八岡. After Kao's death, the sect continued
through at least four branches. The main line of the sect was transmitted through his descendants, and by the early nineteenth century
the head of the sect was a widowed daughter of the Kao family,
Mrs. Kao Chang. Called "Granny Sect Master" (*chiao-chu nai-nai*
教主奶奶) by her pupils, Mrs. Kao Chang lived in the southern
section of Peking with her widowed daughter and her son, both of
whom also practiced the sect. The name they now used was the
Single Stick of Incense, Clean and Pure, Effortless Action sect (*i-chu-
hsiang ch'ing-ching wu-wei chiao* 一柱香清淨無爲教). Mrs. Kao Chang had
in her possession a large number of religious books (at least thirty-
five were confiscated in 1813), and she received contributions
regularly from her followers. These pupils lived in Peking and
elsewhere in north China—in Yü-t'ien (east of Peking), in Chi-nan
prefectural city in Shantung, and in Tsao-ch'iang district in Chihli.

In addition to this main line of the sect maintained by the Kao
family, there was a branch of the original Yuan-tun sect located in
southern Shensi province in Hsi-hsiang district near the Szechwan
border. One of Kao Pa-kang's daughters had married a man named
Ch'en Kuei from this area. Ch'en Kuei was his father-in-law's pupil
and so he carried the sect back to his home and transmitted it there.
His sons and grandsons therefore inherited the position of sect leader
which he had created for himself; by the Chia-ch'ing reign, the sect
in southern Shensi was being managed by Ch'en's great-great-
grandson Ch'en Heng-i. Yet another branch of the Ch'en family's
sect was created when Ch'en Heng-i's brother moved to western
Shantung (to Lin-ch'ing district) in 1811 and there gathered his own
followers. And there was still another offshoot of the original Yuan-

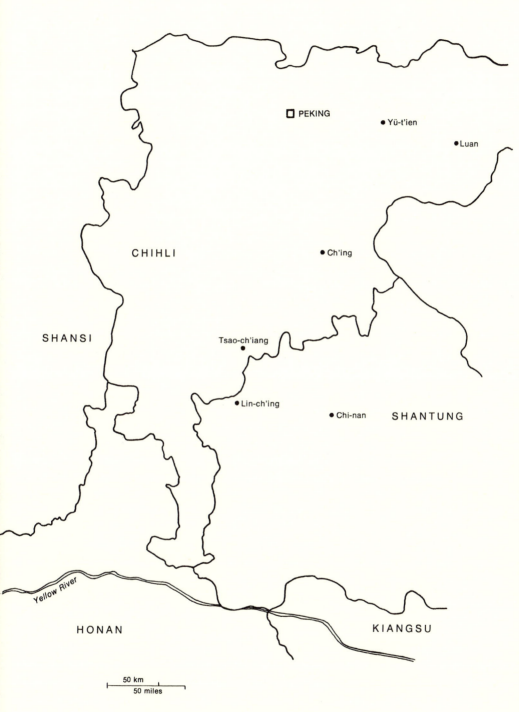

PEKING

• Yü-t'ien

• Luan

CHIHLI

• Ch'ing

SHANSI

Tsao-ch'iang
•

• Lin-ch'ing

• Chi-nan   SHANTUNG

Yellow River

HONAN

KIANGSU

50 km
50 miles

Districts and cities of the north China plain

tun sect located in Feng-t'ien (in Manchuria). That sect was originally transmitted by Wang Ching-ch'ao, a pupil of Kao Pa-kang who
happened to come from that area. One hundred years later, Wang's
great-grandson was still practicing and teaching the sect.

These branches did not remain isolated, despite the distances in
space that separated them and the distances in time from their original association with one another. They were aware of one another's
existence and kept in relatively frequent contact. Mrs. Kao Chang
was acknowledged as the legitimate main-line descendant of the
sect founder, but there was an exchange of information between her
sect and the branches that was more or less between equals. In 1808
the Shensi sect head Ch'en Heng-i came to Peking and stayed with
the Kao family. He told Granny Sect Master that, according to his
predictions, in five or six years there would come a period of hard
times. But, he told her, he happened to know of some spells that, if
properly recited, could help one avoid these troubles. Ch'en taught
her the spells and also gave her several written charms, which, if
burned and taken with water, would help one find enlightenment as
well as avoid "the calamities of fire, flood and the sword." Mrs. Kao
Chang welcomed these new sources of protection and in turn passed
them on to all her pupils. Wang Shih-ch'ing, the sect head in Manchuria, was in the habit of sending money annually to Mrs. Kao
Chang. When one of his pupils came to Peking in the spring of 1813,
bringing with him 30 taels, Granny Sect Master told him about
these new charms and formulas. He returned to Feng-t'ien and
told Wang Shih-ch'ing, who in turn passed them on to his followers.[148] Despite their proximity to the sects that led the Eight
Trigrams uprising of 1813, there is no indication of any involvement
by these people in that rebellion, or even of any connection with the
rebels. It was in the wake of that uprising, however, that Mrs. Kao
Chang and the others were discovered by the government and
prosecuted.

RIGHT BEHAVIOR

Many White Lotus sects practiced some sort of dietary regimen.
Dietary restrictions had long been considered physically beneficial
and a path to long life and possible immortality, and through Buddhism such regimens had also become associated with piety and right

behavior. As it happened, few of those sects involved in the Eight Trigrams uprising put great emphasis on diet—though some of them claimed to abstain from wine[149]—but many other believers were vegetarians.[150] Some believers abstained from eating certain foods,[151] others abstained from meat only on certain days, or ate normally at home but always had vegetarian meals at sect meetings.[152] Abstention from meat for religious reasons turned a hard necessity into an approved and pious gesture. As we have seen, swearing to keep the fast of vegetarianism could be part of the sect initiation ritual, just as public renunciation of such a regimen could indicate severance of connections with a sect.[153]

Most sects encouraged their members to practice a certain code of moral behavior as part of the teachings of the Eternal Mother, though the degree of emphasis on ethical behavior varied from group to group. Some sects prohibited gambling, others forbade alcohol, tobacco, and opium.[154] The Jung-hua Assembly of the Chia-ch'ing period claimed to "abstain from wine, sex, greed, and anger,"[155] while another sect of a later period prohibited "killing, robbing, licentiousness, reckless falsity, and liquor."[156] Wine and alcohol were often considered both unhealthy and evil, but the injunctions against them were not always respected.[157]

In addition to prohibiting what was judged bad behavior, sect leaders encouraged their pupils to live correctly. They were urged to be diligent and thrifty and to "do good deeds" including helping out fellow believers who "were poor or in distress."[158] One man was told, "If you encounter trouble, you should be benevolent, righteous, properly polite, wise, and thoughtful. You should not be a law-breaker or do evil things." Another was told to "respect heaven and earth, be filial toward father and mother, and not cheat those who have more or oppress those who have less."[159]

A common government criticism of White Lotus sects has been that they not only permitted men and women to meet and fraternize with an alarming disregard for social convention, but that the sects sponsored sexual relations outside of marriage and permitted orgies at their meetings. As we have seen, it was certainly true that in these sects a woman's role as wife, mother, or unmarried daughter did not restrict her participation, and as a fellow believer her sex was relegated to a secondary position. By thus liberating women from their normal roles, these sects did indeed run counter to the status quo. Women held positions of leadership, serving as teachers of men, and

they may easily have drawn some sense of importance from the fact
that the Eternal Mother herself, supreme among deities, was of
their sex.

Reliable information about the sexual practices of White Lotus
sects is difficult to obtain, for government accusations cannot be
taken as fact. Certainly there was a tradition of orgiastic meetings by
popular "Taoist" sects extending back many centuries and an equally
venerable association between sexual practices and long life.[160]
Furthermore, evidence from source materials on sects in the Chia-
ch'ing period does suggest that government suspicions may have
been justified.

Members of some Eight Trigram sects practiced a degree of sexual
permissiveness toward which the Ch'ing government, as guardian
of public morality, might justly have been disapproving, even if
orgies were not part of their practices. In two Peking area sects,
fellow believers were apparently encouraged (or at least allowed) to
have sexual intercourse with one another. When the sect leader and
future rebel Lin Ch'ing came to visit one of his pupils, he would tell
(ask?) his pupil's wife and sometimes his daughter-in-law to come to
bed with him. In a spirit of reciprocity which was apparently part of
their morality, Lin Ch'ing offered his own wife and stepdaughters to
this pupil and the latter's son.[161] It is not clear whether the women
were free to refuse. Li Wu, the leader of another sect south of Peking
and a friend of Lin Ch'ing, and his wife evidently had sexual intercourse with various women and men (respectively) who were pupils
in their sect. Not every believer thought this sexual permissiveness
was either right or proper. Wu Hsien-ta was coming to Li Wu's
house for a meeting when he found a fellow believer in bed with Li
Wu's wife. He left immediately and "decided that men and women
in the sect mixing together like that wasn't what I considered 'learning to do right,' so I stopped believing and went no more."[162] Lin
Ch'ing and Li Wu were both influential sect leaders, and it is not
clear if their privileges extended to their pupils.

It is impossible that a tradition as old and as widespread as the
White Lotus religion would not have produced its share of those who
took advantage of these relaxed sexual standards. Hsing Shih-k'uei,
for example, had once belonged to a sect where he had learned to
cure illness by massage. Later, he decided to set up his own sect and,
abandoning the usual practices, he simply invented ideas and activities as he went along. According to his own testimony: "In 1809, Mrs.
Lu Yin from a neighboring village became ill and she came to him

for help. Hsing Shih-k'uei was using massage to cure her when all of a sudden he felt a great desire for this woman, and so he had sexual intercourse with her. After that, he found other occasions to sleep with her. He doesn't remember how many times. . . . Later he came up with the idea of [pretending her son was a god reincarnated in order to increase his following], delude other women, and so make money and have more opportunities for sex."[163]

MONEY AND MEETINGS

One of the more frequent government criticisms of heretical sects was that their leaders wanted only to make money from those whom they "hoodwinked" into believing in them. While the question of true individual motivation is a difficult one, it is very clear that White Lotus sects could and often did generate considerable wealth. Teachers in the sect regularly solicited contributions from their pupils, and this money was passed up along the pupil–teacher chain into the hands of the sect head. These donations were voluntary, but they were usually systematized in such a way as to make refusal by a "sincere" believer very difficult.

There was enormous variety among sects in the procedure by which contributions were elicited, each trying to find the most efficient system for its particular group. Many sects expected an initial contribution by all new members. At least three sects in the Chia-ch'ing period called this donation "foundation money" (ken-chi ch'ien 根基錢).[164] One sect then asked for either monthly or seasonal donations, called respectively "small gifts" and "large gifts" (hsiao li ch'ien 小禮錢 and ta 大 li ch'ien). Another expected "installment money" (ken-chang ch'ien 跟賬錢) twice a year, "according to your ability to pay."[165]

This money was generally used for the benefit of the sect as a whole. Some groups used contributions to buy food and incense for regular meetings where vegetarian dishes were eaten by those attending. One group held banquets each year on its leader's birthday.[166] Although money was used for meetings, the sect heads also benefited. One sect member explained that they believed in their leader and so they had "helped him by giving him money to spend."[167] Contributions were passed up the line of teachers, and although it is not clear how much each teacher took out, the person at the top of a large pyramid of pupils could receive a regular income.[168] The promise of contributions from pupils certainly encouraged all believers to proselytize and expand their own networks.

This system of regular assessments could easily turn into an even more systematic, rebellion-oriented tithing. The new kalpa could arrive at any time, and those sects that expected it to be soon might take specific steps to plan for their own role in this event. One sign of such organizational activity was a difference in the scope of money collecting.

It appears to have been common practice for more ambitious sects to maintain lists of their members' names, and in some cases of their contributions as well. One scripture contained the passage:

> Patriarch Lü established himself in Huang village,
> down to the present he has been prospering.
> All the virtuous people under heaven
> are those who have registered their names [as sect members].
> . . . Go to Huang village to present money and grain.[169]

When plans for an uprising were under way, members were told that their contributions represented more than registration and could now buy them wealth and power in the coming kalpa era. "Lin Ch'ing was always asking for people's money. He said that [giving money] was like sowing the seeds of future benefit (*fu* 福) and in the future [the gifts] would be multiplied tenfold. So people believed and gave money."[170] The benefits promised could be quite explicit. The Eight Trigrams promised that everyone who gave money or grain would later be given land or official position, the amount of land or degree of position depending on the size of the contribution. One group gave each contributor a receipt describing the donation and the promised benefit.[171] Anticipation of rebellion might therefore mean a bias in favor of people who were relatively more useful to the sect: one teacher told his pupil to "bring young and rich people into the sect."[172]

Money raised in the name of rebellion did not simply line the pockets of sect leaders. In the 1813 rebellion, as we shall see, there were a number of necessary expenses met by contributions. Many leaders supplied their pupils either with weapons or with money to buy weapons. Each rebel was to wear at least one and in some cases two pieces of white cloth as a sash or turban; this cloth and the material for many white banners was supplied by the top leadership. For his attack on the Forbidden City, Lin Ch'ing needed assistance from eunuchs who worked inside. Those eunuchs already in the sect were therefore encouraged to convert others, and Lin authorized payments of money to eunuch members—a reverse of the usual flow.[173] In short, there were purchases to be made on behalf of the Eight Trigrams as a whole, and while it is undeniable that the leaders themselves made ample use of contributions to improve their life style, money was spent generously in the interest of their pupils as well.

Even in normal times pressure was exerted on members to contribute, and there were those who left the sect because they were no longer willing or able to do so. Wang Liang, for example, went to a meeting of the group he had just joined. He was told to pay 500 cash in the current year and double that the following year. The next year, however, he refused to pay this much. His teacher told him that he was obviously "not dedicated," and so he "wasn't included in their activities after that, not their meetings or their rebellion."[174] Another man testified that "we had an argument because I had no more money to give him [my teacher], and after that I had no more contact with him."[175] In some ways, the necessity for donations provided a useful weeding-out technique. It discouraged those who were not willing to sacrifice for the sake of the group and provided a regular and escalating test of commitment that served to cement the group. When rebellion was being planned, the leaders were less willing to write off those who would not meet the increased need for funds—they needed all the men they could get and wanted all who knew of their plans to stick with them. At this stage, it was not unusual for warnings and the threat of death to accompany requests. Sect members believed that when the kalpa did come, all nonbelievers would be killed. The fear of being excluded from the ultimate benefits of sect membership and the dread of dying with other outsiders was a powerful weapon in the hands of rebellion-minded leaders, and they did not hesitate to use it: "[My teacher] told me that Li Lao was taking his pupils to rebel. He told me to contribute two strings of cash in order to help Li Lao. If I did so, then Li Lao [and his men] wouldn't kill me. If I didn't give the money, then they would kill my whole family."[176] It was, however, cooperation that leaders wanted, and sect members who had no resources were asked to give their time and energy rather than money by helping run errands, deliver messages, arrange meetings.[177]

Perhaps the most important aspect of this question of contributions is the degree to which they were a hardship for sect members.

This is a difficult problem and this discussion must be regarded as no more than preliminary guesswork based on a small sample. (For details on donations and on the cost of living and sources for this information see Appendixes 2 and 3.) Initial donations ranged from 100 to 400 cash, averaging about 200. If we assume 200 cash to be the very rough equivalent of two days' labor for a poor person, this is high but not outrageous. Annual gifts ranged widely, from as low as 200 cash to nearly 4,000; from two to twenty days' earnings. At the last minute, individuals were asked to make special contributions toward the expenses of rebellion; these also ranged widely, from 20 to 5,000 cash (from less than one to twenty-five days' work). Because teachers expected less money from those who earned less, it is likely that the normal donations by the individual to his sect were not an excessive burden. Demands for cash at the last minute before the rebellion were more of a hardship; but these demands were made in the 8th and 9th months, as the harvest was coming in, and everyone who worked the land had more ready cash at that time. Moreover, it was surely argued that if the new kalpa did indeed arrive, sect members would not have to worry about making ends meet later, and spending one's reserve (if one had any) was quite justified.

Because leaders of small groups were expected to solicit contributions from their pupils and then pass on some of it to the top leadership, their donations were substantially larger. One leader gave Lin Ch'ing over 10,000 cash in the first nine months of 1813, and another was asked to give 4,000 cash every month for the three months prior to the uprising. Lin Ch'ing, who received money from all the groups who participated in the uprising, thus amassed quite substantial sums. The gifts he received included also rolls of pale blue cloth, a cart, a donkey, a mule, a box of silver ingots, five hundred ounces of silver on one occasion, probably the same amount on two other occasions.[178]

These are large sums of money if seen through the eyes of one for whom one or two taels was a great deal. According to Chang Chung-li, the average per capita income for a commoner (based on percentage of GNP) was 5.7 taels a year, and for a member of the gentry class 90 taels a year. On the other hand, the poet and scholar Yuan Mei who lived half a century before Lin Ch'ing would customarily be paid 300 to 500 taels simply to compose a tomb-inscription, and he made 300 taels a month while serving as a prefect. Wealthy salt merchants, admittedly an extreme case, regularly contributed millions of taels to the central government.[179] Thus, a sect leader could become "rich" in comparison with his followers, and a leader at the head of a broad alliance of sects such as the Eight Trigrams could begin to achieve the same income as a member of the elite. Equally important, this system of contributions provided an economic foundation for the sects and gave their leaders a source of income that was entirely independent of government or elite control.

One of the great strengths of the White Lotus tradition was its capacity for both diffused and coordinated activity: meditation, healing, boxing, or vegetarianism could be practiced either individually or in groups. The act of joining a sect and its daily religious activities could involve no more than a few people and could take place anywhere. Nevertheless, these sects were by tradition and by continually renewed choice congregational sects and reflected this fact by calling their groups "assemblies" (*hui* 會). Because "a group which meets secretly at night" was illegal in the eyes of the government, holding such meetings was in itself a dangerous act of defiance.

There was no fixed pattern for sect meetings. Each group assembled whenever and as frequently as it wanted, and within the tradition there was much variety. The most common pattern appears to have been bimonthly meetings, on the 1st and 15th days, which on the lunar calendar represented the nights of the new moon and full moon respectively.[180] Some groups met less often: one, two, three, or four times a year.[181] One sect leader decided to hold eight meetings a year, each of which was called by the name of one of the eight trigrams.[182] Assemblies were usually held in the home of one sect member, often the sect leader. At these meetings, food (brought or purchased with contributions), often vegetarian food, was first offered in sacrifice, and then the sect members sat down to eat.[183] Those attending might then listen to, read, or recite sect scriptures, sometimes meditating or reciting the eight-character chant together. Members of a San-yuan (Three Origins) sect arrested in 1816 stated:

> Whenever there was a meeting, P'ei Ching-i and the others all went to the house of [one of the members]. They contributed money which was turned over to [another member] to buy vegetarian food and an offering. Then, in the evening they burned incense, worshiped, and practiced reciting chants. After the worship was over, they all shared the food. Then they sat and meditated and circulated their breath. On other ordi-

nary days, P'ei Ching-i and some others might meet in one
place in groups of three or five or else they might each individually practice yogic meditation at home.[184]

Sometimes the leader might expound and explain sect teachings or
exhort his pupils to good behavior—"besides, the meetings are
devoted to pious conversation, particularly about the five command-
ments, to the faithful keeping of which they admonish and encourage
each other."[185]

During the Ch'ing dynasty the tension between the individual and
congregational aspects of this tradition was actively encouraged by
the government. It was the policy of the Ch'ing state, as C. K. Yang
has demonstrated, to make "a constant effort to preserve the dif-
fusion of religion . . . and to prevent the development of independent religious organizations which might concern themselves with
affairs of state."[186] The government did not take into account, however, the strength of the White Lotus tradition, for its ideas continued
to be taught even when local assemblies had been dispersed by government investigations. Meetings were important to sect members, for
they allowed their group to congregate as a community with all the
attendant pleasures and benefits for members; but the group could
survive for some time without meetings so long as the assemblies
eventually were able to reconvene.

One final point must be made with regard to the nature of these
White Lotus sects. There are indications, albeit inconclusive, that
these sects conceived of themselves as having, in terms of both organization and practice, two dimensions. These dimensions cor-
respond to the age-old dichotomy between *yin* and *yang* but are here
more often referred to as *an* 暗 (dark or secret) and *ming* 明 (bright or
public). As we shall see, the Eight Trigram rebels used two types of
slogans during their uprising. One was called a "public slogan"
(*ming-hao* 明號) and would be displayed on their banners; the other
was called a "password" (*an-hao* 暗號) and would only be spoken between fellow rebels. In the twentieth century this division into secret
and public organizational systems or into comparable types of activities became even more discernable.[187] This religion does in fact
seem to manifest itself in two ways, as a secret religious organization
in normal times and as a vehicle for open rebellion and revolution at
the time of the new kalpa; it does not therefore appear unusual for
believers to have been conscious of the dual nature of their religion.

The Kao Family's Li Trigram Sect

In normal times, the White Lotus sects scattered about the north China plain appeared isolated from one another, small in size, fixed in one place, and preoccupied only with day-to-day religious activities, unconscious even of their own past histories. The preceding description of sect organization and practices only mirrors this static picture. In order to see how these sects lived and changed, it is necessary to look at them over a longer period of time. We would then see that each sect was in constant motion, expanding, branching out, flowing from place to place, sometimes shrinking to nearly nothing and then rapidly growing again. Each sect member was conscious of this dynamic past. The chain of teacher–pupil relationships of which he was a part encouraged him to forge new links into the future and tied him directly to past prosecutions and rebellions. The emphasis on conversion and the continuity provided by the families of hereditary sect leaders encouraged members to find new pupils in new places. Thus there was a steady pressure away from areas where a sect had become embroiled with the government and toward places where there had never been a sect or trouble before. In other words, these sects were very much alive in time and space. To illustrate this before turning to the Eight Trigrams, let us look at another sect and its various branches as it existed in north China in the late Ch'ien-lung and Chia-ch'ing periods.

The Kao 郜 family lived on the north China plain in Shang-ch'iu district in Honan, near the Shantung border and just south of the Yellow River (which prior to 1850 did not take its present course but flowed due east across the plain and entered the sea south of the Shantung peninsula). This family is known to have practiced the Li Trigram sect 離卦教 "for generations" and is a good example of the hereditary elite who were the carriers of this White Lotus tradition. A member of the family was regarded as sect master and known more formally as the "Immortal of the First Hall of Southern Area Li Trigram Sect." Thus this family saw itself as only one branch of an even larger teaching.

Late in the Ch'ien-lung reign one member of the Kao family decided to move in order to escape the prosecution as a sect member that had befallen most of his immediate family. Kao T'ien-lin's father and two uncles had been executed (they were probably involved in a planned rebellion), another uncle had died in prison, and one of his cousins had been sent into exile. While the Kao family as a whole was able to survive this period of difficulties, Kao T'ien-lin decided to change his name and surname, and in 1787 he moved to Tung-ch'ang prefectural city in west central Shantung, about one hundred and fifty miles away. Kao had by no means turned his back on his family's sect, however, and he continued to take new pupils until his death (of natural causes) twenty-three years later. His son and his nephew, who had accompanied him, were both in the sect, and the latter succeeded his uncle to the position of sect head. Thus, in the early years of the Chia-ch'ing reign, the family maintained at least two centers of sect leadership—the main family in Honan, and Kao T'ien-lin's sect in Shantung. Everyone in the family continued to recruit pupils and to spread the sect, and so branches were steadily established.

One branch was established by a pupil of Kao T'ien-lin, in his own home in Hsin district in western Shantung near the Grand Canal. There this man taught the sect to those who would follow him and acquired many pupils. Further to the south in Chin-hsiang, another branch of the Shantung Kao family sect had been established. Ts'ui Shih-chün was four generations below Kao T'ien-lin and had been teaching the sect since 1804. He had a large network of pupils in his own and adjacent districts, and by 1811 he was regarded as a prominent sect leader there. Leaders of these two branches in western Shantung were acquainted with each other, but contact between them was infrequent.[188]

The Kao family in Honan, in the meantime, had continued to spread and generate its own sect offspring. Through an intermediary teacher from central Chihli, one set of pupils became active in Chü-lu district in central Chihli—the district where Magistrate Huang Yü-p'ien would later seize dozens of sect scriptures. The leader of this Chü-lu group, who was himself at least three generations removed from the Honan leadership, was a healer named Wu Lo-hsing 吳洛興 (also known as Wu Number Two Earthen Pot 吳二瓦罐). In the early years of the Chia-ch'ing reign, Wu had taken a considerable number of pupils from his own district, and through his pupils he spread the sect teachings to at least five more generations of believers in the region to the west of Chü-lu. Some believers from Wu's own district had moved to central Shansi; there they had taken pupils of their own and renamed their group the Hsien-t'ien 先天 (Former Heaven) sect. In 1800 Wu Lo-hsing and two of his pupils were arrested, punished with beatings for the crime of practicing a sect, and then

Districts and cities of the north China plain

released. If this was his sect's first encounter with the law, it was certainly not its last.[189]

In the years after 1800, Wu Lo-hsing's following continued to expand, especially in the Chü-lu area where he lived. A decade later they had more than sixteen hundred members listed in registers as believers in what they had begun to call the Ta-sheng (Greater Vehicle) sect. The use of the new name reflects the fact that Wu's own followers considered themselves independent enough to be more than an extension of the Kao family sect. Every new and full moon the members met in small groups, burned incense, read and recited their religious books, and were urged by their leaders to live properly and to do good works. Contributions were encouraged, and as much as 4,800 taels had been collected.

Given the large scale of these operations, it is not surprising that the sect again came to the attention of the government. A failed exam candidate decided to inform the authorities about these illegal activities. The resulting prosecution, in 1811, was again not especially severe. The sixteen hundred people listed on the membership rolls were not punished at all; their names were noted by officials in their localities and they were instructed to stay out of further trouble. Some of those on the lists came forward voluntarily and swore oaths that they would no longer follow the sect. Other believers continued to practice the sect but held fewer meetings in smaller groups. The leaders of the Ta-sheng sect were treated less leniently than the membership at large. Wu Lo-hsing's pupil and the supposed ringleader of the sect (who had also been prosecuted with Wu a decade before) was sentenced to immediate strangulation. Wu himself, judged a "lesser leader," was sentenced to exile in Kwangsi and died of illness en route there. Four other lesser leaders were sentenced to exile.[190]

These sects were much too resilient to be eliminated by one or even two government investigations, and the prosecution of the Ta-sheng sect in 1811 did little to dampen the zeal of the membership in Chü-lu, although smaller communities were more intimidated.[191] Despite the arrest and removal of several of the highest ranking sect leaders, including Wu himself, there was no shortage of leadership. Only one year after these arrests, a follower named Liu Kuo-ming decided that it was time to revive the sect. He went to a nearby district to consult with Chang Chiu-ch'eng. Chang was a fellow believer, a healer, astrologer, physiognomer, diviner, and boxing expert, as well as a relative of one of the recently exiled leaders. Chang agreed that the sect should begin assembling again and suggested that they send out to the membership announcements of this revival; they could even carve a facsimile of an imperial seal and stamp it on the placards. Liu and Chang set about making these announcements, but not long afterward, one of their followers was arrested in Peking. The placards, with their "presumptuous" seals, were scrutinized by government authorities. Liu Kuo-ming was promptly arrested and sentenced to death. Chang Chiu-ch'eng managed to avoid arrest and remained at liberty and active in sect affairs for several years.[192]

Reviewing the history of this sect, the Chia-ch'ing Emperor decided that the sentences meted out in the past to this group had been too light. He criticized the officials responsible and ordered that the sentences of those punished the preceding year (1811) be now reconsidered. As a result, these punishments were all made one degree more severe. For three of these sect leaders, this meant imprisonment in prefectural jails in Chihli province and possible execution in the fall of that year.[193]

Despite the heavier punishments, these leaders did not "abandon their evil ways." On the contrary, one of those leaders who had been resentenced, a man called Li Ching 李經, actually began to organize an uprising while in prison in southern Chihli. Several years before, the fortune-teller Chang Chiu-ch'eng had made some predictions about the auspicious future of Li Ching's son. He calculated that in 1814 the kalpa calamities would occur, and young Li could be considered the reincarnation of the Buddha who had come into the world at this crucial time. In 1813, therefore, Li Ching sent a message via his jailer to several other sect leaders, reminding them of this prophecy. These men came and visited Li in prison. He told them to make banners on which would be written his son's name and the month and day of the uprising. All members of the sect were to be given these banners, which were yellow in color, and told to acquire weapons and plan for "responding to the kalpa."

Li Ching's plans were disrupted by the Eight Trigrams rebellion in the fall of that year: government investigators again made inquires into the Ta-sheng sect, and the Eight Trigrams' claims to have correctly predicted the coming kalpa had won support from some of Li Ching's own pupils. Despite Li's efforts to change the date and rise up quickly before the Eight Trigrams could "lure away their members," his own plot became known. Angry at these continued and persistent efforts by the Ta-sheng sect to cause trouble, the emperor ordered Li Ching executed immediately by slow slicing (*ling-ch'ih*

凌遲), and twenty-one other sect leaders were arrested and also put to death.[194]

Many members of the Ta-sheng sect, and of its parent Li Trigram sect, knew about the government prosecutions in 1811, 1812, and 1813, but relatively few of them were punished. One follower from Chü-lu, a man called Yang Yü-shan, was certainly quite undeterred. He reestablished a personal link with the Kao family in Honan by taking a young man from that family as his pupil, and subsequently he sent monetary contributions to them. Moreover, having followers who were clearly interested in being saved should the kalpa calamities arrive, Yang made contact with the leaders of the Eight Trigrams and arranged for the participation of his sect in their uprising, and he made sure that the Kao family was notified of these plans.[195] After the enormous loss of life and very intense investigations that accompanied the failure of the Eight Trigrams in the winter of 1813, it does appear that the Ta-sheng sect, the Li Trigram sect, and their various branches, opted for a quieter course, for they do not appear in the historical record in the next decade.

While these Li Trigram sects represent only a portion of the White Lotus sects active during the early Chia-ch'ing reign, this account of several decades of their history should illustrate what life was typically like for such groups and should provide a brief alternative to the more detailed and somewhat different history of the Eight Trigrams during this same period.

PART TWO

Consolidation: The Formation of the Eight Trigrams

To DATE, no one has assembled the primary sources necessary to write a history of White Lotus sects. The secondary source material presently available yields a meager picture, no more than a spattering of unconnected names and dates. Even so, each sect member had his own access to parts of a collective history, through the chains of pupils and teachers reaching back into the past and through the names of the sects themselves that echoed with each successive usage. The Eight Trigrams of 1813 were not the first followers of the Eternal Mother to proclaim the arrival of Maitreya, nor were they the first to be disappointed in their expectations. Before concentrating on their rebellion, let us survey briefly the violent history to which they were heir.

One of the first White Lotus rebellions about which there is information in some detail is that led by members of the Wang family of Stone-buddha village in northern Chihli. This family was discussed previously as an example of hereditary sect teachers whose role in the coming kalpa had been foretold in religious scriptures. The sect leader and family founder Wang Sen had been teaching what he called the Incense Smelling (Wen-hsiang) sect from the 1590s or earlier until his death in prison in 1619. His pupils had branched into several different sects with members in many places in north China. In 1622 his son Wang Hao-hsien 王好賢 and another believer named Hsu Hung-ju 徐鴻儒 spread the word that the kalpa would arrive on midautumn day (the 15th day of the 8th month) of that year. Government investigations forced them to alter their timing, however, and in the 5th month followers of these men donned red turbans and attacked four cities in western Shantung (Yun-ch'eng, Teng, I, and Tsou). The rebels gathered many supporters but were eventually surrounded and besieged in Tsou district city. There they held out for three months before the siege was finally broken and the rebellion shattered.[1]

After the Ch'ing conquest White Lotus teachings continued to be transmitted quietly and, from all available evidence, there were few violent outbreaks in the first century of Ch'ing rule. During the reign of the Ch'ien-lung Emperor (1736–95), for reasons that are not entirely clear, prophecies about the coming millennium and arrival of Maitreya Buddha caught hold once more and were translated into

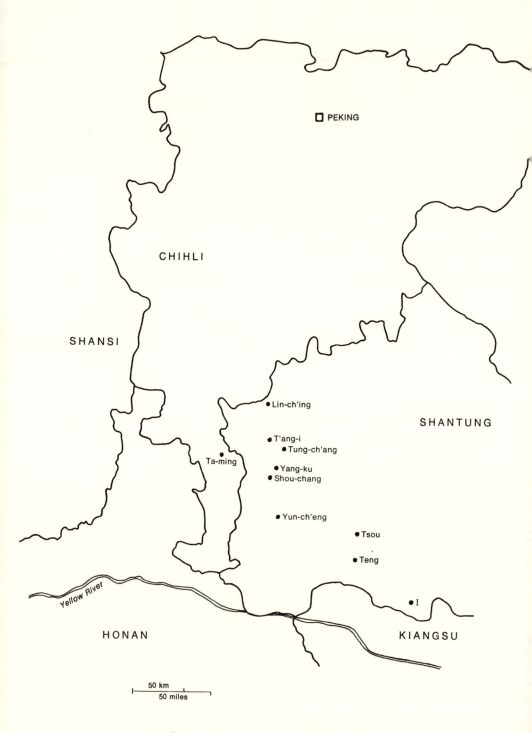

PEKING

CHIHLI

SHANSI

SHANTUNG

• Lin-ch'ing

• T'ang-i
• Tung-ch'ang

Ta-ming

• Yang-ku
• Shou-chang

• Yun-ch'eng

• Tsou

• Teng

• I

Yellow River

HONAN

KIANGSU

50 km
50 miles

Districts and cities of the north China plain

open uprisings. A sect in Hupei that had previously confined itself to teaching fighting skills, curing illnesses, and holding small meetings, began to prepare for the coming kalpa in 1768 (CL 33) by notifying members to prepare red turbans. The government learned of these activities and, before any violence could take place, arrested at least two hundred persons.[2]

In 1774 (CL 39) sect members were more successful. Wang Lun 王倫 was a healer from Shou-chang district in western Shantung, skilled in the arts of boxing and meditation and the leader of a Clear Water (Ch'ing-shui 清水) sect. This group had made plans for an uprising to coincide with the new kalpa, but when a local official learned of their plans, they were forced to act prematurely. On 8/28 of that year, these believers initiated a series of strikes on the district cities of Shou-chang, Yang-ku, Tung-ch'ang, T'ang-i, and Lin-ch'ing, all in western Shantung. The rebels gathered and were quickly besieged in the old city of Lin-ch'ing and within a month the siege was ended, Wang Lun killed, and the rebels defeated.[3]

In 1786 (CL 51), in fulfillment of a prophecy about the kalpa's arriving on the 15th day of the 8th month, an attack was carried out on the government offices in Ta-ming prefecture in southern Chihli (the attack actually took place on the 15th day of the intercalary 7th month). The sect-members-turned-rebels killed more than a dozen official personnel, broke open the treasury and jail, and left the city. At least forty men were subsequently arrested and found to be part of an Eight Trigrams (Pa-kua) sect whose membership came from the Ta-ming area and had links to sects in western and south-western Shantung. There had been a disastrous drought in the plain north of the Yellow River that year.[4]

The largest of the sect uprisings of this period, the well-known White Lotus (Pai-lien 白蓮) rebellion, looked in its early stages like its less successful predecessors. Members of a Pai-lien sect practiced healing arts, ate a vegetarian diet, and recited chants. One of the leaders had been banished to Kansu in 1775 (CL 40) during government investigation of his sect, but he had maintained contact with his pupils and money had been delivered regularly to him while in exile for twenty years. Other members of the same sect were arrested in 1793 (CL 58). Sect leaders then proclaimed that the turn in the kalpa was about to arrive; they declared two young men, sons of leaders, surnamed Liu and Wang, to be the reincarnated Maitreya and a descendant of the Ming royal family, respectively. Uprisings scheduled by these sect members took place in Hupei in 1796

(CC 1). The rebels, pressed by government forces, moved westward into the mountainous border area between Hupei, Honan, Shensi, and Szechwan. There they met with unprecedented success, finding mass support among the poor and immigrant people of this region. Backed by popular support in a terrain more suited to guerrilla than to conventional warfare, the rebels held out against government suppression campaigns with diminishing vigor for eight years (1796–1803, CC 1–8).[5] It is unfortunately not clear how much of the leadership and direction of this rebellion in its later stages came from sect members and how much from the discontented people who had joined them afterward. Regardless of its mixed leadership and ultimate defeat, this rebellion was a powerful advertisement for all White Lotus sects. Equally important, because the military campaigns took place in the mountains to the west of the north China plain, sect networks in Honan, Chihli, and Shantung remained undisturbed by the suppression.

The 1813 uprising of the Eight Trigrams came as part of this surge of millenarian activity. Resemblances among these uprisings are striking, and both the Eight Trigrams and their predecessors confronted many of the same problems: the difficulties of converting a religious sect into a rebel organization, the tension generated by government investigations into plans determined by prophetic inspiration, and the necessity for tactical choices between surgical strikes on government offices, occupation of urban areas, or flight into the mountains.

BUILDING BLOCKS

In the first decade of the nineteenth century there were several White Lotus sects active in the area around the capital city of Peking. Although believers had been arrested periodically, there had been no sect-organized violence in that area.[6] The Eight Trigrams leader Lin Ch'ing united several of these sects and with them built an organization that he would later lead in rebellion. Although our knowledge of the history of these sects is rather shallow, it is instructive to piece together a picture of what they looked like originally, for these sects are important as examples of "normal" sects in "normal" times, the building blocks of higher level sect organizations.

One of these sects called itself the Lao-li 老理 (Venerable Doctrine) Assembly. It had been transmitted five teachers back by a man named Liu Hung from Shantung. Liu Hung's rescue from prison, where he was serving a sentence for previous involvement in another sect case, had been one goal of the Eight Trigrams uprising in southern Chihli in 1786.[7] Around 1810 this small branch of Liu Hung's sect was being practiced under the leadership of a father and son surnamed Wang from Hsin-ch'eng district in Chihli. They transmitted the eight-character mantra, "Eternal Progenitor in Our Original Home in the World of True Emptiness," collected money from their followers, and had four volumes listing the names of all their members.[8]

Not far away in at least eight villages of northwestern Hsiung district, there were members of a Ta-sheng 大乘 (Greater Vehicle) sect. The sect leader, Yang Pao, who was addressed as Venerable Teacher, had been active since at least 1809 and probably for about thirty years. This sect was an offshoot of those Ta-sheng sects in Chü-lu described above that were prosecuted by the government in 1811 and 1812; the Hsiung district group had escaped attention, but members had suspended their congregational activities and the ranks were probably depleted because of this trouble.[9]

Closer to Peking in Ku-an district there was a larger sect under a teacher called Chang T'ien-sheng. Chang was over sixty years old and made his living collecting rents from lands worked by Manchu bannermen; his chief pupil, a man called Li Wu 李五, was from a family that "had money."[10] Although this sect had probably been active for some time, there is no information about them before 1809. The name they were using in that year was Jung-hua 榮華 (Flourishing Flower) Assembly.[11] At that time, the second generation teacher Li Wu, himself in his fifties, was a well-established figure in his own right who collected money from his pupils, held regular meetings, and transmitted the eight-character chant. Sect members lived in Ku-an and adjacent Hsin-ch'eng district.[12]

Most of the other sects mobilized by Lin Ch'ing in 1813 were located within a twenty-five-mile radius on the southern side of the capital. In a small village outside and to the southeast of Peking lived an elderly sect head named Li Kuo-yu 李幗有 and his pupil Liu Hsing-li 劉興禮. They had learned a Hung-yang 紅陽 (Red Sun) sect from a man called Tu Ch'eng-k'uei. In addition to transmitting the eight-character chant, these two men had learned and then taught to their pupils a variety of healing arts, primarily boxing, fencing, and massage. Li Kuo-yu was better known as Li Lao 李老, "Old Li." He was eighty years old in 1813 and had been practicing and trans-

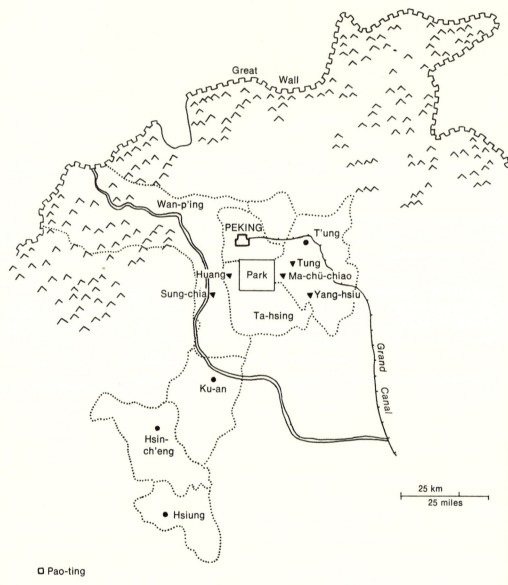

Great Wall

Wan-p'ing

PEKING

T'ung

Tung

Huang

Park

Ma-chü-chiao

Sung-chia

Yang-hsiu

Ta-hsing

Grand Canal

Ku-an

Hsin-ch'eng

Hsiung

25 km
25 miles

◻ Pao-ting

Peking and vicinity

mitting this sect for nearly fifty years. He had chosen a new name for his group, calling it the Pai-yang 白陽 (White Sun) sect, and had at least a dozen major pupils, all of whom had at least one further generation of pupils under them. Li Lao also had a large number of relatives who belonged to the sect, including a son, two daughters, two grandsons, and two brothers (or first cousins), through whom he had six nephews in their forties and fifties and at least five great-nephews in their twenties and thirties. All lived in Yang-hsiu village, where the family had enough land to support this large group and at least four semipermanent hired laborers. Three of Li Lao's older pupils specialized in curing illness, and those pupils who lived nearby would often assemble in the courtyard of a temple near Li Lao's house to practice the boxing and fencing skills he taught them.[13]

Li Lao's pupil Liu Hsing-li was in his eighties, older than his teacher; he had been in a sect for about forty years.[14] Liu Hsing-li had an even more extensive network of pupils than Li Lao, at least one hundred people, and, to mark his independence, Liu had rein-stituted the old name of Hung-yang sect. Liu made his reputation primarily as a healer of illness, and a great many of his pupils had been cured by him before joining his sect. Although Liu Hsing-li was from a village near that of his teacher, most of his pupils lived else-where.

One large group of Hung-yang sect members lived in a small market town called Ma-chü-ch'iao southeast of Peking; they were pupils of Li Ch'ao-tso, who was Liu Hsing-li's pupil and a resident of that village. This group of about a dozen families (between twenty and forty men and women) attended regular meetings of the sect in one another's houses, usually on the 1st and 15th of each month. On these occasions they meditated and had a feast. One member who is of particular interest had been given out in adoption and from his youth had served as a eunuch in the Forbidden City in Peking. This eunuch, Yang Chin-chung 楊進忠 by name, had been ill in 1809 (when he was at least forty years old), and a close friend had cured him and brought him into the Hung-yang sect as Li Ch'ao-tso's pupil. Through Yang Chin-chung, the sect had been extended to at least four other eunuchs who worked with Yang in the Fruit Office of the Imperial Household.[15]

These eunuchs were not the first pupils under Liu Hsing-li who resided in the city of Peking. Many years earlier two brothers, Manchu bannermen and members of the imperial clan itself, had been cured by Liu and joined his sect. Hai-chung, the eldest brother, used the skills he had learned to cure other people but claimed to have taken no pupils and had only distant contact with sect members. His younger brother Hai-k'ang, on the other hand, definitely brought at least a dozen people into the Hung-yang sect, curing most of them first.[16] His pupils were all closely associated with the Peking Manchu elite and included relatives, petty metropolitan officials, eunuchs, and Chinese bondservants.[17] Using his skill at curing illness, the sect leader Liu Hsing-li had built up a following that included both Chinese and Manchu and the bondservants, eunuchs, and servants who formed links between the two.

In addition to the Lao-li Assembly, the Ta-sheng sect, the Jung-hua Assembly of Li Wu, and the Pai-yang and Hung-yang sects, there was at least one other White Lotus sect active around Peking in the years prior to 1808, and it was this sect that was to form the nucleus of the Eight Trigrams rebellion of 1813. Known also as the Jung-hua Assembly, this sect was propagated by the healer Ku Liang 顧亮. Unfortunately, we do not know where Ku Liang came from or the name of his teacher. We do know that as early as 1796 he had taken pupils in the Tung village area southeast of Peking (the most active of whom was a man called Ch'ü Ssu). The majority of Ku Liang's followers came, however, from an area south and west of the capital, in and around Sung-chia village. Ku Liang had come to this village (probably in 1797 but at least by 1804) to stay with some members of the Sung family who were his relatives by marriage. In the 8th month of 1804 Ku Liang took one of his relatives, Sung Chin-hui 宋進會, as his pupil, and other brothers and cousins subsequently followed suit. Ku Liang instructed his pupils in curing illness and in the art of meditation, and he gave them the eight-character chant "Eternal Progenitor in Our Original Home in the World of True Emptiness." He told them to abstain from wine, sex, greed, and anger, and to help out any fellow sect member who was in distress. The group would often meet and meditate together, or they would gather and listen to Ku Liang tell stories about "buddhas and immortals" (probably including tales about the Eternal Mother), leaving the front gate open for the benefit of a regular group of passersby who would stop and listen. By the time of Ku Liang's death in 1807, the sect had at least seventy members, many of them members of the Sung family and most of them from Sung-chia village.[18] One of these followers, a pupil of a pupil of Ku Liang, was Lin Ch'ing 林清, the future organizer of the Eight Trigrams.

In the spring of 1808 (CC 13), the existence of this Jung-hua Assembly was made known to the government. The subsequent disruption of the sect and prosecution of some of its members might be considered the first in a series of events that led these men from meditation and storytelling into violence and rebellion. The trouble had begun with a classic quarrel between two brothers over their patrimony. The younger brother, who felt he had been cheated, reported the Jung-hua Assembly, of which his brother was a member, to the Office of the Gendarmerie. He charged that certain individuals had founded a heretical sect and were using "wrong ideas" to hoodwink people, a crime punishable by banishment to Heilungkiang.[19]

The case was routinely investigated, and by the 6th month of that year, sixteen members of the sect had been arrested and transferred to the provincial capital at Pao-ting (nearly one hundred miles away) for trial. They remained there, apparently not in prison, until early in the 8th month, when the case was formally reviewed by the governor-general of the province and the sentences memorialized to, and approved by, the emperor. The sect founder and "chief criminal" Ku Liang had died the year before and so he was not punished.[20] Three of his pupils who had extended the sect by taking pupils of their own were sentenced to one hundred blows (with the heavy bamboo) and penal servitude for three years. Thirteen others, including both the elder brother and Lin Ch'ing, were sentenced to beatings. The investigators had uncovered no evidence of heretical ideas and concluded that this group was concerned primarily with mutual assistance, charity, and good deeds. For this reason, the sentences were not especially severe. In fact, because of a general amnesty on New Year's Day of 1809 (CC 14/1/1), those three men sentenced to penal servitude were allowed to return home.[21]

Although the sixteen Jung-hua Assembly members from Sung-chia village had escaped with light sentences, this encounter with the law had had a considerable effect on them. Many believers left the sect and refused to have further contact with its members for fear of being implicated; those who chose to remain in the sect despite the danger were correspondingly more committed. More important perhaps, the leadership crisis that had begun to develop when Ku Liang died was intensified when three of his logical successors were sentenced to penal servitude. The issue was finally resolved in early 1809 when the Jung-hua Assembly split. The smaller group followed a sixty-year-old pupil of Ku Liang named Kuo Ch'ao-chün who had escaped involvement in the 1808 case, and the others followed the forty-year-old Lin Ch'ing. It was Lin Ch'ing's assumption of the role of sect leader in 1809 immediately following his experiences as a criminal on trial in the provincial capital that marks the next stage of the transformation of the Jung-hua Assembly from a religious sect into its alter ego, a vehicle for millenarian rebellion. Before describing this transformation, it is useful to look back at Lin Ch'ing's story prior to this decisive moment in his life. It is fortunately possible to reconstruct from the sources this rather unusual Ch'ing biography.

Lin Ch'ing Comes into His Own

Lin Ch'ing's father had originally come from Shao-hsing prefecture in Chekiang province and had moved to the Peking area where he had served as a clerk in two local governmental offices.[22] Both offices were located in Huang village, about ten miles southwest of Peking, where Lin Ch'ing's father lived with his wife and family. Lin Ch'ing was born in 1770 (CL 35). He had three older sisters and was the only son. He grew up on the outskirts of Peking and learned to read and write by studying with a clerk who worked with his father.[23] When he was about seventeen Lin Ch'ing was apprenticed at an herb-medicine shop located in the southwest corner of the northern section of Peking. (See map p. 169.) He spent three years there, studying the trade and learning about life in the capital. When he finished his apprenticeship, Lin Ch'ing took a job as a clerk in another apothecary shop where he earned a monthly salary. Then, according to his nephew, "because he often visited prostitutes, ugly sores appeared on his body" and so the herb-medicine shop fired him. Lin Ch'ing then found employment beating out the night watches outside the southwestern (Shun-ch'eng) gate that divided the northern and southern sections of the capital.

Despite this rather inauspicious beginning, Lin Ch'ing was fortunate in finding another job. When his father died, his mother had arranged for his post as clerk in the subprefect's office to be filled by a person who paid her a substantial sum for the privilege. This man had eventually become impatient with the arrangement and had refused to pay her further. Mrs. Lin, undaunted, filed a charge against him in the very yamen where he worked, asserting her family's right to the post and requesting that it be given to her son instead. Her petition was approved, and thus Lin Ch'ing was able to give up his job as night watchman and take over his father's clerkship.

Unfortunately, and no doubt to the dismay of his mother, who had gone to such lengths to secure this position for her family, Lin Ch'ing was soon fired. Not even a year had passed before an investigation revealed that he had been embezzling money allocated for repair work on the Grand Canal. For this Lin Ch'ing was apparently not prosecuted, but the Lin family claim to the clerkship was terminated. Lin Ch'ing took the money that he had appropriated, having somehow avoided paying it back, and used it to open a teashop in his home village; he even persuaded one of his brothers-in-law to become his partner. During the next six months, however, Lin Ch'ing neglected the teashop and spent every day gambling. When he had gambled away all his capital, his brother-in-law, furious, threw him out of the business.

Unemployed again (and probably unable to turn to his mother for any further sympathy or assistance), Lin Ch'ing decided to try Manchuria, technically closed to Chinese immigrants but in fact a virtually open frontier for those in search of work or opportunity within easy reach of northern Chihli.[24] There Lin found a job organizing a construction project for a Manchu official. But as soon as he had accumulated a surplus he quit and came home. Living off these earnings, Lin Ch'ing continued to do as he pleased for as long as he could, spending his money on food, drink, gambling, and women.

Not yet thirty, without money or firm plans and still restless, Lin Ch'ing next decided to go south and look up another brother-in-law who lived in the city of Soochow, over five hundred miles away in Kiangsu province. Through this relative, he found a position as a personal attendant for the grain intendant stationed in that city.[25] His failure to keep his father's clerkship apparently did not mean that Lin Ch'ing shunned association with the government bureaucracy; quite the contrary, for now he chose deliberately to be part of official life again. When the grain intendant went into mourning and left his post, Lin Ch'ing was able to find another position, again as a personal attendant, this time for the magistrate of Tan-yang district in Kiangsu. Later this magistrate left his post on an assignment and Lin Ch'ing then gave up this type of work.

Lin found that he was able to support himself by using the skills he had learned years before in the herb-medicine shops in Peking. For

the first time since then, he cured illnesses professionally. Nevertheless, he continued to spend his money as fast as he earned it, and
finally he decided to leave the south and to return home. In or before
1797 he hired himself out to haul the grain boats up the Grand Canal
to Peking, and by means of this tedious and exhausting labor made
his way home.[26] His nephew describes Lin Ch'ing's arrival:

> I was only nine years old when he returned. I was out guarding
> the melons in our melon patch about a li from our house. My
> uncle was coming toward our village from the east. His face and
> skin were dark and wrinkled, he hadn't shaved recently, and his
> pants were in rags. He knew me, called me by my nickname, and
> said, "Hey, Dumbhead, your uncle's back!" I didn't recognize
> him, and called him a dirty beggar. But he said, "Go and tell
> your mother and grandmother and they'll tell you I really am
> your uncle." So I went back home and told them, and then my
> father and I took a pair of trousers back to the melon patch for
> my uncle to put on, and we all came back to our house to-
> gether.[27]

Lin Ch'ing rested for a while and then set out once more to find
work. Always persuasive, he was able to obtain gambling quails on
credit from a bannerman he knew who ran a bird shop in Peking;
these he took out and peddled on the streets of the capital, probably
renewing old acquaintances from his earlier gambling days. One of
his customers, a former military officer named Wang, was very
impressed with Lin. Looking at his long face and sharply slanting
eyebrows,[28] Mr. Wang decided that Lin Ch'ing had a promising
future. He loaned him some money and together they opened a shop
selling small birds in the same area of Peking where Lin Ch'ing had
previously beaten out the night watch.

Lin took advantage of his relatively stable situation and got married. He and his wife, a former prostitute, adopted a child and lived
in a rented room near the bird shop. It was clearly not Lin Ch'ing's
fate to become a shop owner, however, and his good luck soon
turned to bad. His adopted child became ill and died. The bird shop
received substantial damage from flooding after some heavy rains.
Then Lin Ch'ing's partner and patron died; his son was less enthu-
siastic about Lin Ch'ing's potential and wanted to sue Lin for
mismanagement of the joint funds. Lin was again able to talk his way
out of trouble and persuaded young Wang simply to dissolve the
partnership and not go to the authorities.

Out of work again, Lin Ch'ing turned to the youngest of his older sisters, the mother of his young nephew, who lived in Sung-chia village, located not very far from their old home in Huang village. Lin rented a room in a temple in Huang village, and he and his wife lived there while he did work for his sister's household. But his troubles were not over. Shortly thereafter his wife died, and it was difficult to find enough money for her funeral. Lin finally managed to collect some back debts from his quail-peddling days; then, in 1806, having buried his wife, he moved into a room in his sister's house in Sung-chia village. His brother-in-law had recently died, and so Lin Ch'ing helped his sister manage her household.[29] Thus he became acquainted with his in-laws and with the other men in that village, many of whom happened to belong to Ku Liang's Jung-hua Assembly.

The relationship between Lin Ch'ing and this White Lotus sect, an apparent attraction of opposites, changed them both significantly. Lin Ch'ing was at thirty-seven a widower, still childless, a drifter and a hustler whose restless life, a series of failures and fresh starts, had been lived in the cities and on the margins of respectable society. The Jung-hua Assembly provided for its members solidarity and mutual support, as well as a sense of exclusiveness and private purpose, and it is easy to see why Lin Ch'ing might have been attracted to it. Here was a new set of friends and acquaintances eager to make converts. Lin Ch'ing could build on his past experience and learn new techniques for curing illness. Moreover, he was apparently stimulated by the religious ideas of the sect and excited by the possibilities for discussion and debate. It was a whole new world.

This is not to say that Lin Ch'ing had nothing to contribute. He was well traveled, having journeyed across the north China plain and spent years in the lush land and cities of the Soochow region; moreover, in addition to having lived for many years in Peking itself, he had crossed the Great Wall and seen the frontier lands of Manchuria. He had worked as a pharmacist-cum-doctor, construction worker, shop owner, peddler, gambler, yamen clerk, and magistrate's attendant and had acquired a variety of skills and experience. Lin Ch'ing was familiar with the city and the countryside, with the life styles of government officials, urban bourgeoisie, peasantry, and hired laborers both rural and urban. It is true that he had no capital, no social position, only a small network of relatives, and a questionable reputation; nevertheless, he did have contacts, much experience, and substantial persuasive ability. He was clearly bright and a man of some presence. He had bounced back from many difficulties and had energy and ability. The sect gave him a structure and purpose, and he developed its potential and transformed it.

When Lin Ch'ing joined Ku Liang's sect, the old teacher was still alive and active. Since many of his oldest pupils were members of the Sung family and lived in the village with Lin Ch'ing's sister, Lin probably heard about the sect as soon as he moved there if not before. Lin Ch'ing's sister's household included her deceased husband's brother and his wife and children and the wife, children, and second husband of her deceased husband's other brother. It was this second husband, one Tung Po-wang, who formally introduced Lin Ch'ing to his teacher Sung Chin-yao 宋進耀, and in the late spring of 1806 Lin joined the sect.

In his first two years as a believer, Lin Ch'ing became familiar with sect ideas and religious practices, but he did not, that we know of, take any pupils. His nephew says that during these years Lin lived at their house and "taught school" (perhaps elementary reading and writing) at home.[30] When Ch'en Mao-kung filed charges against the sect in the spring of 1808, he named Lin Ch'ing as a member of the Jung-hua Assembly. Lin was arrested with the others and taken to Pao-ting for trial. Despite his various escapades, this was, as far as we know, his first experience as a convicted criminal.

It appears that though the sect members were formally interrogated they were not put in prison in Pao-ting; rather they stayed together at an inn run by the Ma family on T'ang-chia alley in the provincial capital. At this time there was a man named Niu Liang-ch'en 牛亮臣 working as a waiter in the Ma family inn. This Niu Liang-ch'en was in his early forties and from a milieu resembling that of Lin Ch'ing's. He had been a treasury clerk in the magistrate's yamen in the district of Hua in northern Honan; he had stolen money and grain from official stores and had left his job and come to Pao-ting in order to avoid being found out. Niu Liang-ch'en and Lin Ch'ing became friends during the months when the sect members were being investigated, and the two used to sit and talk and drink wine.[31] Lin impressed Niu with his knowledge of the legal system and, in the process, related how he himself had come to be on trial. Lin explained the Jung-hua Assembly to Niu Liang-ch'en:

It has been transmitted by a man from south of Peking named Ku. . . . Every day at dawn we pay respects to the sun and recite the Sacred Words. By doing this we can escape the dangers of fire, flood, and war, and if there should come a time of calamity and disorder, then we can use that opportunity to plan and organize the Great Undertaking.[32]

It is probable that Niu Liang-ch'en had been in a White Lotus sect previously;[33] in any case, he was impressed with Lin Ch'ing and wanted to become his pupil.

When the legal proceedings were concluded, Lin received his sentence of one hundred blows with the heavy bamboo.[34] He and the other sect members who had received similar punishments then returned to their homes near Peking, and Lin invited Niu Liang-ch'en to come back with him. In the middle of the 9th month of that year (1808), at Lin's home, Niu burned incense and swore a vow; Lin Ch'ing put his hand on the place between Niu's eyebrows and explained that his nature (*hsing* 性) was located there. He then transmitted the eight-character sacred words, "Eternal Progenitor in Our Original Home in the World of True Emptiness." Niu kotowed to his new teacher. Lin Ch'ing had taken his first pupil.

Lin found employment for Niu as a tutor for an old friend who had run a bird shop in Peking years before and who now lived in a village nearby. Niu Liang-ch'en stayed and worked there for about a year, but early in 1810 he was discharged (the students had become exasperated with his Honan accent) and decided to return home. He asked Lin Ch'ing to come soon to pay him a visit there and meet other sect members from Honan.[35]

In the meantime, Lin Ch'ing and other members of the Jung-hua Assembly were still recovering from the government investigations of 1808. As was indicated above, one effect of this prosecution was to complicate the problem of succession that had developed after Ku Liang's death in the fall of the preceding year. At first Sung Chin-yao—Lin Ch'ing's teacher and one of the earliest converts in Sung-chia village—had more or less taken over direction of the sect, but a year later he was among three arrested and sentenced to penal servitude. In the fall of 1808 (and probably during the preceding months), Kuo Ch'ao-chün, a first-generation pupil of Ku Liang's who had not been arrested, took over as sect head, preventing the sect from fragmenting completely.

That autumn Lin Ch'ing returned home, his ambition and interest in sect activities seemingly stimulated by his experiences in Pao-ting. He challenged Kuo Ch'ao-chün and the latter gave way. By one account, Kuo "was unable to manage things well" and, recognizing that Lin Ch'ing's "influence was great" and that Lin "had a great destiny," he yielded power to his more worthy successor.

A blunter account says that Lin Ch'ing simply "made himself sect head" and forced Kuo Ch'ao-chün out. Lin Ch'ing explained the transfer of power by saying that it was because he was a "good speaker" that the others had "asked" him to be sect head. In any case, Kuo withdrew and took at least five of his pupils with him; they no longer met with or considered themselves part of Lin Ch'ing's sect. Most of the other believers, those who had not been frightened off by the government investigations, kotowed to Lin Ch'ing and formally acknowledged him as teacher and sect head. By the time that Sung Chin-yao returned in the spring of 1809, freed by the amnesty, his pupil was firmly in control.[36]

This change of leadership resulted in a realignment of the pre-existing teacher–pupil relationships. Lin Ch'ing had previously held a position two generations below Ku Liang. Now those generationally his senior within the sect (at least ten men) with their pupils under them formally acknowledged him as teacher. This placed Lin Ch'ing at the top of a sizable pyramid of followers. He had come into his own as a sect leader and "man of respect."

During a period when normal religious practices were disrupted, the old leaders gone, and most followers uneasy, Lin Ch'ing's ability to inspire confidence, convince the doubtful, and convert the skeptic, made him a natural leader. Nevertheless, despite the speed with which he moved to establish himself and was recognized as a leader by others, it should not be assumed that Lin Ch'ing had begun to talk of leading a rebellion. His takeover and subsequent efforts to reach out and contact other sect groups may not have been motivated by anything beyond a desire to ride the wave of power and respect as far as it would take him. While it is certainly possible that Lin had already begun to talk of a coming kalpa and used this idea to clear a path to power and then to inspire an expansion of the sect, there is no evidence that this was the case.

Lin Ch'ing had become familiar with sect practices and religious literature and was serious about reinvigorating the group and about making converts. Once established as head of the Jung-hua Assembly, Lin began to make contact with other sects active in and around Peking. Because of their interest in religious matters, members of one sect were apparently aware, if only vaguely, of the existence of other White Lotus groups. Nevertheless, it took a positive effort, as in this case under Lin Ch'ing's leadership, to find and then activate the connections between the sects. Lin tried deliberately to get in touch with and talk to other sect groups, and at the same time he encouraged his own followers to recruit pupils of their own. Again, it is possible that talk of rebellion and the coming kalpa was used at this stage to arouse interest and to obtain new followers for Lin. His efforts to convert not merely individuals but whole groups does imply that Lin was interested in building a powerful network. Each of the groups whom he now contacted and eventually persuaded to acknowledge his authority was later made part of the attack on the Forbidden City in Peking which was to be Lin Ch'ing's responsibility during the 1813 rebellion. It was at this time that he decided to grow what would eventually become a long black beard, a reflection perhaps of Lin's growing sense of self-confidence and awareness of the necessity of impressing others.[37]

There is relatively little information about exactly how the links between the Jung-hua and other sects were originally formed, or about what spatial or personal networks formed the media for such contacts. It appears that very often it was the man who had lived in several places or been in two or more sects who formed these links. For example, there was a beancurd seller from Hsiung district south of Peking named Liu Chin-t'ing 劉進亭. He had previously been the pupil of Yang Pao, the leader of the Ta-sheng sect that was active in that area. Later Liu Chin-t'ing met the son of a pupil of Ku Liang (we do not know how), became his pupil, and joined the Jung-hua Assembly. He did not, however, forget his past sect associations. On the contrary, Liu Chin-t'ing went to his former teacher and colleagues to persuade them to follow his example and become part of Lin Ch'ing's Jung-hua Assembly. Liu's relationship with Lin Ch'ing appears to have added to Liu's stature at home, and it was he (rather than his former teacher) who organized the Hsiung contingent in the 1813 uprising.[38]

At the same time that Lin Ch'ing was developing this link with the Ta-sheng sect, he also became acquainted (we not do know how) with the sect leader Li Wu 李五 from Ku-an district. Although Li Wu's teacher was still alive at this time and also met and discussed religious matters with Lin Ch'ing, it was Li Wu, the younger man (though older than Lin Ching), who was the real link between the two groups. Like Liu Chin-t'ing, Li Wu used this association to become more influential than his teacher within their sect. Lin Ch'ing often went south to the Hsiung and Ku-an area to see these two men, Li and Liu, and to talk with them about their beliefs and religious organization. He apparently learned much from these sessions, but his nephew says that Lin was no match for either of them in their discussions of religious doctrine.[39]

Prior to this time there are no references to the collection of money in Lin Ch'ing's Jung-hua Assembly. Li Wu on the other hand had been collecting money in his sect for some time. Using these donations and his own resources, he made an effort to gain influence with Lin Ch'ing not only by discussing doctrine but also by acting as a proper pupil and frequently giving money to Lin. Lin in turn used this new income to help his friends, relatives, and pupils, and to better his own life. His financial position certainly improved, although probably gradually, once he had taken over the sect. His nephew Tung Kuo-t'ai said that after Lin Ch'ing became head of the Jung-hua Assembly, he (Lin) had become financially independent.[40]

It was during these years when his position was steadily improving that Lin Ch'ing decided to marry again. Previously, when his prospects had been less than good, Lin Ch'ing had chosen a prostitute for his wife. Now his situation had improved dramatically. It was the sect that formed his world, and it was from among his new acquaintances that he chose his second wife. The object of his attentions was a Miss Chao, the recently widowed wife of a sect member from a nearby village who had by him two daughters of a marriageable age. Tung Kuo-t'ai relates: "So my uncle said to the wife of Liu Ch'eng-hsiang, 'I had a dream, and in the dream I was married to Miss Chao.' That woman told Miss Chao this and the latter said, 'I had a dream too, and it was exactly the same.' So they became engaged, and were later married." Miss Chao's younger daughter, who was in her late teens, came with her mother and moved into Lin Ch'ing's quarters in the Tung family compound.[41]

In addition to setting up close relationships with and a regular channel of funds from some similar sects in the capital area, Lin Ch'ing simultaneously used his new status to attract his own followers and to cement old friendships. One of those with whom he renewed his acquaintance was Ts'ao Lun 曹倫, a Chinese bannerman whom he had met in Kiangsu fifteen years before. Ts'ao Lun was only two years younger than Lin Ch'ing; by 1805 he had risen up the Banner hierarchy and had the fourth-rank title of captain but no active position. During these years Ts'ao was living in Peking, inside the Shun-ch'eng Gate in the same area where Lin Ch'ing had had his bird shop.

In the spring of 1807, still without employment, Ts'ao Lun found himself in a relatively impoverished state. According to his own testimony, his clothing was so ragged that he was embarrassed to go out in public and seek other employment.[42] It was at this time that Lin Ch'ing and another old friend of Ts'ao's came to help out, and Lin Ch'ing redeemed some clothing that Ts'ao had been forced to pawn. Soon thereafter Lin Ch'ing and some other friends invited Ts'ao Lun to become their sworn brother, saying, "You are now in difficult straits. Why don't the four of us swear brotherhood and then we can all help you?" One of these four was also in Lin Ch'ing's sect, while the other was a laborer who worked near Peking.[43] Ts'ao agreed and he and Lin would often have dinner together in a little restaurant outside the Shun-ch'eng Gate, an area of the capital they both knew well. In the winter of 1808, Lin Ch'ing sent water-melon and charcoal to Ts'ao Lun as gifts. When Ts'ao had an op-portunity to go along on the Chia-ch'ing Emperor's Jehol hunting trip in that same year, Lin Ch'ing supplied him with a horse, a mule, and some money. Lin Ch'ing's financial status improved after he took over leadership in the Jung-hua Assembly, and in the spring of 1809 he was able to loan Ts'ao Lun more money. Ts'ao returned some of these favors by using his official seal to authorize Lin to transport rice to outside Peking during the winters of 1808 and 1809 (when such permits were necessary), falsely stating that Lin Ch'ing was carrying soldiers' rations. By 1811 the two men were good friends.

Among the Jung-hua Assembly members who acknowledged Lin Ch'ing's authority in 1809 when he became sect head was a plain-blue banner bondservant named Ch'en Shuang 陳爽. Like many bondservant families in the Peking area, Ch'en Shuang's family was formally attached to an establishment in the capital, but many members were not employed there and lived instead outside the city as "bannermen agriculturists" (t'un-t'ien 屯田) without pay or posi-tion. Ch'en Shuang's family was attached to the household of the Yü 豫 Prince, a descendant of Dodo.[44] Ch'en lived in Sang-fa village, near Lin Ch'ing; he made his living working the land. Ch'en Shuang had been a member of Ku Liang's sect at least as long as Lin Ch'ing, and after Lin became head of the Jung-hua Assembly, the two men became close friends. Ch'en, who was slightly younger than Lin, soon introduced his nephew to Lin Ch'ing and arranged for the young man to become Lin Ch'ing's godson (kan-erh-tzu 乾兒子). Lin Ch'ing used some of the money he had begun to receive from his pupils to buy clothing for the Ch'ens, and the three men often went hunting together.[45] Later, Ch'en Shuang and his nephew Wen-k'uei would become important leaders of the palace attack.

Ch'en Wen-k'uei was not the only person whom Lin Ch'ing had linked to himself with bonds of fictive kinship. He had at least three "adopted sons" (*i-tzu* 義子) who by the summer of 1813 were spending most of their time at Lin's house. Lin Ch'ing had continued to cure illnesses, and two of these adopted sons had been healed by him and become his "sons" (and possibly his pupils) as an expression of gratitude. Both were from families of sect members, as was the other "son."[46] Lin and his second wife remained childless and it seems he was interested in building a family for himself by making an effort to acquire fictive brothers and sons in addition to pupils.[47]

There are no references to Lin Ch'ing's holding meetings of the Jung-hua Assembly prior to 1811. It is probable that as he became increasingly aware of his growing power Lin systematized group meetings and made them occasions for regular contributions by pupils to their teachers. By 1811, for example, Li Wu (the sect leader from Ku-an) had formally acknowledged Lin Ch'ing as sect head and thus linked his sect with Lin's. He told his pupils that there would be a meeting every year on the 1st day of the 10th month, and on that day Lin Ch'ing would come to Ku-an to meet with them. Li Wu and his followers were expected to come to the meeting and to contribute, and indeed such meetings were held on the 1st day of the 10th month in 1811 and 1812. There is also an indication of regular spring meetings in Ku-an, which Lin Ch'ing might not have attended.[48] Lin Ch'ing's birthday was in the winter, and during these years Li Wu and his followers also used this occasion to send gifts and money to their sect head. One participant describes this event:

> Li Wu sent a message that Lin Ch'ing was having a birthday and that we should send presents. I went and took with me two strings of cash as my gift, and two more from my brother. I went to Lin Ch'ing's together with . . . [five other sect members from the village]. We reached Lin Ch'ing's on the evening of that same day. We kotowed to him. He fed us noodles. There were two or three tables full of people. I returned home the following day.[49]

There are no exact figures on how much money Lin Ch'ing was getting from his followers, or on how much lesser leaders like Li Wu were making, but one comment by Lin's nephew indicates the general situation: "The people in the sect all contribute money to Lin Ch'ing in order to show their respect. At first Lin Ch'ing was very poor . . . but ever since he became a sect head, he has had money for all his expenses."[50] Lin used this income to build up his following, and it seems that he did indeed command the respect and admiration of his pupils. Tung Kuo-t'ai, when asked about his uncle's relationship with his followers, said, "My uncle's treatment of the men in the assembly was not at all harsh. There was never any violence or fighting. If a man made a mistake and someone reported this to Lin Ch'ing, he merely called in the man and scolded him a little. The person wouldn't dare reply, he would just kotow." Lin's persuasiveness remained his most useful talent, and it was this that allowed him to grow powerful while expanding the sect. According to his nephew,

> Lin Ch'ing has been trying to convert people to the sect for a long time. He was very convincing. Everyone said that he was constantly asking for money, but he said that making contributions was the same as sowing seeds for future blessings and that in the future such gifts would be multiplied tenfold. So people believed and gave him money. I never saw him give any back.[51]

These promises of future blessings were part of Lin Ch'ing's prophecy about the coming kalpa, and we shall see how he used this beginning to build a foundation for rebellion. In the meantime, during these years between 1808 and 1811 Lin Ch'ing appears to have found a certain ease and contentment in his life. Supported financially by gifts from respectful pupils, Lin allowed himself the luxury of wine and fresh fruit every day. In the winter he went out hunting with his friends, and when the weather was warm he would sit in the courtyard of his home and play his zither or his lute, telling his godsons and nephew to join in. He might have continued to live this way indefinitely but, as he himself later explained, "It was not my fate to be a peaceful citizen (*t'ai-p'ing pai-hsing* 太平百姓)." Aware of the as-yet-untapped potential of sect teachings and structure and always energetic, Lin Ch'ing could not sit quietly for long.[52]

LI WEN-CH'ENG AND HIS FOLLOWERS

Having taken and consolidated power in the Jung-hua Assembly and created a network of supporters and contributors among fellow believers in the Peking area, Lin Ch'ing initiated a series of contacts that dramatically expanded his sect. Early in 1811 he went to northern Honan—over three hundred miles away—to visit his friend and first pupil Niu Liang-ch'en. There Lin was introduced to another large White Lotus sect and to a sect head named Li Wen-ch'eng 李文成 whose ambitions matched his own. Together Lin Ch'ing and Li Wen-ch'eng would provide the inspiration and leadership needed to unite their groups and so build an organization with branches throughout the region and aspirations to even greater power.[53]

Although it is not possible to see into Li Wen-ch'eng's life and personality as we can into Lin Ch'ing's, it is possible to reconstruct the sect to which he belonged, a group which in many ways offers a contrast to the organization built up by Lin Ch'ing. Unlike Lin's sect, which had a short history and whose members came from a few villages over a small area, the Chiu-kung 九宫 (Nine Mansions) sect, to which Li Wen-ch'eng belonged, had a wide geographic base with branches in northern Honan, southern Chihli, and southwestern Shantung and closer ties with sect-led rebellions in the past. Drawing on this larger and deeper pool of experience, leaders of the Chiu-kung sect had instituted a more sophisticated system of sect organization and even before they came in contact with Lin Ch'ing had begun transforming their sect into a vehicle for rebellion.

The Chiu-kung sect had been transmitted in the southern part of the north China plain for at least fifty years and probably was involved or at least connected with those sect members who formed the Eight Trigrams of 1786 and attacked a prefectural city in southern Chihli province in that year. In 1808 the sect master was a man in his sixties called Liang Chien-chung 梁建忠 from Chang-te prefectural city in northern Honan.[54] Together with one of his pupils, Sect Master Liang initiated a series of organizational developments designed to increase both converts and contributions. In 1808 they started keeping a register that listed the names of all sect members and the amounts of their contributions. They devised several pseudo-official ranks, which they promised to those who contributed in sufficient amounts; they even carved seals that they then distributed to believers as symbols of membership. It is also likely that the leaders began to talk about the coming kalpa and the time when believers would be rewarded for their devotion.[55]

These were important and dangerous steps. White Lotus sects that were small and isolated and without incriminating property

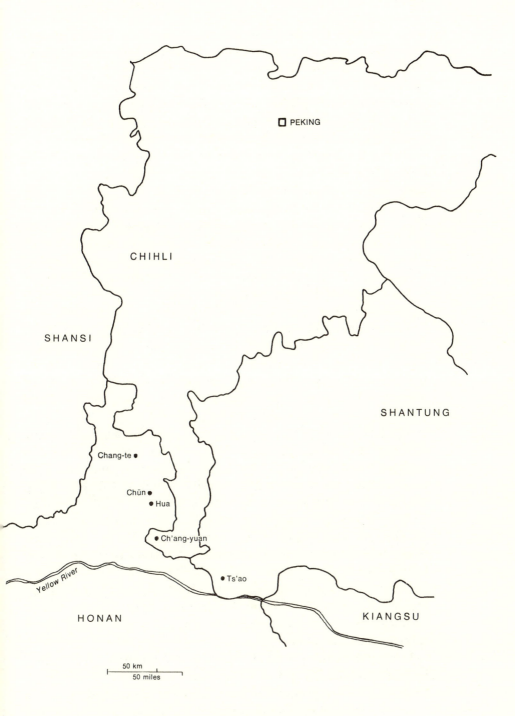

PEKING

CHIHLI

SHANSI

SHANTUNG

Chang-te ●

Chün ●
● Hua

● Ch'ang-yuan

● Ts'ao

Yellow River

HONAN

KIANGSU

50 km

50 miles

Districts and cities of the north China plain

were relatively safe from the interested eye of the Ch'ing government. Sects that emphasized the organizationally and ideologically
"heretical" elements in the tradition and thus developed into widespread networks along which money and "dangerous ideas" could
travel were quite another matter. For the Chiu-kung sect, seals,
the registers of names, and talk of a new system of ranks and titles
marked just such a new and more perilous level of development.

During the next three years Sect Master Liang watched over and
directed the expansion of his sect. Among the new converts was one
man who was single-handedly responsible for the extension of the
Chiu-kung sect into (eventually) at least eight districts of southern
Chihli and Shantung. His name was Hsu An-kuo 徐安國 and he came
from a village in Ch'ang-yuan district in the boot of southern Chihli.
Like many sect members, Hsu An-kuo was a veteran seeker who had
already been in at least one other sect. In 1809 Hsu was introduced
to Liu Kuo-ming, Liang Chien-chung's pupil's pupil, and, persuaded
by him of the superior efficacy of Chiu-kung sect practices, Hsu took
Liu Kuo-ming as his new teacher.[56] Hsu An-kuo made his living as
a healer; he traveled from place to place, staying with pupils and
former patients, curing illness and making converts. In this way he
built up a following that in the next four years would reach six or
seven hundred persons and would provide a base for the Eight
Trigrams in the eastern north China plain.[57]

While Hsu An-kuo was acquiring this large following in Shantung
and southern Chihli, other pupils in the Chiu-kung sect responded to
their teachers' urgings and were making converts (and asking for
contributions) in northern Honan. Hsu's teacher, Liu Kuo-ming,
was from Hua district as were many of his other pupils, including
Li Wen-ch'eng. Li Wen-ch'eng was in his forties, had a wife, teenage
daughter, and an adopted son. His extended family made their
living from the land, but Li's nickname—Li Ssu-mu-chiang 李四木匠
(Li the fourth [son], wood worker)—suggests that he might once
have made his living as a carpenter. By 1811 Li Wen-ch'eng, although formally four generations below Sect Master Liang, was an
established sect leader in the Hua area and may already have been
supported by his pupils.[58]

It was during this period of organizational expansion in the Chiu-
kung sect in the early spring of 1811 that Lin Ch'ing arrived in Hua.
Lin's pupil Niu Liang-ch'en knew Li Wen-ch'eng, and it was in
order to introduce the two men that he had arranged for Lin's visit.
Lin Ch'ing spent a month in Honan, meeting and talking with Li

and other members of the Chiu-kung sect and discussing religious matters with them at length. Circumstantial evidence suggests that they found a common interest in the problem of determining exactly when the turn in the kalpa initiating the third great historical era would come, a matter on which the attention of Chiu-kung sect members had been focused by the talk of future ranks, titles, and other benefits. Lin Ch'ing and Li Wen-ch'eng had different ideas about this problem, but apparently Lin argued very eloquently that the interpretations in which Li had been instructed by his teacher were incorrect.[59] Lin urged Li to break with his teacher and with Sect Master Liang and to adopt instead Lin's ideas on the date of the coming kalpa and join with him in planning for "the great undertaking."

The two men may have been encouraged to consider rebellion (if indeed they needed encouragement) by Feng K'e-shan 馮克善, a brother-in-law of Niu Liang-ch'en who met Lin and Li and took part in these discussions. Although a boxer and only marginally interested in religious ideas and practices, after meeting Lin Ch'ing, Feng became drawn into sect affairs; later, it was Feng K'e-shan, Li Wen-ch'eng, and Lin Ch'ing who became the three highest leaders of the Eight Trigrams. Feng introduces us to yet another type of restless, ambitious personality and potential rebel leader. Because he is also an excellent example of the semiprofessional fighter who concentrated on the military arts associated with the White Lotus tradition, it is worthwhile to pause to say a little about him.

In 1811 Feng K'e-shan was thirty-five years old and lived in Hua, probably in the district city itself. He came from a large lower gentry family and his cousins included holders of military degrees (both *chü-jen* and *chin-shih*). These more respectable branches of the family looked down on Feng K'e-shan and criticized him for being a gambler and a fighter; however, when later asked by government investigators why they had not kept a closer eye on him, the relatives replied feebly that "we each had our own livings to make, and so we couldn't discipline him."[60] Clearly this was a family in which military arts were encouraged, and it is not surprising that although a few members had made their way into the formal elite by earning degrees, others like Feng K'e-shan would find themselves only on the fringes. Feng was a gambler and fighter, a frequenter of the wine-shop, the inn, and the market fair. His friends were restaurant owners, yamen runners, gamblers, and petty swindlers, and he was part of the small-time underworld found in the cities and towns of

China.[61] As we have seen, Feng's brother-in-law, Niu Liang-ch'en, was a treasury clerk in the magistrate's yamen in Hua, and it may have been through Niu or through his relatives that Feng gained a reputation as a "strong man" and informal mediator for local disputes—although his physical skills alone made him a person to be reckoned with.[62]

When he was twenty-one Feng K'e-shan had studied boxing and fencing with a man from Shantung called Wang Hsiang; later he studied with a man from his own district who also taught him how to fight using a spear.[63] Neither of these men practiced a White Lotus sect, and Feng's own "entrance" into a sect was oblique at best. Early in 1810 he simply decided to pretend that he belonged to one. At that time Niu Liang-ch'en had come back from Peking after becoming Lin Ch'ing's pupil, and the two men discussed fighting techniques. Feng K'e-shan narrates:

> My wife's sister's husband, Niu Liang-ch'en, . . . noticed that in my system of boxing there were eight prescribed steps. He said to me, "Is that footwork of yours of the Eight Trigrams type?" I replied, "How did you know it was Eight Trigrams?" Niu said, "I practice the K'an Trigram, and so I understand." So I pretended that I practiced the Li Trigram sect and told him this. Niu said, "So you're in the Li Trigram. We are part of the K'an and Li Linked-Mansions (交宮). Each one can learn what is right in his own way." So after that, they all considered me in the Li Trigram.[64]

When Feng K'e-shan was introduced by his brother-in-law to Lin Ch'ing in 1811, he became drawn even more into the sect network. He began to build his own following and through Lin Ch'ing became interested in the ideas of the sect. It appears to have been Feng's willingness to gamble for high stakes, rather than his commitment to the religious purposes of the sect per se, that led him to associate himself with Lin Ch'ing and Li Wen-ch'eng, and as we shall see he never really stood on equal footing with either of them.

After spending only a month meeting Niu Liang-ch'en's friends and relatives, Lin Ch'ing left Honan and returned to Peking. He was not especially pleased with the results of his trip and told his family that he had not been able to recruit even a single pupil. This pessimistic evaluation of his impact proved premature. Lin Ch'ing's visit had had, on the contrary, a dramatic effect on sect members in Honan. Lin remained in Peking for several months, and then, perhaps not entirely unaware that he had launched a series of far-reaching changes in sect organization, he returned to Hua during the summer of that same year (1811).

On this second visit, Lin learned that in his absence there had been a major reorganization of the Chiu-kung sect. Li Wen-ch'eng had gone to talk with the sect master, Liang Chien-chung. Li had explained the new ideas that Lin Ch'ing had expounded (and that are unfortunately not spelled out in the source material) and, debating in the presence of other members of the sect, Li used these ideas to challenge Liang for the position of sect master. The aging Liang, unable to counter Li's arguments, admitted he was no match for his pupil and "took all his sacred scrolls and name lists and turned them over to Li Wen-ch'eng."[65] Thus Li Wen-ch'eng became the sect master, in possession of religious literature, and head of a realigned hierarchy of pupils. His teacher, his teacher's teacher, and all their pupils now acknowledged Li as head of the Chiu-kung sect. In fact, Li's teacher, Liu Kuo-ming, had been instrumental in helping his pupil during this takeover, and from this point on he acted vigorously as one of Li's chief assistants. More important from Lin Ch'ing's point of view, Li Wen-ch'eng's victory was his as well. It was on the basis of Lin's ideas that Liang Chien-chung was discredited and when Lin returned to Hua, Li Wen-ch'eng, Niu Liang-ch'en, and the others, "having questioned him and found that his doctrine was profound," all kotowed to Lin Ch'ing and "submitted to his authority."[66]

The formation of the Eight Trigrams had begun in earnest, and talk of rebellion, if it had not been explicit before, became so now. Lin Ch'ing and Li Wen-ch'eng began to plan and organize "the great undertaking." It is possible that these deliberations were influenced by the appearance in the sky of a great comet, a portent always taken seriously by Chinese as a reflection of the relationship between heaven, earth, and man. This comet had first appeared in the spring of 1811, and it was at its brightest during the late summer, coming closest to earth at the end of the 7th month. This was exactly when Lin Ch'ing made his second trip south. The Imperial Board of Astronomy declared the comet to be a sign of great glory for the dynasty, but it is likely that Lin Ch'ing and Li Wen-ch'eng considered it support for predictions about the imminent arrival of the new kalpa and an auspicious blessing for their enterprise.[67]

Lin Ch'ing explained to his new pupils that he had "made a prediction according to our sacred writings, namely that Maitreya

Buddha has three sect teachings, the Ch'ing-yang, the Hung-yang, and the Pai-yang. It is now time for the Pai-yang sect teaching to flourish." The turn in the kalpa that would initiate the Pai-yang era was imminent, and Lin explained to his followers that he "must rebel" (該起事).[68]

This decision, it must be emphasized, came as a logical outgrowth of tendencies inherent in the ideas and structure of White Lotus sects. Certain leaders motivated by both conviction and ambition had encouraged these tendencies by stimulating the sometimes dormant anxieties of their followers about the long-predicted arrival of the apocalypse. The belief that this time of great terror and great hope might be finally at hand impelled Lin Ch'ing and Li Wen-ch'eng to move to prepare themselves and their followers. A great comet had indicated heavenly favor, and after five good years there had been a drought in parts of northern Honan that might be interpreted as the beginning of the period of kalpa calamities.[69] Nevertheless, the road toward rebellion was an unpredictable and a dangerous one.

In order to provide coordinated leadership during this period of transition to the Pai-yang era, Lin Ch'ing and Li Wen-ch'eng pooled their ideas and settled on a new organizational framework, that of the eight trigrams. The two men decided that the sect over which Li Wen-ch'eng had recently assumed leadership would henceforth be known as the Chen 震 Trigram sect. Lin Ch'ing's Jung-hua Assembly would be entitled the K'an 坎 Trigram, K'an being the trigram associated with the north. Feng K'e-shan, the boxer, was brought in to fill out the threesome, and he and his followers were to keep the name Feng had been using, the Li 離 Trigram.[70] Other groups who might later join them could be incorporated simply by using one of the other five trigram names. In the meantime, the leaders explained the dominance of these three groups by saying that those other in fact nonexistent trigrams were "decreasing and atrophying" and had few members at the moment. On the other hand, the vigorous K'an, Li and Chen Trigrams could be considered to constitute the "three. powers" (san-ts'ai 三才), symbolizing Heaven, Earth, and Man, and would therefore be more than sufficient for their purposes.[71]

As far as decision making and planning for the uprising were concerned, Lin Ch'ing was to have general authority over the Eight Trigram groups. He was called "the one to whom all the symbols [trigrams] submit," and the "Overall Head of the Eight Trigrams." Lin Ch'ing later told his followers near Peking that he had gone south and assembled the seven trigrams, all of whom now followed him. According to Lin (and corroborated by other evidence), "Li Wen-ch'eng would lead all of the other seven trigrams with the exception of the K'an Trigram, but when there was some business in any of those seven trigrams, he was to notify me."[72]

Although Lin Ch'ing was the acknowledged sect master, Li Wen-ch'eng had much to teach his new mentor. They overhauled and expanded the system that Liang Chien-chung had initiated in the Chiu-kung sect and, by combining this with serious discussions about the approaching kalpa, hoped to increase significantly the number of sect members and the size of their contributions. The ranks established by Liang were set aside and a new hierarchy was introduced. As before, contributions were to be down payments on future benefits.

> It was promised that when Li Wen-ch'eng had risen up, everyone who had given money or grain would be given land or official rank. For every 100 cash, a person was promised 100 *mou* of land; for a certain amount of grain, he was promised a certain official rank. This was all recorded in a register. Moreover, a receipt was made out and given to the donor for him to keep as a guarantee.[73]

The grain would be converted to silver, and all contributions would be passed from pupil to teacher until they reached the top. Li Wen-ch'eng and Feng K'e-shan would forward money from their sects to Lin Ch'ing.[74]

The hierarchy of ranks and titles that Li and Lin created was part of a new system of relationships that would take effect in the coming kalpa. Lin Ch'ing, Feng K'e-shan, and Li Wen-ch'eng were to constitute a triad at the top of this hierarchy. To cement this new relationship they followed the time-honored practice of swearing brotherhood and then, in order to free themselves for these higher positions, formally turned their respective trigram sects over to their chief pupils to run.[75] The three highest offices, derived from the "three powers" of Heaven, Earth, and Man, were known as Controller or King of Heaven (*t'ien-p'an* 天盤 or *t'ien-wang* 天王), Controller or King of Earth (*ti-p'an* or *ti-wang*) and Controller or King of Men (*jen-p'an* or *jen-wang*). They were to be filled by Lin Ch'ing, Feng K'e-shan, and Li Wen-ch'eng respectively.[76]

Despite Lin Ch'ing's preeminence in managing the Trigrams prior to the rebellion, it was agreed from the beginning that the responsibility for ruling in the future would fall to the King of Men, that is to say, Li Wen-ch'eng. Lin Ch'ing himself explained that "when the undertaking is accomplished, all-under-heaven will belong to the King of Men." Lin Ch'ing and Feng K'e-shan were cast in the roles of sages. Lin declared that in the future, when the King of Men ruled, the Kings of Heaven and Earth "would become like the Sage Confucius and the Heavenly Master Chang," and as sages they would "assist" Li Wen-ch'eng.[77]

The tripartite division of power, while important and symbolically necessary, masked the fact that the real axis of power lay between Lin Ch'ing and Li Wen-ch'eng. These two men were to play complementary roles: the sage who was the religious authority but who turned over temporal power to the ruler, and the ruler who had political legitimacy but deferred on religious matters to the sage. Such patterned roles tapped a larger tradition of popular ideas about the ideal ruler–sage relationship dating back at least as far as the Han dynasty[78] and a more specific White Lotus tradition that had manifested itself in previous rebellions. During the White Lotus rebellion in the early Chia-ch'ing reign, the two leaders set up by the sect rebels were a Maitreya incarnate (whose surname was Liu) and a descendant of the Ming ruling house (whose surname was Wang, but who was sometimes called Niu-pa 牛八 or Chu 朱).[79] These two figures, the buddha and the restoration emperor, were reestablished by these Eight Trigram leaders.

Li Wen-ch'eng announced that "he was the reincarnation of the Chen Trigram leader whose surname was Wang"; he later adopted a Ming dynasty era-name and further emphasized his claim to the mandate to rule by declaring himself to be also the reincarnation of the rebel who had overthrown the Ming, Li Tzu-ch'eng. Like these predecessors, Li Wen-ch'eng would rule.[80]

Lin Ch'ing, on the other hand, claimed the role of Maitreya, the one sent by the Eternal Mother to teach the true Way before the new kalpa arrived. The role of Maitreya was apparently blended together with that of sect patriarch and teacher and had become associated with the surname Liu. There was a person called Liu Lin 劉林 who was recognized by these sects as a founder and teacher and as a previous incarnation of Maitreya Buddha; he was called the Patriarch of Former Heaven (hsien-t'ien tsu-shih 先天祖師). Lin Ch'ing was told by Li Wen-ch'eng during these 1811 meetings that he, Lin, had in a former life been mao-chin 卯金, that is to say, surnamed Liu, and was in fact the reincarnation of the famous Liu Lin. Lin Ch'ing was thus to be known as the Patriarch of Latter Heaven (*hou-t'ien tsu-shih* 後天祖師). As Liu Lin had been one incarnation of Maitreya, so "this immortal nature" had been reborn in Lin Ch'ing. Lin was the sagely Buddha come to teach the Way, the sect master who prepared for the millennium; he was "Patriarch of Latter Heaven and Heavenly Controller in Charge of the Faith at the Time When the Eight Trigrams Begin to Practice the Law" (掌理天盤八卦開法後天祖師). When the time came, however, he would play his role and yield this power to the good ruler, the legitimate emperor, the King of Men, Li Wen-ch'eng.[81]

The only suggestion of anti-Manchu sentiment to be found in the ideas or actions of the Eight Trigrams is in a rhyme circulated among sect members in Honan and Shantung describing the role of Lin Ch'ing and his northern contingent in the coming uprising. The rhyme plays on his claim to the surname Liu, which was also the surname of the ruling family of the dynasty that called itself Han 漢; the same character *han* is used to refer to the Chinese ethnic group (in contrast with Mongols, Manchus, and other minority peoples). The rhyme was:

> We wait only for the northern region to be returned
>   to a Han emperor,
> Then all that is will again be under a single line.[82]
> 單等北水歸漢帝
> 天地乾坤只一傳.

The leaders of the newly formed Eight Trigrams obviously wished to expand their claims to leadership as much as possible and did so by tapping a well-known pantheon of popular gods and heroes. Not content with being the reincarnation of several gods and men, Lin Ch'ing also announced that he was "the planet Venus (*t'ai-pai chin-hsing* 太白金星) come down to earth."[83] The rest of the hierarchy that Lin Ch'ing and Li Wen-ch'eng began to set up in the summer of 1811 will be discussed in greater detail below.

By the time Lin Ch'ing had returned to Peking the message had been sent out to all believers and to all possible converts: the devastating calamities accompanying the end of the present kalpa period were on their way; in this time of crisis the Eternal Mother had designated new leaders who would provide deliverance for all who followed their teaching. The foundations had been laid for future growth and cooperation among these sects, and their increasing income fueled a steady expansion of the Eight Trigrams in both the northern and southern parts of the north China plain.

EXPANSION OF THE K'AN TRIGRAM

Through his trips to Hua in the spring and summer of 1811 and the forging of this new relationship with Li Wen-ch'eng, Lin Ch'ing substantially increased the size of his following. By using the new and more systematic form of eliciting and recording contributions, he became the recipient of money from all of the trigram sects. Thereafter, whenever Lin Ch'ing went south he received gifts from Li Wen-ch'eng and his pupils; on other occasions, Li sent men to deliver money to Lin, "the one to whom all the trigram symbols submit."

Lin Ch'ing's changing mode of transportation on his journeys to Honan vividly illustrates his growing power and status. On his first trip, in early 1811, Lin Ch'ing and two pupils had walked to and from Hua. That spring they went again on foot, but their return, after Li and the others had "acknowledged Lin Ch'ing's authority," was financed by their new followers, and Lin Ch'ing rode a donkey that had been presented to him. That fall Lin went again to Honan, riding the donkey while his friends walked; when they returned home a month later, Lin Ch'ing had also acquired a mule. Early the following year (1812) Lin went south again, this time riding in the family cart of one of his pupils, drawn by the mule. They returned in the same cart, now pulled by a horse (and carrying with them a box full of silver ingots). Lin Ch'ing did not make another trip south until a year later, but when he did, in his time of maximum power just prior to the uprising, he rode in a proper passenger cart, with one pupil driving it, one walking as an attendant, and another riding the horse out ahead.[84]

In 1811, 1812, and 1813 Lin Ch'ing used his new prestige and income to expand the sect in the capital area, to regularize meetings and contributions, and to recruit members specifically for the purpose of the uprising. In the spring of 1811, between his first two trips to Honan, Lin Ch'ing introduced his sworn brother the Chinese bannerman Ts'ao Lun to the sect. Ts'ao Lun had become potentially more useful to Lin Ch'ing, for he had recently been promoted and assigned as first captain to a post at Tu-shih-k'ou, a pass north of

Peking on the Great Wall. Ts'ao had come to see Lin Ch'ing to tell
him of his new job and to apologize for still being unable to pay Lin
back the money he had lent him. Lin Ch'ing assured him not to
worry: "I will teach you a system," he said, "by means of which you
can increase your good fortune, avoid any bad luck, and in addition
be saved from poverty." Ts'ao was interested, and so Lin Ch'ing
taught him the eight-character mantra and showed him how to
recite it and meditate. Contrary to usual sect practice, however,
Ts'ao Lun did not become Lin Ch'ing's pupil. But later that year
when Ts'ao complained that he was not especially satisfied with the
"good benefits" promised from recitation of the mantra—"the eight
characters which Third-elder-brother Lin taught me to recite and
which were supposed to save me from poverty don't seem to work"—
he was told that this was because he had not formally become Lin's
pupil.

A year later Ts'ao finally decided to take the step of changing the
relationship. He went to Lin Ch'ing's house and kotowed to him as a
pupil. Lin, as befitting a teacher rather than a sworn brother,
"merely raised his arm, and did not return the courtesy [of kotowing
to Ts'ao]." Ts'ao Lun did bring others to meet Lin Ch'ing and become his pupils. One was his twenty-three-year-old son, Ts'ao
Fu-ch'ang; another was a certain Wang Wu 王五, a household servant for a retired high military official in Peking who had been Ts'ao's
sworn brother for three years. After Lin Ch'ing returned from his
second visit with Li Wen-ch'eng (when the formation of the Eight
Trigrams had begun), he sent Liu Ch'eng-hsiang (who was now
running Lin's sect hereafter referred to by its new name, the K'an
Trigram) to contact Ts'ao Lun and the others, to tell them of Lin's
predictions about the coming kalpa and to ask if they would be
willing to participate. Ts'ao Lun and Wang Wu claimed later that
they had not committed themselves to assisting with a rebellion but
had only asked to be notified when a date for the uprising was
determined.[85]

During this same period Lin Ch'ing began to secure the participation of eunuchs in his sect. Sometime in 1810 or 1811 his friend
Ch'en Shuang had taken as his pupil a thirty-six-year-old fellow
villager named Liu Te-ts'ai 劉得財. Liu had moved to the capital area
and become a eunuch; since 1806 he had been working in the Great
Interior (ta-nei 大內) inside the Forbidden City. In 1809 Liu Te-ts'ai's
adopted father had joined the Jung-hua Assembly; his uncle had

followed suit, and then Liu himself became Ch'en Shuang's pupil.
Ch'en taught him the eight-character mantra and instructed him to
go and convert his own pupils.[86]

During the next few years Liu Te-ts'ai did exactly that, and we
know of at least seven persons, all eunuchs, whom he brought into
the sect. These men worked inside the Forbidden City in a variety
of different offices and had probably been born and raised in the
Peking area.[87] One eunuch revealed the extent to which Liu Te-ts'ai
was proselytizing within the walls of the palace itself as he described
his own conversion.

> I ran into the eunuch Liu Te-ts'ai at the doorway of the Chi-
> shen Office [inside the palace]. I asked him into my quarters to
> drink some tea. At that time there was no one else there. Liu
> Te-ts'ai said to me, "We are very good friends, like brothers,
> why don't you join the assembly and Learn the Right (hsueh-hao
> 學好)." I asked him, "What assembly?" He said, "The Pai-yang
> sect. In our assembly we don't drink wine and don't gamble,
> and in the future there will be money for us to spend." I thought
> this seemed like Learning the Right, so I agreed. He said,
> "There are usually a lot of people coming and going through
> here, so why don't you kotow to me right now. There is no
> point in putting out incense or in burning paper slips." So right
> there in my room in the Chi-shen Office, I kotowed to him and
> took him as my teacher.[88]

These were not the first eunuchs to join a White Lotus sect. In fact,
one of the men Liu Te-ts'ai tried to convert had been in a sect before
(it was this man's uncle whose widow had married Lin Ch'ing),[89]
and as we have seen, the Hung-yang sect of the healer Liu Hsing-li
already counted several eunuchs among its members. Eunuchs did
not live in isolation inside the Forbidden City in Peking. Those who
came from families in the capital area kept in contact with their
relatives and were active links between the palace and the countryside. These eunuchs in general, and Liu Te-ts'ai and his pupils in
particular, were later to play an important role in the attack on the
Forbidden City, and it is difficult to avoid the conclusion that Liu's
followers were deliberately recruited for this prupose.

There is no question that after 1811 Lin Ch'ing cultivated these
eunuchs and did all he could to secure their loyalty. Contrary to
normal sect practice, Lin Ch'ing continually gave gifts of silver to
these pupils, in fulfillment of Liu Te-ts'ai's promises of "money to

spend." Two of the eunuchs testified that they received money from Liu on the 1st day of every month, usually about one tael. It was Lin Ch'ing's practice to deposit the money with a jewelry store (run by men from Shansi) located in the southern section of Peking. Liu Te-ts'ai would then go to the shop and withdraw money as he needed it. Liu told his pupils that this money had been specially given to them by the sect head Lin Ch'ing and that they were to tell no one about it.[90]

During 1812 Lin Ch'ing increased the size of his K'an Trigram dramatically by securing the support of the Pai-yang sect leader Li Lao and all of his pupils. This incorporation of Li Lao's sect into Lin's organization meant increased occupational and geographic diversity: Li Lao's pupils were boxers and healers, eunuchs and Manchus, and they came from villages southeast of Peking and from the capital city itself. The link between Lin Ch'ing and Li Lao was a man called Liu Ti-wu 劉第五, who brought his teacher, Li Lao, to meet Lin Ch'ing.[91] Lin explained about the coming kalpa and persuaded Li Lao that if he and his pupils were to join with him they too could be saved from those great calamities. He was convincing as always and both Li Lao and Liu Ti-wu kotowed to Lin Ch'ing and acknowledged his authority. Lin Ch'ing served them dinner, then they returned home. Thus Li Lao's Pai-yang sect, and the Hung-yang sect of his pupil Liu Hsing-li, were brought under Lin Ch'ing's direction. These men worked in the next year to convert new members in anticipation of the coming kalpa calamities and cemented their relationship with Lin Ch'ing by encouraging contributions from their pupils and passing this money on to Lin.[92]

Liu Ti-wu became caught up in Lin Ch'ing's preparations for the uprising and continued to work to help Lin increase his following. Liu was useful because he had belonged to two sects and because he had lived both southwest of Peking (in southern Wan-p'ing district) and southeast of Peking (in southern T'ung district). He reestablished contact with a branch sect of Ku Liang's Jung-hua Assembly through its leader, a man called Ch'ü Ssu 屈四. Ch'ü Ssu was told about Lin Ch'ing and his plans and was asked to be a part of the K'an Trigram. Ch'ü agreed and worked to make converts in the area of his village so that by 1813 he had tripled the number of his pupils.[93]

Lin Ch'ing was not always successful in persuading every sect he knew about to acknowledge his leadership and participate in the uprising. Contacts were made with a certain Wang Jui, the head of the Lao-li Assembly in Hsin-ch'eng, through his brother-in-law who

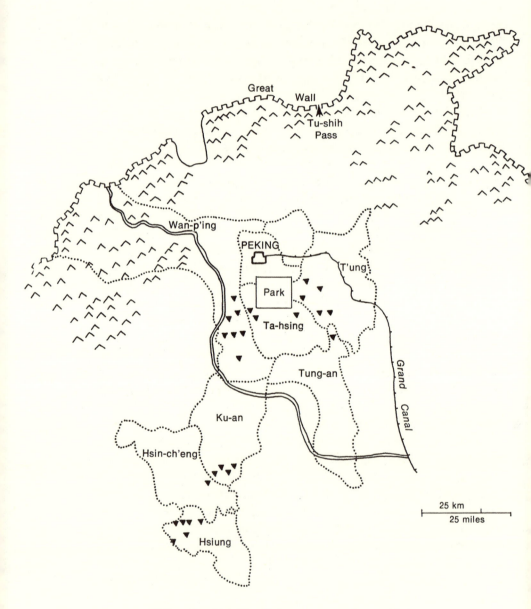

Villages in which K'an Trigram sect members resided

was in one of Lin's sects. Wang Jui, quoting from the literature used by his sect, tried to explain that it was not a good time for rebellion: "If you want to rebel, you must wait a few more years. How can you do it during such a peaceful time? You all are acting too precipitously." The brother-in-law tried to argue that their leader Lin Ch'ing knew what he was doing and had a great many followers. Wang Jui was unimpressed and claimed that his sect was at least as numerous. "I am in the Lao-li Assembly. I don't want to belong to your Jung-hua Assembly. Don't bother me!" Further attempts to persuade Wang Jui also failed, though there is no indication that Lin Ch'ing ever went personally to talk with him, but in the end Lin remembered this group and sent them identifying signs so that they would be spared during the great calamities.[94]

Lin Ch'ing even tried to enlist the support of the man he had ousted as head of the Jung-hua Assembly years earlier. He sent a pupil to see Kuo Ch'ao-chün, to explain the sophistication of Lin's sect and to ask Kuo to come and talk. Kuo claimed later that he had refused to do so, though he had given Lin what was essentially protection money: "He said that Lin Ch'ing was going to rebel and I should give four strings of cash every month; if I did, Lin Ch'ing wouldn't kill me. When I heard these words, I begged him to beg Lin Ch'ing for me, saying 'please spare me!' " Kuo did not participate in the uprising, but, as with Wang Jui, protective banners were sent to him as an albeit uncooperative fellow believer.[95]

Kuo Ch'ao-chün's experience was not atypical. Much of the proselytizing done by Lin Ch'ing and his pupils in 1811 and 1812 was accompanied by increasingly precise promises of benefits to be received "after the affair was successful" and equally explicit threats of the dangers awaiting nonbelievers. Potential converts were told about the turn of the kalpa and its accompanying destruction and were urged to join the sect to avoid certain death. Membership alone was sufficient to place one among those who would be saved, yet Lin Ch'ing made very positive efforts to persuade believers that they should volunteer to take part in the K'an Trigram uprising that would accompany the kalpa calamities. Land and rank were offered as inducements to encourage conversion, contributions, and participation: "Later on there will be unlimited wealth and prestige (wu-ch'iung fu-kuei 無窮富貴)" promised one teacher.[96] Those who assisted actively would be rewarded accordingly, and "those who help a lot will be made high officials, those who help less will be made lesser officials."[97] The usual promise was that one would be given an "official post" (*kuan-tso* 官做), but some teachers were more specific, telling pupils that they would receive "buttons of the first rank," "a first- or second-degree rank," "a soldier's stipend," or "be installed as chief eunuch."[98] These promises were combined with threats: "Whoever doesn't want to help will be treated like a deserter and killed"; "If you don't agree to participate, you won't live long"; "After the affair was completed we would all become officials, but anyone who didn't participate would be struck dead by a thunder-bolt."[99]

The use of these threats and promises implies incorrectly that the many people who joined the would-be rebels at this stage did so entirely out of fear or greed and not out of any faith in sect teachings. It is important to remember that neither these threats or promises were actually carried out prior to the rebellion. Except for the eunuchs mentioned above, no one was rewarded concretely in advance nor was anyone harmed. A potential recruit, in order to be moved by either carrot or stick, had first to believe in at least the possibility that what Lin Ch'ing predicted might actually come to pass. White Lotus sects were fundamentally different from criminal organizations, which normally operated outside the system and whose promises of benefits or violence were carried out immediately. These sects put their challenge to the state and society in the future, and only after a designated time did they openly carry out what had previously been talk. Those who believed and were moved by threats and promises were people who thought that the sect might some day take power as predicted. To those who did not believe this, talk of "official posts" and "not living long" was meaningless.

By the summer of 1813, Lin Ch'ing had built his K'an Trigram into an umbrella over his own Jung-hua Assembly and four other previously separate sects. This network of teachers and pupils numbered more than three hundred men from nearly sixty villages in seven districts.[100] While this network was built by ties between individuals, these three hundred sect members in fact represented nearly that many families. When a male adult joined the sect, his wife, parents, and grown children often followed suit. Even when other members of his household did not formally join the sect, later when the new kalpa came, the protection accorded each member of the sect automatically included his family. Thus the total number of people who could be considered associated with Lin Ch'ing's K'an Trigram sect at this stage was probably closer to one thousand.[101]

Although there were a large number of resident "believer" households in some villages, it should not be assumed that any one village was dominated by sect members. In Sung-chia village where Lin Ch'ing lived, for example, there were at least forty-four adult male members of his sect, one-third of them from the Sung family that gave the village its name. In terms of the sect, this constituted a large number of believers from one place. Even so, there were definitely residents of the village, including relatives of sect members, who did not belong. Without knowing the total number of people or households in Sung-chia, it is impossible to guess at the ratio of believers to nonbelievers. There is no evidence that Lin Ch'ing could (or did) consider this or any other village a solid "base" or "nest." These sects were built up through individual ties, and prior to any rebellion they remained limited by those ties.

Similarly, the links between these villages were created by the sect, and this network appears to have existed independently of other social organizations. It is true that in many cases the sect did expand along lines of kinship or physical proximity: as we have seen, one believer would convert his family, friends, and neighbors. Some of the crucial links in the K'an Trigram network were created, however, between individuals who shared only one thing: their interest in the ideas and practices of White Lotus sects. The crucial association between Lin Ch'ing and Li Wen-ch'eng, brought about through a chance meeting and a mutual friend, would not have been possible without their common involvement in a religious sect. When the teacher–pupil links reinforced preexisting ties, they were stronger by consequence. When they did not, as between chance acquaintances from distant villages, between a visiting healer and his patient, the links were correspondingly weaker, but they existed nonetheless. The sect network grew and spread in the interstices of the larger society, and although technically illegal and sometimes in conflict with normal social relationships, these sects—even those in a state of expansion—did not challenge or openly interfere with the status quo.

NEW GROUPS JOIN THE TRIGRAMS

Having established contact with sect leaders in Honan, Lin Ch'ing kept in regular touch with them during the next three years. For all the trigram sects the years 1811 through 1813 were a fruitful period of cultural interchange, a time when there was speeded-up expansion and increasing travel and communication. It was a time when boxers competed and compared skills, healers traveled and learned new techniques, sect masters discussed predictions and doctrine, and organizers compared systems.

Lin Ch'ing went again to Honan early in 1812. He took three pupils with him, remained there a month, and when he returned brought with him a box of silver ingots and a talisman mounted as an impressive scroll, gifts from pupils there.[102] Lin used some of this new income to improve his living arrangements. He enlarged his quarters and his privacy by building a separate room for himself in the Tung family courtyard, and he hired his niece's husband to come and cook for him so that he could eat separately from his sister and her family. This space was badly needed, for by 1813 Lin Ch'ing had acquired a sizable household. In addition to the Tung family (his sister and all her relatives), Lin had his own wife and two stepdaughters, three pupils who lived with and worked for Lin doing both household and sect chores, plus his friend Ch'en Shuang and three godsons who had more or less moved in by the summer of 1813.[103] In addition, Lin Ch'ing had frequent meetings in his quarters and visitors from the Peking area and from the south.

In the late spring of 1812, three men brought Lin Ch'ing another delivery of money from Li Wen-ch'eng and the trigram sects in the south.[104] In the fall of 1812 two other men from Honan came to deliver money to Lin; they too stayed only a few days and then returned south.[105] Later that fall Li Wen-ch'eng himself came to Sung-chia village. Li brought with him his own right-hand man Yü K'e-ching and Lin Ch'ing's old friend and pupil Niu Liang-ch'en. Yü K'e-ching 于克敬 was originally from Shansi but had moved to a village north of Hua city in Honan.[106] It was to Yü that Li Wen-ch'eng had formally handed over control of his Chen Trigram sect, and Yü was evidently a man of some authority in sect matters. He had in his possession a sacred book that he now presented to Lin Ch'ing. It was entitled "Comprehensive Manual for Responding to the Kalpas of the Three Buddhas" (San-fo ying-chieh t'ung-kuan t'ung-shu 三佛應刼統觀通書), and as far as we know it was the first religious book owned by Lin Ch'ing. (After the uprising it was found by the government wrapped in red cloth and hidden in a bricked-over hole under the eaves of Lin Ch'ing's room.)[107] Later Lin would use this book to make predictions about the arrival of the kalpa and to derive titles for the new Eight Trigrams hierarchy. It was probably at this meeting between Lin and Li Wen-ch'eng that they decided on the "public slogan" (ming-hao 明號) to be used by the Eight Trigrams:

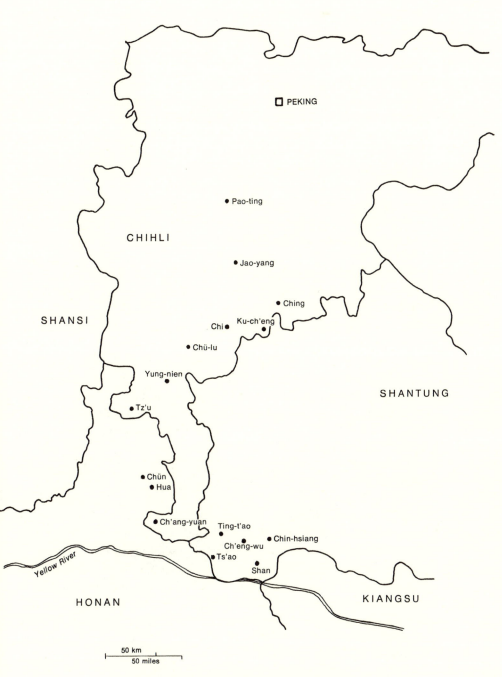

□ PEKING

Pao-ting

CHIHLI

Jao-yang

Ching

SHANSI

Chi

Ku-ch'eng

Chü-lu

Yung-nien

SHANTUNG

Tz'u

Chün

Hua

Ch'ang-yuan

Ting-t'ao

Chin-hsiang

Ch'eng-wu

Ts'ao

Yellow River

Shan

HONAN

KIANGSU

50 km
50 miles

Districts and cities of the north China plain

Entrusted by Heaven to Prepare the Way (*feng-t'ien k'ai-tao* 奉天開道).[108]

The visits by sect leaders to Peking to call upon and deliver money to Lin Ch'ing reflect the process of growth and expansion taking place in those sects during the two years since the first meetings between Li and Lin. This expansion took place in Honan, in southern Chihli, and in Shantung and consisted of the conversion of individuals, families, and entire sects to the cause of the Eight Trigrams. Hsu An-kuo, the healer from southern Chihli, adopted the new system of registering contributions and incorporated Lin and Li's specific plans for an uprising into his own teachings. He worked hard during these years, traveling often and preaching the sect as he went. His activities provide a good illustration of the different ways in which the sect network was extended.

In the winter of 1811 Hsu An-kuo left home to make a trip into western Shantung. He again visited Hu-chia village in Ts'ao district where he had been the previous year curing illnesses. Several branches of a family called Chu lived in this village, and one of these men, Chu Ch'eng-fang 朱成方, was now converted by Hsu and became his pupil. In subsequent months, Chu Ch'eng-fang in turn transmitted the sect to his five cousins. Hsu An-kuo treated him as his "top pupil"—"the one who looks after all the others." Chu and his cousins propagated the sect in Ts'ao and Ting-t'ao districts in Shantung.[109] In the spring of 1812, when Hsu An-kuo was again (or perhaps still) in Shantung, he converted another man from Ts'ao called Chang I, who would later also play an important role in organizing Hsu's pupils in that area. Among Chang I's first converts were his wife's brother and his family, including his five sons.[110]

While Hsu An-kuo's network grew in part by whole family accretions like the Chu brothers or Chang I and his relatives, it also spread by the extension of vertical chains of teachers and pupils. In Ting-t'ao district, for example, one such line consisted of Hsu's pupil Liu Yun-chung, the latter's pupil (one of many) Liu Ching-t'ang, Liu Ching-t'ang's pupil Chou Wen-sheng, and Chou's pupil Li Fa-yen.[111] Although in this case these men were all from the same district, this type of chain often spread the sect over a wide area. Since the process of conversion and introduction to basic sect practices could be accomplished quite speedily, it was easy for new generations to be created very rapidly.

Hsu An-kuo gained followers further east in Shantung not by building up a network from scratch but by converting men who had large sect followings of their own, Ch'eng Pai-yueh in Shan district[112] and Ts'ui Shih-chün in Chin-hsiang.[113] This latter method of expansion brought large well-established blocs into the trigram apparatus.

On another trip to Shantung in the 2d month of 1813, Hsu An-kuo visited each of his senior pupils and began to discuss the planned rebellion quite specifically. He explained to them about the vigorous growth of the K'an, Li, and Chen Trigram sects, and he told them about the sect head in the north known as "Venerable Master Liu" (Lin Ch'ing), and the trigram head in Hua called Li Wen-ch'eng. He urged his pupils to go to Hua and pay a call on Li Wen-ch'eng; in compliance with this suggestion four important pupils went to visit Li in the spring of 1813. Hsu An-kuo took them there and on the way told them more about the coming uprising. He said that the Pai-yang kalpa was about to begin. "Seven days before the Pai-yang kalpa we would have to distribute small white cloth banners. . . . We did not have to prepare or make any knives or swords: when the time came we were just to grab whatever was handy." Sect members would be given these banners to place in the gateways of their houses. The Pai-yang kalpa would come and cut away the past with the black wind that would blow during seven days and seven nights. Sect members would wear white sashes, and when they took action they "were to massacre the residents of any house with no banner at the gate." In this way only sect members would be left and all others would die.[114]

By the time they reached Hua, Hsu's pupils had had an opportunity to get to know one another and to discuss the great undertaking in which they were involved. Arriving at Li's village, they were first introduced to several of Li Wen-ch'eng's pupils and assistants. They were further briefed by Liu Kuo-ming, Li Wen-ch'eng's original teacher and now his assistant and the man who had brought Hsu An-kuo into that sect. Liu told them more about the visits of "Venerable Master Liu" to Hua and about some of the prophecies and scriptural quotations which "proved" that indeed the Pai-yang era was about to begin. Finally, Hsu's Shantung pupils were presented to Li Wen-ch'eng himself. They kotowed. Li remained standing, and then said to them, "You must all work very hard. This kalpa can create endless misery or it can be a preparation for endless blessing. You should all go home now, and if you have any further questions, ask your teacher."[115]

Hsu An-kuo's contacts with the top rebel leadership were all made through Li Wen-ch'eng; he made no trips to Peking and only saw Lin Ch'ing when the latter was in Hua district. On the other hand, Feng K'e-shan, as befitted the future King of Earth, made several trips to Sung-chia village in addition to meeting with Lin Ch'ing in Honan. He went once in late 1811 and again in early 1813; in the time between these visits, he made remarkable progress generating a following and gaining authority as a sect leader.

In 1811, at Lin Ch'ing's invitation, Feng K'e-shan came to Sung-chia village to demonstrate and give instruction in martial arts. Feng brought with him his teacher, an elderly Shantung man named Wang Hsiang, and they taught their boxing system to some of Lin Ch'ing's pupils.[116] It is likely, however, that Lin Ch'ing did not treat Feng with the respect he accorded Li Wen-ch'eng. Although Lin and Li had felt the need to include someone who was proficient at military arts, Lin Ch'ing, who had few purely physical skills, took a patronizing attitude toward such men. Lin's nephew tells of a visit to his uncle by another boxer that illustrates this condescension: Lin Ch'ing's assistant Liu Ch'eng-hsiang introduced this man to Lin as a person of outstanding ability who simply could not be injured by a knife or sword. When Lin Ch'ing wanted to take a knife and try, Liu Ch'eng-hsiang stopped him, saying, "This is serious. You must not treat it lightly." Urged to study with this man, Lin Ch'ing was contemptuous: "Here, ours is the Way of the Immortals; we don't use knives or violence."[117] It is not known how Lin and Feng K'e-shan got along, but it is not surprising that Feng felt the need to demonstrate his usefulness and to build a network of his own comparable to that of the King of Heaven and the King of Men. Furthermore, Feng was intrigued by the millenarian prophecies of Lin and Li and drawn by the accompanying promises of wealth and power. In 1812 and 1813 he worked hard organizing men who would participate on his behalf in the uprising.

In Ching district in central Chihli on the Shantung border there was a large group of sect members who concentrated on the martial arts dimension of the White Lotus tradition. Feng K'e-shan established contact with these men, won their respect for his physical ability, recruited them, and made that network his "base." Their leader, Sung Yueh-lung 宋躍瀧, was forty-three years old and was known for his skill at various forms of fighting, including kicking, the use of fists, staffs, and clubs. Sung had taught these skills to many disciples and called his system the I-ho (Righteous Harmony) school of fighting. They considered themselves a sect but the emphasis was clearly on military arts.[118]

It was this common interest in fighting techniques that eventually brought Feng K'e-shan and Sung Yueh-lung together. In the spring of 1812 a sect member called Huo Ying-fang who lived near Sung but who came originally from Hua suggested a match between Feng K'e-shan and Sung Yueh-lung.[119] Sung was interested, and so Feng came to Ching district to Sung's village to compete with him in boxing and fencing. Feng's abilities were superior and he was acknowledged as the champion. Sung Yueh-lung and his son kotowed to him, took him as their teacher, and joined his Li Trigram sect.[120] The Sungs learned the eight-character chant and thereafter taught it to all their pupils, telling them that they should now consider themselves part of the Li Trigram sect. One of Sung's more important pupils was a military *sheng-yuan* (holder of the lowest military examination degree) from Ku-ch'eng named Li Sheng-te. Li had at least twenty-three pupils under him, from towns and villages mostly in adjacent Ching district[121] Thus, through this one match, Feng K'e-shan acquired all these men as part of his network and thereafter considered them his primary body of followers, his Li Trigram sect. He maintained regular communication with them and began to prepare them for the coming uprising.

Late in the winter of 1812, Feng K'e-shan decided to visit Lin Ch'ing again, perhaps with the intention of impressing Lin with his new following. He stopped off on the way to see his pupils and may have traveled north from Hua together with Huo Ying-fang, who was just returning home after being presented to Li Wen-ch'eng.[122] Feng stayed with the Sung family when he arrived at their village, and they decided that Sung Yueh-lung's son Yü-lin would go with him to see Lin Ch'ing. En route they went through the provincial capital of Pao-ting and stayed there at the same inn where Lin and Niu Liang-ch'en had first become acquainted during the trial in 1808. The inn owner, Ma Lao-t'ai, had later become a pupil of Lin Ch'ing, and he now helped Feng hire a cart to complete the last leg of their journey. When they arrived in Sung-chia village, Sung Yü-lin, who was meeting Lin Ch'ing for the first time, kotowed respectfully to him. The three men discussed the uprising. Lin Ch'ing told Feng that the public slogan for the Eight Trigrams had been decided upon—Entrusted by Heaven to Prepare the Way—and he could begin telling his pupils about it; the secret password and date of the turn in the kalpa, on the other hand, would not be determined until the coming summer. Lin asked Feng how many men he could muster. With some pride, Feng replied, exaggerating, "About three hundred." After several days, Feng and young Sung left and returned south. They stopped in Ching district, and then Feng returned alone to Hua where he informed Niu Liang-ch'en (who had been instrumental in arranging the trip) and through Niu, Li Wen-ch'eng.[123]

In the 4th month of that year Feng returned to Ching, and that spring he and Sung Yueh-lung and one of Sung's pupils traveled to market fairs in the area, demonstrating their skills and attracting potential pupils. By the summer of 1813 Sung Yueh-lung's following included at least fifty men who, together with their families, were prepared to participate in the Eight Trigrams uprising. Although Feng K'e-shan did take a few other pupils, he relied overwhelmingly on Sung to provide men for "his" trigram.[124]

Lin Ch'ing continued to receive callers after Feng K'e-shan left in the 2d month of 1813. Two months later he had a visit from a man called Liu Yü-lung 劉玉隆. Liu is another example of the practicing sect member who through friends who were believers came in contact with Lin Ch'ing and decided to become part of the Eight Trigrams. Liu came from Jao-yang district in central Chihli, but a chance meeting with members of Ku Liang's Jung-hua Assembly in 1808 had led to his conversion to that sect. In 1811 Liu came north to visit his teacher and acquaintances near Peking. He learned about the plans then being made in Hua, was told that there would be an uprising led by all the trigram masters, and agreed to participate. Thus, when Liu Yü-lung came to see Lin Ch'ing in the spring of 1813, he was given more specific instructions: return home and convert more pupils, and when the time arrives, come to Peking and participate in the palace attack with Lin Ch'ing's other followers.[125]

In the 5th month of 1813 Lin Ch'ing received another visit from the titular head of Li Wen-ch'eng's Chen Trigram sect, Yü K'e-ching. Yü brought with him several newly converted pupils from Chü-lu in central Chihli. By including these Chü-lu men in the Eight Trigrams, Yü K'e-ching had tapped a large pool of believers in that area. These men, including the sect leader Yang Yü-shan 楊遇山, had belonged to the Ta-sheng sect in Chü-lu (itself an offshoot of the Kao family's Li Trigram) that had been prosecuted by the government in 1811 and 1812 (see pp. 56-60). After these investigations, Yang Yü-shan and his fellow believers had given up holding meetings and allowed the congregational aspects of sect membership to remain temporarily in abeyance. In the spring of 1813 Yü K'e-ching had come to that district to cure illnesses and find pupils; he and Yang became acquainted and found that they were "in the same sect." Yang began to treat Yü K'e-ching as his teacher and recommended him and his sect to others. Yü was a success as a healer and as a promoter of the Eight Trigrams. He told Yang about the imminent arrival of the Pai-yang era, invited him and his followers to be part of their group, and persuaded them to come to Peking to be introduced to Lin Ch'ing. They did so and Lin explained that the turn in the kalpa was coming that very year, and he was already arranging with eunuchs to capture the Forbidden City in Peking. Lin invited Yang to participate and urged him to go home and "call his pupils together again." The Chü-lu men were persuaded, and so their Ta-sheng sect was reassembled to become part of the Eight Trigrams.[126]

Preparations for the coming uprising had intensified in 1813. As we have seen, word had been sent out during the preceding winter and spring that the new kalpa would arrive that very year. Believers had been alerted, told of a public slogan, and urged to convert and recruit as many people as possible. During the summer Li Wen-ch'eng's adopted son Liu Ch'eng-chang came to see Lin Ch'ing. He stayed for several weeks—from the end of the 6th month until the middle of the 7th. He was accompanied as before by Ch'in Li and brought the customary gifts for Lin Ch'ing, this time 500 taels. Lin immediately took this money and deposited it in a shop in Peking. Lin and Liu discussed the serious matter of determining the precise date of the turn in the kalpa, and Lin decided that he would go to Hua very soon for a major meeting of all the trigram leaders. Liu left immediately to notify everyone of this meeting.[127]

Substantial progress had been made in planning the Eight Trigrams uprising since Lin Ch'ing and Li Wen-ch'eng's first meetings in the summer of 1811. By the fall of 1812 they had agreed on a public slogan and had begun to tell people that the kalpa would come sometime in 1813. The plan of action for responding to the kalpa had been worked out, but in broad outline only. When the signal was given, it was understood that each sect group would move into action and that there would be simultaneous uprisings led by each major leader. With the help of natural and supernatural disasters accompanying the arrival of the new era, nonbelievers would be eliminated and only members of the Eight Trigrams would be left. The details of this plan, including the date on which it would be put into effect, were left to be worked out at the meeting in Honan during the summer of 1813. In the meantime, sect members, though increasingly in contact with one another, were still living normally. Organizationally, a large-scale network linking one sect with another in pyramidal fashion had been created, and previously small and

isolated sects had now become part of a lively whole. Believers waited
only for the announcement from their leaders before openly converting this organization into a vehicle for rebellion.

THE TAO-K'OU MEETING

When Lin Ch'ing left home for the meeting in Honan in the 7th
month of 1813, he was near the peak of his power and prestige and he
traveled in style. Accompanied by three pupils, Lin rode in a passenger cart just presented to him (perhaps specifically for this
journey) by his eunuch pupils. He instructed his godson Ch'en
Wen-k'uei to ride on the lead horse, his pupil Chih Chin-ts'ai to
drive, and his friend and pupil Ch'en Shuang to serve as his personal
attendant. It was a fine contrast with his days in Kiangsu when he
had waited upon other men.[128]

On the way south they passed through Pao-ting prefectural city and
stopped at the Ma family inn; Lin Ch'ing brought Ma Lao-t'ai up
to date on the plans and asked him to prepare his group.[129] Leaving
Pao-ting, Lin Ch'ing continued south to the river port of Tao-k'ou
near Hua city where he stayed at an inn. Li Wen-ch'eng's home was
about five miles away, so Chih Chin-ts'ai rode their donkey there to
tell Li that Lin Ch'ing had arrived. Liu Ch'eng-chang had brought
news of the visit and Niu Liang-ch'en, who had been particularly
active in organizing Li Wen-ch'eng's followers, helped notify and
assemble all the sect leaders in the area. Among those present were
Li's former teacher and present assistant Liu Kuo-ming, the Chen
Trigram sect head Yü K'e-ching, the Li Trigram sect head Feng
K'e-shan, other lesser teachers and leaders from the Hua and Chün
area, Yang Yü-shan and Chao Te-i from central Chihli, and Chu
Ch'eng-fang from Shantung. The meeting lasted from the middle of
the 7th month until early in the 8th.[130]

The most important matter to be settled was the date of the uprising. Word had already spread among believers that the turn in
the kalpa would come very soon. In the early spring, the healer Hsu
An-kuo had told one of his pupils that the kalpa would begin on the
chia-tzu day at the end of the 10th month; he later revised this and
declared that "we would pass through the kalpa" in the 8th month.[131]
As the year went on, an atmosphere of excited anticipation was being
generated, and pressure on the leaders to name a specific date for the
rising increased.

This atmosphere was unquestionably affected by the dismal economic situation in the southern portion of the north China plain in 1813. There had been drought and flood in a few of these districts in 1811 and in many more in 1812, a fact that may have encouraged Lin and Li to expect that the turn in the kalpa accompanying such calamities might not be far away and to anticipate increased support for their enterprise. Since the very early spring in 1813 there had been a severe drought that had continued into the summer without abatement. Lack of sufficient snow the preceding winter had combined with lack of rain in the spring to leave the fields dry and hard; many were not even ploughed and only a few were planted. The price of grain had begun to rise and famine was setting in. "Those who have become impoverished," memorialized a local official, "eat grass roots and tree bark to stay alive. The leaves have all been picked off the willow trees which line the public highways and have been eaten for food."[132] Another official traveling from Peking toward the southwest in the 8th month of 1813, just as the Tao-k'ou meeting was taking place, wrote a poem recording his feelings.

For ten days I have been traveling through Honan,
and I can hardly bear to look at this desolation.
It is easy to gather up the green sprouts, for they are like straw;
but it is difficult to bury the dead in the hard yellow earth.
How long has it been without rain?
No one can do anything but sigh, whether he owns land or not.
Only a few stalks of tough grass can be pulled up,
and these even a passing stranger must use for food.

He went on to describe the empty houses and abandoned villages, the silence with which families left home in search of food and with which bodies fell to the ground beside the road; looters and wolves entered the villages at night, women begged by the highway, children were sold by their parents.[133] Government relief had done little to improve the situation. The disaster area formed a wide belt extending across northern Honan, southern Chihli, and into southwestern Shantung.[134]

A milder spring drought in the Peking area had led to a rise in the price of grain and Lin Ch'ing had taken advantage of this by circulating the rhyme, "If you want cheaper flour, Lin Ch'ing must take power" (若要白麵賤, 除非林坐清了殿).[135] When he visited the south it became even clearer to Lin that there were very practical reasons for fixing a date in the near future.

It was Lin Ch'ing who made this decision and who announced it to his assembled colleagues at Tao-k'ou. He declared that, on the basis of certain passages in the religious books of the sect, he had determined that the new kalpa would begin on the 15th day of the 9th month; at that time members of the Eight Trigrams would "make known the Way" (*ming-tao* 明道). This phrase circulated among sect members as another euphemism for their "great undertaking." One teacher told his pupils cryptically, "There will be Daylight. The Way will be made known" (要天明了，要明道了). As proof of Li Wen-ch'eng's role in the coming kalpa era, Lin Ch'ing cited a phrase from his "Comprehensive Manual for Responding to the Kalpas of the Three Buddhas": "someone named Li would make known the Way" (十八子明道).[136]

Lin Ch'ing explained the choice of date by quoting another passage from sect scriptures:

> Eighth month, midautumn festival,
> Midautumn festival, eighth month.
> It is then that the yellow flowers will bloom everywhere.

The midautumn festival (*chung-ch'iu* 中秋) fell every year on the 15th day of the 8th month. Lin Ch'ing explained that originally he had expected that in 1813 there would be an intercalary 8th month that would have fulfilled the prophecy mentioning two eighth months. When he learned this would not be the case, he had concluded that the 15th day of the 9th month could be properly said to constitute the 15th day of the second 8th month, the time when they would respond to the turn in the kalpa and make known the Way. These phrases involving blooming and brightness both convey graphically the process these sects underwent as they turned from private gatherings to open rebellion.[137] The fact that at least two preceding White Lotus sects had determined that the new kalpa would begin on the 15th day of the 8th month indicates that some sect literature was persuasive on this point.[138] The written prophecy was, however, interpreted in light of other practical considerations.

In the annual agricultural cycle in north China, a slack period in terms of demand for labor on the land did not begin until after the spring crops of sorghum, millet, buckwheat, and beans had been harvested and the winter crop of wheat planted.[139] Until then, all those with land could be expected to be very busy, and those without land who were willing to work as hired laborers found their services much in demand. Normally this busy period fell in August, Septem-

ber, and October (in terms of the lunar calendar, during the 7th
and 8th months plus the 6th or 9th depending on the year). In 1813
the peak period of agricultural activity in the autumn occurred during the 7th, 8th, and 9th months. Lin Ch'ing wanted as many followers as possible to participate in his strike on the Forbidden City,
and the middle of the 9th month, no earlier, was therefore most
practical. These considerations were less relevant in the drought areas
of the southern plain where there was little to be harvested.[140]

Another matter of concern to Lin Ch'ing was the whereabouts of
the Chia-ch'ing Emperor. If Lin was to be responsible for attacking
and occupying Peking, it was essential that he know exactly where the
emperor would be at the time. Every year during the summer the
emperor went to Jehol, north of the Great Wall, to hunt, relax, escape
the summer heat of Peking, and reaffirm his Manchu heritage. These
trips were routine matters, and it is unlikely that the emperor's itin-
erary was a secret within the palace; Lin Ch'ing could have learned of
the plans through his eunuch pupils. In 1813 the Chia-ch'ing Emperor left the capital for the north on 7/18, the same day as the preceding year. If he were to follow the same schedule (as he apparently
intended to), he would arrive in Jehol on 7/24, remain there until
8/15, when he would leave for two weeks at the hunting park at
Mu-lan, return to Jehol, and be back in Peking on the 17th day of
the 9th month.[141] It is clear that when Lin Ch'ing planned the attack
on the Forbidden City, he knew that on the 15th the emperor would
be outside Peking but only a few miles away. The palace would not
be as heavily guarded, and the emperor, despite his retinue of body-
guards, would be more vulnerable while traveling.

Thus, as far as attacking the emperor was concerned, 9/15 was a
convenient date for Lin Ch'ing. In terms of agriculture, it was late
enough so that most of the autumn harvest would have been collected
and if the millennium was to arrive, surely there would be no need to
plant for the spring. In discussing these matters with the other Eight
Trigram leaders in Honan, where drought and famine loomed large
in a way they did not in Peking, Lin Ch'ing could not but have felt
that the sooner they acted the better.

The sect leaders also selected visual and verbal signs by means of
which their followers could identify one another and be protected
from harm. Drawing on a long tradition of using colored turbans as
symbols of rebellion, it was decided that all Eight Trigram members
would tie white sashes about their heads. White, the color of the Pai-
yang (White Sun) era that was about to arrive, would also be the

color of their banners.[142] Houses of sect members would be marked by the presence of a small white cloth banner in the gateway. Women believers would wear small white banners in the lapel of their clothing. Active rebels would use pieces of white cloth as turbans and if possible as sashes about their waists. On those banners belonging to leaders, the public slogan of the Eight Trigrams was to be written— Entrusted by Heaven to Prepare the Way.[143]

These visual signs were not enough; as there was a "public slogan" (*ming-hao*) so there would be a "secret slogan" (*an-hao* 暗號). The latter was in reality a password, not to be written down or broadcast to the world at large, but only to be spoken by one sect member to another. At this meeting, Lin Ch'ing and the others decided that this password would be the phrase "Be Victorious" (*te sheng* 得勝). When one rebel met another he would greet him loudly with these two words, thus identifying himself and by a kind of verbal magic inducing success. When a rebel killed a nonbeliever he was also to speak these words.[144]

Larger strategical matters were also discussed and decided upon at the Tao-k'ou meeting. The leaders determined not only when but precisely how they would respond to the kalpa. Feng K'e-shan alleged in his confession that a territorial division of the spoils was agreed upon, and he reported that the following conversation took place at the summer meeting:

> Lin Ch'ing said, "I want to occupy (*chan* 占) the area of Pao-ting in Chihli. You each can go and occupy some other place. Any place that you don't occupy, I will take over myself." Li Wen-ch'eng then said that he would occupy the area of Chang-te prefecture in Honan. I said that I would occupy the area of Te district in Shantung.[145]

This scheme is more consistent with Feng's far-from-religious attitude toward the entire uprising than it is with the vision of a single system imagined by Li Wen-ch'eng and Lin Ch'ing, and it seems unlikely that any such feudal arrangement was planned. On the contrary, available evidence indicates that it was responsibility for "pacifying" certain regions—not for governing them—that was assigned to each of the participating sect leaders. Judging from their actions, this "pacification" (*p'ing* 平) appears to have entailed primarily the destruction of the symbols of Ch'ing authority, namely the offices and officers of government, and perhaps the massacre of all nonbelievers.

These acts would be carried out on 9/15 when each of the participating sects would "rise up."

Each group was assigned its own targets. Li Wen-ch'eng and his pupils would be responsible for the area of Hua and Chün in Honan and adjacent southern Chihli. Hsu An-kuo's men were responsible for the various districts of southwestern Shantung: Chu Ch'eng-fang in Ts'ao, his cousin Chu Ch'eng-kuei in Ting-t'ao, Ts'ui Shih-chün in Chin-hsiang, Chang Chien-mu in Ch'eng-wu, and Ch'eng Pai-yueh in Shan. The region around Tz'u district in Chihli was assigned to Chao Te-i. There was a leader named Chao Pu-yun who would take care of Chi district in central Chihli. Not far away in Ku-ch'eng there was Huo Ying-fang's sect, and just to the north Sung Yueh-lung in Ching. Yang Yü-shan would handle Chü-lu and Yung-nien, and Ma Lao-t'ai and his pupils would be ready in Pao-ting. Liu Yü-lung and his followers were in Jao-yang. Lin Ch'ing was to be responsible for seizing the Forbidden City and Peking itself.

Because of the importance of Peking to the rebels, it was arranged that Li Wen-ch'eng and all the other trigram leaders to the south would temporarily bring their men and come north to assist Lin Ch'ing. Presumably they intended to make Peking their head-quarters, possibly their "Cloud City." Li and his men would rush northward, stopping en route at the other rebel strongholds to pick up men. Peking would be occupied and the returning Chia-ch'ing Emperor would be attacked outside the capital and killed, and as the present Hung-yang era was completed, Ch'ing rule would come to an end.[146]

It is not hard to imagine how this meeting generated an atmosphere of confidence, optimism, and enthusiasm in which it was easy to believe that cities would fall and armies melt away. Having convinced themselves of how easily it could be done, Lin and Li worked out in a more final form the new hierarchy with which they planned to replace the Ch'ing system. As we mentioned above, the highest positions would be occupied by Lin Ch'ing, Feng K'e-shan, and Li Wen-ch'eng. They were to be known as the Controllers of Heaven, Earth, and Men, respectively; Li Wen-ch'eng would be responsible for governing, while Lin and Feng would serve him as advisers possessed of great skill and wisdom. The two advisers would be a symmetrical pair, Lin the Yin Trigram Master (陰卦主), Feng the Yang Trigram Master (陽卦主). In addition to representing the *yin-yang* polarity, these two also encompassed the dichotomy between civil and military: Lin was known as the Sage of Knowledge (*wen sheng-jen* 文聖人) and Feng as the Sage of Military Ability (*wu sheng-jen* 武聖人). Li Wen-ch'eng took the role of the Emperor of Men (*jen-huang* 人皇) who consulted with them.

As ruler, Li Wen-ch'eng was to be the center of another triad, and he and two pupils (Feng Hsueh-li and Yü K'e-ching) were to be known as the King of Heaven (*t'ien-wang* 天王), King of Earth (*ti-wang*), and King of Men (*jen-wang*), respectively.[147] Presumably these would be responsible for ruling. Underneath these controllers and kings there were to be eight other kings, each named after one of the eight trigrams: the Ch'ien Trigram king (*kua-wang* 卦王), the Kun Trigram king, and so forth. Below these eight kings were sixty-four trigram lords (*kua-po* 卦伯), eight for each of the eight trigrams.[148] Each leader was instructed to prepare registers listing the names of all members so that each could be rewarded eventually.[149]

One point is quite clear. The Eight Trigrams were not introducing a fraternal, egalitarian society. Like the structure of the sects themselves, built by teacher–pupil bonds, the religious structure created for the future was fundamentally and openly hierarchical. The Eight Trigrams offered their members exclusivity and respect, but they did not offer brotherhood and an absence of authority. Li Wen-ch'eng's former teacher and present assistant Liu Kuo-ming explained this to another leader: "At that time [in the new kalpa] only the people who practiced the sect teachings will be left, and they will be divided into upper and lower (*shang hsia* 上下)." To prove this was as it should be, Liu cited the following lines from a sect scripture:

> There are three ranks: upper, middle, lower.
> There are three powers: heaven, earth, man.
> As the five elements gave birth to father and son,
> So the eight trigrams will designate princes and ministers.[150]

Because the new hierarchy created by the Eight Trigram leaders is nowhere described in detail, the lines of authority among the leaders and between leaders and followers are not entirely clear. Nonetheless, there is no indication that teacher–pupil and master–follower relationships would be anything but reinforced under the new system. As with many true believers, the Eight Trigrams built their organization on authoritarianism and orthodoxy.

Finally, the Eight Trigram leaders needed a name for the new assembly of believers that would take place in the Pai-yang era, and they now decided to call this convocation the T'ien-li 天理 (Doctrine [authorized by] Heaven) Assembly.[151] Then, having concluded their business, the sect leaders hurried back to their homes. It was now the middle of the 8th month; they had four weeks in which to notify all their followers about the identifying turbans, sashes and banners, slogans and passwords, and to tell them of the date and their responsibilities for "making known the Way."

As the assembled leaders prepared to leave Tao-k'ou, the heavens finally opened up and rain came. Great downpours fell in northern Honan, southern Chihli, and western Shantung, ending the drought but creating mud and flooding in its stead. These rains continued for weeks and did not taper off until the 9th month, just in time for the Eight Trigram uprisings, as it happened—perhaps another auspicious omen for their enterprise.[152]

It was in this way that the Eight Trigrams were created. Vigorous leaders had used ordinary sect ties to build a sect organization of extraordinary size and scope, and they had emphasized one dimension of the religion—its vision of apocalypse and millennium—to mobilize believers into rebellion. White Lotus sects had always contained the potential for such developments, but only with certain kinds of men and circumstances could this potential be activated and realized. Still operating within the bounds of normal life, sect leaders had created a higher regional network[153] out of small isolated groups, and they had raised their sights accordingly. Their interests were no longer local and private but public and national. Having come this far, however, their task became increasingly difficult. Once in open rebellion, they would have to find ways of using their sect structure to carry out their goals on the battlefield, but even before that time they had to walk a very fine line in order to keep their secret preparations within the limits of what was observedly normal and legal. It was during this period of preparation that the sects were most vulnerable to government discovery. As they changed from being *an*, dark and private, to being *ming*, bright and public, the sects were in great danger of letting their new personality shine through before that designated day when they would all step forward to make known the Way.

PART THREE

Mobilization: Government Investigations and Rebel Uprisings

DURING the month after the Tao-k'ou meeting and prior to the scheduled uprisings, weapons and name lists were prepared, and banners, white cloth, and information were passed along the rebel network from teacher to pupils. At the same time, the Ch'ing government finally learned about the Eight Trigrams' activities, and officials began to interrupt this mobilization. These parallel actions, mobilization and interference, climaxed early in the 9th month of 1813: the rebels were forced to strike prematurely and the scheduled uprisings went off like badly timed firecrackers.

The demanding task of transforming sect members into rebels without alerting the government required a degree of discipline not normal to teacher–pupil relationships, and it strained the entire Eight Trigrams organization particularly at its weakest links. Joining a White Lotus sect was in itself an act of nonconformity, but a mild one compared with the drastic and defiant actions now required of believers. The fears about the future that had motivated many to join the Eight Trigrams could in this crucial moment of transition emerge as timidity and uncooperativeness. Sect members had, therefore, to be moved speedily and unhesitatingly toward the violent acts that would commit them to their new lives. And yet care had to be taken not to rouse these men to total license or anarchy; their hostility and anger had to be directed and channeled so that the movement as a whole would not be fragmented by the unleashed emotions of its individual participants. Against these needs for positive direction and explicit instructions, sect leaders had to balance the increasingly real danger of government discovery. The final preparations for rebellion, involving rapid clandestine communication and the secret procurement of illegal and incriminating objects, were very hazardous. The slowness of the government's response did allow the rebels to sacrifice some secrecy to speed without suffering truly drastic consequences, yet it by no means removed the danger.

The Ch'ing government's problem was not isolation, for as we shall see the lower levels of the Ch'ing apparatus reached directly into the ranks of the rebels, but rather the difficulty with which the attention of the great bureaucracy could be captured by the hints and clues of imminent rebellion and the slowness of its reflexes once a potential problem was spotted. In the end a fair measure of good and bad luck on both sides further hampered both an efficient government response and the smoothly scheduled timing of rebel uprisings. We will look first at the strike against the district cities planned by the various trigrams on the north China plain, and then, because of the incomparably richer source material, examine in greater detail the attack on the Forbidden City in Peking organized by Lin Ch'ing.

Unraveling in Chin-hsiang

In Chin-hsiang district in Shantung, authorities had begun to learn about the planned rebellion even before the Tao-k'ou meeting, and as Eight Trigram leaders were making their final plans, threads of the sect network in this district were already unraveling. In the 6th month of 1813, a *sheng-yuan* (holder of the lowest examination degree) from Chin-hsiang named Li Chiu-piao heard about sect members' holding secret night meetings in a village south of the city (probably near where he lived). Li was concerned about this and informed the Chin-hsiang director of schools. Because the district magistrate was in the provincial capital on business, the director of schools wrote a report and sent it to his superior, the provincial direction of education; at the same time the district constable was told to send a report to the governor. T'ung-hsing, the Manchu governor of Shantung, was at that time at Lin-ch'ing on the Grand Canal supervising the passage of grain boats bound for Peking. He received these reports on the 23d and 24th days of the 6th month and immediately sent a deputy to the scene to investigate and report back.[1]

Two weeks later, on 7/6, Deputy Tso returned and submitted a three-page report to the governor. T'ung-hsing called in an expectant district magistrate named Wu Chieh 吳堦 who was then assisting him and appointed him acting magistrate. Wu Chieh was instructed to go to Chin-hsiang, investigate further, and if necessary make arrests. Wu went first to the provincial capital and then on to Chin-hsiang, arriving there on 7/20. On the way, he encountered the magistrate of Chü-yeh, adjacent to Chin-hsiang, and Wu advised him to return to his post immediately in case arrests needed to be made. In order to learn about the local situation, as soon as he arrived in Chin-hsiang, Wu Chieh went to see an old friend of his, a prominent local dignitary and former official in the Yellow River Administration named Chang Ti-kung. Wu asked to be briefed on the district situation, and Chang told him that "the various localities here are not peaceful. There is

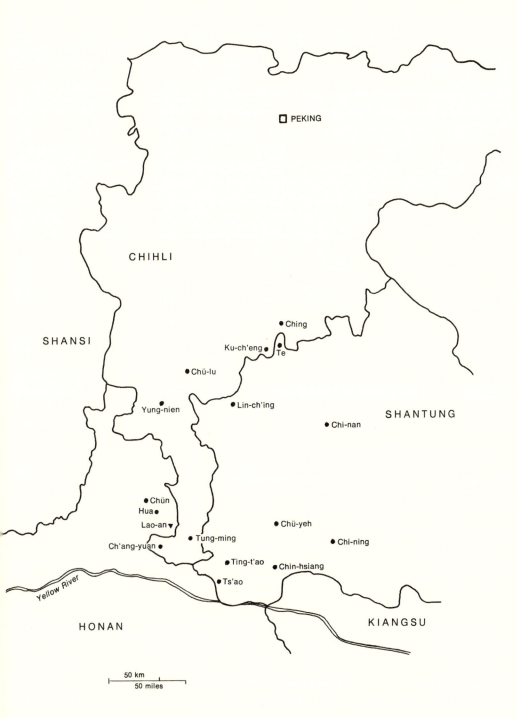

Districts and cities of the north China plain

an evil leader named Ts'ui Shih-chün who has founded a sect and converted many people. Their strength increases like a prairie fire. There is sure to be trouble. The gentry are all just trying to figure out how to avoid harm." According to Chang, this Ts'ui Shih-chün had already held a big feast earlier that month, but when staff from the district yamen arrived belatedly to make arrests, they found that everyone had vanished.

Magistrate Wu decided that these men had to be lured out of hiding, so he ordered notices posted saying that "the charges previously filed against Ts'ui Shih-chün, etc., have been found to be based on groundless rumors started by a person who bore a personal grudge against them"; Ts'ui and the others were no longer wanted for arrest but they should "remain in their proper occupations and cause no trouble." Making other inquiries, Magistrate Wu learned that although most of the gentry in the district were aware of the increasingly public sect activities, they had taken no special steps to put an end to them. He resolved to remedy this.[2]

Wu Chieh had learned previously from the report of the governor's deputy that there was to be a gathering of sect leaders on 7/27. Wu made secret preparations to surprise the "troublemakers" that day and arrest them, but his plans were spoiled by the overeagerness of his associate, the magistrate of Chü-yeh. This man had taken Wu Chieh's advice and returned to his post; on 7/24, eager to get results, he had taken men into adjacent Chin-hsiang and arrested one would-be rebel, luckily obtaining a list of sect members this man was carrying. Magistrate Wu had therefore to act immediately before this arrest could alert Ts'ui Shih-chün and his comrades to their real danger. On the 26th and 27th he sent men and arrested Ts'ui and ten others. They were brought to the distict yamen, but Magistrate Wu cautiously did not imprison or interrogate them there. He let Ts'ui be informed that they were wanted in the provincial capital for questioning on another matter. Thus Wu Chieh hoped to fool Ts'ui's followers into feeling safe once more. Ts'ui and the others were transferred to the prison in Chi-ning, about fifty miles to the east. Wu Chieh meanwhile continued to make arrests, seizing six more sect members on 7/29.

On that day, two commoners from eastern Chin-hsiang district who were evidently aware of the sect activities and of the recent arrests, came to the city. They reported that their sons, together with at least three other men, had joined some religious sect. (In such cases, if relatives of sect members demonstrated their loyalty by reporting the offenders to the authorities before any trouble occurred, all could be spared punishment.)[3] The two sons and the other men were arrested but would admit nothing. Magistrate Wu had their relatives and neighbors brought in to testify against them: these "good people" said to the believers, "At night you all burn incense and recite things. You wouldn't listen to our warnings, instead you just said to us, 'Before long you will have no heads.'" Magistrate Wu ordered torture applied and finally the young men began to confess. They admitted that they had joined a sect in which an eight-character mantra was recited three times a day, and they described how those who contributed money were promised land or office in return. Asked about a possible uprising, these men said that "the Pai-yang kalpa will come in the 8th or 9th month, and it will cut away [the old era] with a black wind which will blow for seven days and seven nights." They admitted that sect members would be given banners just ahead of time so that they would be spared death; everyone else, however, "would suffer under the kalpa and be killed."

Magistrate Wu, now aware of a possible uprising within one or two months, went to Chi-ning city where the eighteen captured sect members were being held. He interrogated them but learned very little—"they hung their heads, closed their eyes, and would only admit that they had encouraged others to do good and to avoid the kalpa calamities, no more." Wu Chieh ordered them transferred to the provincial capital for more professional interrogation.

During the 8th month the pace of arrests slowed. By this time the Tao-k'ou meeting of sect leaders had been held and specific instructions about the uprising were being sent out. A few men were arrested in Chin-hsiang on 8/8 and more ten days later; one of them was Ts'ui Shih-chün's son-in-law Li Ching-hsiu. Li made a detailed and informative statement. He said that Ts'ui had an associate in Ts'ao district named Chu Ch'eng-kuei and a teacher from Ch'ang-yuan named Hsu An-kuo, and he named the villages where they lived. He added, moreover, that he had heard that Hsu An-kuo's teacher lived very near Peking. Li Ching-hsiu admitted that his father-in-law had promised to take the home and estate of the Li family (probably the family that had originally informed on the sect to the director of schools two months earlier) and give it to him as his palace after they had passed through the kalpa.

This information about Chu Ch'eng-kuei and Hsu An-kuo was confirmed when Magistrate Wu arrested five men who had been overheard "talking wildly" in a restaurant a few miles north of the city. These men further confessed that "the overall sect head was named Liu Lin, he lived twenty or thirty li from Peking, and he was in contact with eunuchs." They added that while the date for the turn in the kalpa had been originally thought to be during the 8th month, this had recently (that is, since the Tao-k'ou meeting) been changed to the 9th month.

Wu Chieh "found this very upsetting" and immediately reported the information to the governor. T'ung-hsing, for his part, did not report in turn to the emperor about possible sect organizations near Peking or about rumored eunuch involvement. Instead, he ordered that Ts'ui Shih-chün and the others be interrogated as soon as they reached the provincial capital so that the allegations could first be substantiated; not until 9/11 (when he had already received reports of rebel uprisings) did T'ung-hsing memorialize the emperor about possible Peking or eunuch connections with these sects.[4]

In the meantime, Wu Chieh was trying to expedite the arrests of those named in these confessions. As early as 8/16 he had sent a message to Ts'ao telling the magistrate to arrest Chu Ch'eng-kuei, but nothing was done until ten days later when Ch'eng-kuei's older brother Ch'eng-chen was arrested. Two white banners were found in his possession. Notifed of this, Magistrate Wu realized that the time for the uprising must be very near indeed: "Since I had heard from confessions that these banners would be given out just in advance, I knew it wouldn't be long before something would happen. This business had grown larger and larger during that [the 8th] month." Wu immediately took steps to defend his own district against possible attack. He ordered that all families post the names of their members as part of a *pao-chia* (household registration for security purposes) survey. At the same time, he ordered that able-bodied men be called up and on 9/1 began training them as militiamen. Thus, by the beginning of the 9th month, Magistrate Wu had already arrested thirty-two sect members, including many of the top leaders in that district, he had alerted the gentry and citizenry, and began making military preparations for defending the city. Had all local officials possessed his appreciation of the realities and the same "righteous" assistance of members of the local community, the Eight Trigrams' rising might have been thwarted at an early stage.

PREPARATIONS IN CENTRAL CHIHLI

When the meeting in Tao-k'ou was over, Lin Ch'ing returned

home, traveling in his same magisterial style. Feng K'e-shan accompanied him as far as Ching district, where they stayed with Feng's pupil Sung Yueh-lung, who was finally introduced to Lin Ch'ing. They all discussed their plans and then Lin proceeded north, arriving home on about 8/16.

Feng K'e-shan remained with his pupils. He told them about the Tao-k'ou meeting and the decisions reached by the leaders. Sung and his son were told to notify their followers that the date of the uprising would be 9/15, that the password was "Be Victorious," and that the identifying insignia would be pieces of white cloth and banners on which should be written "Entrusted by Heaven to Prepare the Way." On the 15th, all were to assemble and come to Sung Yueh-lung's village. It had originally been arranged that Sung would then bring his men south to Hua to join with Li Wen-ch'eng, but Feng and Lin Ch'ing had changed this. Sung and his men would instead build a wall around that village making it into a stockade; then they would gather and store food and fodder and wait for Li Wen-ch'eng to come north. When Li and his followers arrived, they would greet them with the password, provide them with supplies, and all would then proceed onward to Peking together. Sung Yueh-lung and his son immediately began purchasing white cloth and making banners, which they then distributed to their pupils with these same instructions.[5]

Sung's son conveyed this information about the banners, password, and date to Huo Ying-fang, the sect leader in nearby Ku-ch'eng district. The source material permits us to reconstruct in some detail, as an example of this process, the way in which these goods and information were then distributed by Huo to his many pupils (see fig. 2). Huo Ying-fang began immediately to make up white banners with the four-character slogan written on them; he distributed these to fifteen people including his teacher's pupils, his own pupils, and members of his family. Huo Ying-fang's pupil Liu K'un had himself a large number of pupils, and so he told them in turn about the date and password and showed them what kind of banner to make. One of Liu's pupils (Su Yuan-mo) then told his pupils. By the time this fourth generation was notified, it was already early in the 9th month and communications became increasingly urgent.[6] Wang Yuan, a participant, described how he was informed:

> Early in the 9th month Su Yuan-mo told his pupil Wang Yuan that sect members were going to rise up, and he had some cloth for banners which could be used to escape being attacked. Su

Yuan-mo gave Wang Yuan pieces of white cloth on which were written the four characters "Entrusted by Heaven to Prepare the Way." Wang Yuan was to wait until the sect rebels arrived, and then place the triangular banner in his gate post. The square banner was to be worn by his wife in the lapel of her clothing as identification. Moreover, Wang was to boil water for tea and to make rice for the sect rebels when they came. Thus he could safeguard himself and his family.[7]

At this point the network began to expand drastically. Wang Yuan, who had been in the sect for less than four months, was much relieved to know this system for saving himself. He quickly made another set of banners, which he gave to a friend, then he passed the information on to yet another friend who was in a different sect. This man was tense and frightened; he knew the day was coming nearer, and he wanted to insure his safety further by becoming Wang Yuan's pupil and being part of the Eight Trigrams. Wang therefore taught him the eight-character mantra, told him the password, and gave him a model of the banner to copy. In his turn this man took as his pupil and passed on all this supposedly secret information to a friend of his, a Taoist priest named Lo Kung. Lo Kung immediately told some of

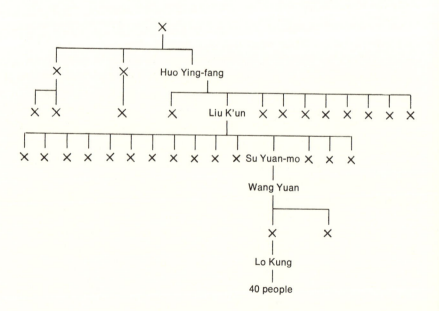

Fig. 2

his friends (none of whom were sect members), so that they too could benefit from this advance warning. They all purchased some cloth and rapidly made up forty banners on which the four-character slogan was written. Lo Kung handed these out to five friends, none of whom bothered to join the sect or become his pupil. Two of them took a dozen banners each, enough to supply all their relatives. None of Lo Kung's friends had apparently any intention of participating in the rebellion, or at least not until someone else took the first step; they were interested only in protecting themselves.[8]

The above account shows how under the pressure of time the normal channels for expansion of the sect became increasingly by-passed. A month was a long time when the danger of government discovery loomed ever larger, but when many links in a chain had to be renewed individually, sometimes necessitating travel from one village or district to another, at a time when interrupting normal activities (such as harvesting one's crops) was a hardship, and when the imagined calamities of the predicted kalpa seemed suddenly possible, a month passed very quickly. Friends and relatives of sect members who had not been interested in the sect suddenly became very concerned about having the option of sect protection if they needed it. As the time for the uprisings approached, sect members first took new pupils so as to extend this protection to them and to gain participants in the rebellion, and then gradually and almost indiscriminately passed on information about the protective powers of white banners, the password, and so forth. What little discipline could be exerted through the teacher–pupil relationship disappeared as word simply spread to friend and neighbor. Of even greater danger to the would-be rebels was the way in which conspicuous objects (such as white cloth banners marked with the presumptuous "Entrusted by Heaven to Prepare the Way") were being prepared and distributed outside the formal sect network. As it happened, none of Huo Ying-fang's followers came to the attention of the local officials; but as we shall see, it was just this hasty last-minute scramble that in other areas alerted the government to the existence of a "rebellious plot."

In the actions of the sect leader Yang Yü-shan and his followers in the district of Chü-lu, we can see another example of the kinds of preparations necessary during the last month. Yang had attended the Tao-k'ou meeting. When it was over, he sent a colleague back to his home in Chü-lu to pass the word to his pupils there; in the mean-time Yang hurried to Yung-nien district, the home of several other of his pupils. He told them about the meeting and said he needed a list of the names of all the Yung-nien group. A list was promptly made up, written not in a register, but in the manner of the "ten family lists" used by the government for tax and security purposes. It is not clear whether this style was adopted out of ignorance or to reduce the danger should the list be discovered.[9]

Yang Yü-shan then returned to his home. He had previously established connections with the Kao family in Honan, the leaders of a Li Trigram sect to which he had once belonged but which had no direct connections with the Eight Trigrams. Now, in anticipation of the uprisings, Yang wanted the Kaos to know and be protected. He had someone write a letter to a member of that family who was one of his pupils. In it he described the coming Eight Trigrams rebellion and suggested that they make up banners to safeguard their families and, when the day came, bring followers and come to Hua to lend a hand.[10] Other fragmentary information indicates that in many cases, Eight Trigram sect members took this generous and rather fraternal attitude toward other White Lotus sects and wanted them to have the option of joining even at the last moment.

In the end, none of these groups from central Chihli—nor two others about which there is no information, those of Chao Te-i in Tz'u and Chao Pu-yun in Chi—ever moved beyond this stage of preparation for rebellion. Huo Ying-fang had been instructed to send his men to Hua to assist Li Wen-ch'eng on 9/15. Early in the 9th month some of his pupils (but not Huo himself) started south, but when they learned of the presence of government soldiers ahead they became frightened and returned home.[11] Yang Yü-shan and his followers never even left their homes, deciding it was far safer to remain where they were.[12] Sung Yueh-lung claimed that he and his pupils had prepared everything as instructed and "when everything was ready, we waited, but we didn't see either Li Wen-ch'eng or Feng K'e-shan come in rebellion."[13]

Although all these men had pledged their support to the Eight Trigrams, when they heard of government soldiers on the march against their colleagues in the south and of the quick elimination of an abortive attack on the Forbidden City by their colleagues in the north, and when they saw that no great calamities were sent by the Eternal Mother to destroy nonbelievers, they changed their minds and remained at home, burning their banners and hoping to cover up their association with the rebels. Although the bonds between the top Eight Trigram leaders and these groups were strong enough to make possible elaborate plans for coordinated action, these links were not so tight that lesser leaders could be compelled to perform as promised. In the cases discussed above, the Eight Trigrams superstructure simply dissolved in the face of the crisis created by the rebellion and government moves to suppress it.

Rebellion in Honan and Southern Chihli

With the reader's indulgence we will change focus once more and look now not at government efficiency or at the prudence of some believers, but at action, at the successful transformation of sect members into rebels through violence.

Liu Pin was the subdistrict deputy-magistrate[14] stationed in the town of Lao-an in southeastern Hua district near the Chihli border, about twenty miles from Hua city. Late in the 8th month, in the pouring rain, after the Tao-k'ou meeting was over and plans for the uprising were in their final stages, Deputy-Magistrate Liu learned about weapons being manufactured in Lao-an market town and somehow he obtained the names of the "criminals" involved. He went to the city and told the Hua district magistrate Chiang K'e-chieh. Magistrate Chiang issued warrants for the arrest of these men and on the 2d day of the 9th month sent out police runners to seize them. Like Magistrate Wu in Chin-hsiang, these officials had been apprised of the names and residences not of rank-and-file sect members, but of the highest leaders. Consequently, it happened that the police runners went to Hsieh-chia village and arrested Li Wen-ch'eng himself and brought him together with Niu Liang-ch'en and several other sect members in custody back to Hua city.[15]

This was a catastrophe for the Eight Trigrams. Magistrate Chiang, however, did not realize how very important his prisoners were. Unlike Magistrate Wu in Chin-hsiang, he made no effort to cover up Li's arrest or to transfer the criminals to a more secure place. Instead, he kept them in the yamen jail and over the next few days tried to interrogate them. Li Wen-ch'eng did not cooperate and so, as was customary, torture was applied. Members of the yamen staff used pincers to squeeze Li's feet and ankles, and then they beat his feet and shins several hundred times with a club. The injuries that Li sustained were very severe. (Three months later his feet were still scarred from the pincers, a thick cotton cloth smeared with a viscous red medicated plaster was still wrapped around the flesh and broken bones of his shins and ankles, and he was still unable to walk or ride a horse.) Li finally admitted that an uprising had been planned but apparently would say no more.[16] He and the others remained in jail as Magistrate Chiang continued to make inquiries but took no military precautions. Several of Feng K'e-shan's more respectable (degree-holding) relatives, hearing of these inquiries, came to the yamen and told the magistrate that Feng was involved in some of these sect activities.[17] On 9/5 more than twenty other sect members were arrested by Hua authorities.[18]

In the meantime, Li Wen-ch'eng's pupils were becoming more and more agitated. They had learned about the injuries Li had received— probably from one of the sect members who worked as a runner in the district yamen[19]—and they were afraid he might die. Yü K'e-ching, who was formally the head of Li's Chen Trigram sect, got together with Li's brothers-in-law and other prominent leaders from the Hua area and decided finally that something had to be done: they could not wait until the 15th but had to take action and rebel immediately. Word was sent out to all believers in the area that the date had been changed, on the 7th day of the 9th month they would attack the city and free their leader.[20]

A man called Chao Te provides one example of how sect members in Honan (and elsewhere) were mobilized for action. Chao Te was an opera performer from a village of Hua district who in the spring of 1813 had been persuaded by his brother-in-law to join the sect. In the middle of the 8th month, Chao's brother-in-law passed the word that Sect Manager Niu Liang-ch'en had decided that the group would take action. A few days later, a fellow believer came to Chao Te's house, bringing a small white banner and ten shares of white cloth, each share consisting of two pieces, and the message that on 9/15 they would rise up. Chao Te was instructed to bring ten men. Chao agreed, took the banner and cloth, and then distributed the latter to two men, presumably pupils, telling them to each find four more men, which they did. All this occurred during the last ten days of the 8th month. On 9/3 Chao Te's brother-in-law sent a messenger again, this time with the urgent news that Niu Liang-ch'en and Li Wen-ch'eng had been seized by Hua authorities and put in jail. The new plan was for Chao Te to go with another sect member (from his village, possibly a relative), bringing his ten men, and enter Hua city on the 7th to free Li and Niu. Chao obeyed instructions and was among those who attacked the Hua yamen.[21]

In a similar manner, other sect members from Hua city and the surrounding countryside were notified and alerted. The arrest of Sect Master Li had exposed their plans and made them very vulnerable, but at the same time this action appears to have stimulated a higher degree of enthusiasm for rebellion. Threatened with the real possibility of imminent arrest, a sect member had less to lose and more to gain by active participation in the uprising. On the night of the 6th, these men left their homes and met with their colleagues in several temples inside the district city. There the plans for the following day were outlined, and at this point, when there was no turning back, some of the rank-and-file members were given their new titles and positions. This further committed them to the cause of the Eight Trigrams and gave them something to fight for. Early the following morning they took the final step and with a burst of violence "made known" their intentions and became rebels.

Members of the Eight Trigrams, perhaps as many as a thousand men, went to the district offices at daybreak. They broke into the jail, carried out Li Wen-ch'eng, and released their other colleagues and over a dozen ordinary prisoners.[22] They were not able to kill Magistrate Chiang, for he had summoned several dozen yamen runners and fled from the compound, by his account fighting rebels all the way. (Chiang reached Feng-ch'iu city about thirty-five miles to the south in safety and three days later hanged himself in disgrace.) The rebels killed the rest of the magistrate's household—two children, six women, and twenty-nine men, over half of them servants. One of the women, the magistrate's daughter-in-law, did not submit passively, and when she fought and cursed the rebels, they furiously nailed her alive to a post, "carved her up," and later ordered her bones thrown away. The rebels also went to the offices of the director of schools and stabbed to death all seventeen people in his household, including his wife, daughters, and grandsons. The education official himself escaped by jumping in the well. Deputy-Magistrate Liu Pin (who had helped arrest Li Wen-ch'eng), the constable, and the resident sergeant were also killed. Finally, the rebels set fire to the yamen buildings. Having destroyed these symbols of Ch'ing authority and left nearly sixty people dead, these men of the Eight Trigrams—who with bloody hands had now become true rebels—spread out to close the gates and occupy Hua city.[23]

In southern Chihli province the mobilization of the Eight Trigrams, its tempo hastily increased when word arrived that Li Wen-ch'eng had been arrested and the date changed, was also interrupted by the government but in a different fashion. As word was being sent out to Hsu An-kuo and others from his district, sufficient care was not taken, and the magistrate of Ch'ang-yuan learned that something was going on. He "heard" that about six miles northeast of the city, in Wei-yuan village, members of a heretical sect were "hatching a plot." On the 6th day of the 9th month, in the middle of the day, he left the city to investigate personally, taking along with him several yamen underlings. When the magistrate reached that village, he found the sect members already alerted: they emerged from the houses wearing white sashes and white turbans and carrying weapons. These men may already have been preparing to go to Hua to free Li Wen-ch'eng, but when they learned of the magistrate's arrival they were spurred to take the first step as rebels then and there. They surrounded Magistrate Chao, stabbed him to death, and cut off his head. They also killed the yamen runners—all but one who managed to escape and run back to the city to report what had happened.

This occurred the day before the attack on Hua city, and the district authorities in Ch'ang-yuan did not yet realize what kind of "plot" they were up against. Two days later a Captain Ch'en, a fourth-rank military official stationed in nearby Tung-ming, came to the village with two hundred men. They opened fire on the house where they had thought the rebels were hiding, but found no one there. They searched the village and were shocked to find the body and head of the magistrate inside one of the houses; these were immediately sent back to the city for a proper burial. Then unexpectedly several hundred rebels appeared and attacked the government force. Other rebels emerged with equal suddenness from the houses of the village. The two groups fought and "both sides suffered casualties." The government was able to capture two rebels alive and to withdraw more or less intact to the district city. Captain Ch'en, now realizing that he was outnumbered, remained in the city "to defend it" and did not venture into the countryside again until reinforcements arrived.[24] Ch'ang-yuan city was never attacked by the rebels, but the murder of the magistrate on the 6th put the city on the alert and the attack on Captain Ch'en and his men forced the city defenders to withdraw behind the walls.

Nearby in Tung-ming district, the local magistrate had also learned in advance about the preparations for rebellion. Sometime prior to 9/10 a blacksmith from a village in western Tung-ming (near Ch'ang-yuan and Hua) came to inform on the rebels. Getting weapons was a problem for the Eight Trigrams, for all so-called deadly weapons were illegal, and they were forced to be somewhat dependent on blacksmiths who were not members of their group. This blacksmith told the magistrate that on the 5th day of that month a man named Chiang from nearby Ch'ang-yuan had come to him, shown him a knife with a steel blade, and asked to have ten made just like it. (Chiang had perhaps thought it would be safer to have the knives made further from home, a mistake in this instance.) Magistrate Chu of Tung-ming immediately had Chiang arrested and interrogated. He learned that Chiang belonged to a group called the T'ien-li Assembly and that they were planning something for the 9th day of the month. Alerted in advance, Tung-ming authorities were able to take elementary steps toward defending the city against attack. The city was put on a curfew, and gentry and merchants gave money and food to hire men to repair damaged places in the city wall and to defend the city if necessary. These preparations plus the fast pace of events in Hua discouraged a secret entry and surprise attack on Tung-ming city, if indeed one had been planned; like Ch'ang-yuan, the city was safe but isolated until assistance arrived.[25]

Surgical Strikes in Shantung

In Ting-t'ao and Ts'ao in Shantung the rebel uprisings went more nearly according to schedule and proceeded without government interference, even though the local officials had been alerted to possible trouble. This is in sharp contrast to nearby Chin-hsiang or Tung-ming, where positive official action prevented secret attacks on the cities. To see what happened, let us to back again to the Tao-k'ou meeting.

Hsu An-kuo, the teacher of all the sects in Shantung, did not attend that meeting. At the time he was staying with the Chu family. his pupils in Hu-chia village in Ts'ao district, and had sent his chief pupil Chu Ch'eng-fang to Tao-k'ou in his stead. On 8/6 Chu Ch'eng-fang returned home with a message from Hsu's teacher Liu Kuo-ming that the date had been set for 9/15. It was at this time that Ts'ui Shih-chün (Hsu's pupil) was being arrested in Chin-hsiang. Notified, Hsu was not pleased by the news; nevertheless, he continued with the plan for uprisings carried out by his pupils in six districts of southwestern Shantung—Ts'ao, Ting-t'ao, Shan, Ch'eng-wu, Chin-

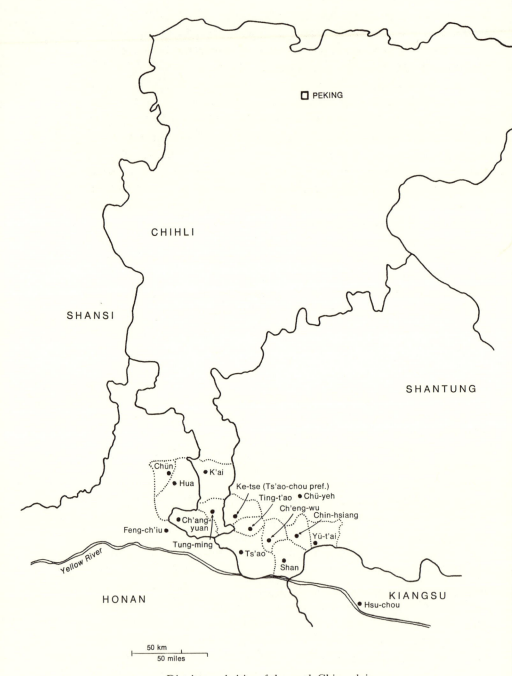

PEKING

CHIHLI

SHANSI

SHANTUNG

Chün

K'ai

Hua

Ke-tse (Ts'ao-chou pref.)

Ting-t'ao

Chü-yeh

Ch'eng-wu

Chin-hsiang

Ch'ang-yuan

Feng-ch'iu

Yü-t'ai

Tung-ming

Ts'ao

Shan

Yellow River

HONAN

KIANGSU

Hsu-chou

50 km
50 miles

Districts and cities of the north China plain

hsiang, and Yü-t'ai. Having risen up, they would join Li Wen-ch'eng and go to Peking with him to assist "Venerable Master Liu"—Lin Ch'ing. Chu Ch'eng-fang had brought back with him a model for the white cloth banners, which were to be prepared immediately. Information about these banners, the password, and the date of the uprising had to be transmitted as fast as possible to all of Hsu An-kuo's different pupils; Hsu gave Chu Ch'eng-fang the responsibility for this while he left and returned home, presumably to coordinate with his other pupils in Ch'ang-yuan.[26]

After Hsu had left, the arrests in Chin-hsiang continued, and as more of the sect network was uncovered and more of their plans revealed, Hsu An-kuo's other pupils became directly threatened. As we have seen, in the middle of the 8th month, Ts'ui Shih-chün's son-in-law was seized and he revealed to the authorities that Ts'ui's teacher was Hsu An-kuo and that Chu Ch'eng-kuei of Ts'ao district was also in that sect. Authorities in Ts'ao were notified of this and on 8/21 the magistrate was able to arrest Ch'eng-kuei's older brother Ch'eng-chen. In his possession were found two white banners, one large, one small, both with slogans written on them. Chu was not imprisoned in the district jail but was wisely transferred to the provincial capital.

The rest of the Chu family, alerted to their danger, left home to avoid being arrested as well. They did not, however, leave the area or abandon their plans. This increased official interest in their activities did put pressure on the Shantung sect leaders, and when Chu Ch'eng-kuei returned home on 9/6 with the news from Hua and instructions from Hsu An-kuo to change the date, they were probably glad to act ahead of schedule. It was impossible to notify everyone in time to attack the following day (to coincide with the Hua attack), but the Chu brothers decided that all could be ready by the 10th, and as the official search for sect members continued, Hsu An-kuo's pupils were notified of the new date.

On the 7th and 8th, the Ts'ao magistrate made seven more arrests; on the 9th, still trying to locate Chu Ch'eng-kuei, he took what looks in retrospect to be the risky step of going personally into the countryside accompanied by only yamen runners, but the expedition was both uneventful and unsuccessful. By the evening of the 9th, when the magistrate returned to his offices in the city, it was already too late for him to halt the planned rebel actions. Members of the Eight Trigrams had entered both Ting-t'ao and Ts'ao cities that night and were ready to strike in the morning. Foolishly, neither magistrate had put his city on the alert.[27]

Hsu An-kuo's pupils from Ts'ao district were responsible for planning and executing the attacks on both Ts'ao and Ting-t'ao cities, which were only twenty miles apart. As elsewhere, those who were staying at home were told how to identify themselves, and those who were participating were told where and when to assemble.

Our clearest view of these events is through the eyes of one of the participants, in this case, Hu Ch'eng-te 胡成德, a pupil of Hsu An-kuo. Hu Ch'eng-te was originally from the same village as the Chu family, but in 1811, after joining the sect, he had left to rejoin his wife and family in southern Honan, where he had spent his youth. As the economic situation became difficult during the summer of 1813, Hu decided to return to his native village in hope of being paid for some work he had done on a relative's land on his last visit. On 8/20 he arrived in Hu-chia village and found himself in the middle of the planning for the uprising, just as the pressure from increased arrests was building up.

Hu Ch'eng-te saw Chi Ta-fu, the man who had originally introduced him to Hsu An-kuo, and he was told, "We will make known the Way. Teacher Hsu is going to assemble enough people and we will rise up." About a week later, Hu was told by Chi that the date had been fixed for 9/10. "We were to go to Ts'ao city and rise up, then later on we would all be given land. I hoped to profit and so I agreed to participate. Later Chi Ta-fu gave me a large triangular silk banner that had six characters written on one side. I can't read, so I asked him what they meant. He told me they said, 'The King who Follows Heaven, Hu Ch'eng-te.' He also gave me about sixty or seventy small pointed white cloth banners." A few days later, Hu ran into Chu Ch'eng-kuei (just back from Hua) and learned that Chu was readying a separate group to attack Ting-t'ao.

On the 9th, as they prepared to leave the village for the city, Chi Ta-fu told his men (Hu says there were about a hundred of them) to bring along whatever weapons they had around—"wooden clubs, knives, spears, or whatever." Hu himself carried a long-handled, doubled-bladed knife, and brought with him a large square yellow banner with a white border. Chi Ta-fu assigned about seventy or eighty men to Hu and told him to be responsible for them. He, Chi, would lead while Hu was to bring up the rear. "So on the evening of that day, I put two knives [which Chi Ta-fu had given me] inside my clothing, and I did the same with the large white banner. I told my relative Hu Kuang to bring a bamboo pole to use later for the banner. I also took the small pointed banners and distributed them among the men assigned to me. There were not enough, so we tore some strips of white cloth which the men could tie in their clothes as a sign. I led the group and we left the village."[28]

The group that attacked Ts'ao city numbered at least one hundred men.[29] Most of them were sect members' of at least several months' standing. Among them, however, was a group of men who were probably not sect members, and who were forerunners of the type of mass following which the rebels would later attract. We have learned about this group from the testimony of one member, a man named Li Ch'eng 李成.

Li lived in Ke-tse district north of Ts'ao. He was physically very strong and had studied boxing and fencing. Chin Lan, his boxing teacher, had not, however, instructed him in any religious practices. At the end of the 8th month, Chin Lan had come to Li Ch'eng and told him that, because of the bad harvest and resultant famine, he and another man had decided to get together a group of men to go and get what they needed by using force, to "plunder" as the government called it. Chin Lan and his men thereupon went out and took food supplies from several different villages in Ts'ao district. Government authorities tried to arrest them, perhaps as part of the general search for dissidents at this time, but without success.

On 9/9 Chin Lan told his followers that there was a man who was assembling some people to go and "cause an incident" in Ts'ao city and that their group was going to go along. It is possible that Chin Lan, being a boxer, was acquainted with some of these Ts'ao sect members, we do not know how the contact was made. Chin was, however, unlike the sect members, already a lawbreaker and outlaw. Now he formally joined the rebels by giving his men white cloth to be tied about their waists for identification and led his group into the city on the night of the 9th.[30]

Not every sect member was willing to take the risks of rebellion. On that same day, 9/9, a sect group was assembling in one village when a believer (and former police runner) named Ts'ai Wu-k'uei was passing through and saw them. He claimed later that he had not known about the rebellion until this time when he was informed about the plans and asked to come along. He refused, but the group told him that if he did not his whole family would (later) be killed. Ts'ai was not persuaded, but he lied, promised to help, and then went home, gathered his family, and fled. He later joined the militia and was helpful in arresting his former colleagues. Ts'ai's decision was not necessarily related to his career as a police runner. Two of his relatives were also runners in the Ts'ao district yamen and in the sect, yet they did participate in the uprising. The risk was great, and as we shall see below in greater detail, commitment to rebellion was not always easy.[31]

Those who were to participate in the Ts'ao uprising were ready by the night of the 9th. They went into the city in different groups either late that night or early the following morning and arrived at the district offices at daybreak. The sixth-rank military official stationed in that city heard them and rushed out; the rebels killed him and three of his men, obeying their instructions to "kill anyone" (luan sha 亂殺). The rebels then entered that lieutenant's quarters and killed his wife and daughter-in-law. Meanwhile, others in the group had already burst into the main government offices. The magistrate came out; he had just risen and was barely dressed. They immediately attacked and stabbed him to death; one rebel cut off his head and took it with him. Using only their spears and knives, the rebels then killed nine other members of the magistrate's household—three men, four women, and two children. According to a government account of the incident, they called out for and sought by name Wu Hsing-tzu, the seventy-year-old cousin of the Chin-hsiang district magistrate (who had been responsible for discovering the Chu family's involvement) who happened to be staying in the Ts'ao yamen. Wu was seized and killed together with his sons and one aide. Engaging anyone who opposed them, the rebels killed another fifteen people, servants in the yamen offices. Since at least two members of their group had worked in the yamen, the rebels had no trouble locating the jail, which they broke open, releasing the forty-one prisoners (ten of whom chose not to flee with the rebels but remained at the yamen). They also broke into the treasury and removed the contents.[32]

As the men left the yamen, they allegedly met Hu Ch'eng-te and his group coming toward them. Hu claimed that he had come to the north gate at dawn and finding it still closed had gone around to the east gate and then into the city. He had tied the white banner with his name and title on to its bamboo pole and then rushed through the streets toward the yamen. There Hu saw Chi Ta-fu, who said to him, "You're too late. The business is done. The men need to get some clothes to wear, so we can take them to the pawnshops at the east gate to get some." It is in fact very likely that Hu Ch'eng-te and his men did take part in the attack on the yamen, for it was easy for Hu to lie later to minimize his involvement. In any case, the rebels proceeded to loot the pawnshops and moneylenders. When they had finished—and presumably could carry no more—they started out the east gate. As they approached the bridge over the moat, they saw that the far end of the bridge had been barricaded. Then someone fired a shot. When the rebels realized that muskets were being used against them, they turned around, hurried along the city wall, and left the city through the north gate.[33] There they broke into smaller groups, each going its own way but arranging to keep in close touch.

While one group of Hsu An-kuo's pupils was carrying out this attack on Ts'ao district city, another large group was executing a similar strike on Ting-t'ao city, only twenty miles away. This group may have been somewhat smaller, perhaps as few as fifty men.[34] The leaders had all been active in planning the attack on Ts'ao. They had notified their followers on 9/6 and distributed banners and white cloth.

Again, let us follow one participant. Chao Chen-wu 趙振五 was from Ting-t'ao district. One day earlier that summer he had met a friend of his called Hsiao Han-san, and Hsiao had said that although Chao was an honest sort, people took advantage of him. He, Hsiao, had a way of getting certain "good benefits," and he promised to make Chao an official and "to put him in charge of things." According to Chao, they were interrupted before he could learn more and because he was at home sick and then busy with the harvest, Hsiao didn't contact him again until the 9th month. (In truth, he had probably joined the sect at that time.) On 9/9 Hsiao Han-san came and invited him to his house. Chao went there, found a dozen other people, and went together with them to their leader Chang Erh-kou-tzu's house. Chang Erh-kou-tzu explained the planned attack to the fifty or sixty men assembled there. By this time it was early evening and so Chang distributed the equipment. He gave Chao Chen-wu a knife, a small triangular white cloth banner, and a white cloth sash. All the other men were likewise given weapons, banners, and sashes.

The group left Chang's house and regrouped again (perhaps joined by others) outside the east gate of Ting-t'ao city. Since it was the middle of the night, the city gates were closed. The rebels had planned for this, however, and knew of a place in the city wall, near the northeast corner, where the wall had collapsed. Chang Erh-kou-tzu sent some men to climb over the wall at this spot, and then to come around from the inside and open the east gate. In this way, the entire group was able to enter the city. They made their way through the streets, stopping briefly to rest in a temple along the way, and finally reassembled outside a pawnshop.

Tying on their white sashes, with weapons ready, the rebels entered the official compound at dawn. The first man roused was a low-ranking military officer who mustered a few soldiers to resist. The rebels wounded him and killed four of his men. The rebel Chao Chen-wu himself went into the main hall of the yamen and smashed the hall drum so that assistance could not be summoned. The rest of the group broke open the jail, freeing fifteen men and setting fire to that building. In the meantime the acting magistrate had heard the disturbance. He quickly took his official seal and gave it to a servant, instructing him to take it to the prefect and report what was happening. Then when he went out into the yamen courtyard to confront and try to arrest the rebels, he was repeatedly stabbed till he died. Half a dozen other men—servants, aides, and relatives—who tried to assist the magistrate were likewise killed.

Their bloody task at the district offices completed, the rebels went about the city taking what they wanted. The leader Hsiao Han-san led his men first to the west-gate area, where they broke into some pawnshops, and then to the south-gate area, where they did the same, setting some buildings afire in the process. Hsiao Han-san himself had some private scores to settle: he went to find some Muslims who he said had refused to join them and he and a pupil beat them up and robbed them. Finished in the city, the rebels left to rejoin their colleagues.

The Eight Trigrams from Ting-t'ao and Ts'ao had accomplished their missions in those two cities, and the success of these two strikes gave sect members who had not dared to participate the courage to commit themselves to the rebel cause. On the other hand, other pupils of Hsu An-kuo in nearby Chin-hsiang were not so successful; let us return to Magistrate Wu's successes in that district.

FOILED IN CHIN-HSIANG

On the 9th day of the 9th month in Chin-hsiang in Shantung, by contrast, everything was quiet. It had rained steadily since the first of the month, and this had inhibited Magistrate Wu's attempts to drill militia. He must have waited nervously during these days of bad weather, worried about the anticipated uprising. The rebels in that district, on the other hand, may have been able to use this interval to collect themselves for the first time since the government began investigating two and a half months before. During that period many sect leaders had been seized, including the sect head Ts'ui Shih-chün, and as news arrived about the premature uprising in Hua city and then a message from Hsu An-kuo telling them to change their date to the 10th, there must have been much confusion and uncertainty about how to proceed.

On the 9th, when the weather finally cleared, the position of the would-be rebels worsened: Magistrate Wu learned about the revised date for the uprising. There was a man named Kao Kuang-kuei who lived in a market town west of the city where he ran a dye shop. On the afternoon of the 8th, an old friend of Kao's had come to see him. This man was a sect member, and he had just received word that the date for the uprisings had been changed to the 10th. He warned his friend Kao that "after noon on the 10th, there would be great turmoil in our district, and massacres everywhere." He urged Kao to bring his wife and elderly mother and move into his house where they would be protected from the kalpa calamities by his identifying white banner. Kao Kuang-kuei thanked his friend but did not take his advice. Having no loyalty to the Eight Trigrams, he went instead to consult with the head of a gentry family in his village. He described the message about the rebellion, said he had seen announcements saying that all "troublemakers" were to be reported to the authorities, and now did not know what to do. The gentry man told him that he should go secretly into the district city and report all this to the magistrate. Kao took this advice and the first thing the following day (the 9th) he presented himself at the yamen of Magistrate Wu and related what he had been told. The magistrate promised Kao a reward for his loyalty and told him to go and get his family and bring them into the city where they would be safe.

Magistrate Wu then immediately notified the two adjacent districts of Chü-yeh and Ch'eng-wu, telling them to ready their city defenses (he probably also notified Ts'ao and Ting-t'ao). Then, that afternoon, he and members of his staff went up on the wall on the north side of the city and, walking along the top of the wall, decided where guards should be stationed. They pretended to be on routine business in order not to alarm the general population. Finishing around sunset, Wu Chieh then went to consult with his old friend gentry-member Chang, briefing him on the latest developments. Chang advised the magistrate to tell "the hundred or so gentry households in the city" to have ready one or two armed men each; if they heard the gong on the treasury building sound the alarm, they were to come immediately to the government offices. Magistrate Wu followed this advice. Furthermore, he instructed all official staff to remain on the job round the clock for the next three days and ordered a halt to routine business. That night, still worried, the magistrate went out after midnight to check on the patrols along the city walls. When he returned he found a report had arrived describing night meetings of sect members in Ting-t'ao and Ts'ao districts. More disturbing, it stated that three days earlier the magistrate of Ch'ang-yuan had been murdered and that a similar event was rumored to have occurred in Hua. Fully alarmed, Magistrate Wu went out again to patrol.

At dawn on the 10th, the magistrate decided with some misgivings to open the city gates as usual. He sent out members of his staff to walk the streets and to look for anyone behaving suspiciously. During the morning Kao Kuang-kuei's sect member friend was brought in and interrogated, but he would say nothing. As the day went on and nothing happened, Wu Chieh, exhausted from being up all night, decided to rest. Not long after he had retired to his quarters, he was awakened by his son, who announced that there were armed rebels in the yamen. Unlike his colleagues in Hua, Ting-t'ao, and Ts'ao, Magistrate Wu did not rush into his courtyard to find a large mob of armed men carrying banners and wearing white sashes. Instead, he found members of his staff holding captive two men who had been secretly carrying knives and banners. Shortly thereafter, a third man who had been caught at the north gate of the city was also brought in. These three sect members had earlier been sitting in a teashop (managed by a former yamen runner) just outside the district offices. As the owner's twelve-year-old daughter brought these men their tea, she had noticed that they were carrying weapons and appeared to be wearing an unusual amount of clothing. She told her father and he sent for assistance in having the men arrested.

The magistrate ordered his staff to break these rebels' shinbones; then he questioned them. He learned that they were indeed members of a religious sect, waiting for the moment to strike. They told the magistrate that it had already been arranged that the group would rise up that very afternoon, attack the city, kill him and his staff, break open the jail, set fire to the city, and murder its inhabitants. The magistrate ordered the men secured in the jail; then he alerted the gentry of the city and instructed his staff to arrest anyone who was not a city resident. A curfew was put into effect, for by this time it was already evening, the gates were closed, and torches were burned along the city walls all night to prevent any secret attacks. According to the magistrate, a group of rebels actually gathered in a village south of the city, planning to enter it that night, but seeing the torches and patrols they decided to wait.

The following day, the 11th, Magistrate Wu sent word to the villages outside the city that they should expect trouble. By noon he had been notified that the preceding day both Ting-t'ao and Ts'ao cities had been attacked and the resident officials murdered. Moreover, there were reports that the rebels had "several ten-thousand supporters" and were "on the rampage" in those two districts. Chin-hsiang city remained on the alert for the next few days and, much to the magistrate's relief, on the 13th government soldiers began to arrive, one hundred fifty that day and two hundred the following day.

Although the rebels continued to make trouble in the countryside of Chin-hsiang for the next few weeks, the city was never attacked. Magistrate Wu, with valuable assistance from gentry and commoners who felt more loyalty to the government than sympathy with the rebels, had uncovered their plans, and by his arrests, interrogations, and defensive measures had drastically weakened the rebel organization in his district and successfully thwarted their plans.[37]

The successful prevention of a rebellion in Chin-hsiang made uprisings by other pupils of Ts'ui Shih-chün in Ch'eng-wu, Chü-yeh, and Yü-t'ai much more difficult. In Yü-t'ai there was an apparent failure of nerve. The magistrate was tipped off to possible trouble by a report of some would-be rebels making weapons in one village. He arrived to investigate and make arrests and encountered no difficulties. The relatively swift appearance of a government army on the scene and the great distance from what was becoming the rebel headquarters in Hua contributed to the retreat from rebellion by sect members in this area.[38] In Ch'eng-wu and Chü-yeh districts a similar situation prevailed. There were some rebels—members of a previously unaffiliated White Lotus sect—who rose up in Ch'eng-wu when they heard of the city strikes in Ts'ao and Ting-t'ao and left their homes to join the Eight Trigrams in the west.[39] Similarly, the Chen Trigram leader Ch'eng Pai-yüeh from Shan who had maintained contact with both the Hua leadership and Lin Ch'ing, mobilized his pupils and, without attempting any military action in his own district, went to Ts'ao district to join his colleagues there.[40]

By the 15th day of the 9th month, the Eight Trigrams rebellion was well on its way in the southern plain. There had been no black wind lasting seven days and seven nights and the Ch'ing regime had not fallen with a single stroke; in fact, the government had learned about the planned rebellion and had been able to prevent many and discourage more from joining it. But Hua city had been occupied and Chün city was being attacked, the magistrates of Ch'ang-yuan, Ting-t'ao, and Ts'ao had been killed, and sect members had risen up as rebels in at least nine districts. Although Li Wen-ch'eng was injured he was still alive, and his followers roamed the countryside in a wide corridor at least one hundred miles across. Should Lin Ch'ing and his men in Peking succeed in taking the Forbidden City according to plan, there was still hope.

The fact that a great many of Lin Ch'ing's followers in the Peking area were arrested and interrogated makes it possible for us to look in far greater detail at the palace attack that he organized—his preparations, the village-by-village mobilization of his followers, the various channels through which information leaked upward to the government, and the entrance into the palace itself. The involvement of the imperial family (and the interest of historians) have forced this part of the Eight Trigrams rebellion into the limelight, and the resulting excellence of documentation compels us to do likewise. Nevertheless, although the target was more majestic, the attack on the Forbidden City should be seen as but one of many provincial assaults, and in terms of rebel mobilization what happened in Peking was not markedly different from events in the south.

PREPARING FOR THE PALACE ATTACK

Lin Ch'ing had returned home from the meeting in Tao-k'ou in the middle of the 8th month and set about preparing his K'an Trigram for their role in the rebellion. The original plan had been for Lin Ch'ing simply to assemble his men outside the Chang-i Gate (the western entrance to the southern section of Peking), wait until the men from Honan had arrived, and then go together to "take care of" the emperor. Lin's friend Ch'en Shuang, who had recruited eunuchs as pupils, had later persuaded him that it was a better idea to enter and occupy the Forbidden City first without assistance. When this plan was discussed by Lin's followers, some agreed with

Ch'en, but there was at least one man, Liu Chin-te, who did not. Liu urged his teacher to persuade Lin to reconsider, saying, "This idea isn't very smart. Why don't you tell Lin Ch'ing that he should first wait for the men from Honan to arrive and then go into the city together." "But," he related, "they all told me that it is said, 'A single man can take Yu-chou [Peking],' and this surely wouldn't be such a difficult thing to do. Because they wouldn't listen to me, I left."[41] Thus it was decided that on the 15th Lin's group would enter the Forbidden City with eunuch help and occupy the city of Peking by taking control of the gates. Within a few days Li Wen-ch'eng and his men would have arrived and with their combined forces they would go out the road to Jehol, meet the returning imperial entourage and "engage and fight them." If the emperor was not killed, he would at least be driven to flight into Manchuria.[42] This was the plan agreed upon at the Tao-k'ou meeting.

When he returned home, Lin Ch'ing considered changing the plan again and taking even more responsibility and possible glory upon himself. He thought that he might even assign some of his men to attack the emperor without waiting for assistance. He sent his friend and pupil Liu Ti-wu to go and talk with the sect leader Ch'ü Ssu about organizing such an expedition. Ch'ü was told to get together as many men as possible and to take and assemble them at Yen-chiao (east of Peking). Lin Ch'ing wanted one or two hundred men but was willing to settle for considerably fewer. Ch'ü Ssu responded to this idea by saying, "The men in my village who are believers are few, and some of them are old people and young children who cannot be of any use [in the rebellion]. If you just want strong and able-bodied young men, then I can only find a dozen. I cannot get even as many as thirty or fifty."

Lin Ch'ing thought about this and reluctantly concluded that he could spare no men from the groups assigned to attack the palace. He sent word to Ch'ü Ssu that if he had only a few men, then the plan would not work, for the soldiers accompanying the emperor were numerous. Ch'ü should therefore forget about making a separate attack and bring his men instead into Peking with the others. "On 9/15 we will just go into the capital and cause this incident (nao-shih 鬧事) there. The government soldiers won't be able to move [into the capital] fast enough, and we are sure to succeed. Then we will occupy (chü 據) Peking."[43] There is evidence that Ch'ü Ssu could in fact have brought more than a dozen men, but obviously and understandably he was unwilling to be the one responsible for attacking the emperor, at least not without assistance. Thus, Lin Ch'ing abandoned the idea of single-handedly both taking Peking and killing the emperor, and he went ahead with his already ambitious plans to occupy the palace and then wait for assistance.

In order to enter and occupy the Forbidden City, Lin Ch'ing needed inside assistance, and for this he relied upon the eunuchs who had joined his sect. It was Ch'en Shuang's pupil Liu Te-ts'ai who had recruited several of his fellow eunuchs and who had secured their loyalty with gifts of money from Lin Ch'ing. Lin had met with these eunuchs twice in 1813, first during the 3d month, and then again on 8/24 after he had returned from the south. Since Liu Te-ts'ai himself worked inside the palace, on those two occasions his father came into Peking, went to the western gate to the Forbidden City, and left a message for his son: Liu was to bring his eunuch pupils with him and come to meet with his teacher's teacher, Lin Ch'ing. These meetings took place in the southern section of Peking, first in a restaurant and then in a large inn. Lin Ch'ing, Ch'en Shuang, Ch'en Wen-k'uei, and Chu Hsien were present, and they met with the four eunuchs brought by Liu Te-ts'ai. They discussed the plans for the palace attack, and Lin Ch'ing promised to make Liu Te-ts'ai chief eunuch if they were successful. It was arranged that at noon on the 15th Liu Te-ts'ai would come out from the palace and lead in the rebels assembled outside the eastern gate; two of his pupils would do the same on the western side, and two others would remain inside and assist from there. Apparently the gates to the Forbidden City and those gates inside it that led to the Great Interior (where the empress, who had not gone to Jehol, was residing) were only scantily guarded during the lunch hour, and the eunuchs, knowing this, may have suggested that particular time of day. Once inside, everyone would go directly to the Great Interior and, joining forces again, would seize and hold the palace.[44]

Early in the 9th month, as preparations were going ahead, Lin Ch'ing received a visit from the boxer and healer from Jao-yang, Liu Yü-lung. Liu was supposed to bring his pupils and participate in the palace attack. Now, however, Liu said that this was not a good idea; he claimed he would not be able to find the way. Lin Ch'ing therefore said that Liu should instead go south and join Niu Liang-ch'en's band. Liu Yü-lung agreed. Bragging that he could "draw charms and recite spells so as to travel like the wind," Liu said he would speed home, get his double-bladed sword and his pupils, and take them to Hua. Liu persuaded Lin Ch'ing to supply him with a new brush, some gold paper, and vermilion ink to make a charm, plus 1,000 cash for traveling expenses, and he left. (Later, Liu Yü-lung had second thoughts, and when he heard about Manchu troops being sent south on campaign against rebels, he decided to go into hiding rather than to Hua).[45]

By the middle of the 9th month of 1813, Lin Ch'ing had contacted at least 360 people in the Peking area about the planned attack on the palace. About one-third of these had been believers before 1811; another third had joined the Eight Trigrams in 1811 and 1812. The last third had joined during the first nine months of 1813 and included nearly 40 people who had been "converted" during the three months just prior to the rebellion. In other words, there had been a steady growth in membership during the years after Lin Ch'ing and Li Wen-ch'eng first met, and a particularly sharp increase during the months just prior to the uprising.[46] The religious commitment of these last-minute converts is open to some question, for they were obviously recruited to fill out the ranks of those who would attack the palace.

Lin Ch'ing decided that at least 250 of his followers could participate in the palace attack. They were to leave home in small groups and come to Peking in time to be outside the Forbidden City at noon on the 15th. Because sect members in one village tended to be all pupils of a single teacher, Lin Ch'ing simply assigned villages or teachers (with their pupils) to either the eastern or the western group and thus divided his followers roughly in half. Of those we know about, approximately 130 were sent to assemble outside the Hsi-hua (West Majestic 西華) Gate, and about 110 to the Tung-hua (East Majestic 東華) Gate. These were the western and eastern gates to the Forbidden City.

In theory, these men were divided into smaller groups of ten, each group led by a leader carrying a white banner.[47] In reality, the groups were by no means so regular. The people sent to the Tung-hua Gate came in three large groups, each under a major sect leader: thirty-one with Ch'en Shuang from Sang-fa village, thirty-eight with Ch'ü Ssu from Tung village, and thirty-eight of Li Lao's men of the Yang-hsiu area came with Liu Ti-wu. Those who were to enter on the western side came in six smaller groups. Li Wu brought twenty-three men from Ku-an district and sent nine more with Hsing Kuei-jung (from Hsin village), and Liu Chin-t'ing brought forty-four members of the former Ta-sheng sect from Hsiung district. Ho Wen-sheng brought sixteen from T'ai-p'ing village, Tung Po-

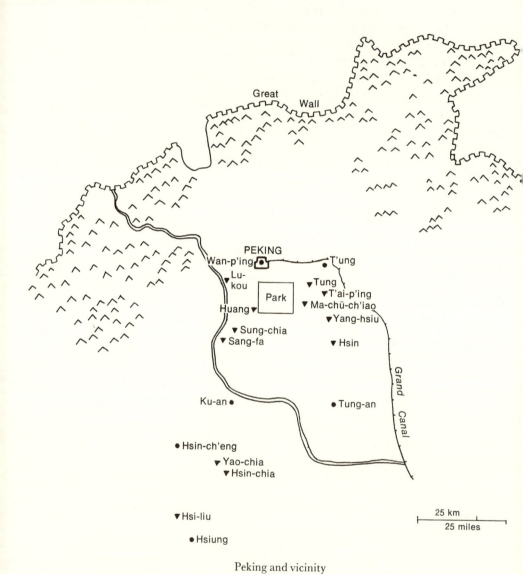

Great Wall

PEKING
Wan-p'ing
Lu-kou
Huang
Park
T'ung
Tung
T'ai-p'ing
Ma-chü-ch'iao
Yang-hsiu
Sung-chia
Sang-fa
Hsin

Ku-an
Tung-an

Grand Canal

Hsin-ch'eng
Yao-chia
Hsin-chia

Hsi-liu
Hsiung

25 km
25 miles

Peking and vicinity

wang brought thirty-four from Lin Ch'ing's home of Sung-chia, and the eunuch Yang Chin-chang brought nine men from Ma-chü-ch'iao. In general villages located southwest of Peking went to the western gate, those to the southeast to the eastern gate. Finally, Lin Ch'ing appointed his close friends Ch'en Shuang and Ch'en Wen-k'uei to be the overall leaders of the eastern and western groups respectively.

All the participants in the palace attack were men. Although many women knew about the planned uprising and had husbands or sons who would participate, no women went along. The men over sixty tended to stay at home, and the majority of participants were in their thirties and forties (62 percent).[48] They were family men, usually with children still living at home. Many had a close relative who was also participating in the rebellion, a father or son, a brother or cousin.[49] There is also some evidence to suggest that sect teachers looked for converts among the agricultural workers hired by their own and other families to help with the harvest: one-third of those who joined Lin Ch'ing's group during the 8th and 9th months were hired laborers.[50] Their inclusion may have been the result of the last-minute increased need for secrecy and manpower. Nevertheless, it is clear that the typical sect member who became a rebel was not a single rootless man with nothing to lose. Most had families and everyone within each village group of sect members knew one another and belonged to clusters of blood relatives, in-laws, and members of the same household.

Once Lin Ch'ing had determined who would go where, he had to send word out from teacher to pupil, notifying each man and telling him where to go and on what day. All participants had also to be given the two-character password "Be Victorious." Each teacher had to make sure that all his pupils had a weapon of some sort and at least one (but preferably two) piece of plain white cotton cloth. This cloth was for the turbans and sashes that would distinguish the rebels from other people. By two descriptions, the piece of cloth to be worn like a kerchief on the head was only about a foot long, and the one to be tied about the waist about two times that length. At about 100 cash a foot, this white cloth represented no small expense, and it appears to have been procured almost entirely by Lin Ch'ing; he had a debt of 50,000 to 60,000 cash for cloth purchases made at a small store near his home during the summer of 1813.[51] Group leaders, of which there were at least ten, were to carry small triangular white cloth banners. Ch'en Shuang, the leader of the eastern group, carried a banner with the slogan "Entrusted by Heaven to Prepare the Way," and it is likely that his counterpart in the west did likewise.[52] One rebel was later found to be carrying a piece of cloth on which were embroidered the lines:

> Be of one spirit with me
> Never be separated
> Always secure.[53]

In addition to white cloth passed down from Lin Ch'ing, teachers provided their pupils with weapons or with money with which to purchase them. The weapons used were in most cases knives, although a few men carried iron bars. Although Ch'ing law prohibited ordinary citizens from owning deadly weapons, knives intended for daily household and agricultural use were permitted, and obtaining knives in small quantities was apparently not extremely difficult. Li Ch'ao-tso, for example, obtained a dozen knives for his men by buying them at small markets "one by one, here and there." The manufacture on demand of large quantities of weapons was more unusual and thus more dangerous. One blacksmith refused to make more than three (and as we have seen, reports from black-smiths to the government about requests for weapons led to arrests in Hua, Tung-ming, and Yü-t'ai districts). Not all smiths were so careful, however, and Li Wu had forty-eight knives made by a blacksmith in his village. There were no known blacksmiths among the sect members, and no specific attempt was made that we know of to convert them and thus obtain an easy supply of arms.[54]

In order to protect the sect members from detection, it was decided that they would not display the knives and cloth that symbolized rebellion until the moment when they entered the Forbidden City. On their way into Peking, the men stuffed these objects inside their clothing and, in some cases, hid their knives under baskets of fruit carried by sect members posing as peddlers.

We can see in detail how the knives and white cloth were distributed by looking at the pupils of the Pai-yang sect head Li Lao. Most of Li Lao's pupils came from four villages in T'ung district. Li Lao took responsibility for procuring knives and cloth for fifteen followers from his own village, including six members of his family. Late in the 8th month, Li Lao told his twenty-two-year-old grandnephew to go to a blacksmith's shop and have some knives made. The black-smith was afraid to make more than three, so Li Lao told some of his pupils to buy knives themselves. On 9/13 and 9/14 these knives and the cloth (which apparently came from Lin Ch'ing) were distributed: either Li Lao sent someone to deliver them or individuals came to his house to pick them up. The rest of Li Lao's followers were the pupils of his pupils, three brothers named Chang. These Chang brothers went personally to the three villages involved on the 13th and 14th to deliver the equipment to their pupils. Li Lao himself, being rather aged, did not go into Peking on the 15th. Instead, Lin Ch'ing chose Li's pupil Liu Ti-wu (the man who had first introduced Li Lao to Lin Ch'ing) to head the group. Liu Ti-wu brought along his two sons, whom he provided with knives and cloth.[55]

Some of the participants were treated to meals in Peking on the day of the attack by their group leaders or were given money in advance to buy something to eat. Nearly everyone stopped to buy something to eat on the morning of the 15th, and these meals fueled their courage, gave them physical energy, and marked the specialness of that day.[56]

Not everyone who knew about the rebellion was supposed to take part in the palace attack. Some men were too old or infirm to take part—Li Lao and Liu Hsing-li were in their eighties, Ch'en Liang was sixty-three and blind, Yü Ch'eng-r was crippled—and they all remained at home that day. As in Honan and Shantung, protection was extended in a fraternal spirit to former believers and to members of other White Lotus sects who took no part in the rebellion itself. Jen Tzu-k'uei, for example, had been in the old Jung-hua Assembly of Ku Liang for more than ten years. He had left the sect during the prosecutions of 1808 and had refused to give money to Lin Ch'ing in subsequent years. Nevertheless, in the 8th month of 1813 a sect member from his village came to Jen's house. "He said that they were going to rebel and kill people. They had kept in mind the fact that I had once been in the sect and so they were going to give me two pieces of white cloth. I was to hide the cloth and then later when the incident began, take it out and tie it on my head. Thus I would be spared and not killed."[57] There were some sect members who told their teachers that they did not want to participate and who were allowed to remain at home. Many of these men lived in Ku-an and Hsiung districts, a considerable distance from Peking. They were told that they should look out for Li Wen-ch'eng and his men as they came toward Peking from Honan. When Li arrived, they were to put the white cloth on their heads and around their waists, come forward, say the password, kotow, and welcome Li by congratulating him. Thus identified as believers, they would be spared death.[58]

Among those told specifically to stay home were several Manchu pupils of Liu Hsing-li. In the 7th month of 1813 Hai-k'ang, Liu's pupil and a member of the imperial clan, had gone to see his teacher. He was told that an uprising was being organized and that they were thinking of including him. The matter was discussed and finally Liu Hsing-li decided that since Hai-k'ang belonged to the imperial clan, it was too dangerous to have him participate. In the 8th month, Hai-k'ang met with Liu again. He was told that the date of 9/15 had been selected and that if he chose to be counted among believers, they would give him a high official position, which, despite his ancestry, he apparently did not have. Hai-k'ang agreed and complied with Liu's request for a 1,600 cash contribution. Later on, when Hai-k'ang saw his relative and pupil Ch'ing-yao, he mentioned that a rebellion was being organized by the sect. He told Ch'ing-yao that if he wanted to be in on it, he should come to Hai-k'ang's house on 9/14 and they would wait for further instructions. Ch'ing-yao in turn told his brother (who had had little contact with the sect in recent years) that on 9/15 "there might be men on the streets, and so he ought to be careful." Ch'ing-feng was not interested and preferring more orthodox means of advancement went ahead with his plans to take the Manchu *chü-jen* degree exams on on the 12th, 13th, and 14th days of the 9th month. Ch'ing-yao and Hai-k'ang, on the other hand, waited all day at the latter's house on both the 14th and 15th.[59] Hai-k'ang had a number of other pupils whom he might also have contacted about the rebellion with similar instructions.

Lin Ch'ing's pupil the Chinese bannerman Ts'ao Lun was also given special instructions for the day of the uprising. In 1813 he was serving as first captain at Tu-shih Pass north of Peking. When he was first informed about plans for an uprising, Ts'ao said that he would not be able to come into the capital. He was therefore told that on that day he should "turn his horse and face south"; later, after the rebels were in control, a messenger would be sent to greet and instruct him. As it happened, Ts'ao Lun was away all summer, accompanying a high-ranking Manchu into Jehol, and he arrived back at his post too late to learn the exact date for the rising.[60]

Despite Ts'ao's absence, his son Fu-ch'ang and his friend Wang Wu were both drawn into the flurry of last-minute preparations for rebellion. Ts'ao Fu-ch'ang (who was then serving as an *orbo*, a private second-class)[61] was told to come see Lin Ch'ing on 9/12, which he did. But Lin was not pleased and "he criticized Liu Ch'eng-hsiang saying, 'Why in the world did you bring him here?' Liu said, 'I was afraid we wouldn't have enough men.' But Lin Ch'ing replied, 'He is a bannerman, you can't have him come along.' " Ts'ao Fu-ch'ang was therefore told to return home. He was given the password and told just to prepare white cloth and wear it on 9/15.[62]

Ts'ao Fu-ch'ang did as he was told, but his father's friend Wang Wu did not. Wang Wu, like his father before him, was a servant in the household of a Chinese bannerman and former military-governor. During the summer of 1813 he had been told about the uprising but he had not kept this matter secret. Instead, he mentioned it to An-shun, the son of his master. Wang had previously admitted to An-shun that he belonged to Lin Ch'ing's Jung-hua Assembly, at which time An-shun told him that such a group had to be a heretical sect. Wang Wu denied this but his young master was unconvinced, though he made no move to report the group. Later, when Wang Wu mentioned that he "had heard" that Lin Ch'ing was going to rebel on 9/15, An-shun refused to believe him, fortunately for the rebels, saying, "You're crazy! This is nonsense! In such peaceful times this kind of thing could not happen. Even if you had a hundred people like this guy Lin Ch'ing, still not one of them would dare to start a rebellion." An-shun turned away angrily and refused to discuss the matter further, nor did he report this "rumor" to anyone.

Wang Wu continued to be uneasy at his own involvement with the Eight Trigrams. Just before the date of the uprising (when An-shun was away collecting rent from their tenants), Wang explained the situation to the wife of his master. He persuaded her that it would be safer to leave Peking temporarily and wait until the outcome of the rebellion was clear. Wang took and pawned some clothing belonging to the family and purchased silver bullion, and early in the 9th month, he and his elderly mistress went to the family graveyard (and country home?) outside the capital. Then, on the 13th, Wang Wu returned to the city, announced that his mistress was ill, and instructed the household staff to bring bedding and belongings and come to be with her. Thus the entire household had left the city before the 15th and all waited in safety.[63]

The most important person to remain at home on the 15th was Lin Ch'ing himself. No specific reason is given for this. Presumably Lin chose the safer course and planned to wait until word came that the Forbidden City had been secured or until Li Wen-ch'eng arrived before joining his followers. He kept his nephew and three godsons

home with him. He told Liu Ch'eng-hsiang, "My godsons and nephew are young. I'm afraid that they can't keep their mouths shut.
There is no point in taking them into the city. When the men from
Honan come, I will tell them to tie on white cloths and go out and
greet them, no more." Lin Ch'ing also kept with him for protection some of the men who had been more or less living at this home:
Tung Po-ying (Lin's brother-in-law), Sung Wei-yin (his pupil and
since that spring his employee), and Liu Fu-shou. Liu Fu-shou was
in his fifties and was the most trusted of those who remained with
Lin Ch'ing that day. He too had been hired by Lin earlier in the
year and had taken up residence with his employer/teacher. While
Lin Ch'ing waited for news on the 15th, it was Liu who was charged
with keeping watch.[64]

By 9/14 everything had been arranged, the symbols of rebellion
had been distributed, and the rebels-to-be had begun leaving their
homes and entering Peking. At the same time, however, the network of secrecy, such as it was, had begun to unravel. As we shall
see, these preparations had not gone unnoticed by the rebels' friends
and neighbors, and Wang Wu was by no means the only sect member who mentioned the plans for a rebellion to an outsider. In
several cases, knowledge of the uprising became public enough to
come to the notice of government officials. As in the case of Li Wen-
ch'eng and his followers, government attempts to learn about and
then prevent trouble paralleled the sect members' efforts to complete their rising before this could happen.

DISCOVERY

We have already noted some of the ways in which hints of the
Eight Trigrams' stepped-up preparations for rebellion reached
members of the government bureaucracy—gentry who lived in the
countryside heard about evening meetings, blacksmiths reported
requests for the manufacture of large numbers of weapons, ordinary
peasants were told by friends of the plans and in turn informed the
authorities. As we look in greater detail at other such channels, it
should become clear that although the government bureaucracy
and official gentry represented a numerically small portion of the
population, they were by no means isolated from the rest of the
society. In the countryside, members of the Eight Trigrams and
members of the elite lived in the same villages, worked in the same

places (for example, the district yamen), and were sometimes related. In the vicinity of Peking, the membership of Chinese bannermen, Chinese bondservants, and Manchus themselves in the sect created even more links between the would-be rebels and the government. Information about their plans filtered upward in many different ways. Sometimes, as in the case of the Chinese bannerman An-shun whose servant was in the sect, revelation of the rebel plans to one member of the elite did not lead automatically to official investigations; in other instances it did, but as it happened, in no case did such investigations disrupt Lin Ch'ing's mobilization of his followers.

Let us look first at what happened in Ku-an district. The sect leader there, Li Wu, despite his relative wealth, was apparently unable to write (or to write well), and having no one among his pupils able to provide the list of sect members requested by Lin Ch'ing, Li Wu turned to a member of the degree-holding elite and a fellow villager. On the 8th day of the 9th month, he sent a relative (and pupil) to try to recruit the village schoolteacher. This man, a fifty-one-year-old holder of the lowest examination degree named Ch'iu Tzu-liang, was promised many benefits if he would join; he claimed he refused. Four days later, on the eve of the rebels' departure for Peking, Ch'iu was asked to come to Li Wu's house. There he was invited to assist Li by writing a list of the names of the people in the sect. Ch'iu claimed, "I realized that there were a lot of people involved, so I thought that if I wrote up the list, I could learn who they were and could then report them." He made up the list as requested and was told about the rebellion scheduled for three days hence. He was also told to keep quiet about these plans.

Li Wu had been brave, perhaps foolish, in flaunting his strength in front of a *sheng-yuan*, for despite whatever promises he may have given, Ch'iu Tzu-liang did not keep their secret. The following day (the 13th), he contacted the *ti-pao* 地保 , the quasi-official government agent in that village,[65] and together with other villagers went to the yamen of the district magistrate. Luckily for Li Wu, the magistrate was away on business. Ch'iu and the others could only inform the clerks about members of this heretical sect "plotting trouble" and did not file a formal report. The magistrate did not return until 9/16, by which time the rebellion had already taken place. No investigation occurred until a month later, when the participation of rebels from Ku-an was uncovered.[66] Ch'iu's "loyalty" had come to nothing and the rebels were very fortunate. This incident indicates that, although it was possible for sect members to survive without literacy, the organizational demands of rebellion forced them to a greater dependency on those with these skills. The physical proximity of sect teachers, members of the lower gentry, and quasi-official personnel within the same village was in itself a danger to a sect intending to rebel.

It has already been pointed out that the Eight Trigram sects in the Peking area had spread to members of that class of more or less hereditary servants to the Peking elite. Family servants for official and Manchu families, the eunuchs who waited upon the imperial family, and the Chinese bondservants who also served the imperial clan all formed links between would-be rebels and the Ch'ing elite. To illustrate this connection, let us look at one bondservant family who formed a channel through which news of Lin Ch'ing's activities spread directly to the highest levels of the Manchu elite. Through Chu Hsien, sect leader and friend of Lin Ch'ing, and his relatives we can see something of the conflicting loyalties that pulled apart this bondservant family.

Chu Hsien 祝現 was a pupil of Lin Ch'ing and had been in the Jung-hua Assembly since at least 1809. He and his family were plain-blue banner bondservants attached to the household of the Yü 豫 Prince, whose palace was located in Peking. (Ch'en Shuang, the leader of the eastern group in the palace attack, was also from a plain-blue banner bondservant family attached to this same princely household.) Chu Hsien himself had no formal employment and lived in Sang-fa village as a "bannerman agriculturalist" (t'un-t'ien). His older cousin was living in the village and serving as ling-ts'ui 領催, the man responsible to his banner company for the banner families in that village.

Chu Hsien's own family was relatively well-off, with a number of hired laborers. Chu's younger brother had been adopted out as a child and was known as Liu Ti-wu. Liu, as we have seen, was a long-standing member of the Jung-hua Assembly, later a pupil of Li Lao, and an active organizer of the palace attack. Chu Hsien himself was forty-six years old; he had remarried after his first wife died and had a son in his twenties and three daughters. Chu Hsien's son became one of Lin Ch'ing's godsons and lived at Lin's house during the summer of 1813. Chu and his son slept with "the women in Lin Ch'ing's household" (probably his two stepdaughters and perhaps his wife), and Chu's wife and daughter-in-law were made available to Lin Ch'ing. In short, the connections between Chu and Lin

Ch'ing were very close, and in consequence Chu had been made a leader for the palace attack and was instructed to organize the men in his village.[67]

Although Chu was not employed by the princely household to which his family was attached, other relatives of his were. His cousin Chu Hai-ch'ing served the Yü Prince in Peking. In the 9th month of 1813 he happened to come to Sang-fa village to visit his family's graveyard; while there he spent the night with Chu Hsien. The two men talked, and Chu Hsien, whose mind was on the coming uprising, asked his cousin many questions about the management and financing of the prince's household—how many people worked there, how many horses, how much did it cost to feed them per day, and so forth. While he was visiting in the village, Chu Hai-ch'ing also talked with another relative who lived there, his uncle Chu Sung-shan. His uncle told him that Chu Hsien had joined a "heretical sect" and had been meeting secretly at night with some person named Lin Ch'ing in Sung-chia village; moreover, they were planning to go into Peking on 9/13, and on 9/15 they were going to rebel. Hai-ch'ing's uncle added that because Chu Hsien had enemies in his village, the rebels were going to attack these villagers, and so he was afraid. He told his nephew to return to Peking immediately and relate this information to other members of the family.

After spending one night in Sang-fa, Chu Hai-ch'ing returned to the prince's palace in Peking. There he told another uncle what he had heard. This uncle said that such hearsay did not constitute evidence and that before they could file a proper report, they had to get sworn confirmation from Chu Jui, the relative of theirs who as ling-ts'ui was formally responsible for all the bannermen in that village. Hai-ch'ing urged his uncle to report this information anyway to Pai-p'eng-a (a bodyguard in the prince's household), which he did. Pai-p'eng-a claimed that this matter did not come within his jurisdiction; however, he did mention it privately to the Yü Prince that night (the 10th). The prince said, "I doubt this is true. Wait until they get sworn statements." Chu Hai-ch'ing and his uncle spent the entire next day, the 11th, trying to find someone to go back to Sang-fa to get these statements. Finally Chu Kuei-shan, the uncle, went himself. He told Chu Sung-shan (the original informant) and Chu Jui (the ling-ts'ui) to come into Peking and sign a statement for the prince.

As it happened, this man Chu Jui was not only the person responsible for bannermen in that village and Chu Hsien's elder cousin, he was himself a member of the sect, as were his wife and adopted grandson. Thus, on 9/12 he found himself in a difficult position. He first stalled for a day, and then on 9/13 went to the home of his wife's brother in a nearby village in order to borrow back a mule to ride into Peking. Chu Jui spent the night there, and he and his brother-in-law discussed the situation. The latter said to Chu Jui, "Those believers in that Sang-fa village of yours are making quite a rebellion —maybe you're one of them!"[68] To this, Chu Jui had no reply. That night his wife said to him, "All you can do is to go and report to the prince. If your report is successful [in preventing the rebellion] then so much the better. If not, then we had better flee, for I'm afraid the Sang-fa sect people won't forgive us when they learn about this."

Chu Jui realized he had to report the sect but he continued to delay as long as possible. On the 14th, as the rebels themselves were leaving for Peking, he rode his donkey and went unhurriedly into the city, not arriving at the prince's household until early morning the day of the rebellion. In the meantime, the prince had been reminded about the rumored rebellion but again had instructed his staff to wait for written statements. Chu Sung-shan, the original informant, arrived at the prince's establishment on the 14th, and everyone spent that day waiting for Chu Jui. When he finally arrived the next morning, Chu Jui was told to write up an account of what he knew. He said that he was unable to write; he asked his cousin to write for him and, claiming he was not absolutely certain about there being a planned rebellion (an obvious untruth), instructed him to put down only that a heretical sect had been uncovered. He and Sung-shan then signed the statement.

Despite their efforts the bondservants were unable to give this statement to the prince right away, for that very day, while the statement was being written, the rebels had attacked the Forbidden City. The prince, Yü-feng, being a ranking member of the imperial family, had gone into the Great Interior of the palace to assist during the crisis, and for security reasons none of his staff was allowed to go in and see him. As a result, it was not until sunset on the 16th, when Yü-feng finally emerged and returned home to get food supplies for some of the soldiers on duty in the palace, that his subordinates were able to present him with the now out-of-date report on a dangerous heretical sect. Yü-feng came in the gate of his residence riding in a sedan chair. He took the report, read it, and then asked, "Is this the matter Hai-ch'ing mentioned before? Some rebels have already taken action. Find out if the people named here are among them. Then let whoever should handle this matter take care of it. Is there anything else?" Yü-feng returned to the Forbidden City that night; the following day, he had second thoughts and sent word requesting that the sworn statement be delivered to him. His intention was not to report the matter to the emperor; on the contrary, once he had the evidence in hand, Yü-feng instructed his staff to "keep it quiet."

(The Yü Prince's foreknowledge of the uprising was successfully covered up for nearly six months. Early in 1814, however, a rumor came to the attention of the emperor that Chu Hsien—who was at the time one of the six most wanted rebels—was hiding in the household of that prince. This rumor was investigated and the story began to leak out. By the middle of the 3d month, Yü-feng had been stripped of his title as prince (ch'in-wang 親王) and sentenced to house arrest. "Let him stay home and contemplate what he has done," said the Chia-ch'ing Emperor.)[69]

In this and the previous example from Ku-an, personal connections between the rebels and members of the establishment led to unsuccessful efforts by ordinary citizens to report the sect and the planned rebellion to the proper authorities. Let us now look at two other cases in which responsible officials were able to learn about the rebellion in advance and yet were unable to mobilize the bureaucracy to take preventive action.

Chang Pu-kao had been serving since the 1st month of 1813 as a subprefect stationed in Huang village, to the west of Peking. (This was the yamen where Lin Ch'ing and his father had served as clerks.)[70] During the night of 9/14, this subprefect received a personal report from a lieutenant stationed there declaring that, according to a man who had come to the yamen for safety, there were people from Sung-chia village who were going to rebel. Subprefect Chang questioned this man and confirmed the lieutenant's report. Immediately he sent two yamen runners to Sung-chia to investigate. This occurred in the middle of the night, just as Lin Ch'ing's men were leaving home and starting into Peking. Nevertheless the runners reported back in the predawn hours that in Sung-chia village all was quiet. Subprefect Chang was not satisfied, and on the 15th he called up some soldiers and sent instructions to the inhabitants of the area to be on the alert. "I could not guess," he later stated, "that the 15th was the very day that those rebels would go into the capital and rebel. I never dreamed that this would happen." The emperor concluded that Chang, who was virtually on the spot, had been unable to discover the obvious, was derelict in his duties, and deserved severe punishment. It does seem difficult to believe that his deputies (if in truth he sent any) had been in Sung-chia village that night and had seen nothing unusual.[71]

Another local official in the capital area also got wind of the Eight Trigrams' plans; he had somewhat better luck in getting results, although he too was unable to interfere with the mobilization of men for the palace attack. In the middle of the 8th month of 1813, the subdistrict deputy-magistrate stationed at Lu-kou was making his rounds through Wan-p'ing district.[72] This official, Ch'en Shao-jung, had just been assigned to this post in the 4th month of that year. He had first toured and inspected the western portion of Wan-p'ing, and then on 9/10 went to inspect the area south of Lu-kou, where Lin Ch'ing's village of Sung-chia and nearly a dozen other villages inhabited by sect members were located. He described what happened:

> I noticed that the people there were not planting their wheat. I summoned and questioned some of the people from that area. They all said that they were afraid and did not dare plant their wheat. When I tried to question them further they all ran off and hid. I became very concerned because they had seemed so agitated.

Deputy-Magistrate Ch'en returned to his office in Lu-kou on 9/12 and sent runners to go and tell the *ti-pao* from the villages in that area to come and report; at the same time he sent out deputies to make secret investigations. Those *ti-pao* arrived on the 13th and all signed sworn statements that they had heard of no trouble. The deputies came back with a different story. They said that in Sung-chia village, they had heard people say, "If you want cheaper flour, Lin Ch'ing must take power." Deputy-Magistrate Ch'en immediately ordered the *ti-pao* from Sung-chia village to come to his yamen and in the meantime wrote a preliminary report. He gave his superior no names or places and said only that a "strange saying" had been reported, one that was "difficult to describe in writing." He stated that he was investigating the matter and would soon interrogate the village headman from that place. Because Sung-chia village was more than twelve miles away from the yamen, this *ti-pao* did not arrive until early afternoon the following day, the 14th. Deputy-Magistrate Ch'en could not see him right away (he had to

meet with the governor-general that afternoon),[73] and so the interrogation did not take place until the evening of the 14th.

The *ti-pao* from Sung-chia village, the commoner who was given
official responsibility for monitoring the local situation, was, like the
bannerman Chu Jui, from exactly that group and class of individuals
who belonged to Lin Ch'ing's sect. This local headman was named
Sung Chin-jung 宋進榮; he was the younger brother of Sung Chin-
yao—one of Ku Liang's relatives and first pupils and Lin Ch'ing's
teacher. While it is possible that Sung Chin-jung was, as he claimed,
not in the sect, the fact that no fewer than fifteen male members of
his lineage were, does make this seem very unlikely. His family was
prominent on the local scene (they were the Sungs of Sung-family
village), though they were not part of the degree- or office-holding
gentry, and they had been the leading sect family in the village for
years. Even after Lin Ch'ing had taken over, the Sungs continued to
constitute a large portion of his followers. Sung Chin-jung had to
know about the case in 1808 when several of his brothers and cousins
were punished for being in the Jung-hua Assembly, and it would have
been very difficult for him not to have been aware of Lin Ch'ing's
increasing wealth and prestige over the last few years. Sung Chin-
jung had been local headman for only a year and a half. He tried
to explain his failure to do anything about Lin by saying, "[I had
seen that] the people who came and went from Lin Ch'ing's house
were a rather motley bunch, and this made me uneasy. After I became *ti-pao* I questioned them, but I never uncovered any hard
evidence. Ever since the 7th month a lot of men from nearby villages
had come to stay at Lin Ch'ing's. I didn't know what they were
doing, but I didn't dare report them."

Summoned before the deputy-magistrate only one day before the
planned uprising, Sung Chin-jung was in an even more unenviable
position. He did his best to feign ignorance when Deputy-Magistrate
Ch'en asked if he knew about anything illegal happening in his
village or about any person planning trouble. Incredulous, Ch'en hit
him across the mouth a dozen times, and Sung finally told him, "In
our village the only person like that is Lin Ch'ing. If there is talk
about anyone causing an incident, it must be him." Since Ch'en had
already heard the saying "If you want cheaper flour, Lin Ch'ing
must take power," Sung's information hardly came as a surprise. He
continued to apply physical pressure and eventually Sung was forced
to name some of the men he had often seen at Lin's house; not surprisingly, none were members of his family.

Ch'en then wrote up a statement for Sung Chin-jung to sign plus his own report for the district magistrate. He placed Sung in the custody of deputies and sent him together with the reports into Peking to the offices of his superior, the Wan-p'ing magistrate. All this took place on the evening of 9/14. Sung Chin-jung did not mention that there was a rebellion planned for the following day, and Deputy-Magistrate Ch'en apparently did not have the authority to issue a warrant for Lin Ch'ing's arrest. By early morning on the 15th, just as the sect members were themselves coming quietly and nervously into Peking, Sung Chin-jung was escorted through the city gates. Shortly afterward, Ch'en Shao-jung, who had become increasingly anxious, came himself by horse into Peking. By 7 A.M. he and Sung had both arrived at the yamen of Ch'en Chü-chou, the newly appointed district magistrate.

Magistrate Ch'en had already received his subordinate's report mentioning a "strange saying," but he had decided to wait for more specific information before taking any action. When the deputy-magistrate and the local headman reported to him in person, the former requested permission to go and arrest Lin Ch'ing and the others. Magistrate Ch'en disagreed and wanted him to go first and report the matter to the prefect. The deputy-magistrate persuaded his superior not to insist on this, saying he had never been presented to Prefect Fei (who was also newly appointed) and had neither proper clothing nor personal credentials. The magistrate was finally persuaded to take responsibility in this matter, and so he wrote out a warrant for the arrest of those men named by the headman and ordered that sixteen police runners be summoned and sent to make the arrests. The deputy-magistrate asked and was granted permission to take along *ti-pao* Sung to identify the offenders, and so they left the city and went back to Ch'en's office in Lu-kou to wait for the arrival of the police runners. These events took place at about 9 A.M. on the 15th.

Sung Chin-jung and the deputy-magistrate waited all day in Lu-kou for the runners, but none came. The magistrate, uneasy about authorizing these arrests, had gone himself to report this matter to Prefect Fei-hsi-chang after Sung and Ch'en had left. By his own account, Prefect Fei had told him that they "must first find out all the facts and for the time being no haphazard arrests should be made. He was afraid that we might be overreacting and that this in itself might provoke trouble. The local headman was to be told to return home and investigate further [before any arrests were made]; then, if the report should turn out to be false, the inhabitants of the area could be so informed [and thus calmed down]." This conference took place between 9 and 11 A.M. on the 15th; as a result Magistrate Ch'en returned to his offices and sent a message to the deputy-magistrate saying, "I have already reported and explained this matter to the prefect. We absolutely cannot make any arrests at this time! It is better instead to issue instructions telling the people to behave, no more. When you get this message, tell the *ti-pao* to come back to my offices, and I will give him further instructions personally."

This message did not arrive until the night of the 15th, and the deputy-magistrate and headman did not leave for Peking until the morning of the following day. It was by then much too late. They found the city gates closed (because of the palace attack) and no one allowed to go in or out. Sung Chin-jung tried to explain that he was being called in for questioning about the group that Lin Ch'ing was assembling in Sung-chia village, and finally later that day they were allowed to proceed to the district yamen. Sung Chin-jung was taken immediately to the office of the military-governor of Chihli, where he was questioned further about Lin Ch'ing. By this time, the palace attack had taken place and government investigators were suddenly very interested in learning the names of sect leaders. Sung Chin-jung was ordered to serve as a spotter for the government and to assist in making arrests. Leaving Peking on the night of the 16th, it was Sung who brought police runners to Lin Ch'ing's house in the early hours of the 17th and made possible his arrest. Later, Deputy-Magistrate Ch'en finally received authorization and personally led about fifty men to Sung-chia village to make other arrests there.[74]

Considering the number of channels that existed for the activities of Lin Ch'ing and his followers to come to the notice of the government bureaucracy, it is remarkable that not a single sect member was arrested prior to noon on 9/15. The fact that men deputized semi-officially by the government to watch out for exactly this type of "troublemaker" were themselves sect members undoubtedly contributed to Lin Ch'ing's security. By having these men and many members of their families in a sect, believers had—intentionally or not—subverted the normal process of government surveillance and created a screen for their activities.[75]

An equally serious problem for the Ch'ing state was the slowness with which its bureaucracy responded. This sluggishness may have been somewhat more pronounced in the capital area where many levels of officialdom resided in close proximity. This concentration of officials may have made the government less rather than more efficient. The sense of urgency was diluted as information passed up the line, and this, combined with each official's unwillingness to take full responsibility unless he had no choice, discouraged independence and inhibited decisive action. The Chia-ch'ing Emperor had some cause to be outraged when he understood the extent to which Lin Ch'ing had openly organized this rebellion—an affair that "suddenly turned up on our doorstep . . . and took place within our very walls!"[76]

Entering Peking

As the hour set for the uprising approached, Lin Ch'ing and his men sacrificed caution and secrecy and concentrated on the tasks of mobilization. The atmosphere of expectation among believers was compounded as more and more other people became aware that something was going on. Unusual conferences, hurried visits from village to village, the strange appearance of quantities of plain white cotton cloth, the unnatural reluctance of some people to plant their winter wheat, a daring rhyme about Lin Ch'ing taking power, and news that a large army was suddenly being readied to march to Honan to "suppress rebels"—all these things contributed to this uneasy mood. Yet official investigations, when they came, were slow and ineffectual, and Lin Ch'ing and his followers were able to proceed unhampered with their plans. Indeed, Lin's problems came more from within his own group than from the government. Many K'an Trigram members became increasingly frightened at their own audacity and at the last minute balked at taking the final step of becoming rebels. This fear ran like a counterpoint to the efficiency and determination of the rebels in the final days before the uprising.

On the 12th day of that month, the sect members began leaving home and traveling in small groups into the great walled city of Peking. Let us look at these clusters of would-be rebels and at their journeys and see how they attempted to maintain a veil of secrecy over what were now the first steps of rebellion, how they found food and shelter in a city where many had never been before, and how their fear grew as they approached the huge walls and gleaming golden roofs of the Forbidden City.

The larger group of rebels had been assigned to the Hsi-hua

(West Majestic) Gate. Of them, the men from Hsiung district were the farthest from Peking, about eighty miles away, and they left their homes early on 9/12, traveled steadily and did not arrive at the capital till the morning of the 15th. This group consisted of the pupils of the former Ta-sheng sect head Yang Pao.[77] They came from eight villages in northwestern Hsiung district. These two dozen men had all met at Yang Pao's house on the night of the 8th and at that time pieces of white cloth and weapons had been distributed. In addition each man was given 200 cash to spend for food en route to the capital. Yang Pao, who was in his sixties or seventies, did not go to Peking himself and delegated responsibility for the group to his pupil Liu Chin-t'ing. They all left from Yang's house on the 12th, at least twenty-two men in all, traveling in three groups. They spent two nights on the way, and by the evening of the 14th, some of them had reached Lin Ch'ing's, where they slept briefly. They were probably very tired. At dawn on the 15th, one group of at least fourteen men had breakfast in a small temple outside Peking and then went on into the city. Of this group, we know that Liu Chin-t'ing and at least four others went all the way into the city and reached the Hsi-hua Gate by noontime; but some of the others had turned back at the last minute.

Li Wu had mobilized a larger group of men from Ku-an district where he lived; at least seventy were involved in the planning of the palace attack, although we only know of forty-five (including Li Wu himself) who definitely left for Peking.[78] Some of those who remained at home had been instructed, as has been mentioned, to come out and greet the rebels from Honan when they came north. Others, like Li T'ien-shou and his brother, backed out at the last minute: "We discussed this [whether or not to go] and thought that if we didn't agree to go, they would kill us, so for the time being we would consent but then we would think about it came more. [In the end] . . . we did not go to Lin Ch'ing's." Li Wu's followers came from at least a dozen villages in the Ku-an and adjacent Hsin-ch'eng area, but most were from Hsin-chia village (where Li Wu lived) and another village close by. They were the pupils of either Li Wu himself or Li Wu's teacher, but it was Li Wu who had done most of the organizing for the palace attack.

Prior to 9/10, Li Wu had had nearly fifty knives made by a blacksmith in his village and he had collected money from his many pupils. On the 10th, 11th, 12th, and 13th, he distributed the knives and pieces of white cloth. It was on the 12th that he persuaded the village schoolmaster to write up for him a dictated list of all the members of their sect. Just before they were to leave, Li Wu invited his followers to a big feast at his house. The food prepared them for the physically demanding trip into Peking, and the event gave a certain honor to their undertaking. On the 13th, these men left for Peking, again traveling inconspicuously (they hoped) in small groups.[79]

As an example, we will describe the route followed by a few of Li Wu's men, people for whom there is good documentation. These men left Hsin-chia village early on 9/13, before it was light. Ts'ai Ming-shan narrates.

> The other four of them went ahead and [my brother-in-law] Shih Chin-chung and I followed. On the way Shih Chin-chung told me that if en route or in the capital I should run into anyone who was in the group, I should say "Be Victorious" and they would know that I was one of them. By the time we crossed the river . . . it was already dark, so we spent the night in O-fang village. We caught up with the others there. We slept on a pile of wood at the west end of that village. During the night [our leader] Wei Pan-r saw some men and women from a nearby village who were frightened and moving away. He was afraid that they would see our knives. Shih Chin-chung, Chang Lien, and I all had knives which were big and long, so we threw them over the dike into the river. Wei Pan-r's knife was short, so he kept it. . . . He told us we could get others in the city.
>
> On the 14th, we left that village and . . . [eventually] arrived on the north road outside the Chang-i Gate [on the west side of the southern section of Peking]. We went into a small inn there where we spent the night. That inn was run by two men, a father and son named Ts'ao; I could identify them.
>
> Early on the 15th we went in that gate to a teashop on the south side of the road at the Vegetable Market where we drank some tea. Wei Pan-r went and bought three knives for us. . . . When we had finished our tea, we went to the other side of the street and had a meal. Then we went in the Shun-ch'eng Gate [into the northern section]. It was nearly noon . . . when we got to the front of the Hsi-hua Gate.[80]

Li Wu and his other pupils went first to Lin Ch'ing's and spent the night of the 14th there. On the 15th Li went into Peking, met the rest of his group at the Vegetable Market, and then led them to the

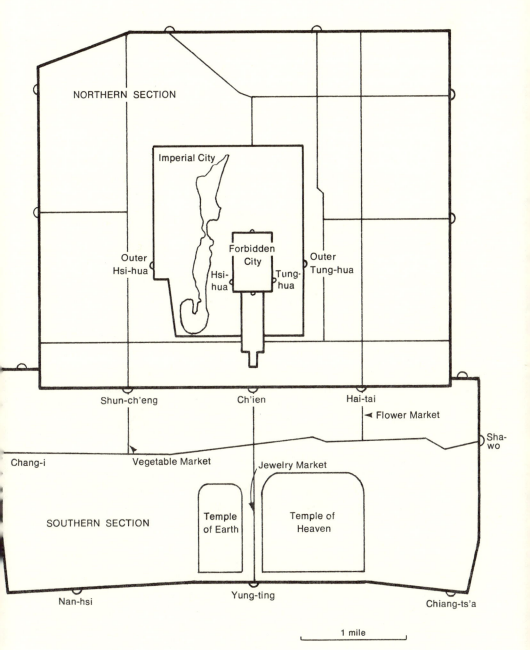

NORTHERN SECTION

Imperial City

Forbidden
City

Outer
Hsi-hua

Hsi-
hua

Tung-
hua

Outer
Tung-hua

Shun-ch'eng

Ch'ien

Hai-tai

◄ Flower Market

Sha-
wo

Chang-i

Vegetable Market

Jewelry Market

Temple
of Earth

Temple of
Heaven

SOUTHERN SECTION

Nan-hsi

Yung-ting

Chiang-ts'a

1 mile

City of Peking

Hsi-hua Gate. Of those forty-five who left home for the city, we know of at least twenty who definitely made it into Peking, and most of them went on to the Hsi-hua Gate itself.[81]

A small branch of Li Wu's group lived in Hsin village in Tung-an district, southeast of Peking.[82] Although it would have been closer for them to be part of the eastern contingent of the palace attack, they were assigned to the western side together with their teacher Li Wu. The leader of this group was Hsing K'uei-jung 邢貴榮, who was Li Wu's pupil (and also Li Lao's son-in-law). Hsing held a meeting at his home for the men from his village on the night of the 13th. They all left the following morning, carrying their knives and white cloth hidden in their clothing. That night they stayed at an inn run by a man called Yang Ssu-pa, located in the southeastern corner of the southern section of Peking to the east of the Temple of Heaven. Although there is no indication that Yang was in the sect, at least a dozen rebels from different villages stayed at his inn on the 13th and 14th.[83] The following morning, early on the 15th, Hsing K'uei-jung and the five others left the inn and went through the Hai-tai Gate into the northern section of the city and then around to the Outer Hsi-hua Gate. It is not clear how many of them went any further.

Ho Wen-sheng 賀文升 was the leader of the sect members from T'ai-p'ing village, many of whom were his relatives. Ho had been in the sect since at least 1808, knew Lin Ch'ing, and was active in planning the palace attack. He and eleven (possibly fifteen) others left their village (east and south of Peking) on the 14th. They went around and into the city from the southwest, may have stayed at Yang Ssu-pa's inn, and the following day assembled with men from other villages for a last meal at the Vegetable Market in the southern section of Peking. There is unfortunately no firsthand account by any member of this group.[84]

One other group assigned to go in through the Hsi-hua Gate was led by the eunuch Yang Chin-chung, whose office was on the west side of the palace, and who came from the area of Ma-chü-ch'iao (east of Peking). These nine men were organized by their teacher Liu Hsing-li, following instructions from his teacher Li Lao.[85] Liu Hsing-li was rather elderly and relied for assistance on his son and on his pupil's pupil Yang Chin-chung. Yang's family, the Chaos, lived in a small village near Ma-chü-ch'iao, and this house became the center for the prerebellion activities. These men had met with their teacher Liu Hsing-li in the 6th month of 1813 to discuss the uprising, and most of them met again at Yang Chin-chung's house on 9/9, which happened to be Yang's birthday. On the evening of the 14th they all came again and, like many of their colleagues, had a big dinner and discussed plans for the following day. Yang Chin-chung's coworker, the eunuch Chao Mi, who was to help the rebels inside the palace the next day, left early that evening to return to his post inside the Forbidden City.

On the morning of the 15th, after they all had eaten breakfast, Yang Chin-chung left with his adopted son; they went into Peking through the Yung-ting Gate (in the center of the southern wall), walked straight north, in the Ch'ien Gate into the northern section of Peking, and then around to the eastern gate to the Forbidden City. Being a eunuch Yang went directly in that gate and to the Fruit Office, where he reconnoitered with Chao Mi. Yang then proceeded to the western side, to the Hsi-hua Gate; there he waited until noon when he was to go out and lead his colleagues back inside.

In the meantime, the others of this group had left the village and followed a similar route. They traveled in small groups and met one another again at the Ch'ien Gate. Li Ch'ao-tso and his son, carrying two baskets of persimmons in which thirteen knives were hidden, pretended to be peddlers. All went to the area outside the Hsi-hua Gate, where they too waited nervously.

The group from Lin Ch'ing's own village included thirty-two men who went into Peking and seventeen who did not.[86] Most were actually from Sung-chia but some were from adjacent villages. Lin Ch'ing made his brother-in-law Tung Po-wang 董伯旺 (the man who had originally introduced Lin to the sect, seven years before) the leader of this group, while Lin's friend and the head of the K'an Trigram, Liu Ch'eng-hsiang, was responsible for organizing them. Ch'en Wen-k'uei, the overall head of the Hsi-hua Gate contingent, also went to Peking with this group. These men, together with batches of men from other villages, came to Lin Ch'ing's house on the evening of the 13th. Tables had been set up, and from late afternoon on, they sat drinking tea and wine and discussing the attack. That evening, Lin Ch'ing outlined the plan of action, assigned ranks and titles to some of the men, and distributed pieces of white cloth and knives.[87] The Sung-chia group did not leave until the following evening, the night of the 14th, some early that evening, others just before dawn on the 15th. (It was this night that the runners sent by Subprefect Chang Pu-kao came to Sung-chia village and found that "all was quiet.") It had been arranged in advance that they also would all meet at the Vegetable Market in Peking.

One of these men described his journey:

> During the fourth watch [on the night of the 14th] Hsiung Wu and Li Liu came to my house, each carrying baskets of persimmons. We lied to my father and mother and said that they had asked me to go into the city with them to buy some things. We left the village together, and then went to get Chin Lao-hu and [his younger brother] Chin Lu-r to join us. . . . We went to the Nan-hsi Gate [in the southern wall of Peking] and waited there for the gate to open. Then we entered Peking and went to the Vegetable Market. When it was light, we saw that Tung Po-wang was already there, so we all went to a restaurant and had something to eat.[88]

Men from the neighboring villages joined them at the Vegetable Market; they had left home during the fifth watch (that is, near dawn) and had also waited outside the city for the gates to open. After Tung Po-wang and his men had eaten, sometime during the 9–11 A.M. hour-period, they went in the Shun-ch'eng Gate into the northern section of the city, to and through the Outer Hsi-hua Gate, and gathered near the Hsi-hua Gate proper.

While these men were assembling on the western side of the Forbidden City, other sect members were on their way to the other side to the Tung-hua (East Majestic) Gate. The overall leader for this group was Lin Ch'ing's close friend Ch'en Shuang, who was from Sang-fa village and brought with him into the city at least thirty-one men.[89]

Although Sang-fa village was located near Sung-chia to the southwest of Peking, these men went with their leader to the Tung-hua Gate on the eastern side. This group included two eunuchs and a few people from small villages near Sang-fa. One member was Chu Hsien, the blue banner bondservant whose relatives were at this time trying to report him to the Yü Prince. Perhaps knowing of these efforts and unnerved by the tension and fears about the future of these final days before the uprising, Chu Hsien had begun to have second thoughts. He talked with his family, saying that this whole business was very dangerous. In tears, he confessed that he was afraid that "now that they had mounted the tiger, there would be no way to dismount." They all cried and agonized together, and finally Chu declared that he would simply tell Lin Ch'ing that he was quitting. He went to Lin's house to do so, but Lin Ch'ing talked with him, encouraging him to go with them, perhaps reminding him of the benefits to be won, reassuring him, and telling him that to be so concerned about one's wife and family was not acting like a real man. Eventually Chu Hsien was brought around. But as he left home on the 13th he said to his family, "If it is fated that we meet again, then I will see you all once more. If it is not so fated, then this is our last time together." Everyone cried bitterly as he left.[90]

Many of the men in the Sang-fa village group had attended the meeting at Lin Ch'ing house on the evening of the 13th, and most of them left for Peking the following night. At least six of them stayed at the San-ho (Three Harmonies) inn at the Jewelry Market. In order to find lodgings for the others, the group leader Ch'en Shuang made use of a relatively recent convert to the sect, a theater owner named Liu Ch'ao-tung. Liu was an old acquaintance of Ch'en Shuang's nephew, and it was the latter who had first approached him, probably with the explicit intention of having a Peking resident in his group. In the 8th month, the two Ch'ens had come to visit Liu and had told him, "[Lin Ch'ing] sent us to get you to join our assembly, and in addition he wants you to become his godson. Later on there will be infinite wealth and high position for you." Liu Ch'ao-tung had agreed, and so on the eve of the rebellion, he was ready to assist. The night of the 14th, Ch'en Shuang and his nephew came into Peking early and watched a play at Liu's theater. Then they all went out to dinner at a Muslim restaurant (in other words, to eat mutton or beef), and afterward Liu found a place to stay for at least five of Ch'en's group.[91]

Early on the 15th part of this Sang-fa group assembled at the Jewelry Market, where knives and cloth were distributed to those who needed them. One of the subleaders of this group took most of them on into the northern city, but he first instructed about ten of them to remain where they were, saying that he would be back to get them later. (These men waited there until noon, but no one ever returned for them, and they made no attempt to find the Tung-hua Gate themselves.) The others went ahead in the Ch'ien Gate and around to the eastern side of the Forbidden City. Four of them went into a wine shop there for something to eat and drink. Another five men in this group had camped out south of the capital, bought something to eat there, and then came into Peking that morning. They also passed through the Ch'ien Gate and sat for a while on the main street just inside that gate; it was not until nearly noon that they went to the Tung-hua Gate itself. We know that at least a dozen men of this group arrived outside the gate; inside, the two eunuchs, pupils of Ch'en Shuang, were waiting to lead them.

Another group of rebels consisted of the members of the old Pai-yang sect; they were from four villages southeast of Peking, and were all pupils under Li Lao. These are the people for whom we described distribution of cloth and knives. They were Li Lao's family, the pupils of his pupils the Chang brothers, and their leader Liu Ti-wu and his family.[92] Li Lao, though the leader, did not go. This group was rather well organized and nearly all made it to the gate itself.

Two brothers who were from Ma-chü-ch'iao left home on the 13th and spent the next two nights in Peking (one at Yang Ssu-pa's inn, and one at the San-ho inn). At least seven of the Yang-hsiu village group (that is, Li Lao's village) came into Peking on the 14th; they stayed at Yang Ssu-pa's inn as well. Chang I-fu, the senior Chang brother, led in most of the others; they left home in the middle of the night of the 14th, came into the southern section of the city, then straight north and in the Hai-tai Gate or the Ch'ien Gate. One man described his trip as follows:

> At just past the third watch I followed Chang I-fu and we all set out. We went to the Chiang-ts'a Gate, but they hadn't opened it yet. I saw [others in the group] also waiting there. When the gate opened, everyone went into the city. We split up, and I went with Chang I-fu [and some others]. We bought some dumplings to eat on the way, and then went in the Ch'ien Gate. We followed along the eastern Ch'ang-an street, walking at the foot of the wall of the Imperial City, going around to the Outer Tung-hua Gate. Then we went in this three-arched gate and arrived outside the Tung-hua Gate. . . . There we went into a teahouse which was on the south side of the road.[93]

In the teashop, Chang I-fu bought tea for his men, and together with the other pupils of Li Lao who had assembled near the gate, they waited for noon.

The third and last group to make up the eastern contingent was from Tung village in T'ung district and came with their leader Ch'ü Ssu. Although Ch'ü had told Lin Ch'ing he had only a dozen able-bodied men among his pupils, there were thirty-one (possibly thirty-eight) who came with him into Peking. One member of Ch'ü Ssu's group was his fellow villager An Kuo-t'ai, who made his living as a puppeteer in Peking. He had been asked to join the rebellion specifically because he was familiar with the streets of the capital and could help the others find their way in what was to many a bewildering maze.[94] Most of this group went to Ch'ü's house for a meeting on the night of the 14th. There, in a pattern identical to that of many of their comrades, they had some dinner—noodles in this case—and were given knives, pieces of white cloth, and instructions for the following day. At this meeting Ch'ü outlined what would happen and urged everyone to participate; to those thinking about backing out at the last minute he counseled, "In this business it might be death if you went, but it would certainly be death if you stayed. If we are successful after all, then everyone will obtain both wealth and position." He asked who wanted the task of carrying banners for the group (a dangerous privilege), and two men volunteered. The banners were marked with the slogan "Entrusted by Heaven to Prepare the Way."

The men in this group went into the city through the gates along the southern wall of the capital and assembled at the Flower Market. At this point, Ch'ü Ssu instructed at least five of his men to remain behind, waiting there for men who would come from the south to assist them. "There would be men and horses coming from Hua," he explained. "Bring them into the city, taking the Chiang-mi lane as far as the Tung-hua Gate, and they will be reinforcements for our men."[95] (Like another group told to station themselves in the southern city on the western side, these men waited and finally fled when they learned the palace attack had been unsuccessful.) The others went ahead with Ch'ü Ssu. One man carried a basket of dates under which he had hidden knives for the group. They went to outside the Tung-hua Gate, where some went into a teashop, some into a wineshop, each drinking for courage and to pass the time until the signal was given for action.

There were many who never came as far as these two gates to the Forbidden City. In testimony after testimony, those who were to have been rebels stated that they had had second thoughts as they made their way into Peking, and "the more I thought, the more afraid I became." Some of these men turned back before they reached the palace gates; others hung back and, hoping "that when they got their 'benefits' they would not leave me out," looked for an excuse to flee. The tension and suspense, only partially relieved by the alternation of much walking with frequent pauses to eat and drink, undermined morale and ate away at the conviction that this deed must be done. When the noon hour finally arrived, many had lost their nerve, and we shall see that in the forward movement, the rush to enter the gates, there was an undertow, a simultaneous pulling back which weakened the force of that attack.

INTO THE FORBIDDEN CITY

Of the intended Tung-hua Gate rebels, between thirty and forty had stayed at home. Of the ninety to one hundred who had left, at least thirty-four never made it to the gates, but at least sixty-one did arrive in the immediate area just to the east of the Forbidden City. Most of them had come in plenty of time and were, as we have seen, sitting in different teashops and wineshops, eating, drinking, and waiting nervously for the moment when they would act. Early that morning the eunuchs Liu Te-ts'ai and Liu Chin had come out from the Interior (where they worked) and exited through the Tung-hua Gate. As arranged, they went to the wineshop just outside and met Ch'en Shuang, their teacher and the overall leader for this eastern group. The eunuchs joined Ch'en and his men, reviewed their plans, and then they too sat and waited, drinking for courage.

Finally, at noon, the two eunuchs rose and walked toward the gate; word was passed that the time had come. The rebels took out their banners, tied on identifying white cloth, drew out their knives, and, following the eunuch leaders, walked rapidly toward and then through the open gate. At that time seventeen men were supposed to be on guard duty at that gate, and though many were eating their lunch, sleeping, or talking with friends, some were at their posts. As the rebels hurried inside, those guards—with little effort—simply closed the doors of the gate. This turn of events almost epitomizes the naiveté and ultimate hopelessness of the rebels' plans. Besides the two eunuchs, only five rebels were able to enter; all the rest were shut out.[96]

The rebels who were at the gate saw it close, and those who were farther away heard the noise of the great doors swinging shut. One participant described how he carefully preserved the options of advance and retreat and watched what happened:

> At the Outer Tung-hua Gate, I saw [some of the others] drinking in a wineshop, but I went ahead in that gate. Just to the south of the stone bridge [leading to the Tung-hua Gate proper] there were some men selecting horses, so I watched them for a while. Then I went forward onto the bridge and then stood

there and waited. At noon official soldiers began grabbing people, and I heard the noise of the gate closing, so I turned and ran.[97]

The guards outside the gate shouted, "Seize them! Seize the rebels!" There was noise and commotion as many turned to flee. Word quickly spread: "There's trouble at the Tung-hua Gate." "They're rebelling, someone's rebelling!" Some rebels did not arrive at the gate until the last minute (at least so they claimed), and when they got there it was already too late. Several men who had stopped for tea and were just coming toward the gate encountered some of their colleagues "running frantically" in the other direction. They too turned around, frightened, and made their way home as fast as they could. All those who fled from the scene disposed of their incriminating paraphernalia as best they could, throwing knives and white cloth by the roadside, into moats, streams, graveyards, sewers, or the deep ruts made in the road by carts. Word was carried to those who had been waiting in the southern section of the city: "I hear the Tung-hua Gate has been shut. Things are not going right. Let's get out of here!" At least three rebels were arrested near the palace gate, but the others all returned home unhindered. Those from the Sung-chia village area came back in a group and shamefacedly presented themselves at Lin Ch'ing's quarters to bring him the bad news.[98]

In the meantime, the two eunuchs and five other rebels who had made it through the gate found themselves alone inside the Forbidden City. Among them was Ch'en Shuang, the leader of the entire attack. Their plan a near failure, they still followed the eunuch Liu Te-ts'ai and turned toward the north intending to kill anyone who got in their way. Their goal was the Great Interior, where they hoped to find their colleagues from the western side. Along the way they encountered resistance: two palace personnel grabbed clubs and tried to stop them. Ch'en Shuang and another drew their knives, stabbed them, and ran on. They turned up a narrow passage along the eastern wall of the Interior, heading for the only gate in this wall, the Ts'ang-chen Gate. They were pursued, and Ch'en and two others were stopped and seized. The remaining four, including the two eunuchs who were still leading the way, reached this gate to the Interior.

Sixteen men were assigned to guard duty on the Ts'ang-chen Gate. On this day, five of them were on their lunch hour and had left the palace. Ten others had, contrary to regulations, left the gate—some were resting, others were sitting around, talking, or writing up

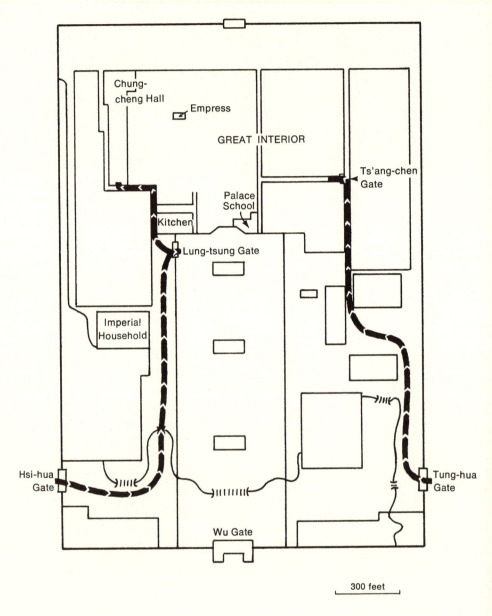

Forbidden City, with paths taken by Eight Trigram rebels

reports. Only one man, the Manchu soldier Kuan-lung, was on duty. When the rebels entered the Ts'ang-chen Gate, he claimed he saw nothing unusual. They appeared to be just three or four eunuchs; no one had white cloth or weapons, though it did look like the first eunuch was carrying some cabbage, and they did not look like rebels. So Kuan-lung did nothing to stop them. Shortly afterward, however, he realized something was wrong. Someone from the Interior called out for help. "There are bandits inside the Interior!" Those gate guards who should have been on duty were alerted and, together with Kuan-lung, rushed in the gate to see what had happened. In the meantime, palace eunuchs had fought with and successfully tied up two rebels with no help from the guards, although several of them were injured in the process. The two rebel eunuchs had escaped detection entirely. One simply walked on through the Interior and made himself scarce elsewhere in the palace. The other turned upon his rebel comrades and, grabbing a staff, began to swing it at them.

The Chia-ch'ing Emperor's second and third sons, Mien-ning (the future Tao-kuang Emperor) and Mien-k'ai, were at this time in the Palace School next to the southern wall of the Interior. They heard the commotion and quickly came out to see what was happening. They encountered the chief eunuch accompanied by other eunuchs and the bound captives. The rebels had been searched and their knives and white cloths discovered, and the princes were assured that everything was under control. Of the three other rebels who had come in the gate, two of them had already been caught before reaching the Interior, and the third was caught and apparently killed. No one involved in making these arrests realized that there were—or would be—rebels also coming in the western gate. The Tung-hua rebels had been taken care of with dispatch, and calm had apparently been restored.[99]

At least seventy or eighty men, possibly as many as one hundred thirty, had gathered outside the Hsi-hua Gate. The eunuchs who were to lead this group inside—Yang Chin-chung, Kao Kuang-fu, and Chang T'ai—came out through the gate to meet their associates. Although both attacks were to take place at noon, there is some indication that this Hsi-hua group's attempt to enter occurred after the entry on the eastern side. Either one was early or the other late. At least four men were carrying peddlers' baskets of persimmons and sweet potatoes under which they had hidden knives. Some of the men from Sung-chia village gathered around the man who was carrying their knives and pretended to be buying persimmons from him. Instead, each reached under the fruit and took a knife. The group from Ma-chü-ch'iao, when they realized it was time to go through the gate, surged up behind the young man who was carrying their weapons, knocked him and his baskets over and, as the bright orange persimmons spilled out into the street, grabbed their knives from the baskets and rushed in the gate.

At least seventy men took this step and committed themselves to rebellion. The Hsi-hua Gate was supposed to be guarded by twenty men, but none of them did anything to oppose the rebels. Once inside, the leaders hastily decided that most of their men had made it, and closed the gate. In fact there were a number of sect members who had perhaps intentionally lagged behind and who were shut out. The gate guards, finally roused, called out, "These are rebels!" and so everyone left outside hurried away.[100]

Inside, the rebels tied on their white sashes and turbans; the leaders of each village group carried small white banners, and everyone had his knife ready.[101] One of the leaders immediately went up onto the wall and planted a banner there as a signal of welcome to the Honan men who, according to plan, would soon arrive as reinforcements. Then the group headed toward the north, now totally dependent on their eunuch guides to show the way within the immense and unfamiliar palace complex. They were going toward the Great Interior just as the rebels on the eastern side had done. They passed the offices of the Imperial Household near the Fruit Office where Yang Chin-chung worked and where several other eunuchs who were sect members were now waiting. They encountered staff and palace personnel and, now fully committed and their lives at stake, attacked and tried to kill them.

It took this large group at least a half hour to reach the next set of gates leading into the Interior, but by this time the palace staff had been alerted and these gates were closed. (The eastern group had apparently all been seized by the time the western group reached this point.) When the rebels arrived at the Lung-tsung Gate on the edge of the Great Interior (just inside of which were the offices of the Grand Council) they found it closed. They tried to open it by banging on the gate door and even tried to burn down the door but were unable to get a proper fire started. Finally they seized the bows and arrows there for use by the gate guards and fought with those guards who advanced against them. As this fighting was going on, the Manchus had begun to mobilize their defenses.

That morning the emperor, returning from Jehol, was about fifty miles from Peking. The head of the Peking Gendarmerie, which was responsible for maintaining order in the capital city, had left early that morning to go out and greet the imperial retinue. His number two man, who had been with the emperor, came back to Peking to take charge temporarily. This man, Yü-lin, arrived in Peking during the 1–3 P.M. hour-period on the 15th. He was immediately notified that there had been trouble at the Tung-hua Gate of the Forbidden City; word of the more serious trouble on the western side had apparently not yet reached his office. As the highest ranking Gendarmerie official in Peking, Yü-lin had the authority to put the city on the alert, which he did immediately. Soldiers were sent to each of the four gates to the Forbidden City, and guards were instructed to close the thirteen city gates earlier than usual and to halt any suspicious-looking persons.

At the same time Yü-lin assembled soldiers and proceeded directly into the Forbidden City, entering from the north. He met with other high Manchu princes (including the Chia-ch'ing Emperor's brothers Yung-hsing and Yung-hsuan), who had already been alerted. They began to search for rebels and arrived to find that some of the Hsi-hua Gate group had come as far as the gate to the Chung-cheng Hall, part of the Great Interior, while others were "causing a disturbance" outside the Lung-tsung Gate. The Gendarmerie soldiers were well armed and came immediately to the assistance of the palace guards. Some of the rebels had abandoned the attempt to storm the Lung-tsung Gate and had gone instead toward the north. When they ran directly into the approaching soldiers, they were forced to turn southward again, away from the Interior.

At about this time, the two sons of the emperor again became involved in the action. Earlier they had seen that the rebels who had come in the Ts'ang-chen Gate had been caught and bound, and they felt the situation was under control. They had talked about it and decided that they would go and inquire after the empress (who was the mother of the younger of the two, eighteen-year-old Mien-k'ai) to make sure that she was unharmed. As they walked toward the northwest, still inside the Great Interior, they found themselves directly inside the Lung-tsung Gate, outside of which the fighting with the second group of rebels still continued.

At least three rebels, unable to enter the gate, had climbed the wall instead and were jumping down onto the roof of the imperial kitchen, which was just inside the wall. At this time there no soldiers inside the Interior; only eunuchs, already on the alert but armed merely with clubs and staffs, were patrolling up and down the lanes and standing on lookout duty on some of the walls and roofs. Seeing the rebels coming over the wall, the elder son and future emperor, Mien-ning (then age thirty-one), immediately sent an aide to fetch his knife, musket, and powder. He realized that the rebels might be trying to head north deeper into the Interior and that the men on the inside could do nothing against those on the walls and roofs without using muskets. Therefore, he explained later, he broke the rule forbidding anyone to shoot a gun within the Interior, and when his musket was brought, he fired upon the rebels. He hit one who fell to the ground outside the wall. This shooting from the inside convinced most of the rebels outside not to continue scaling the wall, but there were already several rebels on their way. Mien-ning ran into a nearby courtyard, where he shot and killed another rebel on the wall—a leader who was carrying a white banner and calling out orders to the others. Those rebels who had dropped down onto the roof of the imperial kitchen, jumped to the ground and found hiding places temporarily.

The emperor's nephew, Mien-chih (son of the I Prince Yung-hsuan), had previously arrived on the scene, and now he borrowed his cousin's musket and began shooting at other rebels upon the wall. killing at least one more. Mien-chih then went to join in the fighting outside the Lung-tsung Gate and in the course of the day stabbed one rebel and shot two more. The two imperial sons in the meantime went as they had previously planned to see the empress. Mien-ning insisted that his younger half brother remain with his mother, just to be safe, and then he went back to where there had been fighting, accompanied all the while by the chief eunuch and several other eunuchs.

The rebels had given up their attempt to enter the Interior, and finding soldiers to the north and rifle fire coming from within, they turned back toward the south, the way they had come. The eunuch Yang Chin-chung was still acting as a leader, and with him there were at least twenty rebels still alive and increasingly desperate. Yang went south with them, but realizing that the situation was hopeless, he abandoned the group and ran to the Fruit Office, where he worked. The staff there (some of whom were in the sect) had closed their gate and were waiting fearfully inside. Yang Chin-chung climbed the wall and jumped down into the courtyard. He went to his room to get a knife and then put a ladder up against the wall

and climbed up to see what was happening. When he saw the Manchu princes leading soldiers and searching for rebels, he descended
and tried to go about normal business, hoping to avoid detection.
(His name came out a few days later and like the other eunuch rebels
he was eventually arrested and executed.) Without their leaders and
guides, the remaining rebels scattered and found themselves trapped.
Some tried to hide, others committed suicide.

Under the leadership of the I Prince, Ch'eng Prince, Mien-chih,
Mien-ning, other lesser princes, officers of the Imperial Household,
and the staff of eunuchs, the surviving rebels were hunted down and
one by one found and arrested. During the night of the 15th, the
palace and the city were patrolled regularly and though there was
some fighting during the night, by morning all was calm.[102] The
entire Forbidden City was carefully searched in the course of the
next two days and few rebels escaped. Two were found hiding in the
imperial kitchen, one young man was discovered inside a shed near
the Hsi-hua Gate, two bodies were found in the canal near that gate,
and twenty or thirty bodies were lying about on the ground outside
the gates to the Interior. Three other rebels were found alive three
days later, hiding in the ceiling space of the Wu Gate.

While most of the rebels were caught or killed, a few did manage
to find their way over the walls and escape from the palace. One,
Fan Ts'ai, ran to the southern side of the Forbidden City and spent
the afternoon of the 15th hiding under a bridge. After dark, he crawl-
ed onto the palace walls and made his way along the top. In the
morning he tried to jump down, but fell, hurt himself, and was soon
caught.[103] T'ien Ch'i-lu was luckier:

[After fighting at the Lung-tsung Gate] I went back to the
Hsi-hua Gate and went up the horse ramp. Then I jumped
down onto another building [still inside the palace] and hid
there for several days. Early on the 18th, I climbed a large tree
that was next to the wall and jumped from the tree down onto
the wall itself. I headed toward the north, walking along the
wall for about one li, crossing over one gate. I saw that there
were some piles of loose dirt along the base of the wall, so I
jumped down onto them. I climbed over some bricks and up
over a storage place for grain, then I jumped down from there
onto a broken-down house which was filled up with dirt. I
swam across a river and then climbed up some rocks and up the

riverbank. I followed along the side of the wall there and squeez-
ed through an opening. [Once in the city itself] I went out
[various] gates and then back home.[104]

T'ien was not arrested for two months, but then he was caught and
executed like the others.

AFTERMATH

Nearly all the rebels who entered the Forbidden City were either
killed or captured. The government stated that thirty-one rebels
were killed and forty-four captured alive, some of whom were seriously injured and soon died. Nevertheless, the Ch'ing side did suffer
more than their share of casualties, for these seventy-five rebels,
armed only with knives, had been able to kill or injure more than one
hundred of the palace defenders.[105]

Around six P.M. on the 15th, the Chia-ch'ing Emperor himself
learned about what had occurred in Peking. That afternoon two
low-ranking Manchu officials had by chance gone to the Tung-hua
Gate. Finding the gate closed, they went around to the northern
entrance to the Forbidden City. There they learned of the disturbances within and arming themselves with knives, went inside to
assist. They witnessed some of the fighting, and respectfully inquired
of the Manchu princes who were in charge if there was anything
they could do. The emperor's brother Yung-hsuan (whose son Mien-
chih had already distinguished himself in fighting the rebels) gave
them a brief draft memorial drawn up and signed by the seventeen
princes and ministers who were there in the palace. He dispatched
the two men to deliver it to the emperor as fast as possible. They left
the palace immediately, commandeered horses at the Board of War,
and rode rapidly out of the city. When they reached the imperial
entourage, then less than fifty miles away, they presented the memorial and described to the emperor and grand councillors present
what they had seen personally of the situation.[106] In this manner
the emperor learned within a few hours, that there had been trouble
caused by men wearing white sashes and turbans, that his son and
nephew had behaved outstandingly, and that the situation was under
control.[107]

The Chia-ch'ing Emperor had known about the disturbances in
Honan and Shantung for several days (since the 12th), and the com-

mon use of white sashes may have already suggested a link between these events and the palace attack. The possibility of a close connection between these uprisings had since become clearer. On the 15th the emperor had received a memorial from the governor of Shantung finally reporting the confessions of Chin-hsiang sect members who claimed that the leader of their sect lived near Peking. One Shantung sect member had stated that this man was a reincarnation of Maitreya Buddha, called by many names, sometimes Lin, sometimes Liu. He lived twenty-eight li south of the capital near the main thoroughfare. He had previously visited Honan, conferred with sect leaders there, and was planning his own uprising in the Peking area.[108] Very soon the emperor received other evidence indicating the existence of a "mastermind" named Lin. The Sung-chia village *ti-pao* had named Lin Ch'ing several days before, and by the 16th his testimony began to be taken seriously. He was taken along as a spotter to identify and arrest Lin Ch'ing the following day. (Some of the rebels captured inside the palace were already being informally interrogated, but apparently none of them mentioned Lin Ch'ing's name before the afternoon of the 17th.)

The days prior to his arrest were difficult ones for Lin Ch'ing. The men from Sung-chia village had left from his house for Peking in the middle of the night on the 14th. The following morning, with the village relatively deserted, Lin Ch'ing left home briefly but returned just after breakfast time. When he returned to his quarters in the Tung family courtyard, he instructed his nephew and some of the others who remained at home with him to take out and play some cymbals and a trumpet while he beat out a drum beat on a board. At noontime, when the attack on the palace was scheduled to begin, Lin Ch'ing, a picture of calm, retired to his room to rest saying, "If people come, wake me up." Tung Kuo-t'ai and Sung Wei-yin stood at the gate to the house, watching the street. While they were standing there, they saw Ho Shih-k'uei, a sect member who was supposed to have gone into Peking. He had been too afraid to go and was on his way to market instead. Sung Wei-yin pulled Ho Shih-k'uei over under a tree next to the temple nearby and asked him why he had not gone with the others. Not sympathetic with Ho's weak explanation, Sung told him that "because you didn't go into the city today, that means that later our people are going to kill you." Ho Shih-k'uei hurried away.[109]

At dusk, as the lamps were being lighted, Lin Ch'ing arose. He told some of the others that now they could sleep. Sung Wei-yin and six of those staying at Lin's house were given knives and clubs and told to stand guard. Rebels began to return from Peking during the night and early morning. As these men, at least eleven of them, arrived at Lin Ch'ing's house, alone or in small groups, they gave their leader the bad news. Lin fatalistically explained to one of them that it was because their basic foundation was weak that they were unable to be successful. Realizing that he was truly in danger now, Lin insisted that everyone spend the night guarding his house.

The following day, the 16th, other rebels who had fled from Peking also returned to their villages.[110] Lin Ch'ing stayed at his house and spent the day with a few friends in almost total silence, sitting, smoking, and thinking. Lin had already received some word about the progress of the uprising in Honan, and for a while he considered going there himself. Finally he decided to send instead his friend and fellow villager Chih Chin-ts'ai, who had accompanied Lin on each of his visits to Hua and who therefore knew the way. He told Chih to take the horse, go first to notify Sung Yueh-lung in central Chihli, and then go to Hua and tell Li Wen-ch'eng that the attack on the Forbidden City had not been successful.

Lin Ch'ing had just this one day in which to consider his options, and he chose to remain at home. Early the next morning the governmental machinery that had been set in motion seven days before finally caught up with him. Before dawn on the 17th, the *ti-pao* Sung Chin-jung (Lin's fellow villager and the brother of his teacher) arrived in Sung-chia village accompanied by one sublieutenant, several soldiers from the district garrison, and three men from the police bureau of the Imperial Household. The arrest was quickly made and there was no opposition. The only other person in the household awake at this early hour was Lin's nephew Tung Kuo-t'ai, who happened to be on his way to the outhouse. He saw his uncle being led away and as soon as the arresting officers spotted Tung, he was seized as well. The two were bound, put in a cart, and taken off.[111]

The rest of the household awoke almost immediately. Lin Ch'ing's sister, Tung Kuo-t'ai's mother, took charge of the situation. She aroused everyone and ordered them all—at least twenty men—to grab knives and clubs and staffs and to chase the cart and rescue her son and her brother. A neighbor, out early in his buckwheat field, saw these men in the distance, running after the cart waving their weapons, but the attempted rescue was less than wholehearted. Most ran only as far as the edge of the village, and everyone had an excuse not to go farther: "The cart was going too fast, and we couldn't catch up." "I hurried to the entrance to the village, but because I'm not very brave, I then ran back home."[112] For security reasons, Lin Ch'ing and his nephew were taken to Peking via the extensive Southern Park (Nan-yuan), off-limits to commoners, which lay south of Peking and just east of Sung-chia village. Then Lin was taken to the offices of the Gendarmerie for interrogation. The southern route subprefect Chang Pu-kao had arrived with some men to accompany the prisoners into Peking.[113] The following day, the 18th, Subdistrict Deputy-Magistrate Ch'en Shao-jung finally arrived in Sung-chia village empowered to make arrests. He found Lin Ch'ing gone but searched his quarters and arrested members of the Tung family and eight sect members who were still at the house.[114]

In the meantime, after a preliminary interrogation in which Lin Ching did admit to organizing the palace attack—"he stood up and straightforwardly admitted he was the head of the rebels, but when we questioned him about how many people there were in his group and where they were now, he equivocated and would not give us any information"—Lin Ch'ing was transferred to the Board of Punishments. There he underwent intensive questioning by senior board officials and special deputies of the emperor.[115] In these subsequent confessions, Lin Ch'ing did give the names of other sect members, but he used nicknames and was very vague; his information was relatively useless, especially compared with that supplied by his nephew, whose statements were long, detailed, and reliable. (Tung Kuo-t'ai remained in the Board of Punishments prison nine years before being executed. He was periodically interrogated and asked to describe or identify wanted rebels or to confirm the testimony of those arrested later.)[116]

On the 21st, Lin Ch'ing was again interrogated by the highest Board of Punishment officials. They lectured him, saying, "Our emperor loves the people as if they were his own children. Anyone with a human heart would certainly have been grateful. You even live in Wan-p'ing district, which is an area on which the emperor has repeatedly bestowed special favors, and this is nothing like being from a distant province. You had to be aware of this. How could you organize people and charge into the Forbidden City armed with knives? Even brutes and beasts would not go this far! Exactly what did you intend to do?" To this Lin Ch'ing replied, "When I thought up the idea of organizing an assembly, I intended it as a way of making money. Later on, the people who believed grew numerous, and then, because I wanted to acquire wealth and honor, I started in on this business [of rebellion]. It is my fate to die. It is not my fate to be a peaceful commoner. I sought this end myself. What else is there to say?"[117]

On the 23d day of the 9th month, Lin Ch'ing was brought before the Chia-ch'ing Emperor himself and questioned by him and the assembled Manchu princes and ministers. With Lin were two eunuchs and another rebel; Lin's friend Ch'en Shuang was also to have been present at this court interrogation, but he had just died of wounds received during the attack on the palace. The four were questioned, particularly about the extent of eunuch involvement in the rebellion, and then taken away to be executed. Thus Lin Ch'ing did have the privilege of seeing the man he had hoped to oust before being executed by slicing. His head was subsequently taken to the battlefields in Honan, where it was displayed for the rebels there as proof of his death.[118]

The bodies of all those rebels who died during the palace attack had already been taken to the execution grounds and "chopped into ten thousand pieces." Those K'an Trigram sect members and their relatives who were subsequently arrested were interrogated and then sentenced with meticulous attention to the extent of their knowledge of or participation in the abortive uprising. Over the next four years, more than eight hundred people were arrested and punished by the Board of Punishments, the majority with some form of banishment.[119] The networks of White Lotus sects around Peking, even those having no connections with Lin Ch'ing, were decimated. Because of what was felt to be a pressing need to restore the security of the capital city and its environs, the policy of leniency toward sect members who did not join the rebellion, the rule in the areas to the south where Li Wen-ch'eng and his followers had risen up, was not applied.[120]

In retrospect, the assault on the Forbidden City by this handful of poorly armed and inexperienced rebels appears almost pathetic. It is true that in Shantung a few hundred men had entered two cities and massacred the residents and staff of the magistrates' yamen, but they had not even tried to occupy those cities. In Honan it took thousands, not hundreds, of men to seize and hold the city of Hua. The evidence suggests that the planning of the palace attack had been entirely unrealistic, and the responsibility for that planning lay with Lin Ch'ing. It seems to have been Lin's ambition that blinded him. He may have been the victim of his own propaganda, forced to attempt a deed commensurate with a "Patriarch of Latter Heaven and Heavenly Controller in Charge of the Faith," a deed that would outdo those of his colleagues and continue to earn him respect and deference from members of the Eight Trigrams. Lin Ch'ing ignored the weaknesses within his own group and the strengths of his opponents. The fact that he remained at home rather than leading his men into the palace is certainly not to his credit; his participation might actually have helped overcome the fragmented organization and lack of discipline that debilitated the attacking groups.

Under the best of circumstances, however, the rebels faced very difficult problems. The sheer physical presence of the Forbidden City put them at a disadvantage. After the dusty and crowded streets of village and city, the emptiness, the stillness, the dramatic colors, and the solidity of the buildings must have been overwhelming, almost paralyzing. The massive walls and gates and the immensity of the palace complex might be to an outsider an awe-inspiring maze and ultimately a trap. Even had the full complement of those sent by Lin Ch'ing been able to enter the palace, they would have still been outnumbered, and in terms of discipline, arms, and military experience, the rebels could not compare with the bannermen who served as palace guards. Other soldiers were stationed in great numbers all around Peking. Did the rebels not expect that they would be called in? Even had they been able to kill most of the palace personnel and members of the imperial family, could the survivors have held the four gates to the Forbidden City against large armies determined to enter?

Knowing nothing of the palace itself, Lin Ch'ing relied entirely on his eunuch pupils for assurances that this assault was possible. It is true, however, that there was some cause for their belief that the palace could be entered. Investigating the state of palace defenses after the event, the Chia-ch'ing Emperor, although proud of the quick suppression of the rebels, found much to criticize. For at least a year afterward, memorials and edicts were exchanged on ways to improve surveillance of the gates, to assure the availability of arms in good condition and in sufficient numbers, to regulate the movements of eunuchs in and out of the palace, and so forth.[121] Yet no matter how careless the palace staff had become, when pressed they rose to the occasion and responded swiftly and very vigorously. Unused to such violence, the imperial family and princes of the imperial clan could justly feel a surge of confidence in their ability to meet and deal with crises as men and as Manchus.

Looking at the Eight Trigram uprisings as a whole, the difficulties involved in turning these White Lotus sects into instruments of rebellion are striking. In order to prepare many groups of ordinary people for violent uprisings in different places on and not before a designated time, sect members had to begin to engage in dangerous and illegal activities that in themselves made discovery by government agents increasingly likely. The acquisition of the physical implements of rebellion involved risk. The stepped-up efforts by sect leaders to convince their followers of the rightness and inevitability of rebellion—to make them psychologically ready to give up what security they had and adopt a way of life built initially on violence— these were even more dangerous to the security of the movement as a whole. Friends and relatives and neighbors could not help but be aware of the tense, expectant, fearful, and excited behavior characteristic of believers about to become rebels. This mood spread outward in waves around the centers of sect activity, inevitably coming to official attention. In short, both the attitudes and physical objects which needed to be prepared in advance of the rebellion had to be and yet could not be secret.

Information about the "rebellious plot" traveled upward through individuals who served officially and unofficially as links between the government and the people. The eunuch who worked for the imperial family, the Chinese bondservant who served the Manchu elite, the servant in a wealthy household, the poor member of a rich lineage, the country neighbor of a gentry family, the degree-holding village schoolmaster, the semiofficial government agent in a village, the deputies of provincial officials stationed in market towns—these and other individuals had access to the official elite as other ordinary people did not, and this access made them possible conduits for information.

The near impossibility of secrecy and the existence of these upward channels meant that an extensive "plot" such as that of the Eight Trigrams could not be kept entirely secret. It was speed on the part of the rebels and slowness on the part of the government that allowed rebels to act without advance interference. As we have seen, if the officials were alerted to a possible threat, the seats of the Ch'ing government could be well protected by their high walls, men, and money. The Forbidden City, admittedly a special case, was defensible even in a surprise attack. By contrast, district cities operating normally were more vulnerable to sudden, violent attacks.

For those Eight Trigrams who survived the transition from the *an* (dark, secret) to the *ming* (bright, open) phase, an entirely new set of problems awaited them. The competition between these sects and the government, though indirect and muted in normal times, became now an open contest fought on the battlefield. Let us turn to that struggle.

PART FOUR

Survival: The Contest for
Popular Support

THE magistrate of Ch'ang-yuan district in southern Chihli had been surprised and killed by a band of Eight Trigram rebels in a village of that district on the 6th day of the 9th month of 1813. The following day, rebels who had secretly entered Hua city in northern Honan attacked the official compound there and then occupied the city and the adjacent port town of Tao-k'ou. Three days later, on the 10th, other rebels carried out surprise attacks on the magistrates' offices in Ting-t'ao and Ts'ao in southwestern Shantung but did not attempt to occupy either city. On the 15th, the date originally designated for these uprisings, another band of rebels entered the Forbidden City in Peking with the intention of seizing it but were instead killed or arrested.

During the rest of the 9th month the rebels in Shantung and southern Chihli formed small bands and were involved in a continuous search for food and supporters. Government soldiers were gradually mobilized and by the end of the month drove these rebels out of Shantung toward the west. From their base in Hua city and in villages nearby, the Eight Trigrams in Honan also went out in search of men and supplies. They attempted to seize the city of Chün but were unsuccessful. A large Ch'ing army was slowly assembled during the 10th month, and pressure was put on the Honan rebels from all sides, with the spearhead of the government's attack aimed at Hua city. Assisted by local militia, Ch'ing soldiers gradually recaptured rebel-held villages and, as surviving rebels fled into Hua city, regained control of the countryside. At the end of the 10th month the river port of Tao-k'ou was recaptured by the government and the encirclement and siege of Hua city was begun.

In order to escape, the rebel leader Li Wen-ch'eng took several thousand men and left the city. After first attempting to go toward Shantung, they were forced to swing south and then west and finally sought the comparative security of the mountain foothills on the Honan–Shansi border. Trapped there in a small fortified village, Li Wen-ch'eng and his men were surrounded and wiped out by pursuing soldiers late in the 11th month. The siege around Hua city had meanwhile tightened, and on the 10th day of the 12th month, when fifteen thousand soldiers from as far away as Manchuria had been assembled, the Ch'ing armies attacked and recaptured the city. The Eight Trigrams rebellion had lasted for three months and had cost the Ch'ing government some four million taels. More than one hundred thousand people had been involved in the uprising, some of them against their will, and at least seventy thousand had died.

Once the Eight Trigrams had risen in rebellion, the nature and scale of their undertaking changed radically. Committed sect members, now the core of a wider and more heterogeneous movement, had at once to hold their rebellion together and to defeat militarily the forces of the Ch'ing government. All else had been a prelude; this was the real test. We will look first at how the rebels tried to win popular support and at the life they offered to recruits. Then we will examine the problems that faced the Eight Trigram leaders as they tried to adapt their ambitious goals and strategies to the disappointing realities of their situation, and at the new life style enjoyed by these leaders. We will discuss in more conventional terms the Ch'ing suppression of the uprising, their use of both large armies and militia. Finally, we will look at the last days of the rebellion, Li Wen-ch'eng's flight from Hua and the bloody recapture of that city by Ch'ing forces. The following account, concentrating as it does not on the government but on the struggles and painful collapse of the rebel movement, should help us understand how the Eight Trigrams tried to survive as rebels and why they failed in this, their final metamorphosis.

ROUNDING UP SUPPORTERS

Once they had risen in rebellion, the size of the Eight Trigrams multiplied rapidly. Hsu An-kuo had about six hundred pupils who were involved in planning the uprising. Within one month, nearly six thousand rebels had been killed or captured in Shantung, and an equal number had allegedly fled the province.[1] The one or two thousand Eight Trigram sect members in Hua and Chün districts in Honan later attracted between seventy and eighty thousand followers and were in effective control of urban populations of an additional twenty thousand.[2] In short, the core of believers who initiated this rebellion amassed ten times as many new followers and eventually themselves constituted only a fraction of the total rebel population. How did they attract and secure the loyalty of these new recruits? How did they organize and direct them? To answer these questions we must look both at the occupied cities and at the villages in the countryside, for each presented the sect members and rebel leaders with somewhat different problems of recruitment.

Unfortunately, information about the occupation of Hua city is distressingly sparse. Only a few rebel leaders lived to be interrogated; the others died when the city was retaken in the 12th month. There are only a few descriptions of what this occupation meant for the inhabitants of the city and of the relationship between rebels and those "good people" (liang-min 良民) whose loyalty they hoped to win.

As we have seen, on the morning of 9/7 Li Wen-ch'eng's aides and pupils from Hua and Chün districts broke into the Hua yamen buildings and freed their leader. They attacked the symbols of Ch'ing authority, opening the jail, breaking into the treasury, destroying tax and household registers, and burning down the compound buildings.[3] Toward the resident Ch'ing officials they were equally fierce. Magistrate Chiang was able to escape, but his servants and relatives, thirty-seven people in all, were killed. The director of education was dragged from the well into which he had jumped and later killed together with seventeen members of his household. His corpse was thrown over the city wall, while the bodies of his relatives were simply left inside to rot. The rebels announced that anyone who tried to bury them would be killed. Director Lu's subordinate, the eighth-rank subdirector of schools, fared somewhat better. He claimed later that he had refused when the rebels tried to force him to serve as magistrate; but nevertheless he was merely imprisoned in an apothecary shop for the duration of the rebellion. His unwillingness to cooperate may have been exaggerated, for he was the only official so spared.[4] It is noteworthy that this rebel violence against Ch'ing officials extended automatically to their administrative assistants, relatives, visiting friends, and household servants, regardless of their age, sex, or social position. The prisoners, on the other hand, were freed by the Eight Trigrams and most of them appear to have joined the rebel cause.[5]

Initially rebel attitudes toward city residents were hostile. Following the yamen attack, bands of armed rebels rushed through the streets of the city, and if the following account is typical, they brought terror to the inhabitants of Hua. The Wei family belonged to the urban bourgeoisie: old Mr. Wei owned a store in the city where he sold shoes and hats, his son managed a wineshop, a nephew had earned sheng-yuan status, and a grandson had been studying for the civil service examinations since he was twelve years old. Early on the morning of the 7th, just as it was getting light, the wineshop owner, Wei Ping-ch'ün, was awakened by the shouting of the ti-pao out on the street. The constable cried out that members of a White Lotus sect had rebelled and come into the city, and he told everyone to grab clubs and other weapons and come to chase and capture the rebels. Wei Ping-ch'ün followed the *ti-pao* toward the yamen compound, but when they found themselves being fired upon with rifles, the attempted resistance was abandoned and everyone scattered. Wei immediately left the city, apparently not even returning to check on the welfare of his family. His father also left the city while escape was still possible, and Wei Ping-ch'ün's wife and son were left at home unprotected.

Later that morning, when the young man was at his studies as usual, waiting for his tutor to arrive, seemingly unaware of the attack on the yamen, he suddenly heard sounds of great confusion in the streets. Having finished at the government offices, the rebels had now dispersed through the city. Young Wei related: "Then some people shoved open our gate and ten or twenty rebels came running in. I rushed inside the house but they ran after me. They grabbed a lot of our clothing and supplies of food. They had knives and were going to kill me when my mother cried out, 'He is my only son. Spare him!' But then the rebels stabbed my mother three times and she fell to the ground. They bound me and took me away with them." After the city was retaken, surviving members of this family found that their house had been destroyed and the boy's great-grandmother, grandmother, uncle, and two aunts were all dead.[6] Obviously official and urban leaders were caught by surprise and were unable to mobilize effectively against the Eight Trigrams. If those with money and power, such as the magistrate or the Weis, chose to flee at the outset rather than to resist, it is not surprising that those with less leverage acquiesced to the new state of affairs.

As the Eight Trigrams occupied the city, property was confiscated, buildings were seized, and city residents were forced to serve the rebels. Although there does not appear to have been a general massacre as the sect members themselves had predicted, nevertheless assistance and active participation in the rebellion were demanded and those who refused were summarily killed. The rebel leader Huang P'an-kung, for example, was given charge of a team of two hundred men and sent out to search the city for valuables. As they were confiscating the property of a certain Chang family, Mrs. Chang screamed curses at them. Huang thereupon ordered his men to kill her and then the twelve other members of her household.[7]

The young son of the Wei family, on the other hand, was one of many who chose instead to obey the Eight Trigrams. He was bound and taken to the courtyard of a store taken over by the rebels. There he and several dozen other men—all also bound—were imprisoned for several days and so given time to consider their options, which were not numerous. "A rebel came who was armed with a knife. He asked us if we would obey his orders or not. Those who did not want to obey, he explained, had merely to say so—but they would be killed on the spot. So all of us agreed to comply and chorused yes! Then they untied us."[8] Those whose compliance was given only grudgingly and who could not be fully trusted were given commissary jobs involving the procuring and preparing of food for rebel leaders and for the city population and fodder for the livestock.[9] Sang Te, for example, had been stopped on the road by a rebel band outside a village near the city. "They wouldn't let him pass and forced him to go with them into Hua city. There he heated water and cooked for them. They said they would kill him if he didn't cooperate."[10]

In addition to the dedicated rebels and their families, who moved into the safety of Hua city in increasing numbers,[11] and the able-bodied men who were useful to the rebels, a large portion of the city population consisted of women, children, and old people. Though obviously important as symbols of popular support for their cause, these dependent groups were of limited practical use to the rebels; nonetheless they required attention, food, and shelter. Children in particular appear to have been left unharmed as the following not untypical testimony from a child who lived in Tao-k'ou suggests: "In the ninth month of [1813], a White Lotus sect came in rebellion to Tao-k'ou. They came in the south gate killing people. My grandmother told me to flee, but a large group of rebels came and made me and my grandmother go with them. Since she was over seventy years old and could not walk, they killed her. They seized me but did not kill me because I am a child."[12] Homeless children slept in broken-down buildings or near the city wall and lived by begging and by eating the offerings still being placed in the city temples.[13] In general, however, the rebel leaders established a system of procuring, cooking, and distributing food to the city residents. Survivors testified that they were given something to eat once and sometimes twice a day; this food was at times precooked (steamed dumplings are mentioned in one instance) but in general consisted of rice or millet in daily allowances.[14]

The city of Hua became increasingly crowded as the rebellion progressed. The original population appears to have been about ten thousand. Nearly sixty thousand, a third of them women and children, were living there when the city was retaken in the 12th month.[15] Raiding expeditions brought back provisions and supporters from the countryside, rebels from nearby areas fled into the city, and all contributed to the swelling population. The disruption and confusion of life in the city of Hua during the three months of rebel occupation could only have been compounded by this influx of residents.

Nevertheless, by occupying Hua and Tao-k'ou, the Eight Trigrams had put themselves in control of large stores of grain. Inside the cities grain was commandeered from homes, shops, and markets.[16] When Tao-k'ou was being attacked during the 10th month, the rebels moved all the provisions accumulated in that grain storage depot into Hua city. As a result, even after Hua itself was besieged, the inhabitants—despite the increased numbers—were in no immediate danger of being starved out.[17]

During the entire three months Hua was occupied the Eight Trigrams guarded the gates to the city and permitted no inhabitants to leave. Rebels themselves, identified by their white cloth sashes or by the password "Be Victorious," and others who were involved in importing grain into the city for food (and who may have been under surveillance), were permitted to pass through the east gate, the only one open for traffic. The initial period of strict control, perhaps terror, was probably followed by a general relaxation of discipline as the situation in the city stabilized. Later, however, as government pressure on the city mounted, especially after Hua was besieged, controls over the city population tightened again. Despite unspecified stern measures to keep them from leaving, there were people who climbed onto the city wall and let themselves down on the other side on ropes in order to surrender themselves to the Ch'ing authorities.[18]

Prior to the uprising, new sect members were in some measure converted to the White Lotus religion and bound together organizationally by pupil–teacher bonds. The prophecy of apocalypse and death for nonbelievers was strong encouragement for joining, and yet secrecy had necessitated private and low-keyed proselytizing. After sect members had publicly declared themselves rebels, they were still bound to one another by these ideas and ties. In contrast, new recruits joined the Eight Trigrams on an entirely different basis. They did not take as their teachers men with whom they had established a firm personal relationship. If they were taught meditation, yoga, boxing, or healing techniques, there is no mention of it in the historical record. Their knowledge of White Lotus ideology, even the ideas of apocalypse and millennium, was probably quite superficial. There is no indication that any kind of religious instruction was arranged in the occupied cities or in the countryside. The force of the millenarian message of the Eight Trigrams was perhaps more terrifying as a prediction; once manifested in events, the prophecy became more or less convincing in direct ratio to the progress of the rebellion itself. Success would generate confidence and momentum, failure would even more speedily breed pessimism and doubt. But in either case the new recruit's understanding of the historical vision of the White Lotus sects would not be profound, and as a result the religious message of the movement as a whole was greatly diluted once the rebellion began.

Although the Eight Trigrams were able to secure control over the inhabitants of Hua and Tao-k'ou, their fate ultimately depended on their success in the countryside. There it was necessary not only to dominate and control territory, but also to continuously attract large numbers of new supporters. It was not enough merely to survive the mounting Ch'ing counterattack; the Eight Trigrams had also to grow vigorously and to generate and maintain the momentum and the appearance of a victorious movement.

This kind of success was in large measure dependent on the free and effective use of violence by the rebels. The Eight Trigrams had used force to destroy the symbols of Ch'ing authority, killing officials, burning buildings, and occupying walled administrative and commercial centers. To survive, the rebels would have to eliminate local opposition, defeat Ch'ing armies on the battlefield, and resupply themselves with food and weapons; all required the use of force. Equally important, the unrestrained violence and even brutality that was generated by rebellion and that marked the life style of the rebels would themselves contribute to the persuasiveness of the rebel cause. This violence not only exposed weaknesses in the Ch'ing "order" and commanded fear and respect from the population at large, it laid the groundwork for the subsequent recruitment of many who would not normally have joined a rebellious group.

Any disruption of the routine of normal life in and of itself encouraged people to reassess their habits and values; when combined with the presence of an openly advocated alternative to the status quo, such dislocations multiplied and further unraveled the fabric of normal life. The Chinese called such a condition *luan* 亂 (disorder, chaos, confusion), and it was a state of affairs greatly feared by those advocates of the established order who made up the ruling elite in

China. The appearance of the armed and determined Eight Trigram rebels accompanied and created disorder, and it was in the rebels' interest to shatter the status quo and so make possible a realignment of loyalties. The fact of this ongoing rebellion, an alternative to and in open defiance of the government, created a tension that forced each person affected to reappraise his interests. In such a referendum, the Ch'ing system might collapse, or it might be further strengthened by a strong show of approval. In either case, there was no hope of success for the rebels without loosening and then redirecting traditional loyalties.

In areas where the Eight Trigrams rose in rebellion, the local gentry often took the initiative of organizing militia to defend their homes against the rebels. By attacking and defeating these forces, the Trigrams were not only eliminating their enemies, they were discrediting the local pillars of the Ch'ing order, and they did so with vigor. In Shantung, for example, a family named K'ung had rallied the people of their village in support of the government. To punish them, Trigram rebels came there deliberately and killed the members of that family and everyone in their village, more than five hundred people. In Honan, the rebel Wang Liang-tao had come with his band to a village where he urged the residents to join him. He was met instead by active resistance led by a *sheng-yuan* who had organized his fellow villagers into a militia, and was driven away. Wang Liang-tao did not forget this challenge. Later he brought his teacher, Chen Trigram King Sung K'e-chün, and a force of several thousand men back to that village, and the rebels looted and burned it down.[19]

The Eight Trigrams did not restrict the use of violence to those who opposed them in battle. The decision to take up the life of a man in rebellion against the state was a liberation for the individual from the constraints of normal life, and one dimension of this new freedom was the possibility of venting through violence one's grievances, grudges, and hatreds. Rebels captured later testified readily to having used their new power to attack and kill personal enemies, particularly those who had previously refused to cooperate with them, and not surprisingly many of these enemies were members of the local elite.

We have seen that when the rebels originally attacked Ts'ao city, the leader Hsiao Han-san went directly from the district yamen to the residences of some people he knew who had refused to join their sect: he and a pupil beat them up and robbed them.[20] The sect teacher Hsu An-kuo stated that when he took command of his pupils, the first thing he did was to lead his men to the residence of an old enemy of his, a military *chin-shih* named Hsu (perhaps a relative?), where they killed that man and the members of his family.[21] The rebel Tsung Yuan-te described another incident in which an unsuccessful attempt had been made to recruit a military *sheng-yuan* and a *chien-sheng* from Tsung's village. These degree-holders had refused to cooperate with the Eight Trigrams, and later a rebel force came to the village to show their anger and burned these men's houses and killed them and their families.[22]

One of the villages in Chin-hsiang district that was attacked by rebels was the residence of a *sheng-yuan* named Li Chiu-piao. It had been Li who had reported the suspicious behavior of sect members in his village to the district authorities in the 6th month of 1813; this report had led directly to the investigations of Magistrate Wu and to the subsequent arrest of the sect leader Ts'ui Shih-chün and about fifty of his pupils. The Li family, aware that their actions might call for reprisals, had left their homes in the countryside early in the 9th month and moved into the district city. Later they learned that the rebels had come to Li Chiu-piao's village, and to revenge their colleagues, had killed the seven members of the Li household who had remained behind, even destroying a coffin that was there awaiting burial, and burned not only the house but the entire village.[23]

Although rebel attacks on members of the local elite are recorded with particular thoroughness in the source material, there is no question that the Eight Trigrams used equal violence against ordinary people. Old enemies were punished, uncooperative residents of rebel-occupied villages were eliminated, and support for the rebel cause was often forced at gunpoint. Children whose parents were harmed by the rebels testified later with similar stories, of which the following are typical. Wang Kuei-ni was a young girl from a village outside Hua city. When the Eight Trigram rebels came to her village, her older brother was killed by them. Her father and another brother fled (or perhaps were frightened into joining). She and her mother and her sisters-in-law, separated from the men, were forced to go into Hua city. There her mother jumped into the water (perhaps a well) and drowned. One sister-in-law became ill and died; the other killed herself.[24]

Liu Hsi-r, a ten-year-old girl from another village, described her experiences:

Last year hundreds of White Lotus sect people came and surrounded our village. A dozen or so rebels came to our house to take our grain. They asked my grandfather, my father, and my mother if they would join them or not. They said no. The rebels tied the three of them up and said they were taking them into Hua city to kill them. My twelve-year-old sister Lien-r and I were terrified and ran and hid in the muddy waters of the marsh nearby. That evening the rebels found us and forced us to go into the city too. . . . We went to the gate of our godmother's house and next to the wall we saw our grandfather's, our father's, and our mother's bodies. That is when we knew that they had been killed. Dogs had torn their clothes apart and eaten at their hands and feet, but you could still recognize the faces.[25]

On the other hand, violence was not always necessary. The threat of force or simply the arrival of the rebels themselves and the atmosphere of *luan*, confusion and disruption, which they symbolized could be frightening enough. T'ien Lien-yuan and his family were in the process of gathering their belongings and moving away from their now-endangered home when members of the Eight Trigrams arrived in their village. "Suddenly nine men appeared, mounted on horseback. They told us that the White Lotus sect really did not kill people, and so there was no need for us to run off; all they wanted was some food to eat. But along with everyone else in the village, I was terrified and rushed to find a place to hide. Later on those men on horseback left. We were talking about it afterward and [someone] said he thought he recognized one of the men—he looked like Chao Erh of Wang-chia village."[26]

It is important to remember that the rebels had a decided advantage over villagers whom they encountered. The Eight Trigram bands were concentrated groups of able-bodied men, often mounted on horseback, armed, and prepared for violence. The villagers by contrast included many people unable to resist effectively (women, children, old people). Villagers were not by law permitted to have weapons in their homes, and if taken by surprise even the men were not organized for resistance. (The great importance of officially sponsored militia organizations was that they encouraged village leaders to take an active role and, by supplying food and weapons, enabled the men of the village to put aside their normal tasks and concentrate on fighting.) The rebel life itself was an advertisement for their cause and a way of winning adherents. Those who joined the Trigrams could participate in their roaming and freebooting and could share in the opportunity to eat, dress, travel, and behave publicly as important people. This opportunity for power and prestige was a strong magnet to many, even in the face of mounting Ch'ing opposition.

The rebels offered not only freedom from normal restraints and access to new power; equally important, they provided a source of food in a time of drought and famine. The north China plain has always been subject to a vicious cycle of flood and drought, both accompanied by famine, and, as we have seen, Hua and Chün districts had had a series of bad years (with only a short respite in between) for at least a decade.[27] The other districts affected by the rebellion had not suffered as long, but they too had been hurt by the drought that began in the early spring of 1813.[28] The rain that finally fell in this drought-stricken area during the 8th and 9th months, coming as it did in too great a volume and too late to improve significantly the agricultural situation, probably only contributed to the disaster conditions.[29] In and after the 9th month, as winter approached, the people's desperation could only increase. The Eight Trigram rebels, on the other hand, were from the start relatively rich in food supplies. They used violence with impunity to take what they pleased, and their occupied cities and villages became storehouses for grain and provisions.

As the Trigrams moved about the countryside, plundering with strength and confidence, they surely tempted many famine victims into joining their movement. Indeed, the quickest (and least permanent) source of rebel support came from the bands of men who, while unwilling to join the Eight Trigrams movement, used the occasion and the cover of rebellion to undertake their own robbing and looting. One rather unlikely rebel was a man called Liu Chü from Ch'eng-wu district in Shantung who had been a seventh-rank preceptor at the Imperial Academy. Nevertheless, when Liu saw the district city under curfew, other cities attacked by rebels, and bands of people plundering in the countryside, he arranged with his son and nephew to take advantage of the situation. Following Liu Chü's instructions, the two younger men organized the people of the village, who were probably in economic difficulties, and led them out to take what they wanted from others. At least sixteen men were nvolvied, most of them surnamed Liu and probably members of Liu Chü's lineage. Liu composed a rhyme or slogan of encouragement, but he himself remained at home. The others brought their booty back for him to divide up. This group went out many times, "preying on adjacent villages," but when word of this reached the magistrate, he

was able to make arrests without encountering resistance.[30] There
were surely many other groups like this one whose appearance, often
indistinguishable from those who called themselves Eight Trigrams,
served to bolster the size of the rebel population and to contribute to
the breakdown of law and order in the countryside. The support
provided by these looters was, however, only transitory. As government control was reestablished (and with it, often, famine relief),
these bands, especially those on the fringes of the rebellion, simply
melted away and disappeared.

Given their relative power, it is not surprising that many villagers
chose willingly to join the Eight Trigrams. The Shantung sect leader
Chu Ch'eng-kuei was leading his band of men from place to place in
search for food and supporters and came to the fortified village of the
Pi family in Ke-tse district. Members of that family related what
followed:

> On 9/13 the Chen Trigram sect head Chu Ch'eng-kuei and his
> younger brothers . . . came to Pi-chia village, leading a group
> of men. They burned down the gate to the village and raised a
> white banner on which was written "Entrusted by Heaven to
> Prepare the Way." They forced everyone to accept this. Be-
> cause it was difficult to resist so numerous an enemy, and because
> everyone was afraid of being killed, Pi Kuang-ju [the senior
> member of the lineage that dominated the village] led the others
> in bowing and welcoming Chu Ch'eng-kuei.

The eagerness with which the Pi family joined the Eight Trigrams
became apparent when with little hesitation eighty men in the
family left home to plunder under the banner of Trigram Lord
Chu.[31] In this case, the threat of violence and the promise of plunder
were enough to win the defection of the entire village, and this
example gives credence to an official report that the Eight Trigrams
sometimes "practiced a policy of not killing or burning at all in order
to gain popular support."[32]

Although the great mass of followers of the Eight Trigrams were
apparently motivated by combinations of fear, hope, greed, and
hunger, there were also those who had previously belonged to a
White Lotus sect and who dared commit themselves to rebellion only
after others had taken the first step. These believers may not have
been very numerous, but they did supplement the pool of available
leaders. A believer named Wang Sen described the arrival of an
Eight Trigram band in his village soon after the occupation of Hua

city. At that time many of the sect leaders had returned to their own villages rather than remain in the city, and there they raised white banners to proclaim their presence. Wang Sen had, in the meantime, remained at home to see what would happen.

> On 9/10 [the rebel] Chang San-yang led men from his village to [Wang Sen's home of] Wang-chia village nearby. Chang was calling himself the Ch'ien Mansion King. He announced that the Hua magistrate had been killed and he urged the villagers to join his sect and thus avoid a similar fate. Some villagers like [so-and-so] heard this and were afraid, and so they kotowed to Chang San-yang. Chang San-yang then distributed white cloth to the group so that each person could tie some around his waist, and he gave each household a small white banner to be placed at its gateway. He told everyone that if they met with other rebels they were to say the password "Be Victorious." He made Wang Sen an important leader with the title Ch'ien Trigram Lord, and gave him a large white banner on which were written the words "Ch'ien Trigram Lord Wang Sen, Entrusted by Heaven to Prepare the Way." Wang Sen was put in charge of sixty men, including those [from his village] who had been coerced. Chang San-yang also named [three other men] as leaders. Each of them led a group and all went out to take supplies and provisions.[33]

The integration of new supporters into the hierarchy of titled positions created by Li Wen-ch'eng and Lin Ch'ing was as simple as the brief instructions about banners and slogans and identifying sashes. The recruits were simply assigned to groups under the trigram kings and lords. The eighty-odd members of the Pi family in Shantung who joined the band of Trigram Lord Chu Ch'eng-kuei were divided into groups of ten men, each one having a designated leader, with one man, Pi Ch'ou (畢臭, Stinking Pi), appointed as overall leader. Chu Ch'eng-kuei gave Pi Ch'ou white cloth and instructed him to distribute it; the men were to tear the cloth into strips to make identifying white sashes. Thus organized, these male members of the Pi family left their village and went on with Chu's band. As they came to other villages and found more men willing to join them, they incorporated them in the same manner. The new recruits from each village were split into groups of ten to twenty men, each with one leader. These additional groups were also assigned to Pi Ch'ou's command until he had a hundred men in his charge.[34]

Another rebel described a similar arrangement of men into simple ten-man groups. In this case, Liu Kao-yü was assigned to carry a small triangular white banner and lead ten men. His teacher in the sect carried a large square white banner and led one hundred men, ten groups of ten; his teacher's teacher had a large triangular white banner and was in command of a thousand men. The sect member Chao Te stated that his teacher had given him a small banner and instructions to bring ten men to participate in the rebellion. We have seen that those of Lin Ch'ing's followers who were part of the palace attack likewise came into Peking in groups of roughly ten, each with a leader identified by his banner.[35] It is not surprising that this simple decimal system should be employed, nor is it surprising that, as was the case in Peking, the actual size of each group varied and the neat theoretical arrangement was not reflected in reality.

As we have seen, the Eight Trigrams used banners made of white cloth to signal their different levels of organization. Lesser leaders had unmarked banners or banners reading either "Commander" (ling 令) or "Commander [so-and-so]." Higher leaders had large and small banners of different shapes on which were written the Eight Trigrams' public slogan, "Entrusted by Heaven to Prepare the Way." Those rebels with titles had this slogan, their titles, and their names written on their banners. Some leaders made their banners of silk rather than cotton. The rank-and-file rebels looked to these white banners on the road and in battle to find their place and instructions.[36]

New recruits were assigned to a leader and given weapons (usually spears or knives, but sometimes guns) and, in lieu of a uniform, white sashes. Four men testified that a portion of the hair on the underside of their queue was shaved off as another secret identifying sign, but this may not have been common practice.[37] Chang Wei-han lived in a village of Hua district.

> On 9/8 [one day after Hua city was occupied] Li Mei, a sect rebel from Chiao village came there riding in a cart and carrying a large white banner on which was written "Chen Mansion Lord, Entrusted by Heaven to Prepare the Way." He was leading seventy or eighty men. They surrounded the village where Chang Wei-han lived and ordered the villagers to come along with them if they wanted to avoid being killed. They seized Chang Wei-han, and because he didn't want to die, he cooperated. Li Mei took them all back to his own village. Behind Chang Wei-han's queue they burned away some of his

hair with moxa and gave him a white banner. They put him in
charge of the village gate. Three days later Chang Wei-han
accompanied Li Mei [and others] and went to join Li Wen-
ch'eng's followers in attacking Chün city.[38]

Most of the men who joined the Eight Trigrams were assigned
military tasks. Several peasants testified that they had been forced
to serve on the front lines and were given a special name meaning
"those who get there first."[39] Those followers not involved in fighting
or guard duty, which is to say those who were older or less trusted,
were put to work doing menial tasks in the rebel camps, often under
supervision. They cut fodder, fed and cared for the livestock, ground
flour and prepared meals, drove carts, or carried baggage for rebel
leaders.[40]

Because of the difficulty of securing commitment from "good
people" forced into rebellion, the Eight Trigrams often used violence
to seal this relationship. New recruits were encouraged (or compelled) to demonstrate loyalty to their new leaders, and the more
"crimes" in which they were involved, the greater their stake in the
rebel cause. Trigram leaders used recent recruits to carry out threats
against those who were less willing to join up. Ch'en Chin-kuei, a
herdsman, and Ch'en Ch'en, a butcher, told of their experiences. An
Eight Trigrams band had come to their village and had forced many
of the villagers, including the two Ch'ens, to go along. Ch'en Chin-
kuei was given a musket and Ch'en Ch'en an iron spear. The following day, the rebel band and their new members went to another
village looking for food and supporters. Some of those ordered to join
the rebels refused, and so the rebel commander ordered Ch'en Chin-
kuei to use his gun and shoot one of them as an example to the
others. Ch'en fired and killed the man. When this did not produce
the desired effect, Ch'en Ch'en was told to use his spear and kill
another of the villagers, but he merely stabbed him in the leg without
killing him.[41] On a different occasion, another man, similarly
"forced" to join, was instructed to use the knife with which he had
been supplied to execute two prisoners.[42] A recruit named Wang
Wen-cho watched his new comrades as they tied up and stabbed
a recalcitrant individual to death with their spears, and then he
was given the task of cutting off the dying man's head with his
knife.[43]

There were many who, having lived and fought with the rebels,
eventually decided to abandon their cause. It was particularly after
military defeats that rebel followers fled for their lives, and this

occurred with increasing frequency as Ch'ing armies arrived on the scene. Some, probably those who had truly been forced to join against their will, took aggressive action against their captors. Ch'eng Chin-hsiu, for example, arranged with several relatives, all of whom had been compelled to join the same Eight Trigrams band, and made specific plans to go over to the government side. When a well-organized militia force advanced to attack their camp, Ch'eng left secretly, surrendered himself to the militia commander, and promised to rally the others and fight for the government the following day as a fifth column within the camp. Ch'eng then crept back into the rebel village, gathered and hid over two dozen muskets; the next day during the battle, he started a fire inside the camp and, arming himself and the others, turned on the rebels and killed at least one of them. (He later joined the militia and fought against the Eight Trigrams on several other occasions.)[44]

Although it is true that the Eight Trigrams gathered over one hundred thousand supporters in the course of their rebellion, it is important to remember that the country villages of the north China plain were affected by the rebel presence with far less concentrated intensity than the residents of the occupied cities. The sudden rebel seizure of the major commercial centers of the region, the occupation of villages throughout the area, the disruption of communication, transportation, and marketing—not to mention the fear generated by the presence or merely the rumored presence of bands of armed men killing, looting, and burning as they pleased—must have been a frightening experience. Nevertheless, comparatively few people were directly involved in the rebellion itself. Hua district, which felt the rebellion most intensely, was densely populated and had between 700,000 and 800,000 inhabitants.[45] Admittedly rough estimates suggest that only about 10 percent of these people came in direct contact with the Eight Trigrams.[46] Even if the actual figure were two or three times as large, we can still see that the great majority were not ultimately forced to confront the rebels personally.

If some Eight Trigram supporters were hungry or displaced individuals, as certainly seems likely,[47] there is some evidence that famine alone was not a sufficient condition for successful recruitment. When Li Wen-ch'eng took a band of several thousand followers and left Hua city early in the 11th month, he led these men in a broad semicircle through the districts of Wei-hui prefecture in northern Honan. The districts through which the rebels passed had suffered greatly during the famine of 1813. Feng-ch'iu, Yang-wu, Yen-chin and Huo-chia (see map p. 252) had all experienced severe drought, and in Hsin-hsiang and Hui districts this had been compounded by flooding in the fall of that year.[48] One would expect—and certainly Li Wen-ch'eng hoped—that Li's band might have gained new support in these districts, perhaps enough to infuse new vigor into the faltering uprising. Yet this did not happen. Rebel numbers increased hardly at all: Li rallied no more than fifteen hundred or two thousand men at the most in the course of his flight.[49] Apparently neither the persuasiveness of the rebel cause nor the pressures of economic distress was compelling enough to induce large numbers of people to join the rebels as they had done earlier in districts to the east.

It is perhaps of interest that there is no evidence of the wholesale defection to the rebels of preexisting ethnic or occupational minority groups as fueled the fires of rebellion at other times and places in China. The reason for this may be very simply the absence of such groups in north China, which was relatively speaking an economically and racially homogeneous region. The rebels could rely on no ties between their members other than those created by the sect organization and the rebel hierarchy, and the fragility of these networks, particularly in the face of powerful opposition, contributed to the weakness of the Eight Trigrams. In contrast, to suppress this rebellion the Ch'ing government could and did rely on social organizations of great strength—the government bureaucracy, two separate military establishments, and time-honored local networks of gentry power and prestige. Before turning to those defenders of the established order, however, let us first return to the outbreak of this rebellion and look at Li Wen-ch'eng and his colleagues and at the attempts of these Eight Trigrams to deal with their new mass following and with government opposition.

REVISED STRATEGIES

Few large-scale undertakings proceed according to schedule, and that of the Eight Trigrams was no exception. From the moment their plans were formalized during the Tao-k'ou meeting in the summer of 1813, sect leaders were forced to make adjustments and alterations. Indeed, the lack of coordination between the various uprisings, the failure of many groups to act at all, the fiasco in Peking, Li Wen-ch'eng's injuries, disputes among the leaders, and successive defeats on the battlefield made it necessary for the rebel leaders to reappraise continually their options and their goals.

It is not clear exactly what was supposed to happen after the district officials had been killed in a dozen cities, the Forbidden City taken by Lin Ch'ing, and with assistance from Li Wen-ch'eng the emperor killed and Peking occupied. We will probably never know. Indeed, we cannot be sure that the decision to occupy the city of Hua—a tactic of major consequence for the course of the rebellion— was even part of these original plans. It may have been Li Wen-ch'eng's unforeseen arrest two weeks before the scheduled date that determined this particular strategy. It was Li's relatives and chief pupils who made this decision, arranging to change the date and move ahead of schedule to free their leader and occupy the city, but there was evidently some last-minute disagreement with this plan. On the day before the rescheduled attack, a sect member of long standing from the Hua area, a man called Wang Hsueh-tao, tried to persuade the others to abandon the idea of seizing the city. Wang told them that "he had a thorough knowledge of the areas of war, and he believed that after they had broken open the jail, they should not occupy the district city. If they were to occupy it, then they would certainly be surrounded and attacked by government soldiers and eventually all killed." Wang considered himself an expert on military strategy—he even carried a small book in which he had written down brief accounts of campaigns and battles in the past—but to his disgust, his advice was ignored.[50]

On 9/7 those Eight Trigram sect members from Hua and Chün districts entered Hua city and released Li Wen-ch'eng and Niu Liang-ch'en from the jail. They sealed off and took control of the city and then moved immediately to do the same to the nearby port city of Tao-k'ou. Tao-k'ou was a grain and rice storage depot and an important commercial center for the region; it served Chün and Hua in particular and was located on the Wei River, halfway between the two cities and no more than ten miles from either.[51] Sect members from the area were obviously familiar with the place and its resources, and it was there that the summer meeting of the assembled Eight Trigram leaders had taken place. Using at least two thousand men, the rebels occupied Tao-k'ou on 9/7 or 9/8, and if they met with resistance, none is recorded. Rebel bands moved across the Wei River into the villages of southern Chün district, raiding some and setting up camp in others.[52] Similarly, Eight Trigram bands appeared and took over villages elsewhere in Hua district, to the east and south of the city particularly.

At this stage, it was still their intention to try to rendezvous with Lin Ch'ing in Peking: one rebel commented that "from Hua we wanted to go toward Chün, and then cross the mountains and go to Peking."[53] In any event it was strategically important to the rebels that government authorities be driven out of Chün city. Chün was only fifteen miles from Hua; to have had hostile armies there would have been (and eventually was) too close for comfort. On the other hand, for the rebels to have held all three cities—Hua, Tao-k'ou and Chün—and to have controlled the Wei River running between them would have strengthened their position immeasurably, whether or not they chose to go on to Peking. In short, Chün city was very important. It therefore seems somewhat surprising that no attempt had been made to attack Chün secretly on 9/7 simultaneously with Hua. More than a dozen high-ranking sect leaders came from that district, including Li Wen-ch'eng's adopted son and at least one trigram king.[54] Perhaps the leaders had decided to concentrate all their strength on freeing Sect Master Li and occupying Hua, preferring to try later to take Tao-k'ou and Chün by military force. It

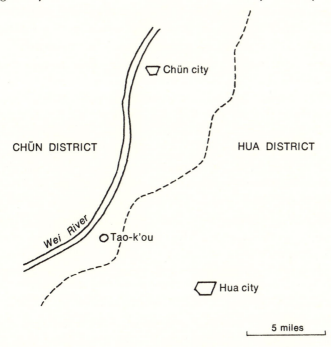

Hua and Chün cities

is true that once Li Wen-ch'eng had been arrested, their advantage of surprise was diminished, for Magistrate Chiang of Hua had notified his colleague in Chün by the 5th day of the month, and that magistrate had begun immediately to make his own investigations and arrests.[55] Nevertheless, the rebels may have miscalculated, for even a very careful and stealthy entry into Chün and elimination of the magistrate would have been far easier than the open military attack on the city that now became the rebels' only recourse.

As soon as Hua city was seized on 9/7, Magistrate Chu Feng-sen of Chün closed his city and readied what defenses were available. Following Li Wen-ch'eng's directions, Niu Liang-ch'en, together with other rebel leaders and several thousand men, moved swiftly to capture the walled city. Fresh from their successes in Hua and Tao-k'ou, they camped on the slopes of the low hills to the south and east of Chün and blockaded the stone bridge across the moat that constituted the city's main entrance. Other small bands assembled in and occupied villages nearby.[56] The city was defended only by a small garrison force; nevertheless, the initial rebel attacks (inadequately documented in the sources) were completely unsuccessful. Despite initiative, momentum, and superior numbers, the Eight Trigrams were unable to break into the city. Was this a result of their lack of military expertise, a failure of nerve, or a testimony to the security of a walled city no matter how lightly staffed?

Although the rebels threatened Chün city for ten days they were unable to seize it; finally, on 9/17, the first outside detachment of Ch'ing soldiers arrived. A thousand Green Standard soldiers from western Honan reached the outskirts of Chün, attacked, captured the main western entrance to the city, and cleared that area of rebels.[57] Another thousand soldiers arrived later, and Niu Liang-ch'en had to call for reinforcements from Hua. By the 26th, there were eighty-five hundred rebels, including some who had come from Shantung, camped south of Chün with cannon now in place ready to attack again. They were opposed by only two thousand government soldiers, and yet the rebels were still unable even to regain their previous positions, much less to capture the city. They attacked on 9/26, storming the main government camp located on a hill just to the south of Chün, sending a smaller force to locate and destroy the official supply depot. The government position was a good one, however, and the rebels lost a thousand men that day without being able to dislodge the Ch'ing forces from their hilltop. Although government soldiers did not dare pursue the rebels as they withdrew, they had in fact carried the day.[58] This was the last rebel attempt to take Chün city. They had fought there for two weeks, lost between three and four thousand men, and been unable to achieve their objective.[59] Furthermore, this prolonged and ultimately unsuccessful contest for Chün city gave the Ch'ing government a place on which to concentrate their counterattack and a chance to gain a militarily and psychologically important victory.

Thus, by late in the 9th month, rebel leaders must have realized that a victorious northern expedition was virtually impossible. Niu Liang-ch'en had planned an attack on the prefectural city of Wei-hui and had sent scouts there to survey the situation; this plan was now abandoned.[60] The rebels may even have heard rumors about the abortive attack on the Forbidden City and of Lin Ch'ing's death, for the emperor had ordered that Lin's head be taken south and displayed publicly so that all would know he had been executed. More important, Ch'ing soldiers had begun moving into northern Honan with the specific aim of defending the urban centers and blocking the rebels' path. Official soldiers arriving at Chün city made good use of its proximity to Tao-k'ou and Hua, and during the 10th month they gradually reclaimed rebel-held villages and closed in on the rebel strongholds.

Increasingly pressed on their northwestern flank, the rebels considered expansion toward the south instead and sent out scouts in that direction. In the middle of the 10th month, as government pressure intensified, the rebel general Wang Chin-tao told some of his men to go to and cross the Yellow River. "If the soldiers on the south bank are not numerous, then the rest of us will come and we will all cross the river," he told them.[61] Such a crossing would have been even easier once the river had frozen over, but regular government patrols along the Yellow River, the absence of boats for crossing, and the presence of heavy concentrations of soldiers in the area of the provincial capital of K'ai-feng (see map p. 228) were effective barriers against rebel movement in that direction. Another plan considered and then rejected during this same troubled 10th month was movement toward the southwest. A scout captured in western Honan confessed that his superiors were considering occupying the prefectural city of Huai-ch'ing, located about one hundred miles southwest of Hua, and "digging in there." "Huai-ch'ing prefecture," he said, "relies upon the T'ai-hang mountains at the north and is protected by the Yellow River to the south. Saltpeter and iron weapons are its chief products. Its territory can be readily defended and fought for."[62] This plan was thwarted by movement of government soldiers into this part of Honan and into adjacent Shansi and by the presence of Ch'ing armies and well-organized militia along the western border of Hua district. The rebels' two-week abortive attempt to take Chün city had eaten up their momentum and spent the advantage of surprise and preparedness that they had had with regard to their official opponents. In consequence, they soon found themselves blocked to the north, west, and south.

Even without such problems, these could not have been easy weeks for Li Wen-ch'eng. The injuries to his feet and legs received at the hands of Magistrate Chiang were extremely painful; he could not walk and remained confined to his bed during this entire period, living in his own village, which had been occupied by the rebels. He appears to have given orders and made decisions, but he was necessarily dependent on those close to him for information and for the execution of his instructions. Sometime during this time, Li's adopted son Liu Ch'eng-chang left Hua and was not seen again. In his thirties, Liu was active in the sect and had been a leader during the occupation of Hua city. It seems very probable that Li had sent Liu north to Peking to find out about Lin Ch'ing and to inform Lin about events in Honan. In any event Liu vanished and never returned.[63] For Li Wen-ch'eng this meant the loss of one of his most trusted aides and close associates.

Equally unfortunate for Li was the death, during the battle for Chün city, of his assistant, Yü K'e-ching.[64] It was Yü who had obtained a copy of the scripture "Manual for Responding to the Kalpas of the Three Buddhas" and presented it to Lin Ch'ing; he was an active recruiter and appears to have been knowledgeable about and committed to sectarian religious practices. It was to Yü K'e-ching that Li Wen-ch'eng had turned over management of his sect in 1811 when he and Lin Ch'ing began planning "the great undertaking," and Yü was among those who organized the attack on Hua that freed Li and probably saved his life. Both Liu Ch'eng-chang and Yü K'e-ching had numerous contacts all over north China and considerable organizing experience; their loss so early in the rebellion must have been very distressing for Li Wen-ch'eng.

It was probably with less personal grief that Li viewed the departure of Feng K'e-shan, "Controller of Earth" and "Sage of Military Ability." It is not clear what happened between Feng and Li, for we have only one side of the story and that is the unreliable testimony of Feng himself. He later told government interrogators that at the time of the attack on Hua city, he, Feng, had been in Shantung. He had then rushed back to Hua, arrived two days after the attack, and gone into the city. "I went to my home and saw that my wife and son and daughter had all been stabbed to death, and their bodies were lying on the ground. Then Niu Liang-ch'en came, on orders from Yü K'e-ching and Liu Ch'eng-chang, to seize me because I had not been at home and had not helped rescue Li Wen-ch'eng. I cried bitterly and begged Niu Liang-ch'en to spare me. So he forgave me and told me I must work hard serving Li Wen-ch'eng." Feng was, by his own account, put to work transshipping grain to Li's village, but Li continued to refuse to see Feng, using his injuries as an excuse. As time went by and pressure from government soldiers on Hua city increased, Feng became concerned about the future. "Besides," he explains, "I was still angry because Li Wen-ch'eng had had my wife and children killed. So I thought about fleeing to Te district [where his followers were] and finding [his pupil] Sung Yueh-lung. Then I would organize my people there and rise up and come and kill Li Wen-ch'eng and so get revenge."[65]

Appealing as this account may be, it is at least in part a complete fabrication. There is ample evidence that Feng K'e-shan was not only present during the attack on Hua city but, as befitted his rank, a leader of it. The wife and children and their alleged murder by his friends to punish Feng for not helping were in fact invented by Feng.[66] Nevertheless, something did go wrong between Feng and Li, Feng did not take part in high-level decision making, and in the middle of the 10th month he left Hua city. Another rebel described the dispute with frustrating economy, saying "Feng K'e-shan had been in disagreement with Li Wen-ch'eng (與 Li Wen-ch'eng 不和) and had therefore gone to Te where he had pupils of his own."[67] Feng's identity as a skillful itinerant boxer and local tough guy does not seem to have been changed by his association with believers of the Eight Trigram sects. He had apparently been willing to cooperate with religious leaders for their goals primarily in order to satisfy his own ambition and competitiveness. He had brought few followers into the sect and none into the rebellion. It is not surprising that he did not get along with the Trigram leaders after the rebellion had begun. His departure was probably not much regretted.

Without Lin Ch'ing or Feng K'e-shan, or even his close friends Yü K'e-ching and Liu Ch'eng-chang, Li Wen-ch'eng, himself ill, was very much alone in dealing with the deteriorating military situation. Similarly, on him alone devolved the responsibility for providing symbols of leadership that could rally his pupils and their followers. The new hierarchy outlined in advance for the Pai-yang era was drastically reshaped by the realities of the situation as it developed after 9/15, just as the rebels' goals and ambitions had been tempered by less than auspicious military conditions. Without Lin Ch'ing and Feng K'e-shan, the triumvirate of the Controllers of Heaven, Earth, and Men (*t'ien-p'an, ti-p'an,* and *jen-p'an*) dissolved. It had previously been planned that as Emperor of Men (*jen-huang* 人皇) Li Wen-ch'eng would rule and in this role would be assisted by Yü K'e-ching and Feng Hsueh-li; by the end of the 9th month, Yü K'e-ching (who may have been one who helped formulate such titles) had been killed. It was nevertheless essential that some kind of new hierarchy be established, no matter how truncated, both to satisfy the expectations of believers and to provide the entire rebel group with its formal alternative to the Ch'ing system. Li Wen-ch'eng therefore emphasized his own role as ruler, apparently sweeping aside all other sets of titles, and he created a working apparatus that would meet the needs of the current situation. Available information about the new system is limited and confusing. We do not know if Li followed blueprints drawn up prior to the uprising or if he improvised on his own, nor is it clear whether he intended this system (or some part of it) to be temporary, limited only to the period of transition, or permanent, extending into the Pai-yang era.

Li Wen-ch'eng's first official act after he was freed from prison was to formalize and confirm ritually his own position and that of his subordinates. A knowledgeable aide of Li's said that "Li Wen-ch'eng was honored (尊) as Master (主), and then he enfeoffed (封) [his subordinates with the various ranks here named.]"[68] This could not have been an elaborate ceremony, considering Li's weakness, but it was an important one. Li claimed to be the "True Master" (*chen-chu* 真主) of the sect, a supreme teacher and authority on religious doctrine and practices. He also laid claim to the legitimacy of the preceding Ming dynasty and simultaneously to the most famous of the rebels against that dynasty, calling himself, "True Master Li of the T'ien-shun Era of the Great Ming" (大明天順李真主). Capitalizing on his surname, Li Wen-ch'eng also asserted that he was a reincarnation of Li Tzu-ch'eng, the rebel who had overthrown the Ming dynasty and founded (but was unable to perpetuate) his own state of Ta-shun 大順, Great Accordance (with Heaven's

Will). Moreover, Li proclaimed the reestablishment of the Ming dynasty and took the traditional step of a dynastic founder and selected an era-name. He chose one—Heaven's Accordance—that was reminiscent of that of both Li Tzu-ch'eng and the Ming Emperor Ying-tsung.[69] Thus he cast himself in the dual role of rebel and restorer and used both to create an additional aura of legitimacy about his claim to power.

Li Wen-ch'eng followed previously formulated plans at least with regard to one set of titles set up for his subordinates. He established the trigram kings (kua-wang 卦王), one for each of the eight trigrams: Li 離, Ken 艮, Chen 震, Ch'ien 乾, K'un 坤, Sun 巽, Tui 兌, and K'an 坎. Under each of the kings there were eight trigram lords (kua-po 卦伯), sixty-four in all.[70] At least some, perhaps all, of these titles had been assigned prior to the uprisings, but the act of investiture did not take place until after the sect members had openly committed themselves to rebellion. These titles were intended for use only during the period of transition to the Pai-yang era. Ultimately, the Eight Trigrams, with Li Wen-ch'eng at their head, were to become the Nine Mansions (chiu-kung 九宮),[71] and accordingly each of the trigram kings and lords would have his title changed to mansion king or lord (kung-wang 宮王 or kung-po). It is nowhere stated that Li Wen-ch'eng ever declared the formal beginning of the new era, but it is likely that he had done so with his first formal ceremony, for these rebel leaders are referred to by both titles (trigram and mansion) during the months of rebellion.[72]

It is not clear how well structured the relationship was between Li and the kings and lords. It appears to have been one of loose association rather than tight command and, relatively speaking, the position of trigram lord was one of considerable independence. Both kings and lords inscribed their names and titles on white banners, which they displayed prominently as symbols of their authority.[73] During the uprising rank-and-file rebels were assigned to the command of one of these seventy-two kings and lords. The relationship between the king or lord and his fighting men was relatively close, and most rebels knew their commander and his trigram by name.[74]

These kings and lords, in addition to Li Wen-ch'eng and several of his chief assistants, all had the power to assign titles and positions to people who had served them and proved themselves worthy.[75] Other rebels simply selected titles for themselves. Thus a hodgepodge of titles was generated during the rebellion, creating a mixture of dissimilar terms whose relationship to one another and whose part in a larger structure is not known. Part of this problem is historiographical, for most information about these titles comes from lists compiled by government military commanders containing the names of dead or captured rebels followed by their title, in a orderly but uninformative fashion. On the other hand, the rest of our information comes in confused and contradictory fragments. There is only a limited amount of sense to be made from this data, and as a summary I have therefore drawn up the following table, giving Chinese terms and tentative English translations:[76]

Chief Minister*	*tsai-hsiang* 宰相 or *ch'eng-hsiang* 丞相
Chief Commander	*tsung yuan-shuai* 總元帥
Commander*	*yuan-shuai* 元帥
Assistant Commander*	*fu yuan-shuai* 副元帥
Brigade-General* **	*tsung-ping* 總兵
Lieutenant-Colonel* **	*ts'an-chiang* 參將
First Captain* **	*tu-ssu* 都司
Captain of the Forward Bureau	*ch'ien-pu tsung t'ou-ling* 前部總頭領
Captain of Musketry	*niao-ch'iang tsung t'ou-ling* 鳥鎗總頭領
Adjutant*	*hsien-feng* 先鋒
Adjutant Who Leads the Way	*k'ai-lu hsien-feng* 開路先鋒
Adjutant for Transferring Soldiers and Horses	*t'i-t'iao ping-ma tsung hsien-feng* 提調兵馬總先鋒
Advance Officer*	*hsien hsing kuan* 先行官
Grain Supervisor*	*tu-liang kuan* 督糧官
Superintendent*	*tu-tsung kuan* 都總官
Assistant Superintendent*	*fu-tsung kuan* 副總官

Titles Only Promised by Rebel Leaders

Military Governor of the Nine Gates	*chiu-men t'i-tu* 九門提督
Great Commander Who Summons Men and Horses for the Pacification of All under Heaven	*t'ien-hsia tu-chao-t'ao ping-ma ta yuan-shuai* 天下都招討兵馬大元帥
Chief Eunuch* **	*tsung-kuan t'ai-chien* 總管太監
Prefect**	*chih-fu* 知府
Magistrate**	*chih-hsien* 知縣

*Titles assigned to more than one person
**Titles also used by the Ch'ing government

In general, most of these titles had the virtue of being easily understood and important sounding, and none was likely to be beyond the understanding of the ordinary rebel. All were clearly working titles, and they reflect the primarily military and logistical activities that dominated the rebels' lives during the uprising. At least ten of these titles (marked with an asterisk) were assigned to more than one person. The total number of men (and there is no indication of any woman holding a position) holding an office of some sort numbered at least one hundred.

Despite the only partial response by Eight Trigram groups to the call for rebellion on 9/15 and the disappointing performance by rebels in Peking and in Chün, Li Wen-ch'eng had proclaimed his challenge to the Ch'ing government and retained the support of his subordinates and tens of thousands of followers. He had scaled down his goals and his organization to fit the new situation, but as the 10th month passed, government pressure increased and it became increasingly apparent that the tide had somehow to be turned quickly if the rebels were to survive at all. In the final section of this part we will return to Li Wen-ch'eng and his attempts to save himself and his movement. First, let us look in more detail at the new life sect members had created for themselves and for their followers.

A NEW LIFE

No matter what their expectations, members of the Eight Trigram sects who had discarded the known and familiar to act the roles of rebels in the name of the Eternal Mother could not but have been astonished at the excitement, the fierceness, and the unpredictability of their new lives. And although in time many surely realized that the creation of a Cloud City where "everyone was in the sect" was beyond their power, what was to have been a period of transition was a new life nevertheless, a radical break with the past and an emancipation in its own right.

The problem of survival was a paramount one, for the rebels had not only to secure food and shelter in a world now completely disrupted, but they had to defeat hostile military forces in armed combat. They needed men, ammunition and weapons, efficient organization and realistic plans if they were to vanquish Ch'ing armies. These were not tasks for which life as a believer in a White Lotus sect was appropriate preparation. Not only had the sect structure to be changed to fit the demands of this entirely new situation, but the attitudes of the sect members themselves were forced to shift. The devotion and discretion of the believer had to be replaced by the determination and defiance of the rebel. Free from restraints and reprisals, these rebels had an extraordinary opportunity for courage and independent action, if they could take advantage of it.

For the organizers and leaders of the rebellion, this new life consisted of an endless series of orders to be given and decisions to be made. The occupation of Hua and Tao-k'ou and of villages in the countryside was a demanding business. Both cities had to be closed off and all exits guarded. Granaries and stores, pawnshops and loan houses had to be emptied and the contents stored. Food had to be made available to the rebel leaders and their fighting men, and to the tens of thousands of dependents (old people, women, and children) who were brought into the rebel strongholds in increasing numbers. This work had to be organized by the rebel leaders and executed by their followers in orderly fashion if the movement was to be successful. New recruits had to be incorporated into the rebel organization and persuaded to fight for its cause.

During the first two months of rebellion Li Wen-ch'eng remained at home in his village just north of Hua city, lying in bed and allowing his broken legs, ankles, and feet to heal.[77] He entrusted the administration of Hua city to two men: Niu Liang-ch'en, who was his chief minister (*tsai-hsiang*), and Sung Yuan-ch'eng, who was his chief commander (*tsung yuan-shuai*). Sung Yuan-ch'eng, in his forties, was a craftsman from Chün district who had done painting work for a living. He had been to visit Lin Ch'ing early in 1813 and was among those who made the decision to move ahead of schedule to free Li Wen-ch'eng from prison. Niu Liang-ch'en was the Hua district treasury clerk who had met Lin Ch'ing in 1808, become his pupil, and arranged the first meeting between Lin and Li Wen-ch'eng in 1811. He had been arrested early in the 9th month and was freed together with Li on 9/7. These two men supervised the provisioning and defense of the city; when Li Wen-ch'eng fled from Hua early in the 11th month, he left them in charge.[78]

The sources yield few personal details about Sung Yuan-ch'eng's role, but Niu Liang-ch'en, who was ultimately captured and interrogated, talked freely about his life during this period. Niu had been very active in planning the rebellion before his arrest, and unlike Li he was not injured by torture during the five days in the Hua jail. He took over the job of chief minister and went with the rebel armies to supervise the capture of Chün city. The rebel failure there does not speak well of Niu's ability as a commander, but more bureaucratic skills learned while serving as a treasury clerk may have made him more successful at the task of supervising the occupation of Hua city that absorbed his energies thereafter.[79]

For Eight Trigram leaders like Niu, their new life as rebels meant prestige as well as power and an opportunity for public display of their high status within the sect. Niu alone of the Hua rebels could claim a special relationship with Lin Ch'ing, and Niu made the most of his status as Lin's pupil. He had made and publicly displayed banners reading "Pupil of the Lin [Ch'ing] School" (林門弟子) or in a longer and more impressive form "Niu, the Chief Pupil of Lin Who Is the Patriarch of Latter Heaven and the Heavenly Controller in Charge of the Faith at the Time When the Eight Trigrams Begin to Practice the Law" (掌理天盤八卦法開後天祖師林大弟子牛). Seemingly not content with his practical job as Li Wen-ch'eng's chief minister, or with the prestige of his position as pupil of the Heavenly Controller himself, Niu Liang-ch'en chose to act out yet another role. He explained that previously his teacher Lin Ch'ing had consulted his "Manual for Responding to the Kalpas of the Three Buddhas," and from it determined that in addition to the three great Controllers of Heaven, Earth, and Men, there would be a Controller of the Immortals (hsien-p'an 仙盤), Niu Liang-ch'en. Accordingly, during the months of the rebellion Niu dressed himself in robes elaborately decorated with the symbols of the eight trigrams and the square cap of a Taoist priest. He was addressed by everyone as "Honored Sir" (hsien-sheng 先生).[80]

It is possible that other rebel leaders did as Niu had, altering their life style and appearance so as to be in keeping with new religious roles. (Niu was particularly willing to talk about religious matters and did not share what seems to have been a prevailing attitude among his colleagues not to speak of such things to the authorities.)[81] Other rebels used titles that either had unexplained religious significance or were simply made up on the spot by men eager for prestige. Some used the title General (chiang-chün 將軍), for example, including one who was known as the Great General of the Middle Era (chung-yuan 中元 ta chiang-chün), which may have referred to the second and present great kalpa period, and another was called the Great White General (ta pai 大白 chiang-chün), which may have referred to the White Sun era to come.[82]

There were also a number of men who called themselves "king" (wang 王) without reference to the Eight Trigram kings selected by Li Wen-ch'eng. Some of their titles included: The King Who Follows

Heaven (*shun-t'ien wang* 順天王), or The King Who Pacifies the West (*p'ing-hsi wang* 平西王).[83] Other men simply were called by their surname and a number, as Second Great King Hsiao (Hsiao Erh Ta-wang 蕭二大王) or Fourth Great King Ts'ai (Ts'ai Ssu Ta-wang). The latter, a man called Ts'ai Ch'eng-kung, was a person of no prominence in the sect whose confession (and possibly his life as a rebel) reflects his strong desire to appear important and impressive. He claimed to have given orders to men like Niu Liang-ch'en and Feng K'e-shan, though apparently he simply made up his title himself.[84] A monk who joined the sect and rebellion claimed to have been installed as The Ch'an Master Who Protects the State (*hu-kuo ch'an shih* 護國禪師). Not surprisingly there were other rebel leaders who took and wore the clothing of members of the elite or arrogated imperial titles to themselves.[85]

In order to describe the kinds of activities in which rebel leaders were engaged, we will look at one set of leaders for whom relatively more information is available: the Tui Trigram king and his lords. Liu Kuo-ming 劉幗明 was the Tui Trigram (or Mansion) king, one of eight kings selected prior to the rebellion. Liu had been Li Wen-ch'eng's teacher in the past, but he had acknowledged Li as sect master when Li had taken over in 1811. Liu Kuo-ming had converted Hsu An-kuo and was responsible for the participation in the Eight Trigrams of Hsu and his vast network of pupils in Shantung. He had taken part in the entry into Hua city to free Li Wen-ch'eng but, having been confirmed in his position as king, he then took his men and left Hua. Liu and two of the Tui Trigram lords (Wang Hsueh-i, who was Liu's pupil, and Wei Te-chung, who was Liu's teacher's pupil) set up camp in the villages of Ssu-chien-fang, P'an-chang, and Nan-hu in northeastern Hua district, erecting poles to display the white banners that proclaimed their titles. During the 9th and 10th months they remained there, raiding other villages in Hua and adjacent K'ai districts for food supplies, and engaging local militia and government soldiers whenever necessary. Trigram King Liu appears to have had a force of at least three thousand men under his command: Trigram Lord Wei named at least eight men, including himself and Wang Hsueh-i, who had been named "leaders" (*t'ou-mu* 頭目) under Liu's authority and each of whom commanded three hundred to four hundred men. There was communication but apparently no formal or regularized chain of command between Liu and the other rebel leaders in Hua city; between Tui Trigram King Liu and the six men designated as Tui Trigram lords, there were no visible organizational links.[86]

These six other lords consisted of three sets of brothers (or cousins) who apparently worked together in pairs. Shen Kuo-hsien and Shen Kuo-chen were pupils of Niu Liang-ch'en from a market town in the far northeastern corner of Hua district. Unfortunately nothing else is known about what they did or where they were during the rebellion. They could have been with Liu Kuo-ming, for they did finally join Liu when he accompanied Li Wen-ch'eng on the latter's flight from Hua in the 11th month. Huang Hsing-tsai and his brother Huang Hsing-hsiang were also Niu Liang-ch'en's pupils and Tui Trigram lords. They came from a market town in southeastern Hua and had brought their followers to assist in freeing Li Wen-ch'eng from jail. Both were among those put in charge of the port town of Tao-k'ou, and Hsing-hsiang died in the battle for that city on 10/27. Hsing-tsai had an unspecified number of men under his command, had "fought many battles," assisted with the unsuccessful defense of Tao-k'ou, and moved into Hua city and remained there until it was retaken and he was captured. There were no visible connections between either brother and the Tui Trigram king. The last two Tui Trigram lords were Chu Ch'eng-kuei and Chu Ch'eng-fang, cousins from Shantung, pupils of Hsu An-kuo, and the leaders of the rebellion in that province. Having organized and carried out the attacks on Ts'ao and Ting-t'ao, the two Chus and their followers had raided the villages of those districts for several weeks, using their own home village as a base. Late in the 9th month, following instructions from Hsu An-kuo, they brought their followers and came to Hua city. They joined in the attack on Chün city and then together with Hsu An-kuo went to Tao-k'ou to prepare its defenses. Chu Ch'eng-fang remained in Hua with Hsu An-kuo until the end, while Ch'eng-fang went with Li Wen-ch'eng. While the two Chus might have coordinated their activities with the Huang brothers—for all were involved in defending and losing Tao-k'ou—there is again no evidence of any upward connection with the Tui Trigram King Liu Kuo-ming.[87]

This admittedly rough picture should illustrate the looseness with which king and lords of a given trigram related to one another. Generally speaking, the position of trigram king had been assigned to eight sect teachers active in planning the rebellion (and all from Li Wen-ch'eng's group), and the other sixty-four positions had been distributed among their highest-ranking pupils. In reorganizing the chains of teachers and pupils in the various sects to fit the structure of eight kings and sixty-four lords, it appears that family and sect ties were respected, but the power of a trigram king over his followers was diluted by the addition to "his" trigram of those whose sect loyalties went to other leaders. The resultant organization was flexible and apparently not unmanageable since teacher–pupil relationships did continue to be operative as chains of command supplementing those of king to lord.

Some of the organizational and command problems experienced by the rebels can be further illustrated if we look at four brothers named Chang, all pupils of Li Trigram King Wang Tao-lung. The third brother, Chang Feng-hsiang, had originally been designated by Trigram King Wang as a Li Trigram lord and in that capacity he had "managed things" (possibly in Hua city). Chang Feng-hsiang did not manage things properly, however, and when Wang Tao-lung found out that he had been "privately accumulating part of the money" (taken from city residents?) and not turning it over to rebel authorities, Wang forced him to relinquish his position of trigram lord. The title was not assigned to a stranger, however, but was taken by Feng-hsiang's older brother, the second of the four sons. It is not said what happened to Feng-hsiang, but his other two brothers were also given posts. The youngest had been made adjutant (hsien-feng), while the eldest had been promised by his teacher that he would be given a leadership position "after the period of rebellion (luan) was over," presumably in the new Pai-yang era. All four brothers remained in Hua city and lost their lives there.[88]

The dispute described above suggests that "looting" by rebels may have been organized and systematic. This picture is confirmed, at least in the case of Hua city, by the testimony of the rebel named Huang P'an-kung. Huang's story can also illustrate how rebel leaders lived and worked in Hua. Huang P'an-kung was one of several clerks and runners in the Hua district yamen who were in a sect and in the rebellion—Huang himself was a yamen runner. His teacher, relaying instructions from Niu Liang-ch'en, had arranged with him about participating in the uprising, and Huang later helped free Niu and Li Wen-ch'eng from prison. Huang received no title after the rebellion, but Chief Commander Sung Yuan-ch'eng assigned him the task of emptying and cataloguing the contents of a pawnshop appropriated by the rebels. Chief Minister Niu Liang-ch'en came later and made an inspection of the pawnshop, commended Huang on his handling of the task, and formally promoted him. Huang says that he became a "big leader" (ta t'ou-mu 大頭目). In this new capacity, Huang P'an-kung took charge of two hundred men and went through the streets and houses of the city, looking for and taking objects of value, and, as we have seen, this authorized plunder included the power to kill those who resisted.[89]

In addition to the systematic looting of Hua and presumably of Tao-k'ou, many rebels were engaged in the transshipping of grain from Tao-k'ou into Hua city during the 10th month. From the beginning, those rebels involved in transporting grain had been allowed to pass freely through the city gates, and when Ch'ing pressure on Tao-k'ou mounted, the rebels decided to move all of that town's sizable grain reserves into Hua. This operation was assigned to several trigram kings, trigram lords, and their followers.[90]

Although a great many rebels were involved in securing and defending Tao-k'ou and Hua, the majority of Eight Trigram commanders spent their days as rebels living in the countryside. Making camp in villages and market towns, they took what they wanted and lived as they pleased. Many sect leaders from Hua and Chün district preferred this life and did not go into Hua city until forced there by irresistible pressure from advancing Ch'ing armies.[91] Rebels in southwestern Shantung were likewise free from harassment for a time, though a considerably shorter time, and lived a similar life of foraging expeditions and sporadic battles, a life in which they too were put increasingly on the defensive before being driven out of their camps altogether. We will look in greater detail at these rebels in Shantung, for the documentation permits us to see into the life of these lower level, village based, and eventually beleaguered rebel bands, and their experience can stand as representative of that of their comrades in southern Chihli and northern Honan.

The Shantung rebels had a period of only three weeks before they were driven to take refuge in Hua by a closing circle of government soldiers, but during these weeks they were particularly free to do as they pleased. They were connected with the top level Eight Trigrams leadership only through their senior teacher Hsu An-kuo, and Hsu, who had left his home in southern Chihli only to join his colleagues in Hua, offered his pupils little instruction or direction during this period. Although all the Shantung leaders and many of the followers had been sect members, there appears to have been little interest in translating into reality the religious ideas of their sects. Instead, the rebels concentrated on staying alive and if possible enjoying life.

A government scout described their life as follows: "They are confining themselves to Ts'ao and Ting-t'ao district. In the daytime they loot shops and at night they drink wine with their women. They have forced others from the villages [of those districts] to join them. Now they roam about, hesitating and not daring to approach the cities." A local magistrate gave a similar picture: "The rebel group from Chi-t'ieh village had eaten early, divided into groups, and then gone out to burn and plunder. . . . In the evening, after they had eaten, they made plans to attack the [district] city; however, when they heard that our defenses had been increased, they dared not."[92]

Our best rebel source, the testimony of the leader Hu Ch'eng-te, presents a slightly more colorful picture. Hu Ch'eng-te was among those who attacked the government offices and the pawnshops of Ts'ao city. He and his group of seventy men left the city that same day (9/10), and went, apparently on foot, to Fan-chia village. They were joined by others, and by the time they reached the village, their group numbered about two hundred. Outside the house of Fan Ta-p'i-keng, who was one of Hu's lieutenants and for whose family the village was named, they constructed a makeshift shed. There the men sat and rested until evening and, using Fan Ta-p'i-keng's supplies (perhaps stockpiled in advance), cooked noodles in broth for everyone to eat.

After relaxing for a day or two, the group mobilized themselves and marched to Ma-chia village about six miles away. That market town contained several pawnshops and these were broken open and emptied by the rebels. They helped themselves to the clothing for which the pawnshops were serving as summer storage.[93] Hu Ch'eng-te took a blue padded-cotton robe and a green padded-cotton riding jacket and immediately put them on. He also obtained for himself a more dignified means of transportation, commandeering a passenger cart with a mat awning. Along the way that day, Hu encountered an old acquaintance whom he had persuaded to join their group; this man had been a cart driver, and so now Hu told him to drive his cart. To another recent recruit, Hu assigned the task (or privilege) of carrying the banner inscribed with the title Hu's teacher had given him, "The King Who Follows Heaven, Hu Ch'eng-te." That night Hu came back to Fan-chia village in style, sitting under the awning of a horse-drawn cart with his banner carrier walking out front.

The rebels were by necessity concerned with subsistence as well as style, and finding that Fan Ta-p'i-keng's supplies had been exhausted, they then went to the other houses in the village and took flour and dumplings. The following day they again stayed in the village, resting and enjoying themselves. This was their pattern during these early days of their rebellion. They would leave the village one day to obtain food, clothing, and supporters and then return to relax for a day or two. Each night when the men came back to the village, they would greet one another by bowing deeply, saying "Be Victorious," and laughing.[94]

What did they take in these foraging expeditions? The primary object of rebel "looting and plundering" was food, necessary in large quantities to support each growing rebel band. They took grain and other provisions from people's houses and from grain shops. (There is surprisingly no reference by rebel or official to the opening of government granaries.) In addition to food, the rebels helped themselves to other valuables. As we have seen they removed the contents of the treasuries (presumably silver and copper money) when the government offices were attacked. Inside the cities and later in smaller market towns, they broke into loan houses (*ch'ien-p'u* 錢鋪) and into pawnshops (*tang-tien* 當店). From the pawnshops and from people's homes, the rebels took clothes, particularly those made of silk or of padded-cotton—luxuries beyond their previous means. To make the white banners carried by rebel leaders (and captured in great quantities by the government), we presume that cloth was taken whenever possible. In order to transport themselves and their supplies, the rebels took horses and mules and carts of all sizes. Similarly, they armed themselves and stockpiled weapons and ammunition, taking knives, spears and muskets, and from the cities, cannon.[95]

At first the prospect of a good fight with Ch'ing soldiers was a welcome one for those rebels who had attacked Ts'ao and Ting-t'ao cities and who were riding high on a wave of excitement and self-confidence. Several days after the attacks on the cities, a third-rank military officer from the Green Standard garrison in Ts'ao-chou prefectural city ventured southward into Ting-t'ao district with two hundred men, some of whom were militia. The rebels learned of this, and word was sent out to all of the various bands in the Ting-t'ao area (we know of at least four) telling them of the approaching soldiers and asking everyone to assemble and fight them. The rebels attacked on the 12th or 13th (of the 9th month) in a place called K'ung-lien-keng. The soldiers, though better armed (with muskets), were outnumbered: "Because the rebels were many and the soldiers few, the few could not hold off the many," and the rebels won handily. Nearly one-fourth of the soldiers, including their commander, were killed or wounded.[96] One Ch'ing agent sent in disguise to spy on the rebels reported that at this stage "the villages where the bandits were gathered extended over an area of about forty or fifty li across. The rebels go out in the daytime and rest at night. They have forced young and able-bodied men to join them and fight on the front lines.

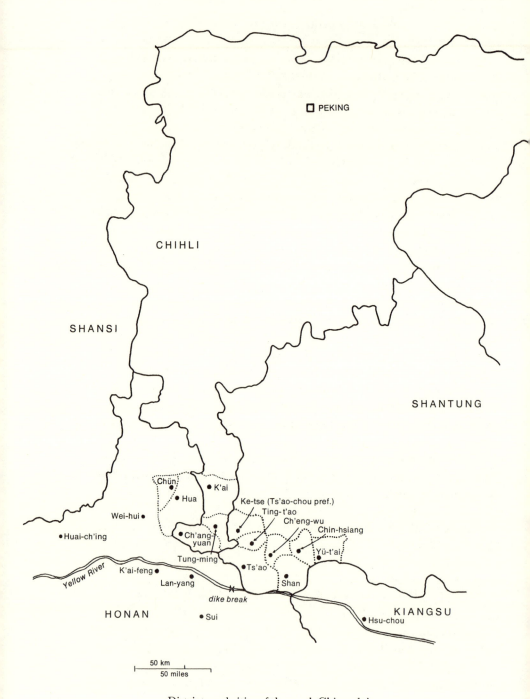

Districts and cities of the north China plain

Labels within map:
□ PEKING

CHIHLI

SHANSI

SHANTUNG

Chün
Hua
K'ai
Ke-tse (Ts'ao-chou pref.)
Ting-t'ao
Ch'eng-wu
Chin-hsiang
Wei-hui
Ch'ang-yuan
Yü-t'ai
Huai-ch'ing
Tung-ming
Yellow River
K'ai-feng
Ts'ao
Lan-yang
Shan
dike break
KIANGSU
HONAN
Sui
Hsu-chou

50 km
50 miles

They have also sent out men to different places to reconnoiter and get in touch with other [rebels]."[97]

The Shantung rebels remained unchallenged in Ting-t'ao and Ts'ao districts for several weeks, but toward the end of the 9th month this situation began to change. On 9/21 the governor of Shantung and a veteran general arrived in Ts'ao-chou prefectural city, bringing with them footsoldiers and cavalry transferred from elsewhere in the province. These soldiers began to attack and engage small rebel groups, as did soldiers from Kiangsu who had also moved into Shantung. At about this time, the sect leader Hsu An-kuo sent word to his major pupils in Shantung that they should come to Hua to confer with him and assist in the faltering attack on Chün city.[98] These two developments—the arrival of Ch'ing soldiers and the request for assistance from Hsu An-kuo—would eventually put an end to the period of free and unhindered plundering, but those rebels who went to Hua to aid their colleagues still exhibited the exhilaration characteristic of this initial phase of rebellion.

The rebel Hu Ch'eng-te, whose own teacher had relayed to him the message from Hsu An-kuo, again narrated what happened to him. When Hu and his men got the message, they spent the rest of that day getting ready and by evening were prepared to leave for Hua. "Along the way we took dumplings for food and mules to ride. We also took ten or twenty passenger carts. I continued to ride in my cart. . . . At that time our men. . . numbered about five hundred or so." Hua city was seventy miles away, and by dawn two days later Hu and his men had arrived about five miles from the city walls. Hu's aide Fan Ta-p'i-keng volunteered to take a horse and ride ahead to announce their arrival to Hsu An-kuo. Later as Hu Ch'eng-te approached the east gate of the city, he saw a group of men walking toward him. Fan Ta-p'i-keng was leading his horse in one hand and walking respectfully behind "Teacher Hsu." Hu Ch'eng-te and the others greeted Hsu An-kuo, described the villages they had looted and the battles won, and then they kotowed to Hsu. "When we stood up again, we put our hands together and shook them, congratulating one another, said 'Be Victorious,' and then everyone laughed."

Later Hsu An-kuo spoke to them and said,

> You've been very successful in doing this job for me. In the future, those who can read will be given official posts, those who cannot will be given land. However, right now I am afraid that the government soldiers will be making many arrests. For this

reason, you should now, without delay, go back to your homes and get your families and move them here [into Hua city] as quickly as possible.[99]

Some of the rebels chose to remain in Hua and assist in the fighting; Hu Ch'eng-te and others returned to Shantung to get their relatives and colleagues. But when they reached Shantung, early in the 10th month, the balance of power had already changed and they found Ch'ing soldiers waiting for them. In this less happy phase in the life of the Shantung Eight Trigrams, they became engaged in increasingly desperate battles against superior armies.

The pacification of the rebels in Shantung was undertaken by the veteran general and Shantung Salt Commissioner Liu Ch'ing. On 9/27 he first ventured into the area of rebel-held villages with five hundred soldiers, one-fifth of them cavalry. Thereafter he continued to attack and scatter rebel camps and whenever a large group of rebels came to their comrades' assistance, the Ch'ing armies held their own and forced the rebels to leave and regroup elsewhere. A battle in Ts'ao district on 10/1 was typical. Ch'ing soldiers advanced and "the rebel group rushed out to resist. The government soldiers attacked them. More than one hundred fifty rebels were killed and the rest—more than one hundred people—fled into the multistoried building in that village. They closed the gate to that building and threw down a rain of stones from above. The government soldiers were hit and injured by the stones but regardless . . . they rushed forward and set fire to the building." Those who jumped down and survived were captured, but the rest were burned to death inside.[100] After they were repeatedly defeated by Ch'ing soldiers, some rebels chose not to fight; frightened by the news that more armies were approaching, some "threw down their weapons and fled for their lives"; others came forward, removed their white sashes and ko-towed to the soldiers.[101]

By the first week in the 10th month, the rebels in Shantung had been reduced to two large camps, one in Hu-chia village, and a smaller one in nearby An-ling village. Realizing the danger of their position, they attempted to fortify these villages and to turn them into stockades. At An-ling there was an earthen wall of a mile or more in circumference around the village. Although none of the four gates in the wall had wooden doors, the rebels had filled them up with brambles and thorny branches. Hu-chia village, which was the home of Chu Ch'eng-kuei and his brothers and cousin (Hsu An-kuo's chief pupils in Shantung), had been made even more inaccessible. There, the earthen walls had been built up all around the village, the gates were closed, and tree trunks, branches, and bramble bushes were piled outside the walls. Earlier Trigram Lord Chu Ch'eng-kuei had taken many of his followers and gone to Hua, but his brother Ch'eng-liang had been left behind with nearly two thousand men to protect their home.[102]

On 10/4 the larger camp at Hu-chia village was attacked. As the Ch'ing soldiers cut through the brush, the rebels were forced back inside the village wall. They soon found that fireballs were being thrown over the wall. The thatch houses began to catch fire and flames, spread by the wind, soon enveloped the village. The rebels could not muster an organized counterattack; most who tried to flee were easily cut down. A few did manage to escape and, though pursued by government cavalry, made it safely to An-ling village. Those who remained inside were either burned to death or captured as the soldiers entered the village.[103] After this battle, the backbone of rebel strength in Shantung was broken.

Once word spread of the destruction of Hu-chia village, many of the rebel bands still in Shantung decided to seek safety in Hua. The rest congregated in An-ling village. Although they were joined by one of the Chu brothers who had come from Hua to assist his relatives and pupils, the initiative had already been lost. The remaining rebels were sitting ducks, isolated and vulnerable, and the Ch'ing soldiers moved quickly to attack. A cavalry officer from Ts'ao-chou prefecture led soldiers and approached the beleaguered village. He climbed up onto a small mound outside the earthen wall around the village and threw copies of an announcement of clemency over the wall, hoping to undermine rebel morale. The village was soon surrounded by Ch'ing soldiers, including crack Manchu troops led by an imperial bodyguard of the first-rank sent specially from Peking. Early in the morning on 10/7 the government attacked, stormed the village, and killed and captured its defenders.[104] In the face of these defeats, surviving Shantung rebels, disillusioned and afraid for their lives, rid themselves of weapons, banners, and booty, and either left the area as soon as possible or made their way home and hoped that their involvement would remain undetected by the authorities.[105]

The experience of the Shantung rebels paralleled the pattern of the rebellion as a whole, for once they had lost their forward momentum, they were attacked, pursued, and eventually besieged. Inexperienced in warfare and without an efficient command system, the rebel leaders were neither imaginative nor flexible in their military strategy. As Ch'ing armies approached, the rebels merely withdrew into their poorly defended villages. Beleaguered and on the defensive, they soon could only flee or fight to the death. Over the next two months, those Trigram rebels who occupied villages of Honan and southern Chihli found themselves in exactly the same position, and their pride and delight with their new status soon turned into anxiety, fear, and even panic.

THE CH'ING GOVERNMENT STRIKES BACK

Most histories of rebellions in China consist largely of accounts of how the rebels were suppressed by the government. Here, however, matters peripheral to the uprising itself such as government decision making, finance, communications, military preparedness, or the personalities of the emperor and his chief officials, will not be discussed in any detail. Instead, I wish to concentrate on the Ch'ing defeat of the Eight Trigram rebels insofar as it relates to the nature of the contest between rebel and government and their competing strategies for getting or holding power. We will look first at the Ch'ing government's measures to win renewed commitments of allegiance from the local gentry and "good people" in the country-side, and then at their overall plan for defeating the rebels on the battlefield.

In order to quell the Eight Trigrams rebellion, the Ch'ing government undertook both organizational and propaganda measures to counteract rebel claims to legitimacy. In the first place, it was necessary for the government to secure the loyalty and assistance of the nonrebel population, particularly the local elites. In the second place, it was important to induce the majority of rebel followers to "return their allegiance" to the Ch'ing.

The emperor and his officials appear to have divided the population into categories along a spectrum of varying degrees of allegiance to the government: (1) "righteous citizens" (*i-min* 義民), those who supported the state with money and energy and actively rallied others to oppose the rebels; (2) "good people" (*liang-min* 良民), those who refused to join either a heretical sect or the sect-led rebellion; (3) "good people" who had been "tricked" into joining a sect but who repented of this and did not participate in the rebellion; (4) "re-fugees" (*nan-min* 難民) and "coerced people" (*hsieh-min* 脅民), those who had unwillingly joined the rebel side, who as rebels may have robbed or set fires or killed people, but who eventually surrendered to the government and refused to do battle with Ch'ing soldiers; (5) rebel followers who, no matter how persuaded to join the rebel cause, took up arms against government soldiers in battle; and (6) rebel leaders and sect members who actively directed others in the rebellion against the Ch'ing state. The first two groups were to be rewarded, the third and fourth forgiven for their mistakes, and the fifth and sixth punished or killed.

The policy of sparing all rebels who abandoned that cause and surrendered to the government was designed to create a wedge between dedicated Eight Trigram leaders and their less committed followers and to discourage any new defections to the rebel side— "those among the rebels who are fierce will become fearful, and those who are timid will flee." This policy of leniency and amnesty was posted on bulletins, distributed through leaflets, and announced aloud before battles. During a battle the government set up special red banners, visible at a distance, where all "coerced people" and "refugees" could come and surrender themselves.[106]

While they attempted on the one hand to persuade rebel supporters to surrender, the Ch'ing simultaneously sought to enlist the assistance of local elites in the process of restoring the order in which they too had a vested interest. The essence of these measures consisted of allowing power—in the form of initiative, money, and weapons— to flow down and out from the center to the local level. It was normal Ch'ing policy to retain this power in the hands of district, provincial, and metropolitan bureaucrats and soldiers; local leaders and men of wealth or prestige below the level of the district and outside the government were discouraged from taking any action that might lead to the creation of an independent power base. During the crisis of rebellion, however, the central government made an exception to this rule and bought the loyalty of families and individuals who were normally outside the power structure (or only marginally within it) by allowing them new scope for legitimate independent action at the local level.

As soon as the Eight Trigrams rebellion broke out, the Chia-ch'ing Emperor called upon local gentry and wealthy merchants for support by encouraging all threatened localities, villages, and cities alike, to "organize and train militia (*i-yung* 義勇) and to dig out trenches and moats." "This," declared the emperor, "is the excellent policy of 'strengthening the walls and clearing the countryside.' "

According to this policy, militiamen trained "solely for the defense of their own localities (*hsiang* 鄉)" could give the people a source of protection and a means for repulsing rebel attacks on their homes if larger armies were not on the scene.[107] This officially sponsored organization of militia also gave the people a way of demonstrating their loyalty and using their power in the interest of the central government; in fact, it clearly put pressure on them to do so. By "donating" time, manpower, money, and supplies, all "righteous citizens" could expect to earn concrete rewards from the government in the form of money, titles, or positions.[108] In the districts of Shantung, Chihli, and Honan that were either attacked or threatened by the Eight Trigrams, the creation of local militia and the readying of village and town defenses, and with them the rallying of local support, was both policy and practice. Under local leaders, these militia guarded the cities, arrested sect members and rebel scouts, and fought with rebel bands that entered their districts. When the danger was past, the militia were dissolved.[109] Let us turn to the events of 1813 for a closer look at how this policy worked.

We have seen that in Shantung, the district magistrates in Yü-t'ai, Ch'eng-wu, Shan, and Chin-hsiang were alerted to potential danger and had effectively discouraged the rebels from causing trouble in their districts. In general, the representatives of Ch'ing authority in those areas had shown leadership and confidence convincing to the general populace. In Ch'eng-wu city for example, where markets were closed and a militia organized, the city defenders were at first very uneasy, conscious of being isolated in what might become hostile countryside. Those men who were patrolling the city walls at night to prevent a surprise attack claimed to have seen a strange firelike light in the sky, an evil omen which frightened them. To counteract this growing unease, one of the local education officials lectured the militiamen, describing the government's great strength and comparing it with the weak and disorganized rebels. This heartening shift of perspective, combined with a stable and then improving situation, gradually restored public confidence in Ch'eng-wu.[110]

We have seen how the aggressive actions of Magistrate Wu of Chin-hsiang disrupted and demoralized the network of would-be rebels in his district. Not until 9/15 did sect members from Chin-hsiang, encouraged by the successes of their colleagues in Ts'ao and Ting-t'ao, dare to become rebels. But when the magistrate sent out the small detachment of soldiers from the city to make more arrests, the rebels fled rather than fight. After this, the people of the countryside realized that the government, not the rebels, was the dominant force there, and they began taking the initiative themselves. Villagers located and seized rebels and sect members and brought them to the city to be put under arrest. In this manner, forty prisoners from six villages were turned in between the 18th and the 20th of the 9th month. The large bands of rebels left the area, and by the 24th, Magistrate Wu could claim that "things have settled down, even though there are still a few rebels in hiding or in flight."[111]

Ke-tse district, located directly north of Ting-t'ao, was the seat of Ts'ao-chou prefecture, and it is not surprising to find that the gentry there had organized themselves quickly and in large numbers. One group of rebels from Ts'ao district ventured into Ke-tse following the attacks on the cities on 9/10, and they met with immediate resistance. Members of the local gentry (holding the rank of military *chü-jen* and below) had organized and coordinated militia from over a dozen villages, a force of more than a thousand men according to official sources. This militia engaged the rebels in several battles over a period of days in the middle of the 9th month, killing several hundred and driving the other rebels southward back into Ting-t'ao. On the 13th, a force of only two hundred soldiers from the local garrison and some militia, emboldened by these successes, ventured deep into Ts'ao district, but they were attacked by several combined rebel bands and defeated.[112] Thereafter, Ke-tse district forces continued to defend their own district successfully but waited for large detachments of soldiers to move into rebel territory.

The events in these districts of southwestern Shantung should illustrate that leadership from local officials, swift organization of city defenses, and a firm commitment against the rebels did have the effect of generating public confidence in the government. Sect members were discouraged from becoming rebels, and rebels were discouraged from entering these areas. The atmosphere of initial nervousness and anxiety which, if prolonged, could have been disastrous for the government, was swiftly dispelled and replaced with a realization of Ch'ing strength and of the unlikeliness of rebel success.

In the 9th and 10th months, Eight Trigram rebels had moved freely from their bases in Hua and Shantung into the adjacent districts of southern Chihli. There their superior numbers had left local garrisons powerless. The cities and villages were isolated and helpless until outside soldiers could be transferred to the scene. "Since for the moment my military force is not yet consolidated," memorialized the governor-general of the province, "everything depends on the gentry in those localities themselves doing the defending. We must assist them with provisions and so I have sent a rapid order to [the financial commissioner] saying that each of those districts should be given between one thousand and two thousand ounces of silver."[113] In K'ai district, which shared a thirty-mile border with Hua on the west, a curfew was put into effect in the city, and men were called up and paid to defend the city. The gentry of K'ai(the local gazetteer, an important medium for commemorating acts of local heroism and patriotism, gives biographies of seven men) immediately called for volunteers and led these men to attack the rebels. The militia were repelled with apparent ease, and many of the gentry leaders were killed or wounded.[114] Although authorities in K'ai admitted their helplessness after this initial setback, they continued to do whatever they could. They filed reports naming which villages had been entered by rebels, encouraged residents of the countryside to dig trenches around their villages and to resist all rebel attempts to recruit them by persuasion or force, and arrested individual rebels whenever possible.[115] These acts were important as symbols of continuing Ch'ing authority, but an army capable of dealing effectively with the rebels on the battlefield was a necessary complement to local efforts.

Like villages in southern Chihli, the villages of Hua district were powerless against superior rebel numbers. Moreover, they were deprived even of the leadership provided by the magistrate (who had killed himself in disgrace after fleeing the city) and city gentry—a situation symbolized by the district city itself, now in rebel hands. The large armies necessary for elimination of the rebels from the countryside were needed first to form the government spearhead against Tao-k'ou and then Hua, and therefore the villages of Hua could not even count on receiving outside military assistance. In order to provide these localities with a military force capable of dealing with the rebels and to give the gentry of that area a focus for their activities, the emperor allowed a special kind of militia to be formed.

Militia, when permitted at all, were normally to be organized and financed locally and used only for the defense of their own localities. It was the firm policy of the Chia-ch'ing Emperor not to permit the organization of higher-level militia that would operate outside and be financially independent of the locality where they were formed or that would "follow along with the army." After the massive White Lotus rebellion (1796–1803) was suppressed fewer than ten years earlier, there had been many problems demobilizing militiamen of this sort who had been organized and used successfully during the campaigns in the mountains of Shensi, Szechwan, and western Hupei. Nevertheless, in light of the special and urgent situation in the district of Hua, one officially sponsored exception to this policy was permitted in 1813.[116]

As soon as Hua city had fallen, the prefect of Wei-hui ordered Meng Ch'i-chan 孟屺瞻, an expectant official then in the provincial capital of K'ai-feng, to go to Hua and organize militia there. On 9/20 Meng, a Shantung man in his early fifties, arrived at the market town of Niu-shih-t'un in southwestern Hua district. Following instructions, he called up men from about 180 villages and from them selected 5,200 able-bodied "braves" (yung 勇). A training camp was established in that town and there the men were given weapons and instruction and supported by local contributions. This large militia force was to oppose any rebels who came in the direction of either Wei-hui prefectural city (to the west) or the Yellow River (to the south).[117] Meng Ch'i-chan and his men took to the field and fought several small engagements in western and southern Hua district during the 10th month, killing more than 1,300 rebels during the first three weeks of that month.[118] This obvious effectiveness against the rebels on the battlefield was in part possible because, unlike militia in Shantung and Chihli, this one was allowed to be both larger and more professional. Meng Ch'i-chan and his force also became an actual and symbolic rallying point for "loyal citizens," a source of food and work, an opportunity to earn rewards and reputation.

After the large government army had arrived within a few miles of Hua city, Meng's militia also joined with these soldiers in combined operations in the countryside. For example, on 10/18 Yang Yü-ch'un, the military-governor of Shensi and Kansu, in command of two thousand Shensi soldiers (one-fourth cavalry) joined with some of Meng's militia and engaged a rebel band of about the same size south of Hua. They pursued these rebels, driving them back to their camps, and then attacked those camps, forcing the rebels to abandon them and retreat into Hua city. The following day Military-Governor Yang again took his men into the field to attack a large rebel camp at Ting-luan village. Because he had learned through rebel testimony that it was the government soldiers, not the militia, who were truly feared by the rebels, Yang dressed his soldiers as militia. The rebels from that village, seeing that it was "merely" the militia attacking them, rushed forward confidently. Confronted with soldiers who were apparently the better trained and more effective fighters, the rebels quickly fell back. Yang's combined force was not strong enough to surround or destroy the rebel camp, but it was able to compel most of the rebels to take refuge in Hua city.[119] Meng Ch'i-chan's militia continued to engage in this kind of harassing activity, clearing the countryside by encouraging rebel bands to regroup elsewhere rather than trying to defeat them thoroughly on the battlefield.[120] During the 11th and 12th months these militiamen joined with the massive government army and assisted in the recapture of Tao-k'ou and the city of Hua. For their labors, many received rewards and Meng Ch'i-chan became magistrate of Hua.[121]

Although the organization of local militia and even of special militia such as that of Meng Ch'i-chan's was useful for rallying the local population and defending village and town against small-scale rebel attacks, these measures were by no means enough to suppress the rebellion as a whole. The primary responsibility for the suppression of the Eight Trigrams rested with the Ch'ing armies. In order to understand this other dimension of Ch'ing policy and to see how large armies were deployed, it is first necessary to look at the Ch'ing military apparatus as a whole and at the general pattern for its handling of large-scale disturbances on the north China plain.

The Green Standard army (lü-ying 綠營), manned by Chinese and staffed by Manchus at the highest levels, was deployed in small units (averaging fewer than a thousand men) at regular intervals across the plain. The arrangement was such that few localities were more than fifty miles from any garrison force. The largest garrisons were along the Grand Canal and in the provincial capitals of K'ai-feng (Honan), Chi-nan (Shantung), and Pao-ting (Chihli); here were garrisons of one or two thousand men. On a second, higher level, there were Manchu soldiers of the Eight Banners (pa-ch'i 八旗) stationed in three strategic cities: K'ai-feng near the Yellow River, Te on the Grand Canal in Shantung and Peking itself. Finally, there were large concentrations of special Manchu soldiers in Peking, along the Great Wall north of the capital, and in Manchuria.[122]

These three levels of deployment can be seen as reflections of three different levels at which the Ch'ing government was able to check rebellion. The small Chinese garrisons were for minor disturbances, those larger Chinese and Manchu brigades at strategic places were for large-scale trouble, and those in the north constituted the emergency reserves. The regularly spaced garrisons of at least several hundred Green Standard soldiers were capable of handling only rebel groups of equal or smaller size. Because the command structure of the Green Standard army prevented any single commander from marshaling large numbers of soldiers, and because many localities were several hundred miles from the handful of large garrisons (one thousand or more men), it was important for these forces to defeat and disperse dissident groups before they started to grow. Constant vigilance and readiness at the local level could keep dissident groups from getting too big to be handled by local garrisons (often with the assistance of local militia). Once a rebel band passed the level of several hundred men, however, a second line of defense had to be called into action.

The mobilization of the larger garrisons stationed at strategic points could be slow (if they were far from the scene of action) and inefficient, especially if more than one province were involved, because of the fragmented command structure. This line of defense was in fact of limited usefulness. Rebels whose numbers increased slowly or not at all could eventually be suppressed locally, but a rebel group of several thousand that continued to attract followers could easily reach ten thousand or more before a large and coordinated government force could be assembled against them. In that situation it was necessary to call in the third line of defense, Manchu soldiers from the north, sometimes almost immediately. Ideally, these soldiers from Peking and Manchuria, together with local and regional garrisons and local militia, could combine to make up a force of sufficient number and skill to suppress even a very large rebellion. The command problem was solved by the appointment of a Special Imperial Commissioner (ch'in-ch'ai ta-ch'en 欽差大臣) who was given temporary command of all these soldiers for the purpose of suppressing one particular rebellion.

In the case of the Eight Trigrams, all three levels were called into action almost immediately. On the periphery of the rebel area, local garrisons were of some use, but where rebel bands were large, even government forces of several thousand men were at best only able to drive the rebels out of the area rather than to defeat them in battle. In the area of Hua city, the rebels grew quickly to numbers far exceeding available regional forces, and the Eight Trigrams won for themselves the time and freedom to grow until a sufficiently large force under a single commander and including troops from beyond the Wall was mobilized against them, and then the rebels were defeated.

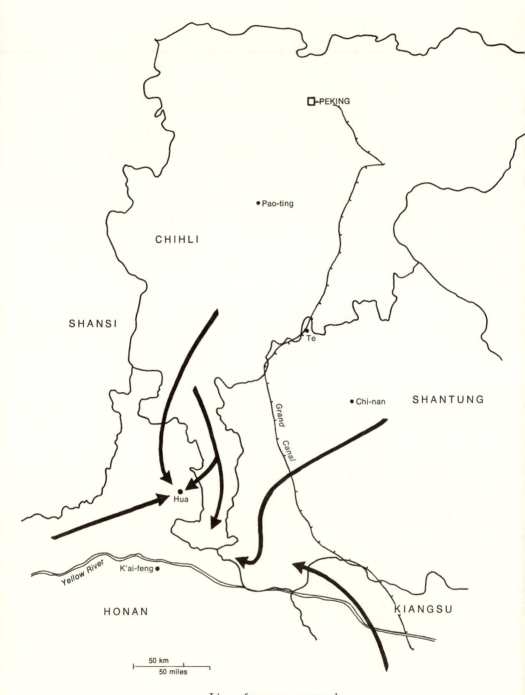

Lines of government attack

The government's overall plan for the suppression of the Eight Trigrams was quite simple. The Yellow River, extending in a west–east line across the north China plain, south of which there had been no disturbances, would be a southernmost barrier against rebel expansion. North of the river, Manchu Banner and Chinese Green Standard soldiers would be transferred into the area from northern Kiangsu, eastern Shantung, Peking and Manchuria, Shansi, Shensi and Kansu, and northwestern Honan. Forming a great arc and moving inward by stages, these soldiers would form a net, limiting rebel expansion in all directions. Like hunted prey—"fish in a kettle or animals in a trap"—the rebels would be driven into a smaller and smaller area until they were held at bay in Hua city. In order to counter the massive concentration of rebel forces in the area of that city, and in order to protect particularly vulnerable cities nearby (such as Chün and Wei-hui), additional soldiers would be sent directly to Hua, to blunt the force of any rebel drive outward and eventually to go in for the kill. As Hua was attacked, soldiers ringing the periphery would be ready to capture any who fled and tried to escape. The scenario was developed early in the campaign and agreed upon by the emperor and Special Imperial Commissioner Na-yen-ch'eng; little occurred to upset their plans. The Chia-ch'ing Emperor's main complaint was that the suppression took much longer than he had hoped; yet these delays were due primarily to the slowness with which Manchu troops from outside the Great Wall were moved south to participate in the final assault on Hua city.[123] Let us now look at the implementation of this policy.

In 1813 the Yellow River ran from west to east in an almost straight line across the north China plain. Cutting through northern Honan and running along the southern border of Shantung, the river was a natural deterrent against rebel expansion toward the south (and against the government transfer of troops to the north). Upon hearing of the initial uprisings, the emperor immediately ordered that all boats be anchored on the south bank for the entire length of the great river in those two provinces so that rebels would have no means of crossing or escaping downstream. The boats bearing the precious copper from the mines of Yunnan were ordered to anchor immediately and to proceed no farther until it was safe to do so.[124] The magistrate of Lan-yang district in Honan did decide, despite these orders, to ferry across to the southern bank some two thousand "refugees" who had gathered on the north bank at the end of the 9th month: "They had waded out onto the sandy flats of the river and were standing in the mud and shallow waters, crying out for help." For this he was dismissed and orders were given for all the alleged refugees to be interrogated and the rebels among them arrested.[125] In general this policy of containment was quite successful, possibly because the rebels themselves do not appear to have thought in terms of travel by water.

Unfortunately for the government, there had been a break in the dike of the Yellow River in Sui district in Honan late in the 8th month. The river had burst through the southern embankment and was flowing south of its regular course. The main channel that ran due east was nearly empty.[126] Efforts to repair this breach had begun prior to the rebel uprisings, but now this construction site became a point of government vulnerability. A number of rebels from Shantung and a few from Honan had learned about the construction work and had gone to the site with the express aim of destroying government equipment and material. For example, Chu Te-san, who was arrested at the site on 10/7, stated that the leader of his group had given him explosives and told him and at least five others to go to where the construction was being done and pretend to be beggars or carters. They were then to "find a chance to set fire to the walls of the dike which were made of thatch."[127] These and other small groups of scouts were vulnerable to arrest because they traveled individually or in small groups, and many were seized by authorities on the spot. In the end no disturbances took place at the construction site.

The suppression of the Eight Trigram rebels in Shantung was accomplished with apparent ease and dispatch, but the task had been made considerably easier by the departure of most of the large bands of rebels from the area. We have seen that in the districts of eastern Ts'ao-chou prefecture, a display of confidence on the part of the government officials and people had discouraged some sect members from taking any action and encouraged others to leave to join their colleagues in Ts'ao and Ting-t'ao. This movement of the rebels toward the west was speeded by the swift appearance of Ch'ing soldiers on the scene. To contain the rebels and protect the area exposed by the break in the dike, a second-rank military commander from Hsu-chou in Kiangsu was ordered into the area. By 9/18 he had arrived near the borders of Shan district with four hundred men (soon increased to a thousand), and he remained there for the next few months deterring large bands from coming his way and mopping up smaller groups that came within reach.[128] (Also see map p. 228.)

As we have seen, the Ch'ing counterattack in Shantung was under-taken by the salt commissioner of that province. Commissioner Liu Ch'ing 劉清, then in his seventy-first year, was a former military official and veteran of the campaigns against the White Lotus rebels in Szechwan and was respected as an able commander.[129] Both the governor and salt commissioner had come to Ts'ao-chou prefectural city, just north of the area where rebels were living and raiding, arriving there on 9/26. Commissioner Liu decided to attack immediately. He moved southward into Ting-t'ao district, leading five hundred Chinese and Manchu soldiers, including some cavalry.[130] In a series of skirmishes that day and with the assistance of another government force of two hundred men who came from the east, Commissioner Liu supervised the killing of three hundred rebels out of a group of at least one thousand, and he captured another hundred. More impor-tant, he forced these rebels to leave that part of Ting-t'ao and move to the south and west. Over the next two weeks Liu Ch'ing pursued and attacked the rebels wherever he could find them. When the rebels withdrew into a village and tried to defend it, he surrounded them and relied on muskets and fire to break through their defenses. When they fled, he used cavalry to pursue them. In battles at Han-chia-ta-miao (9/30), Hu-chia village (10/4), An-ling village (10/8) and Hao-chia village (10/9) the rebels in Shantung were gradually pushed out of the province, nearly five thousand of them losing their lives in the process.[131] In these battles it was the government soldiers (mostly Green Standard with some Banner troops) who did the fighting; mopping up was left to the local militia, which were not capable of handling the large rebel bands. After the 10th month, when rebels from Honan and Chihli tried to come to Shantung, they found their way blocked by these Ch'ing soldiers. Those scattered rebels still left in Shantung were "exhausted," and their groups broke apart as each man tried to save himself.[132]

The beleaguered cities of southern Chihli did not receive the same swift assistance as those in nearby Shantung. The governor-general of Chihli, Wen Ch'eng-hui 溫承惠, had begun transferring soldiers to the south as soon as the initial uprisings occurred. On 9/12 he was named Special Imperial Commissioner and he and the military-governor of Chihli, Ma Yü 馬瑜, were ordered to go in person to supervise the sup-pression campaigns.[133] On 9/16, after the palace attack, the emperor punished Wen Ch'eng-hui by removing him from his post and appointed a new special commissioner. Wen was told to continue to the battlefield and to assist with the campaign in order to make up for

his negligence. He and Ma Yü and their 4,200 Green Standard soldiers did not, therefore, arrive at Kai district city until 10/2, more
than three weeks after the murder of the magistrate of Ch'ang-yuan
by rebels. At this time, the situation around Chün city was still
considered critical, and since the threat to that administrative center
took precedence over that posed by the roaming bands of rebels in
southern Chihli, the emperor ordered Wen Ch'eng-hui and Ma Yü
to take their men westward instead. They were to help the governor
of Honan relieve the pressure on Chün.[134] Ten days later, the situation
had improved and the emperor realized that "if the rebels were to
move northward, we would be unable to halt them." He ordered Ma
Yü to return to the K'ai area and begin clearing the rebels out of
southern Chihli.[135]

Ma Yü was instructed to be ready to cut off any rebel movements
away from Hua and to move with his two thousand men down the
boot of southern Chihli, retaking rebel-held villages and driving the
larger rebel bands westward to Hua. He finally reached K'ai on
10/21. The rebels in southern Chihli had had no serious opposition
for six weeks. Meeting only minor challenges from militia, rebel bands
of five hundred to a thousand men had come freely into Chihli from
their camps in Hua district, dominating the countryside—"their
strength was frightening."[136]

Strengthened by another one thousand soldiers from Shantung (no
longer needed in that province), Ma Yü finally led his men into battle
on 10/23. They attacked a rebel camp at P'an-chang village about
ten miles away inside the Hua border. The government appeared to
have the upper hand; the rebels defended the village from a small
ridge but were eventually forced to take refuge inside, and nearly a
thousand died when the soldiers set fire to the thatched houses inside.
But just as the Ch'ing soldiers were counting the bodies, gathering up
firearms, banners, and captives, they were suddenly attacked by two
thousand rebels who had come belatedly to their comrades' assistance.
Ma's men "had been fighting all day and were like a bow which has
already been shot, and so they could not be victorious." It was nearly
dark and the government army beat a hasty retreat back to K'ai.[137]
Realizing that his three thousand men were inadequate against large
rebel armies, Ma Yü concentrated on smaller villages, engaging the
rebels, killing some, but trying to drive most of them westward to
Hua city.[138] Pressure on the rebels from this direction was important,
for it came at a time when the Eight Trigrams were feeling increasingly beleaguered. On 11/1 Grand Councillor T'o-chin 托津 arrived

in K'ai to take charge of the campaign in Chihli.[139] When Li Wen-ch'eng took his followers and tried to escape from Hua early in the 11th month, these soldiers were waiting for them. After that, only mopping up was necessary as the rebels were caught in the trap in Hua city.

Rebel bands were driven into Hua city during the 9th and 10th months by these government actions in Shantung and Chihli. This centripetal movement was also encouraged by the growing need to defend Tao-k'ou and Hua against the increasingly pointed attack by armies concentrating on those cities. A thousand Green Standard soldiers under the command of the brigade-general stationed in Huai-ch'ing prefecture (to the west of Hua) arrived outside Chün city on 9/17.[140] The governor of Honan, Kao-ch'i 高杞, arrived on the 20th, bringing another thousand men. As we have seen, this force was sufficient to blunt the rebel attack on Chün city and force a standoff. During the 10th month, more soldiers hurried to the scene: two thousand Green Standard soldiers from Chihli, and five hundred crack cavalry from Kansu.[141] The government attack was effectively directed during these weeks by the commander of that cavalry, the military-governor of Shensi and Kansu, Yang Yü-ch'un 楊遇春. Like Salt Commissioner Liu, Yang was a veteran of the campaigns against the White Lotus rebels, as well as of other Ch'ien-lung period campaigns in Kansu, Taiwan, and Nepal and against the Miao rebels in the southwest. The emperor had ordered him to the scene as soon as word reached him of the loss of Hua city.[142] During the 10th month Yang Yü-ch'un, Kao-ch'i, and Wen Ch'eng-hui positioned themselves between the rebels and the mountains, fearing that the rebels might try to abandon Hua and head for the T'ai-hang mountains less than fifty miles to the west. There was only one large engagement during this time: on 10/9 Yang Yü-ch'un led the assembled soldiers and succeeded in driving the rebel bands out of the area on the west bank of the river across from Tao-k'ou.[143] Yang then took some of these soldiers and joined with Meng Ch'i-chan's militia in minor engagements in southern Hua district, but the main thrust of the attack was stalled temporarily, pending the arrival of the new special commissioner.

When he fired Wen Ch'eng-hui on 9/16, the Chia-ch'ing Emperor had replaced him with Na-yen-ch'eng 那彥成 as Special Imperial Commissioner, and a month later Na was also made governor-general of Chihli province. Na-yen-ch'eng, then forty-nine years old, was a plain-white banner Manchu, the grandson of the official and general of the Ch'ien-lung period A-kuei. He too had commanded troops in Shensi during the suppression of the White Lotus rebellion and had served as grand councillor, as governor-general of Kwang-tung and Kwangsi (where he dealt with the problem of coastal pirates), and since 1810 as governor-general of Shensi and Kansu.[144] He had high office, experience, and the personal confidence of the emperor. All the soldiers transferred to Honan and Chihli for the campaign against the Eight Trigrams were placed under Na-yen-ch'eng's supreme command.

It took quite some time for both commander and troops to reach the scene of the fighting. Na-yen-ch'eng did not leave his post at Lan-chou (Kansu) until 9/26. Delayed by rain and mud, he passed through Tung-kuan (at the juncture of Shensi, Honan, and Shansi provinces) only on 10/4. From there he moved more rapidly east-ward, along the Yellow River, and reached Wei-hui prefectural city on 10/8. Another ten days passed as Na regrouped, and finally on 10/19 he arrived in Chün district. Together with Yang Yü-ch'un and the others, he immediately set up camp at Hsin-chen, across the river from Tao-k'ou. Na had brought with him thirty-five hundred soldiers (five hundred Green Standard, the rest Manchu); Kao-ch'i had three thousand Honan soldiers; and Wen Ch'eng-hui com-manded two thousand (all Green Standard).[145] Thus by the middle of the 10th month, there were eighty-five hundred men in position to the west of the rebel-held villages and cities, on both sides of the river, ready to attack. (See map p. 211.)

On 10/21 the commanders learned that three or four thousand rebels had "poured out of their nest at Tao-k'ou" and dividing into two groups had gone south and east. In fact, a third band had been prepared secretly and the rebels were hoping to lure the Ch'ing soldiers into a trap. Na-yen-ch'eng and Yang Yü-ch'un both went into battle. Attacking alternately with cavalry and infantry, one detachment of soldiers forced the rebels to scatter and return toward Tao-k'ou. The would-be trappers were themselves caught, for they found Yang Yü-ch'un and his men waiting for them. The battle lasted all day and was the biggest government success to date: more than fourteen hundred rebels killed, five cannon recaptured, and a thousand "coerced people" surrendered to the government (and were allowed to go free). Those rebels who survived the battle retreated into Tao-k'ou and Hua.[146]

This battle, seven weeks after the initial uprisings, showed the Eight Trigrams that not only had they lost the initiative but that

Tao-k'ou was now seriously threatened. They began to improve the town's defenses: deep trenches were dug around it, the gates were closed, large bands of rebels were no longer sent out on raiding expeditions, and the remaining grain stores in Tao-k'ou were moved to safety in Hua. The government countered by shutting the locks on the Wei River downstream outside Chün city; this forced the upstream water to back up, widening the river at Tao-k'ou and making it more difficult for the rebels to cross the river and escape toward the west. When the Tao-k'ou rebels tried to build a pontoon bridge of wooden planks at a fording place near the city, in what was their final attempt to maintain an open avenue toward the mountains in the west, they met with immediate resistance. Kao-ch'i had moved his men to the west bank opposite Tao-k'ou and together with Yang Yü-ch'un destroyed the bridge, drove the rebels back into the port town, and killed another thousand rebels in the battle.[147]

The government armies, numbering some eighty-five hundred men, moved against Tao-k'ou itself on 10/27. This was their first direct attack on a major rebel stronghold, and they did so against far superior numbers, hoping to ride the tide of their series of victories. There were from seventeen to twenty thousand people in Tao-k'ou, and at least half of them took up arms to defend the city, assisted by several thousand reinforcements from Hua. The Ch'ing armies set up cannon across the river and sent soldiers to attack from both the north and the south; the rebels were left with one escape route, southeast to Hua city. Meng Ch'i-chan and his militia had been called to the scene to assist. The government attacked early on the 27th, and as the rebels began to retreat toward Hua, the soldiers entered Tao-k'ou and set it afire. By the evening of that day, five or six thousand rebels had been killed in battle, and an additional four or five thousand people were burned to death. Following the policy of leniency toward those who were "coerced," the government had set up prominent banners and announced that all "good people" should come there if they wished to be spared. Eight to nine thousand "refugees" from the city refused to fight and came forward begging for mercy.[148]

After resting that night, Ch'ing forces entered Tao-k'ou the following morning to seize those still hiding in the ruined city. A small band of about five hundred rebels made a break for it and fled toward Hua city, luring government soldiers after them. Na-yen-ch'eng and Kao-ch'i pressed onward after them, but the sudden appearance of first three thousand rebels coming from a rebel-held village nearby and then five thousand more coming from Hua city forced them to pull back to Tao-k'ou. There the two commanders personally inspected the carnage; they found bodies everywhere, filling the streets and the houses. Contrary to their orders, the soldiers had killed anyone who opposed them, making little effort to spare any remaining innocent city residents or coerced rebel followers.

With the capture of Tao-k'ou the government net around the Eight Trigrams tightened significantly. Although rebel bands did continue to camp in villages near Hua, their movements were increasingly circumscribed. By the 1st day of the 11th month, Na-yen-ch'eng's men were pitching camp outside the walls of the city. The rebels were forced to close all but two city gates. A thousand more government soldiers had arrived, boosting the size of the Ch'ing army to nearly ten thousand men.[149] It would take Na more than a month to fully close the siege and assemble the additional five thousand soldiers transferred to his command. In the meantime, rebel leaders inside the city had taken stock of their situation and decided to take drastic and dramatic action.

TRAPPED

At the end of the 10th month, Li Wen-ch'eng decided to take a few of his followers and flee from Hua city before it was attacked by government soldiers. Li had previously been living in his home village north of Hua city, trying to recuperate from his injuries. Sometime during the 10th month he had moved to the nearby camp of Chen Trigram King Sung K'e-chün at T'ao-yuan village. At this time Tui Trigram King Liu Kuo-ming was camped not far away, and he and Sung K'e-chün had both been involved in increasingly frequent battles with soldiers in northeastern Hua district.[150] After Ch'ing forces attacked and retook the port of Tao-k'ou on 10/27, no rebel camp outside Hua was secure.

At about this time, Feng K'e-shan, who was to have been King of Earth, quarreled with Li Wen-ch'eng, thus further fragmenting the rebel leadership. He left Hua city on horseback in order to organize his own people in Shantung and then "rise up and come and kill Li Wen-ch'eng and so get revenge." Early in the 11th month, Feng arrived in Ching district near the Shantung border at the home of his pupil Sung Yüeh-lung. Sung later described Feng's journey for government interrogators (the constant insertion of personal names and place names was surely at the insistence of the investigators who feared Feng might start another rising and were doggedly tracking him down):

> [After leaving Hua city] Feng K'e-shan had fled to Nan-kuan-t'ao at Ho-wang-tzu where he spent the night. At daylight the next day, he crossed the [Wei] river, using a boat prepared by a pupil named Chao. . . . After crossing the river, they went together to Tung-tien-tzu to Chao's home where Feng had stayed for three days. Because it was dangerous to be traveling with a knife and a horse, he gave them both to Chao. His clothes and books had blood on them, so he rolled them up in a ball and threw them in the river. He traded his saddle and a riding jacket for some clothing, shoes, and socks belonging to Chao. He left there on 10/27.

Two weeks later Feng arrived at Sung Yueh-lung's home. He explained to Sung why he had left Hua city, and asked for help in revenging himself against Li Wen-ch'eng. He discovered, however, that the power base he thought he had created for himself was non-existent without the support of religious leaders such as Li or Lin Ch'ing, for Sung replied flatly that he did not have enough men for this undertaking. Feng K'e-shan kept up a brave front in the face of this refusal and declared that he would instead go and find his first boxing teacher who lived in Shansi (in fact this man lived in Honan and had no interest in rebelling) and with his help and the assistance of others from Shensi province, "where there were still big leaders with several tens of thousands of men under them," would return to Hua and "compete with Li Wen-ch'eng for mastery." Feng promised Sung a high title should he be successful, and Sung was thus persuaded to give him 16 taels for traveling expenses. Feng's talk about Shansi and Shensi was only bluster; he had no other supporters. A few weeks later he was arrested in a small village about fifty miles to the north, where he was selling medicines and curing illnesses.[151]

Meanwhile on the 29th day of the 10th month Na-yen-ch'eng had ordered his men to begin laying siege to Hua city. This city was surrounded by a wall about three miles in circumference in which there were five gates, two on the western side (which faced Tao-k'ou and the Wei River) and one in each of the other sides. The rebels, in anticipation of a siege, had begun clearing out the moat, which was about twenty feet across, and had piled up earth on at least three sides of the city to strengthen their defenses; moreover, they had set up carts in a circle around the outside as a further line of defense.[152] Government soldiers had been able to blockade the east, south, and southwest gates, leaving the rebels with access only through the north and west gates. Through these gates, however, the rebels in the city maintained contact with Li Wen-ch'eng and with other leaders still camped in villages north and west of Hua.

On 10/29, two days after the loss of Tao-k'ou, two thousand men from the camp of Trigram King Sung at T'ao-yuan, assisted by a thousand men from inside Hua city, converged on the area outside the northern wall in an effort to drive away the government soldiers positioned there. With the assistance of cannon and musketfire from the city walls they were able to stave off the Ch'ing advance that day, but the land outside the north gate was muddy and marshy, poor for fighting and difficult to hold. The next day, the 30th, the T'ao-yuan and Hua city rebels had to fight again to keep that area clear. From early morning until late afternoon a thousand men from T'ao-yuan and two thousand from inside the city did battle with soldiers under the command of Yang Yü-ch'un and several imperial body-guards. The rebels lost more than a thousand men, and government soldiers were able to push close to the northern city wall before they were again driven back by the hail of rocks and gunfire from above. At the end of the day, the rebels still had access to the city through the north gate, but the west gate had been closed.[153]

That night, Trigram Kings Liu Kuo-ming and Sung K'e-chün and Trigram Lord Wang Hsueh-i, each riding in carts, approached Hua from the north, bringing between seven and eight hundred men with them. They made camp less than a mile from the city. In the middle of the night Sung K'e-chün went to the north wall, called to his comrades inside to open the gate, and then he and Liu Kuo-ming went inside. Li Wen-ch'eng either came with them now or had been brought into the city the day before. During that night, the last day of the 10th month, the surviving Eight Trigram leaders—Li Wen-ch'eng, Liu Kuo-ming, Sung K'e-chün, Sun Trigram King Wang Hsiu-chih, Chief Commander Sung Yuan-ch'eng, Niu Liang-ch'en, and Hsu An-kuo—discussed their alarming situation. What could they do? Liu Kuo-ming felt that Li Wen-ch'eng and a core group of followers could be saved, and he wanted to take them to Shantung to hide at the home of Hsu An-kuo's chief pupil Tui Trigram Lord Chu Ch'eng-kuei. Chu had been in Hua since late in the 9th month, but had left his brother in charge of their village of Hu-chia in Ts'ao district. No one knew the current situation in Shantung, so scouts were immediately sent out. In the meantime, the leaders agreed that Liu Kuo-ming would take Li Wen-ch'eng from the city. They intended eventually to return with all available help to relieve those left behind.[154]

Before dawn, Liu, Li, Chu Ch'eng-kuei, and Sung K'e-chün left through the north gate, taking some additional men with them. With about a thousand followers, they went to Liu Kuo-ming's camp at Nan-hu village, which as yet had not been attacked. Li Wen-ch'eng, still unable to walk or even ride a horse, rode in a large cart drawn by four horses. They stayed at Nan-hu for several days, awaiting word from Shantung.[155]

In the meantime, Grand Councillor T'o-chin had arrived in Ta-ming prefectural city to direct the pacification of the rebels in southern Chihli belatedly undertaken by Ma Yü.[156] Ma Yü was at that time attacking rebel villages on the border between K'ai and Hua districts. On 11/1, just as Liu Kuo-ming and the contingent from Hua city were arriving at his camp, a group of his followers under Trigram Lord Wei Te-chung encountered Ma Yü's force nearby. About five hundred rebels died in the battle; five cannon, hundreds of light arms, and two large carts packed with clothing, dried provisions, guns, and ammunition were lost. Some rebels tried to take refuge but were burned out.

Li Wen-ch'eng and Liu Kuo-ming could not have been encouraged about their chances of escaping to the east when they realized how near this army was. Within a few days they learned from their scouts that the situation in Shantung was hopeless anyway: all large bands of rebels had been driven out of that province, Chu Ch'eng-kuei's home village had been burned a month earlier, and Ch'ing soldiers were positioned on the borders in case anyone should try to cross into Shantung. There was not much time to consider where to go, but it became imperative that Li Wen-ch'eng and his men set forth as quickly as possible. Li Wen-ch'eng's condition was not improved by an eye injury received about this time.[157]

On 11/3 Ma Yü learned that there were about three thousand rebels camped at Nan-hu, though he did not realize that the "chief rebel" himself was among them. In preparation against attack, a deep trench had been dug around that camp and the two other villages nearby, and when Ma Yü attacked on the 3d, the rebels were able to hold out. It is likely that Liu Kuo-ming, Li Wen-ch'eng, and the others fled that evening. The next day Ma Yü attacked again. The government soldiers cut down trees, dragged the tree trunks to the

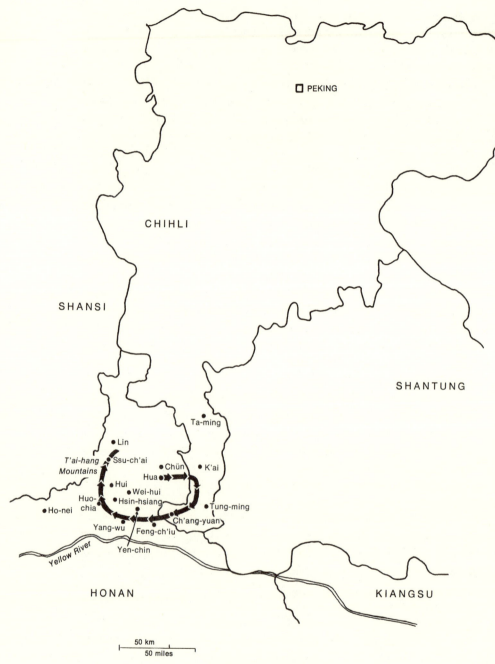

PEKING

CHIHLI

SHANSI

SHANTUNG

Ta-ming

Lin

Ssu-ch'ai

*T'ai-hang
Mountains*

Chün

K'ai

Hua

Hui

Wei-hui

Huo-
chia

Hsin-hsiang

Ho-nei

Tung-ming

Ch'ang-yuan

Yang-wu

Feng-ch'iu

Yellow River

Yen-chin

HONAN

KIANGSU

50 km

50 miles

Li Wen-ch'eng's flight

trench, and laid them across. Then they rushed across, simultaneously hurling fireballs to inflame the thatch buildings. The villages were
burned and five or six hundred rebels died and more than a thousand
people left behind, including women and children, were taken
prisoner.[158]

All the important rebel leaders and their most devoted followers
(probably fewer than a thousand men) had fled. Liu Kuo-ming and
Li Wen-ch'eng had decided that their only chance for survival lay in
reaching the safety of the T'ai-hang mountains on the western border
of Honan: there they would camp, reassemble, gain strength, and
when they were ready (and presumably when Li Wen-ch'eng was
well) would rise up again and return to Hua to save those holding out
in that city.[159] The only way to reach these mountains and avoid the
closing government net and the fierce concentration of soldiers in the
Hua city area would be to make a sweeping semicircle to the south,
west, and then north. Li and his band traveled along the border
between Honan and Chihli; they were "sighted" by local officials
on 11/4 on the border between K'ai and Hua districts, then on the
Hua border farther to the south, and on 11/6 they entered Feng-ch'iu
district in Honan. At this time their band was said to consist of about
fifteen or sixteen hundred men on foot, two hundred more on horseback, and some seventy or eighty carts—perhaps two thousand men
at the most. There they were joined inadvertently it appears by
another rebel band of about five hundred men who had just been
driven out of their camp (with large losses through death and defection) by Meng Ch'i-chan and his militia, still mopping up in central
Hua district.[160]

It had been six days since the band left Hua city, and in the last
three days they had traveled some seventy miles. At first the rebels
had surrounded and looted some of the villages through which they
passed; later they tried to avoid battle and did not risk attacking any
place that had the forces to resist them. Provisions and ammunition
and weapons were carried in carts, as were women, some of the high
leaders and Li Wen-ch'eng. As many as possible rode on horseback,
and the rebels tried to steal horses and mules whenever they could.[161]

Gradually the government commanders at Hua learned of the
existence of this rebel group, but they did not realize immediately
that it was a single band traveling speedily and purposefully westward. At first small detachments were sent after them, but these were
unable to halt the rebels.[162] Na-yen-ch'eng, having finally received
a variety of reports and confessions convincing him that Li Wen-

ch'eng was traveling with this band, decided to take more forceful action, even though it meant reducing his strength outside the besieged city. On 11/11 he ordered the recently appointed Brigade-General Yang Fang 楊芳 to take two thousand soldiers and, leaving at night so that Hua city rebels would not see them depart, to go speedily to intercept the fleeing rebel band.[163] In the meantime a brigade-general in command of a thousand soldiers had come from Shansi to be stationed temporarily in Ho-nei district in Honan; he heard of the approaching rebels and moved to cut them off from the west.[164]

The rebels had moved along the borders between Yen-chin and Yang-wu, and they continued traveling due west along the southern boundaries of Hsin-hsiang and Huo-chia.[165] Finding that government soldiers were ahead of them in the west, the rebels changed directions once more. Part of the band remained behind and returned eastward, "causing disturbances" in the Yen-chin area. The main band, including Li Wen-ch'eng and all the top leaders, turned north and, proceeding along the border between Hsin-hsiang and Huo-chia, aimed for the mountains just north of Hui city. By 11/11 they had traveled fifty miles from Feng-ch'iu (more than one hundred and twenty miles since they left Hua) and arrived in southwestern Hui district. According to official reports, the villages along this portion of the rebels' flight had been "ravaged, attacked, burned, and plundered, and their inhabitants forced to join the rebels or die." If true, these reports may indicate the rebels' lack of supplies and increasing sense of desperation.[166]

The rebels were certainly not greeted by a wave of public support during this rush toward the mountains. They gained no more than one or two thousand new followers despite the fact that these were districts where drought and flooding had left many starving. It is not known how Li Wen-ch'eng and his men tried to rally support. They did carry Li's banner reading "True Master Li of the T'ien-shun Era of the Great Ming" with them for all to see, but they may have been a clearly losing cause and could not have been welcome after they began to prey on the villagers and villages for supplies.[167]

On 11/12 as they entered the foothills of northern Hui district, the rebel band numbered about four thousand men. In order to cross the low mountain passes, their carts had to be abandoned, and men and provisions traveled by horseback and on foot. Li Wen-ch'eng was still unable to ride a horse and was instead carried in a large winnowing basket slung on poles between two men. The rebels continued north, close to the Shansi border and finally decided to pause and set up camp at a village called Ssu-ch'ai, "Fourth Stockade." There they rested for several days, perhaps imagining that they were safe. Half the group, several thousand men, went on an expedition eastward into Lin district on 11/17 looking for supplies. They burned and looted two markets, but when they learned that government soldiers were approaching, returned rapidly to their camp with the bad news. Ssu-ch'ai was a fortified village; it had mountains behind it, a deep moat, sturdy walls, and access to fresh water. Exhausted and now surely pessimistic about their chances for survival, Li Wen-ch'eng and the others decided to stand and fight.[168]

Yang Yü-ch'un's protégé Yang Fang had been sent from Hua to pursue the rebels, and quickly traversing the fifty-mile distance, he and his men entered the mountains on the 18th. The following day, Yang Fang arranged an ambush. He lured the rebels out of the stockade by sending only four hundred men to attack it. Nearly the entire rebel force, three thousand men including about three hundred on horseback, hoping perhaps for a quick victory, rushed out of the fort to attack. They pursued the soldiers as Yang Fang had planned and rushed straight into the trap. As the four-hundred-man bait halted and turned against them, several hundred other soldiers appeared to the right and to the left. The rebels were hemmed in, despite their superior numbers, and when six hundred crack Manchurian cavalry suddenly attacked, the rebels tried desperately to retreat. They fled to a nearby ridge and held it for a while, throwing down bricks and stones upon the soldiers, but they were again surprised by an attack from the rear by cavalry led by imperial bodyguards that had circled around behind them. Attacked from above and below, the one thousand rebels still alive tried to descend from the ridge and return to their camp. Only a few hundred made it. Between 2,200 and 2,500 rebels were killed that day; uncounted others fell to their deaths on the rocks and into the stream, and several hundred were captured alive.[169]

This was a disastrous defeat for the rebels; in a single day their fighting force had been cut to one-quarter its size. The government troops were fresh, as they had traveled only fifty miles since leaving Hua; the rebels, in contrast, had been on the move for nearly three weeks and had covered three times that distance. It was the able Manchu cavalry only just arrived from Kirin and Heilungkiang to assist in the campaign and the infantry and cavalry from Shensi and Kansu that had made the victory possible. Nevertheless, the battle had not been an easy one. There were reports later that some of the other soldiers (both Chinese and Manchu, both provincial and capital soldiers) had refused to attack the rebel-held ridge when ordered to do so and were galvanized into action only by the execution of two soldiers on the spot by their commanders. It is said that Yang Fang's whiskers "turned white overnight" on this expedition at Ssu-ch'ai.[170]

Inside the fort were Li Wen-ch'eng, Liu Kuo-ming, a few other leaders, and about eight hundred of their followers. They had occupied the several hundred houses, most of them made of stone and brick, as well as the seven or eight high stone towers from which they were able to watch as Ch'ing armies surrounded them.

Yang Fang did not lose his momentum, and the following day, the 20th day of the 11th month, he attacked. Government soldiers jumped the moat and tried for the entire morning without success to break through the wall of the stockade, being continually fired upon by rebels on the wall and beaten back by a hail of bricks and stones. Finally the soldiers were able to ram through one section of the wall, and as the rebels rushed to fill the breach with planks and bricks, the soldiers charged inside, firing bullets from their guns and arrows from their bows as they went. The rebels had to come down from the walls and the fighting continued in the narrow streets and alleys of the mountain village. Realizing that the end was near, the rebels fled back into the towers and houses. From the towers they fired their guns and cannon and threw down bricks and tiles. By this time it was already evening and both sides were exhausted, but Yang Fang, not wanting to give the rebels a chance to escape that night, ordered that the buildings be set afire immediately. His soldiers gathered wood and thatch and built fires around the stone buildings. Some rebels braved the smoke and made a rush for the gates of the stockade, but they were intercepted and caught or killed.[171]

Captured rebels were asked about Li Wen-ch'eng, and Yang Fang, learning that he was in one of the towers still standing, hurried to the spot. According to his report, he led a small group of soldiers into the building and

> from above there emerged a rebel leader who identified himself as Liu Kuo-ming. He leaped out, holding a knife, and stabbed two soldiers one after another. Other soldiers fired their guns and killed him. Then [the Ch'ing commanders] called to the other rebels, saying that if Li Wen-ch'eng would come out and give himself up, then those with him would be spared death.

That head rebel [Li] himself came out, and pointing to himself he said "Li Wen-ch'eng is right here. All you have to do is come up and get me. I'm not coming down." When the soldiers heard this, they all rushed in, holding ready their knives. But that rebel then started a fire, and in the fire the rebel group of forty or fifty men in that place surged to surround him and he was crushed to death.

One of those followers who escaped from the building explained that "when Li Wen-ch'eng saw that there was no way to save himself, he shouted to the group that they should all immediately set fire to the place, and so those leaders . . . were all burned to death."[172]

The fires burned all night; the next day, the Ch'ing forces inspected the ruined fortress and its dead. Another forty rebels were captured that morning—they had been hiding all night in manure pits and in stacks of grain—and a few others who had escaped from the fort were quickly rounded up. Li Wen-ch'eng's body was found in a pile of charred wood and bricks. He was easily identified by the eye injury he had received and the leg and foot wounds from his torture in Hua three months before. He had a turban on his head and wounds from both guns and arrows on his face. "His body was intact. . . . He was wearing a lot of fur clothing. His face looked alive. His left eye had a white film over the pupil. His ankles were wrapped in cloth bandages and inside there was broken bone, rolls of flesh, and scars from the pincers [of torture]."[173] The large white banner bearing his title was found nearby. Besides Li, the bodies of all of the high-ranking sect leaders were located and identified. There were between seven and eight hundred bodies lying about inside the fort; few had survived.

It had been a little less than three months since Li Wen-ch'eng was first arrested. His flight from Hua was a gamble against high odds. He had been able to outwit the Ch'ing generals only temporarily. If his group had originally gone directly westward into the mountains, without making the long detour toward Shantung, perhaps they could have preserved the vigor needed to hold off pursuing armies and win new supporters. Now without Li or any of the kings and lords who had accompanied him, the position of those Eight Trigram rebels still trapped in Hua city became even more hopeless.

While Li Wen-ch'eng was in flight, Special Imperial Commissioner Na-yen-ch'eng had been proceeding with the siege of Hua

city. His first job was to close off the city completely by preventing
the rebels from leaving or entering through the north gate. Because
there was marshy land along the north wall, Ch'ing soldiers had
difficulty controlling this territory, and when they approached the
gate they were continually driven back by the hail of gun and cannon
fire from the city walls. Moreover, they were occasionally harassed
by attacks from the few rebel bands still camped in villages nearby.
Na-yen-ch'eng therefore decided first to clear the countryside of
these remnants; he sent out large concentrations of soldiers to attack and destroy their camps. Under pressure from these armies,
from Ma Yü's force in southern Chihli, and from Meng Ch'i-chan's
militia in southern Hua district, most of the scattered rebel bands
abandoned their camps in the course of the 11th month and either
retreated into Hua or joined Li Wen-ch'eng's band as it fled west.
Once their allies nearby had been swept away, the Eight Trigrams
in Hua closed the north gate, themselves sealing the siege.

By early in the 11th month Na-yen-ch'eng had assembled about
thirteen thousand soldiers, nine thousand of whom were available
for combat. Although no attacks on the city took place for nearly
three weeks, Na-yen-ch'eng explained to the impatient emperor
that this was a trick calculated to fool the rebels into feeling over-
confident. The rebel population inside Hua numbered at least fifty
thousand people, and Na prudently wanted to wait until the cavalry
had arrived from Manchuria before attacking.[174] In the meantime,
he prepared for the assault on the walled city. The moat was cleared,
fierce wooden barricades called "deer antlers" (consisting of rows
of sharpened poles planted in the ground at an angle, pointed
toward the city) were set up around the city, and cannon were
arranged on platforms aimed at strategic places in the walls.[175] In
order to demoralize the city inhabitants, Na-yen-ch'eng ordered
that some of the "good people" from villages in the district who had
chosen to surrender to the government after being "coerced" by
the rebels go and appeal to city residents to do likewise. These
people were sent to walk outside underneath the walls of Hua,
carrying banners of imperial yellow. They were to call out in loud
voices to the people within and encourage them to surrender themselves, promising that they would be spared punishment. And indeed
some (apparently not many) did climb over the walls to do exactly
this.[176]

Finally, on 11/19 Na-yen-ch'eng ordered a general attack on all
five gates of the city. (He did not know it, but this was the day Yang

Fang was inflicting the disastrous defeat on Li Wen-ch'eng's band in the hills outside Ssu-ch'ai.) Cannon were fired and soldiers charged the city gates. The rebels rang their gongs to signal the alarm, threw down huge stones and flaming reeds from the walls, and shot bullets, arrows, and cannonfire "like rain." Despite the protection of wooden shields and boxes, the soldiers could not withstand the hail of objects from above and were unable to make any progress toward the goal of undermining the city wall.[177]

The attack had been a failure. Na-yen-ch'eng began to realize that the walls and gates could not simply be stormed, nor could they be broken down by occasional cannonfire, a technique he tried next. Therefore, he ordered that tunnels be dug near each of the gates, extending right up to the city walls, inside of which land mines and explosives would be placed. This work was begun early in the 12th month. Yang Fang had meanwhile arrived back from his victorious expedition against Li Wen-ch'eng, and Na-yen-ch'eng soothed the increasingly angry emperor with a list of the eighty-one important rebel leaders killed or captured to date. Digging the tunnels was a difficult undertaking; some were dug secretly and others openly in hope that only the latter would attract rebel attention and bombardment. Those inside the city did throw down rocks and bricks upon the soldiers, and they fired on those within range. One night (12/2) they threw down burning bunches of reeds, and these flaming torches chanced to set off some of the land mines that had just been installed. The explosion did not achieve its full force because the tunnel had not yet been sealed off at the other end, so only several feet of the thick city wall were destroyed, but all the workmen and soldiers at work inside the tunnel died.[178]

The Eight Trigrams may have been cornered but they had not given up. Late on the night of 12/3, when there was no moonlight, Hsu An-kuo led some six hundred of his comrades and came quietly out the north gate; their goal was the destruction of the cannon and gun emplacements that they feared could break through the city walls. Hsu and his men attacked the cannon platform located near the northwest corner of the city, hurling explosives at it in order to burn it down. Ch'ing soldiers stationed there were taken by surprise but sounded the alarm and prepared to counterattack. The commander in charge of the gun emplacement ordered that the cannon be fired upon the rebels. Unable to withstand the bombardment, Hsu and his men turned around and headed back toward the north gate, pursued at least part of the way. Na-yen-ch'eng reported the next day that there was blood all over the ground along the north wall, but one rebel stated that fewer than one hundred and fifty of his comrades had died.

Memorializing, Na-yen-ch'eng summarized the situation at Hua at this point:

> The rebels inside the city know that their highest leaders have been killed and that their outside assistance has been cut off. They realize that a large force surrounds them and that there is no route of escape. For this reason they are fighting like cornered animals. I should point out that during the period when they occupied Tao-k'ou, they took all the grain and provisions which were stored there and moved them into Hua city, and so they should still have enough food to eat. Their supply of fodder, on the other hand, appears to be deficient. When they came out of the city [to attack], their horses were in poor condition, and the great majority of the rebels were on foot. Thus they will not be able to escape from our cavalry.[179]

Na-yen-ch'eng was feeling increasingly confident, and when the last of the Manchurian cavalry arrived, he prepared for the final assault on the city. Deer antler barricades had been set up in two rows outside the gates (especially on the western and eastern sides where the ground was firm) to halt any rebels who might try to escape. Militia were positioned in many of the nearby villages and told to be ready to round up remnants who would inevitably flee when the city was taken.[180] The Chia-ch'ing Emperor, still displeased at the delay and hoping to have the business over with before the new year, sent repeated edicts ordering an immediate attack.[181]

The rebels inside continued to fight back. Great Commander Sung Yuan-ch'eng, who together with Niu Liang-ch'en and Hsu An-kuo was in charge of the rebels left in the city, told Trigram Lord Huang Hsing-tsai that now it was his turn to try to destroy the gun emplacements. On the night of 12/7, while another group created a diversion on the eastern side of the city, Huang led four hundred men to the cannon platforms at the southwest corner of Hua. The government soldiers again responded quickly and, assisted by militia, forced the rebels to retreat again into the city without achieving their goal. Huang Hsing-tsai, who was shot twice in the arm by arrows and once in the leg by a bullet, fell to the ground and the following day hid among the militia in hope of escaping undetected. But when a head count was made, Huang was discovered and later interrogated and executed.[182]

Yang Yü-ch'un and Yang Fang had been directing the tunnel digging near the west and southwest gates, and Na-yen-ch'eng now ordered that all energies be concentrated on those tunnels. This work was completed on 12/9 and finally the land mines and explosives were placed inside the tunnels, the fuses extended, and the tunnels sealed off. That night, all government soldiers were ordered into place. Na-yen-ch'eng positioned his men at the southwest corner. Kao-ch'i was stationed on the east side, Yang Yü-ch'un along the western side, and Ma Yü together with Meng Ch'i-chan and his militia along the north. Each force had other soldiers positioned behind them as reinforcements and each was equipped with scaling ladders and sandbags. The Manchurian and Shensi cavalry were positioned in various locations around the city in order to round up any who managed to escape. By early morning on the 10th, all was ready. The cannon were to be fired, land mines exploded, and everyone would attack simultaneously.

The order was given to begin. At first the Ch'ing soldiers made little headway against the continuing hail of rocks and bullets from the rebels on the walls. Finally the land mines at the southwest corner went off with a great explosion, hurling bricks and stones in all directions and destroying twenty feet of the city wall. As Na-yen-ch'eng and Yang Fang led men to occupy the breach, the land mines at the northwest corner also went off. The tide of battle began to turn; government soldiers scaled the wall and fought hand-to-hand with the rebels at the top. Yang Yü-ch'un and his force broke through the south gate, and gradually the other gates were forced open as well. The rebels retreated into the walled houses of the city. By this time it was evening and the fighting had raged for over twelve hours. As it was clearly going to be necessary to retake the city house by house, Na-yen-ch'eng decided to call a temporary halt for the night. He ordered the city gates closed, placed guards outside each gate and outside the breach in the wall, and instructed his men to rest.[183]

Inside the city, the rebels were still not ready to surrender. Li Wen-ch'eng's wife, Miss Chang, whom he had left behind together with his daughter, was among those still alive. Hsu An-kuo, Niu Liang-ch'en, and Sung Yuan-ch'eng had survived and were still in command. They had urged Miss Chang to mix in among the refugee women who were leaving the city to surrender so that she could escape safely. According to Na-yen-ch'eng, "Miss Chang listened to what they had to say but declared that she wanted to die with them and refused to flee. That night [12/10] Hsu An-kuo told her to get on horseback and, with several thousand men as support, she left the city." It was during the second or third watch that night that this band of two or three thousand rebels came rushing through the breach in the wall at the southwest corner of the city, shouting, yelling, and charging through government barricades. Ch'ing soldiers, jolted awake by this sudden attack, held them off nevertheless, and when a nearby building caught fire and visibility improved, the soldiers again gained the upper hand. They killed more than a thousand rebels and drove the rest, including Miss Chang, back into the city.[184]

The following day, government soldiers reentered Hua and closed in on about fifty houses where rebels were still hiding; they surrounded them, set fires, and eventually smoked out the rebels. This house-by-house recapture of Hua continued for three days. When it was over, the city was in ruins. Buildings that had survived the rebel occupation did not survive the battle and, like the city wall, barely stood intact. Bodies filled the moat outside the city, clogged the streets, the gutters and the wells, rotted in cellars, and hung from the trees.[185]

More than twenty thousand people had fled the city during the battle, claiming to be refugees and begging to be spared; of these, five hundred were discovered to be "genuine rebels," two to three thousand were young male children, and the rest were women. About two thousand other rebels were captured alive on the day of the big battle, but after that those left in the city were assumed to be rebels and were killed. According to government figures, nine thousand rebels died on the 10th, an equal number were killed in the next few days, seven to eight thousand more were burned to death inside the city, and several thousand others were buried under the rubble. In sum, about thirty-five thousand people had died.[186] Miss Chang hanged herself rather than be taken prisoner, and government soldiers cut off her head. Great Commander Sung Yuan-ch'eng, K'un Trigram King Feng Hsiang-lin, and Ken Trigram King Liu Tsung-shun all were killed. Hsu An-kuo and Niu Liang-ch'en were captured.[187]

All government commanders had been given explicit instructions to seize alive the top rebel leaders so that they could be interrogated and then publicly and painfully executed. A certain Colonel Chang had learned the location of Hsu An-kuo's home and, taking soldiers, had surrounded the grocery store above which Hsu and his family had lived. Hsu was not there, however, and his relatives refused to surrender and threw down bricks and tiles in defiance. The soldiers then burned the building and all those inside.[188]

Hsu An-kuo had, together with Chief Minister Niu Liang-ch'en and K'an Trigram King Yin Ch'eng-te, been holding the northwest corner of the city. Hsu described what happened when the city was attacked: "Our men had tied white cloth at their waists and when the government soldiers entered the city, they killed anyone with such a sash. I was wounded and fell to the ground. My older brother . . . and his son . . . dragged me into someone's house, and we hid in the cellar. [Sun Trigram King] Wang Hsiu-chih's younger brother . . . moved a millstone over the entrance as a lid and then piled earth on it to disguise the place." Two days later, the Manchu commander Ke-pu-she captured a rebel named Wang Te-feng (who was also hiding in a cellar) and questioned him about the whereabouts of the top leaders. Wang said that Hsu An-kuo was hiding in an underground room and "if you won't kill me, I will find him for you."

Wang Te-feng led the way and brought the Ch'ing soldiers to the disguised entrance. As the dirt was shoveled away above them, Hsu and his brother and nephew realized that they would be discovered. According to Hsu, "I saw that the situation was a very bad one, and so I killed my older brother and my nephew by cutting their throats and was going to cut my own throat." Simultaneously, the stone was being removed and the soldiers were pulling out the bodies, first Hsu's brother and his sixteen-year-old nephew, and before Hsu could kill himself, he too was seized and dragged out by the shoulders. The informer Wang Te-feng confirmed that this was Hsu An-kuo. Hsu said to him, "Did you actually tell them where to find me?" Wang replied, "There were a dozen people in my family, and you killed half of them. Why shouldn't I revenge myself by telling them where to find you."[189]

Hsu was already seriously wounded: he had a severe head injury from a brick, a spear wound in the ribs, a smashed right leg, and burns on his back and left leg. The officials were worried he might die before being transferred to Peking for punishment: "He is in pain and moans all the time. We are afraid that the rocking and bumping of the carts might make him die of his wounds, which would mean that he would escape being punished for his crimes." For this reason, after a brief preliminary interrogation, Hsu was placed in a wooden cage and carried by bearers to Peking; there he was treated medically, interrogated in detail, and eventually executed.[190]

Niu Liang-ch'en, who like Hsu had been hiding underground, was also found and arrested. He too had been wounded in battle and had a bullet in his upper arm; to avoid execution Niu also had tried to commit suicide, and though he managed to inflict a very severe injury on himself, he did not die.[191] Like Hsu, he was cared for, taken to Peking, interrogated by the Board of Punishments and then by the emperor, and finally executed by slicing on 1/12 of the new year.[192]

While Niu and Hsu were singled out for interrogation and execution in Peking, all other leaders were summarily killed during the recapture of the city. On 12/17 Na-yen-ch'eng memorialized a list of 191 rebel leaders whose bodies had been identified at Hua; he explained that this did not include the lesser leaders, because in the morass of rotting bodies "identification was difficult."[193]

By the middle of the 12th month, just three months since its beginning, the rebellion of the Eight Trigrams was over. Nearly forty thousand people had surrendered to the government and been spared, but more than seventy thousand others had died. The campaign to suppress the uprising had cost the Ch'ing government at least four million taels[194] and the fighting compounded the natural disasters that had already affected the north China plain. The sects whose members had had faith in and followed the Eight Trigram leaders were destroyed. An appropriate epitaph was pronounced by Ch'in Li, Li Wen-ch'eng's captured aide: "The people in our sect believed what Lin Ch'ing and Li Wen-ch'eng said. Now those two men who were our leaders are dead and our sect is disbanded and scattered."[195]

Conclusion

THE EIGHT TRIGRAM leaders failed in their attempt to respond to the kalpa and make known the Way. Lin Ch'ing's attack on the Forbidden City in Peking had been swiftly and decisively halted, and in a matter of days he and his pupils had been killed or seized. Li Wen-ch'eng and the Eight Trigram leaders from southwestern Shantung, southern Chihli, and northern Honan had been more successful in carrying out their plans. They created a public challenge to the Ch'ing regime and backed their challenge with the recruitment of more than one hundred thousand followers, but in the end Ch'ing strength and their own weaknesses brought them to the same fate as their comrades near Peking.

Like the palace guards taken by surprise in Peking, the Ch'ing civil and military establishments in the provinces were slow to respond to the crisis posed by the rebel uprisings. It was a matter of months before large numbers of soldiers could be brought in, and during this time the Eight Trigrams were able to grow, consolidate, and test their strength against generally weaker opponents. Yet even before a large army could be assembled, the Ch'ing government was able to turn to members and would-be members of the local elite— men and families who looked to the state for power and prestige and protection—and demand their assistance. Well-developed gentry and merchant networks were tapped and used to encourage the "good people" to remain loyal, to defend the urban centers, and to check the expansion of the rebels on a limited basis. When trained soldiers finally arrived to relieve beleaguered cities and villages, the rebels were no match for them. The Ch'ing court was furthermore able to draw on the experiences of the campaigns against the Shensi– Szechwan–Hupei White Lotus rebels a decade earlier, using generals who had gained expertise in that fighting, following its administrative precedents, and remaining alert to the dangers of mistakes they had made in the past. For the Chia-ch'ing Emperor and many of his officials, those campaigns were a fresh and vivid memory on which they all could draw.

The Eight Trigram rebels, on the other hand, had had no such valuable experience. They were men of diverse backgrounds, and though a few were bannermen or had military degrees and others

265

vaunted their swordsmanship, the rebel rank-and-file—and most leaders—had absolutely no experience in basic military tactics. Moreover, many of those sect leaders who planned the rebellion did not live to direct its progress, and in the end Li Wen-ch'eng alone, ill and without the ideas, good judgment, and companionship of his closest colleagues, bore the weight of this responsibility. Unlike the Ch'ing bureaucracy, which was designed to deal with logistics and decision making, the Eight Trigram sects were normally intended to serve very different purposes; converting a diffuse secret religious network into the core of an aggressive armed rebellion presented many difficulties for sect leaders. It is in fact rather remarkable that the Eight Trigrams succeeded as well as they did with the military and administrative tasks of rebellion. They relied on teacher–pupil bonds to provide links between the leaders and used other simple organizational systems to produce a decentralized structure that was still quite responsive to orders given at the top. Individual leaders were willing to do as instructed by Li Wen-ch'eng, quick to come to the assistance of their comrades—even when the prospects for success were doubtful—but were also able to shoulder the responsibility for dealing with their own bands' particular problems. The relationship between lower level leaders who were sect members and their followers, most of whom were new recruits, posed more serious difficulties. Those who made up this mass following were not well integrated ideologically or organizationally, and some had been coerced into joining in the first place. As a result, many recruits stayed with the rebels while they were winning but quickly abandoned them when government victory seemed likely.

In short, the Ch'ing government knew what it had to do to suppress this rebellion, and it had the civil bureaucracy, military apparatus, local support, access to funds, and ready propaganda necessary to do it. The Eight Trigrams had no such sophisticated appreciation of the nature of their enemy and were comparatively naive about the task they had undertaken. They had ideas with which to rally supporters, but they lacked an efficient system for propagandizing among new followers. They had some resources accumulated in advance, but once in rebellion they were dependent on what they could forcibly seize to feed, finance, and arm their movement. They had a pool of leaders committed to the cause and loyal to one another, but these leaders lacked the military expertise necessary for battle against a vastly stronger opponent, and only a small percentage of these men had the administrative skills needed to organize the movement not simply at the center but in all its decentralized components.

For the followers of the Eternal Mother, both personally and as a group, the Eight Trigrams rebellion was a catastrophe. In areas affected by the uprising, those believers lucky enough to survive remained in constant danger of arrest—even if their sect had had no contact with the Trigrams. For the next ten years Ch'ing officials searched for criminals on the lists of wanted rebels issued frequently by the emperor.[1] Many sect networks were uncovered and uprooted and others chose to disband temporarily in order to avoid a similar fate. In addition to the death of many believers and the scattering of sect congregations, the failure of the Eight Trigrams could not help but result in the discrediting of White Lotus teachings. Although the uprising itself could be seen as evidence of the potential rightness of sect doctrine, its failure was a powerful reminder that the prophecies of sect teachers could be disastrously wrong.

Although the Eight Trigram leaders prepared for rebellion with a surprising ease and lack of secrecy and could not be prevented from making their initial strikes on government offices, the picture of a decrepit and collapsing dynasty painted by those who see the late Ch'ien-lung reign as the beginning of the end of traditional China is not corroborated by the events of 1813. Furthermore, the suppression of this uprising was an acknowledged triumph for the Chia-ch'ing Emperor, his family, and his officials. The campaigns were tainted by no major scandals and the expense does not appear to have been considered excessive. Bannermen, Green Standard soldiers, and local militia carried out their responsibilities without major difficulties.[2] Provincial bureaucrats became—at least temporarily—more conscientious, and for the next decade White Lotus sects throughout north China were brought under closer scrutiny. Nonetheless, although the suppression of the Eight Trigrams does indicate a certain vigor in the Ch'ing government, the fact of an uprising of this scale also suggests some degree of dynastic weakness. Other research on the Chia-ch'ing reign could indicate the true extent of dynastic decline and the extent to which this rebellion and its pacification were typical of the period.

This study has described the life style and social milieu of the men and women who became the Eight Trigrams and of the bonds made and cemented between them; as such it is simply one case study, a sample of White Lotus sect organization and membership. During the Ch'ing dynasty the networks of people bound together by the ideas and practices of this religion constituted one of the few social institutions not dominated by the orthodox elite that existed on a regional scale in north China. Although normally diffuse and unobtrusive, these sects were an important element in the competition for power and influence in village and urban communities, and as such they were the rivals of those groups whose position derived from other socially sanctioned sources—landholding, governmental office, profitable commercial business, or examination degrees. Studies of Ch'ing society should not ignore the money-making and prestige-conferring alternative presented by these sects, though it is obvious that much research will be required before their place in the Ch'ing social structure can be fully understood.

A cursory comparison of these White Lotus sects with another "secret society" network, that of the Triad societies of sub-Yangtze China, is perhaps instructive. Like the White Lotus sects, the Triads appeared as a group of autonomous assemblies sharing common ideas and organizational features but only loosely associated in normal times. The Triad brotherhoods transmitted to their members a tradition of ongoing resistance to the authority of the Manchu dynasty. The societies attracted small merchants, yamen workers, professional gamblers and gangsters, pirates and smugglers, and gave them a certain mystique, organization, and a source of mutual protection against more powerful social groups.[3] White Lotus sect members, on the other hand, did not as a rule live by either violence or crime. They congregated for religious purposes, were linked to one another in vertical chains of teachers and pupils, and judged both membership and authority within the sect in terms of mastery of certain secretly transmitted religious ideas and practices. In normal times believers accepted the authority of the Ch'ing state; it was only in the new kalpa era—whenever it arrived—that this authority would be rejected. Their strong vertical ties and persuasive historical vision gave the White Lotus sects a greater capacity for unified action, however poorly sustained, than the south China Triads.

As this study presents only one example of White Lotus sect organization, so it describes only a portion of the diverse and changing body of White Lotus teachings and illustrates but one instance of a sect-led rebellion. Further investigation into the beliefs and practices of this religion can reveal how it originated and then grew and changed in reaction first to the Ch'ing conquest and then to the years of peace and prosperity, the upheavals of the nineteenth century, the arrival of foreigners and foreign religions, and the disorders and new orthodoxies of the twentieth century.

Similarly, the Eight Trigrams uprising in 1813 must be placed in the context of a long series of sect-inspired rebellions. As rebels, the Trigrams were relatively successful and managed to mount and sustain their challenge to the Ch'ing state for nearly one hundred days. Nevertheless, the preliminary reorganization, mobilization, and transformation of small scattered sects into a united rebel movement followed a pattern that was repeated in many less successful sectarian uprisings during the dynasty. The Ch'ing government, engaged in an almost perpetual if sometimes muted contest with these sects, usually interrupted at earlier stages the complete (or nearly complete) mobilization so well illustrated in 1813. While the formation of the Eight Trigrams can stand as an example of the potential inherent in other aborted sect uprisings, comparison with equally successful risings—such as those of Hsu Hung-ju (1622), Wang Lun (1774), or the three-province White Lotus rebels (1796–1803)— could, on the other hand, suggest the different factors that made possible the effective transformation of these sects. The Taiping rebels of the mid-nineteenth century illustrate yet another set of possibilities for a well-integrated movement inspired by a millenarian vision though their rebellion was founded in the solidarity of the Hakka minority community and their vision strongly influenced by Christianity.[4]

White Lotus rebels, like the Taiping but unlike the Triads, were *hsieh-fei* 邪匪, "heretical rebels." The belief in the Eternal Mother and her promise of protection and salvation for her followers, the predictions of an approaching apocalypse, visions of a future millennium, and the anticipation of a divine leader who would save all believers were ideas justly considered inflammatory, defiant, and subversive by the state. The existence of this religion in premodern China and the history of repeated contests between government and believers suggest that the Ch'ing elite was not entirely unfamiliar with fundamental challenges to its political and social system. The hostility of the elite toward this subversive religion is perhaps some indication of the danger it posed. The continued hostility of both the Republic of China and the People's Republic of China toward most of these sects today is evidence that the long battle between orthodoxy and heterodoxy in China, of which the events of 1813 were only a minor skirmish, is still being waged.[5]

Finally, the Eight Trigrams may be considered from a wider comparative perspective. Most of the millenarian movements now being studied with increasing interest by historians and social scientists were generated as a response to the ideas and technology of modern Western civilization.[6] The Eight Trigrams uprising and the White Lotus sects that produced it illustrate a different phenomenon, that of a millenarian alternative existing within and in partial reaction against a great religious tradition. White Lotus sects, considered in the context of Ch'ing orthodox thinking, may be comparable to the heretical sects of medieval Christianity, to the Mahdist movement or the Sufi orders of Islam, or to the various messianic traditions within the Hindu and Buddhist cultures of India and southeast Asia.[7] These popular sectarian religions, often ruled heterodox or illegal, were usually long-lived but only briefly institutionalized; the social movements they generated were repeated and ever hopeful, oblivious to their history of defeat and disappointment. The tensions between each of these great traditions and their many little traditions will require further scrutiny if we are to understand this type of powerful and persistent millenarianism.

APPENDIX 1: Sample Confessions

CH'Ü SSU 屈四 was a sect teacher from a village southeast of Peking. He was arrested in the fall of 1813. The rebels had considered and then rejected a plan for Ch'ü Ssu to lead his men in an attack upon the imperial entourage as it returned from Jehol, and Ch'ü was interrogated repeatedly about this plan. His various confessions about this and other matters, taken together with those of some of his associates, illustrate the kinds of information contained in confessions, the reliability of such testimony, and the judicial process that produced them.

A. First Interrogation of Ch'ü Ssu

Memorial from the Grand Council and the Board of Punishments (KKCK 207.1, CC 18/9/24):

. . . . On 9/23 we received a report from the censors for the south city [of Peking] saying that they had seized the criminal Ch'ü Ssu and [others]. They have been interrogated. . . . The text of Ch'ü Ssu's confession is attached.

Confession of Ch'ü Ssu (KKCK 208.1, 18/9/24)

From T'ung district. Age thirty-six. Mother Miss Meng. Older brother Ch'ü Wen-hsiang. Wife Miss Ts'ai. My son Ch'ang-yu-r is ten. I was born the son of Ch'ü Te-hsin but then I was adopted by Ch'ü Wu.

When I was nineteen, Liu Ti-wu brought me and Ch'ü Wen-hsiang to take Ku Liang (who has since died) as our teacher. I entered the sect and recited the eight characters "Eternal Progenitor in Our Original Home in the World of True Emptiness."

On the 14th day of the 8th month [of 1813] Lin Ch'ing told Liu Ti-wu to put me in charge of one to two hundred men and lead them to Yen-chiao [outside Peking] to rise up there. Later on I didn't have this many men and could only bring fifty or so. For this reason, they decided not to go ahead with that plan. Instead we chose ten men from those fifty to come into the capital and enter [the Forbidden City] through the Tung-hua Gate. He also gave me two knives and a white banner with "Entrusted by Heaven to Prepare the Way" written on it. The other men each had a knife and two pieces of white cloth.

I led Li Yuan-lung, Teng Erh, Chou San, Chou Ssu, Chang Yung-jui, Chu Liu-t'ao, Jen Erh, Kao Wu, An Ta, and Chang Yung-kuei, and we all came into the capital to start this affair. Kao Wu, An Kuo-t'ai, and Chang Wu were afraid and didn't come. Li Yuan-lung and the other six men and I all went in the Sha-wo Gate. Then we went in the Ch'ien Gate to outside the Tung-hua Gate, where we were all to assemble. We saw the group of our comrades who were all in front of us go in the gate and initiate the incident. The gate was then closed and so we all scattered and fled. At sunset I arrived back at home and I hid. On the 17th I was seized by some official men. Liu Ti-wu also sent the men under Li Lao (who is from Yang-hsiu village) in the Tung-hua Gate. Ku Ssu and Li Erh's men went in the Hsi-hua Gate. This is the truth. 24th day of the 9th month.

B. *Second Interrogation of Ch'ü Ssu*

Second confession of Ch'ü Ssu [submitted by the Grand Council and Board of Punishments] (KKCK 227.3, 18/10/21):

On 8/14 of this year, Liu Ti-wu brought me to Sung-chia village to see Liu Ssu (who is also known as Liu Ch'eng-hsiang). The two of them said to me, "Those of us in Sung-chia and Sang-fa villages now number fifty or sixty men. You all at your place must select between thirty and fifty. Altogether that would make over one hundred. Assemble at Yen-chiao." I said, "The men in our village who are believers are few, and among them there are some old people and young children who are of no use for this. I could only find ten strong and able-bodied men. I can't get as many as thirty or fifty." They told Lin Ch'ing what I had said, and Lin Ch'ing told me to come and see him. He said to me, "So you all there can't get together thirty or fifty men. I can't spare you any of my men here. The [Ch'ing] soldiers accompanying the emperor on the hunt are numerous, so I've decided that we can't go to Yen-chiao [to ambush the emperor]. Instead, on 9/15 we will just go into the capital and cause our incident there. The soldiers will not be able to move fast enough [to get back to Peking], and we are sure to succeed. We will occupy the capital, and then everything will be fine. You just bring ten men, and follow Liu Ssu and go in the Tung-hua Gate."

Aside from what I've already told you, I really don't know any more about how many men there were in the capital area. Lin Ch'ing truly did not tell me when the men from Honan would arrive to give us reinforcements. I have committed a serious crime, so how could I dare hide anything now?

C. Third Interrogation of Ch'ü Ssu

Memorial from the Grand Council (CFCL 17.4–7, 18/11/6):

We questioned Ch'ü Ssu once more. He said: On 8/14 Liu Ssu (also known as Liu Ch'eng-hsiang) transmitted a message to me from Lin Ch'ing saying that I was to assemble people and go to Yen-chiao. The people in my village were few, and I couldn't mobilize many, so I told them this. Later on Lin Ch'ing told me to come see him and said, "Since you can't get together a lot of people from your place there, then the people you can get should follow Liu Ssu and go in the Tung-hua Gate and rise up. We will occupy the capital city. Don't be afraid of the imperial entourage. Don't go to Manchuria." [I came out of his house] and Liu Ssu said to me that the men from Honan would come on 9/15, for the Trigram Master himself had arranged this. At that time we would kill the officials and people inside and outside of the capital city. On the 17th we would all surge out to Yen-chiao and do that business [killing the emperor]. And so on 9/15 I led Chang Shun and the others, ten men, and went into the city to rebel. This is the truth.

(CFCL 17.23–24, 18/11/9)

On this day there was a court interrogation [in the presence of the Chia-ch'ing Emperor] of Ch'ü Ssu and Ts'ao Lun. Both were then executed by slicing and their heads displayed publicly.

D. Interrogation of Yen Ch'i 閻七

Confession of Yen Ch'i [submitted by the Grand Council and Board of Punishments] (KKCK 225.1–2, 18/10/18):

Also known as Yen Cheng-li. From Ta-hsing district: Lao-chun-t'ang. Age forty-three. Parents are dead. Younger brother Yen Lao. Wife Miss Ch'ü. Elder son Liang-r, younger son Shan-r. Elder daughter Wu-chieh, younger daughter San-lan.

This Ch'ü Ssu is my wife's younger cousin on her father's side. On 9/10 of this year, Ch'ü Ssu sent a message that I should go to his house. There he urged me to join his assembly. I didn't want to. He said, "If you decide you want to join the sect, come again to my house on the 14th of this month and I will have some special confidential things to tell you." Because I didn't want to join the sect, I didn't go on the 14th.

On the 15th, before dawn, my wife's younger brother Ch'ü Ming-r came and said to me, "Today Ch'ü Ssu is going to rebel. He wants you to help him. Get a knife and some white cloth and wait at the teahouse on the main street at the Flower Market. Then go quickly with me and together we will go in the Tung-hua Gate to start the incident." I said I did not dare go along. Ch'ü Ming-r said, "If you don't, then later on when Ch'ü Ssu is successful, the lives of your family will not be safe." I was so afraid that I went along with Ch'ü Ming-r, in the Sha-wo Gate. All the time, the more I thought about it, the more afraid I got. When we reached the Flower Market, I ran off and returned home. That day I didn't even see Ch'ü Ssu, or any knives or white cloth. After a few days, official people came to my house and arrested me.

E. Interrogation of Tai Wu 戴五

Memorial from the prefects of Shun-t'ien [prefecture, Chihli] (KCT 015579, 19/2*/16):

We received a report saying that a bannerman from Wu-ch'ing had given information that a rebel in the Lin Ch'ing case named Tai Wu was hiding in his district near Wang-ming village. Tai Wu was arrested on the 12th, . . . and interrogated.

He says he is from Tung village and had in the past worked for Li Yuan-lung's household. He had followed Li Yuan-lung and joined the sect. He had driven a cart for Ch'ü Ssu. In the 9th month of last year, Li Yuan-lung had given him a knife and white cloth and arranged that on the 15th he was to go in the Ch'ien Gate and wait for Ch'ü Ssu, and then go with him in the Tung-hua Gate. Early on the 15th, he and Chang Shun, Chang Liang, Li Ta-po, and Wang Po entered the city. They didn't see Ch'ü Ssu but went themselves to outside the Tung-hua Gate. There they saw Liu Ssu. When they went in toward the Inner Tung-hua Gate, it closed and they fled; he went back to Li Yuan-lung's house. Afterward, he hid in various places, and now has been arrested.

F. First Interrogation of Ch'ü Ming-r 屈名兒

Memorial from the Grand Council (SYT 227–34, 22/11/20):

Ch'ü Ming-r has been arrested, and we interrogated him. He testified:

From T'ung district. Age thirty-three. Father Ch'ü Te-min died in the 6th month of CC 6. The older woman you have in custody is my mother Miss Ma; the younger is my wife Miss Wen. The eight-year-old child is my son Mo-r. I said before that they were dead because I was afraid they had died when Tung village burned down.

In the 4th or 5th month of CC 14, I was brought into the sect by my elder cousin Ch'ü Ssu. I recited the eight-character chant "Eternal Progenitor in Our Original Home in the World of True Emptiness." Together with Ch'ü Ssu I often did meditational yoga and "learned the good." Yen Ch'i is my older sister's husband and he is in the same sect.

On 9/14 Ch'ü Ssu told me to come to his house. There I saw my fellow sect members Kuo Shuan-r, Chiang Sheng (also known as Chiang Li-sheng), Yang Tung-r (also known as Yang Kuang-pi), Kao Wu, Chang Erh-t'u-tzu, Chang Wu-t'u-tzu, Wang Chu-r (also known as Wang Po), Chang Erh-chu (also known as Chang Hsi-ch'eng), Ts'ao Wu, Li Wen-lung (also known as Li Yuan-lung), Chang Shun, Tai Wu, and a lot of other people I didn't recognize. Each person was given his own knife and cloth. It was arranged that we would go together into the city. I received a knife and two pieces of white cloth, plus a white cloth banner on which were written some words I couldn't read. Ch'ü Ssu asked who wanted to carry the banners when we went into the city, and Yang Tung-r and I each took one.

I left early on the 15th. We went in the Kuang-chü Gate to Lu-lu-pa at the Flower Market outside the Ch'ung-wen Gate. Ch'ü Ssu led some of the men and went on into the city. He told Yang Tung-r, Chang Erh-chu, Wang Chu-r, and me to wait at the Flower Market for several dozen men carrying small blue cloth bundles on their backs who would be coming from the south. These would be the men and horses from Hua. We were to bring them into the city via the Chiang-mi lane to the Tung-hua Gate as reinforcements. We waited quite a while there but saw no one. It got to be noon. The time was wrong, and Ch'ü Ssu, Kuo Shuan-r, and the others came back in great haste and agitation. They cursed us and called us useless things and said that everyone had better flee. I went home. I gave the knife, cloth, and banner back to Ch'ü Ssu.

During the day I would hide in the manure pile, and at night I sneaked home to get food. Then, after Tung village was burned, I fled to the south and lived by begging.

G. Second Interrogation of Ch'ü Ming-r

Memorial from the Grand Council (SYT 245–48, 22/11/21):

We again questioned Ch'ü Ming-r, saying to him: Ch'ü Ssu wanted to take men to Yen-chiao in the 9th month of CC 18. He went as far as Pa-li bridge, where he met an old man who told him that there were already government soldiers at Yen-chiao, and so he didn't dare go any farther. You are Ch'ü Ssu's cousin, you must have been among his men. How many men did Ch'ü Ssu have at the time? Who were they? How did the old man persuade you not to go? Did Ch'ü Ssu give drugs to his group to make them weak-willed but physically strong? You must have taken some, what were the drugs like?

Ch'ü Ming-r testified: When I first followed Ch'ü Ssu and prac-ticed the sect, I didn't know he was going to rebel. On the 14th day of the 8th month of CC 18, I returned home from the temple of the God of Wealth at Erh-li-kou, and it was then that my mother told me that Ch'ü Ssu was in the Pai-lien sect and she had heard that they were going to rebel. I had fifty to sixty *mou* of land and was coming back from taking care of the crops on it there near the temple of the God of Wealth. I lived at the south end of Tung village and Ch'ü Ssu lived at the west end. We were separated by over twenty houses and I certainly didn't see him every day.

On 9/14 at Ch'ü Ssu's house he told us that it was necessary for us all to go into the city. In this business, it was death if you went, and death if you stayed. However, if we could be successful, then every-one would get wealth and position. I wanted these things and so I agreed to participate. He said that we were to take out our knives when we went into the Forbidden City and stab anyone we met. I only saw Ch'ü Ssu a few times between 8/14 and 9/14. . . . I don't know about any group going to Yen-chiao. . . . I heard nothing about any drugs. On the evening of 9/14 we just ate some noodles at Ch'ü Ssu's house, that's all. I didn't feel any drugs.

H. Interrogation of Wang Po 王博

Confession of Wang Po [submitted by the Grand Council and Board of Punishments] (KKCK 215.1–2, 18/10/11):

From Tung village. Age thirty-two. Father dead. Mother Miss Wu. Younger brother Wang Shih-tse. No wife or children.

In the 11th month of CC 16 Li Yuan-lung brought me into the Pai-yang Assembly. He transmitted to me the eight characters "Eternal Progenitor in Our Original Home in the World of True Emptiness." On 9/11 of this year, Ch'ü Ssu sent me and Ts'ao Wu with more than ten others to go and help Lin Ch'ing rebel. It was discussed and decided that at noon on the 15th we would go in the Tung-hua Gate and start the incident. I prepared a knife myself, and two pieces of white cloth.

Before dawn on the 15th I took the knife and white cloth and went in the Sha-wo Gate and the Hai-tai Gate. I went to outside the Outer Tung-hua Gate. I looked for Ch'ü Ssu but couldn't find him. At noon I heard someone say that rebels had gone in the Inner Tung-hua Gate. I didn't dare go in. So I waited some more and then ran away. I went to the big street by the palaces and there I ran into Ts'ao Wu. He said, "Government soldiers outside the Tung-hua Gate are arresting people. Let's get out of here." So I went with him to the Flower Market. We had a meal and then we went back home.

I. Three Interrogations of Chung Yu-i 鍾有義

Memorial from the Grand Council (SYT 15–17, 19/10/3):

Confession of Chung Yu-i. From T'ung district: Tung village. Age sixty-two. Wife Miss Hsu. Son Hei-r; I heard that he was arrested last year. Daughter is Erh-ke, she is married to Ch'en Erh, who is the son of Ch'en Hei-tzu.

In the 10th month of CC 8 my son Hei-r and I took Ch'ü Ssu as our teacher and joined the Pai-yang sect. Ch'ü Ssu taught me to recite the eight characters "Eternal Progenitor in Our Original Home in the World of True Emptiness." In the 8th month of CC 18 I brought my relative by marriage, Ch'en Hei-tzu, into Ch'ü Ssu's sect. At that time my son-in-law was running a restaurant at Liu-li-ch'ang in the capital and was not living at home, so I didn't instruct him in joining the sect. I remember that in the 7th month Ch'ü Ssu, Chang Shun, and Li Yuan-lung discussed making knives and rebelling, using white cloth as identification. They told all the people in my village who had joined the sect to give money and go with them to help. If you didn't give money, they would kill you. I was afraid and paid 160 cash. Ch'en Hei-tzu paid 200 cash. They gave each of us two pieces of white cloth. Ch'en Hei-tzu and I both took them.

On 9/10 Ch'ü Ssu and the others arranged with Tai Wu, Kao Wu, Li Ta-po, Li Erh-po, Little Ch'ü Ssu (also known as Ch'ü Fu-r),

Ch'ü Ming-tzu (also known as Ch'ü Ming-r), Ts'ao Erh-wu (also known as Ts'ao Erh), and Ts'ao Hei-tzu to go into the city on 9/14 and cause the incident. They said that we would go in the Sha-wo Gate to the Tung-hua Gate. They also gave me a knife and wanted me to go with them. I was afraid and didn't want to, so I didn't take the knife. On 9/16 I fled to the area of . . . and lived by begging. . . . Little Ch'ü Ssu (also known as Ch'ü Fu-r) is from Tung village, age twenty-seven or twenty-eight, tall, light complexion, pointed chin, and whiskers.

Memorial from the Grand Council (SYT 197, 19/11/16):

Confession of Chung Yu-i: I live in Tung village and have known Ts'ao Hei-r for a long time. He is called Hei-r, or Ts'ao Lao-ta. Not Hei-lien-r. He has two younger brothers, Little Ts'ao Erh and Ts'ao Liu. Both were in the sect. The people I know in the sect surnamed Ts'ao besides them were old Ts'ao Erh and Ts'ao Feng-wen. . . . My wife did not join the sect.

Memorial from the Grand Council (SYT 229–30, 22/12/22):

We brought in Ch'ü Ssu's pupil Chung Yu-i. He states that Li Yuan-lung, Ts'ao Feng-wen, Chang Shun, Chang Erh-t'u-tzu, Chang Wu-t'u-tzu, Ts'ao Hei-tzu, Ch'ü Ming-r, Tai Wu, Kao Wu, Li Ta-po, Li Erh-po, and Kuo Shuan-r were all in the sect and were pupils under Ch'ü Ssu.

J. Interrogation of Liu Kou-r 劉狗兒

Confession of Liu Kou-r [submitted by the Grand Council and Board of Punishments] (KKCK 215.1, 18/10/9):

Also known as Jen Erh, also as Jen Fu-r. From T'ung district: San-cha [village]. Age twenty-five. Parents are dead. Have no brothers. Wife and child are dead. When I was four years old I was adopted by Jen Feng-li of Shen-shu village, and I changed my name to [Jen] Fu-r. When I was older I changed and went back to my old lineage, so everyone still calls me by my old name Liu Kou-r.

In the 9th month I was doing short-term hired labor for Ch'ü Ssu's household. Ch'ü Ssu invited me to join the assembly. He transmitted to me the eight characters "Eternal Progenitor in Our Original Home in the World of True Emptiness." On the 13th I went to market with Ch'ü Ssu. Ch'ü Ssu told me to buy a butcher knife, saying that he was going to use it to slaughter a pig. On the 14th, Ch'ü Ssu told me that on the 15th they were going to enter the city and rebel, and he told me to help. Moreover, he gave me two pieces of white cloth. When the affair was successful, he promised to give me a soldier's stipend. This persuaded me, and so I agreed.

Early on the 15th I went with Ch'ü Ssu in the Sha-wo Gate and the Ch'ien Gate to the Tung-hua Gate. Of the men under Ch'ü Ssu's command, I recognized only Chang Shun and Li Yuan-lung. I didn't know the others. I saw them run in the Tung-hua Gate. The gate was then closed, and so I decided to run off. Then official men seized me. They confiscated the knife and cloth which I was carrying.

APPENDIX 2:   Donations to Eight Trigram Sects

Initial contributions:[1]
    100 cash
    100 to 200 cash
    200 cash
    "several hundred cash"
    400 cash
    400 cash

Other contributions:

Twice a year:[2]	100 cash
Monthly:[3]	30 cash
Once a year:[4]	80 cash
	200 to 300 cash
	500 cash
	1,000 cash
	2,000 cash (birthday gift for leader)
	4,000 to 5,000 cash (from two people)
	4 taels and 4,000 cash (from leader)

Last-minute contributions(for the purpose of rebellion):[5]
    "anywhere between 20 or 30 and several hundred cash"
    160 cash
    200 cash
    1,600 cash
    2,000 cash
    4,000 cash (from each of two leaders)
    5,000 cash

A NOTE ON THE CURRENCY: A *wen* 文 or "cash," the unit of money mentioned most frequently in confessions, was formally worth one thousandth of a tael(*liang* 兩)or ounce of silver. A thousand *wen* strung together formally made up one "string of cash"(*tiao* 吊).

Unfortunately, these ideal equivalencies were not reflected in reality. The number of cash considered to make up one string of cash does appear to have been approximately one thousand in 1813, but the amount varied with time and place, and a string of cash in "capital money" 京錢 contained fewer than the ordinary string.[6] Similarly, the number of strings of cash which could buy one ounce or tael of silver also varied, and as silver became more expensive, the amount rose. One informant stated that in 1813 (in Peking) he purchased 700 ounces of silver with 1,200 strings of cash; that is, he paid 1,700 cash (instead of the ideal 1,000) for one tael.[7]

APPENDIX 3: The Cost of Living in the 1810s

Purchase price of land: (cash per *mou*) [1]
    Northern Chihli: 6,000
                            1.81 taels (approximately 3,000 cash)
    Southern Chihli: high quality land, good year: 10,000
                            high quality land, bad year: 1,000
                            low quality land, good year: 3,000–4,000
                            low quality land, bad year: 300–400
    Mortgage on land (near Peking):[2] 1,666

Land rents in Honan:[3]
      500 cash/*mou*   (1st grade land)
      400 cash/*mou*   (2d grade land)
      300 cash/*mou*   (3d grade land)
   1,000 cash/*mou*   (temple land)
      400 cash/*mou*   (temple land)

Wages:
    Bondservant in a prince's household: 4 taels (in money and grain) per month[4]
    Agricultural laborer during harvest time: 100 cash per day[5]
    Agricultural laborer during slack season: 70–80 cash per day[6]
    Feeding mules in a cart shop: 1,500 cash capital-money per month[7]
    Clerk in apothecary shop (Peking): 6,000 cash capital-money per month[8]
    Soldier: 1.8 taels (approximately 3,100 cash) and 2 piculs (石) of rice per month[9]
    Income from a sinecure clerkship in a district yamen: 50,000 cash per month[10]

Room and Board:[11]
    Room rent: 150 cash per month or 200 cash per month
    Room and fuel: 600 cash per month
    Militia men paid for food: 50 cash per day

Militia instructor given for food: 200 cash per day
Food for last meal in Peking before attack on palace: 200 cash
Soldier's daily allotment for food: 150 cash

Goods:[12]

Knife: 500 cash
One foot of white cotton cloth: 100 cash
14-year-old boy: 4,000 cash
11-year-old boy: 1,000 cash
Woman: 10,000 cash

Abbreviations Used in Notes

CITATIONS from documentary collections are followed by a date given according to the Chinese calendar, that is, year of reign/lunar month/day. Unless otherwise noted, all years refer to the Chia-ch'ing reign (1796–1819), abbreviated CC. The Ch'ien-lung reign (1736–95) is abbreviated CL. An asterisk next to the month indicates the intercalary month that followed the regular month. Following the date is an indication of the type of document cited, that is, an edict, memorial, list of names, or confession. Instead of stating "confession," I have indicated the name of the person whose testimony is being cited. "Composite confession" refers to a statement combining the testimonies of different individuals and summarized by the memorializing official. Women are referred to as Mrs. (married name) (maiden name): Mrs. Liu Kung is Mrs. Liu née Kung. The particle *erh* 兒, which is added to many proper nouns in the Peking dialect is here indicated as "-r," as in the name Liang Chuang-r. Where two or more texts exist for a given document, I have cited the more complete one.

CFA   *Chiao-fei an* 教匪案 [Documents relating to the case of the religious rebels]. Wade Collection B. 750a–751a, Cambridge, England. Miscellaneous handwritten copies of memorials from the period CC 19/2 through 20/4.

CFCL   *Ch'in-ting p'ing-ting chiao-fei chi-lueh* 欽定平定教匪紀略 [Imperially authorized account of the pacification of the religious rebels]. 1816. Memorials and edicts from CC 18/9 through 21/6.

CPT   *Chiao-pu tang* 剿捕檔 [Suppression and arrest record book]. National Palace Museum, Taiwan. Memorials and edicts for CC 18/9, 18/10, 18/11, and 18/12.

CSL   *Ta Ch'ing li-ch'ao shih-lu* 大清歷朝實錄 [Veritable records of successive reigns of the Ch'ing dynasty]. Mukden, 1937; reprint ed., Taipei, 1964. Edicts.

KCT   *Kung-chung tang* 宮中檔 [Palace memorial archive]. National Palace Museum, Taiwan. Memorials for the period

CC 19/6 through 20/12. An "E" following the number of the memorial indicates an enclosure (附片) to that memorial.

KKCK   *Lin-an kung-tz'u tang* 林案供詞檔 [Confessions from the Lin Ch'ing case]. National Palace Museum, Taiwan. Texts of confessions submitted by the Grand Council in CC 18/9 and 18/10. This material was published in *Ku-kung chou-k'an* 故宮週刊 [Palace Museum Weekly] 195–236 (1931–33) and is here so cited.

NYC   *Na-wen-i-kung tsou-i* 那文毅公奏議 [The collected memorials of Na-yen-ch'eng]. 1834; reprint ed., Taipei, 1968. Three volumes of this set cover Na-yen-ch'eng's tenure as Special Imperial Commissioner for Rebel Pacification and as Governor-General of Chihli province. Memorials sent (with imperial rescripts) and edicts received, CC 18/9 through 21/6.

PHHP   Huang Yü-p'ien 黄育楩, *P'o-hsieh hsiang-pien* 破邪詳辯 [A detailed refutation of heterodoxy]. 1883. Quotations from sect scriptures confiscated in the 1830s.

SSTC   *Sui-shou teng-chi* 隨手登記 [Daily record]. National Palace Museum, Taiwan. A record of all edicts sent by and memorials sent to the emperor, with brief summary of their contents and imperial rescripts. Entire Chia-ch'ing reign.

SYT   *Shang-yü-tang fang-pen* 上諭檔方本 [Imperial edict record book, long form]. National Palace Museum, Taiwan. Edicts sent by the emperor and memorials sent to him by the Grand Council. Entire Chia-ch'ing reign.

Notes

1 The best English accounts are in Arthur W. Hummel, ed., *Eminent Chinese of the Ch'ing Period* (1943–44), pp. 585–86, where the rebellion is described in Fang Chao-ying's biography of Na-yen-ch'eng; and in J. J. M. de Groot, *Sectarianism and Religious Persecution in China* (Amsterdam, 1903–04), pp. 401–69. The best Chinese language account is *Ching-ni chi* [Account of the suppression of the rebels] (1820) written by the scholar Sheng Ta-shih under the pseudonym Lan-i wai-shih. This is an excellent and detailed description of the rebellion that includes an account of government campaigns and brief biographic sketches of the major rebel leaders. A more conventional version may be found in Wei Yuan, *Sheng-wu chi* [Record of imperial campaigns] (1842), *chüan* 10. Chao-lien's account in his *Hsiao-t'ing tsa-lu* [Miscellaneous notes from the Hsiao pavilion] (completed ca. 1814–15), 4:44–59, is colorful but unreliable. Two articles have been written about this rebellion by contemporary Chinese historians: Chang I-ch'un, "Kuan-yü T'ien-li-chiao ch'i-i erh-san shih," [A few things about the T'ien-li sect uprising], *Li-shih chiao-hsueh* (1962), and Hsiao Yü-min, "Ch'ing Chia-ch'ing T'ien-li-chiao ch'i-i" [The T'ien-li sect rebellion in the Chia-ch'ing reign of the Ch'ing dynasty], in *Chung-kuo nung-min ch'i-i lun-chi* (Peking, 1958). There is one that I know of in Japanese: Onoda Sayoko, "Kakei jūhachinen no tenrikyōdō no ran ni tsuite," [A study of the rebellion by the T'ien-li sect in the year Chia-ch'ing 18] *Shisō* (1966).

Sheng Ta-shih, the author of *Ching-ni chi*, states in his preface that he met and talked with contemporary observers and participants in the suppression of this rebellion in 1814 and that he consulted the documents published in CFCL in 1816. None of these authors consulted the documentary material now located in the National Palace Museum archives in Taiwan.

2 See Jean Chesneaux, "Secret Societies in China's Historical Evolution," pp. 1–22 in *Popular Movements and Secret Societies in China, 1840–1850*, and Jerome Ch'en, "Secret Societies," *Ch'ing-shih wen-t'i* 1, no. 3 (1966): 13–16, for English summaries of the controversy that has taken place largely in Chinese. Two of the most important Chinese articles on this subject are T'ao Ch'eng-chang, *Chiao hui yuan-liu k'ao* [A study of the origins of sects and societies] (Canton, 1910), and Hsiung Te-chi, "Chung-kuo nung-min chan-cheng yü tsung-chiao chi ch'i hsiang-kuan chu wen-t'i," [Several questions on the relationship between peasant wars and religion in China], *Li-shih lun-ts'ung* (1964).

3 For example, see Richard Yung-deh Chu, "An Introductory Study of the White Lotus Sect in Chinese History" (Ph.D. diss., Columbia University, 1967).

4 Documents that I consulted contained a total of 471 confessions from 367 different individuals involved in the 1813 rebellion. Sixty percent (or 221) of these people lived in the Peking area; the rest were from Honan, Shantung,

and southern Chihli and were not involved in the palace attack. (See explanation in Part One, n. 5.) The location of these confessions, broken down by documentary collections, is as follows: local gazetteers 8, CFA 41, NYC 31, CFCL 83, KKCK 92, SYT 140, KCT 76. Nearly 50 percent (the memorials cited as SYT and KCT) are available only in the National Palace Museum in Taiwan.

Naturally most sect members or rebels tried to deny or minimize their own involvement in any criminal activity and on this point their word alone cannot be trusted. In the case of sect members and rebels from the Peking area, however, corroborating testimony by other participants was available in almost every case. Government interrogators asked repeatedly and particularly about the activities of other people, and in the case of the Peking sects, the evidence from two hundred people testifying about each other is consistent and altogether credible. I have assumed that each individual would if possible lie to minimize the involvement (or existence) of his relatives. Many sect leaders revealed as few of their followers' names as they could, and some of the highest leaders gave the most worthless information on this point. For example, see CFCL 3.9-13, 18/9/18 Lin Ch'ing, and also CFCL 4.5-9, 18/9/19 Lin Ch'ing; or KKCK 207.1, 18/9/24 Liu Hsing-li. The latter confession is corroborated by no one except Liu's son, whose confession is nearly identical. In Peking, nearly all arrested sect members were interrogated first by the staff of the Board of Punishments and then by the Grand Council. The officials in charge were experienced investigators and interrogators and appear to have had an excellent command of all the evidence; false or unreliable confessions made at a lower level were usually reversed at this stage.

In order to demonstrate the judicial process involved in acquiring these testimonies and to show how overlapping information from several individuals can build a multifaceted and credible picture of an event, I have brought together from different sources a dozen confessions in Appendix 1.

PART ONE

1 In my Ph.D. dissertation I gave a new name to the sectarian stage of the White Lotus religion that developed in the late Ming; I called it, after its central deity, the Venerable Mother religion. In the interest of clarity, I have here returned to the more conventional name White Lotus. See my "Millenarian Rebellion in China: The Eight Trigrams Uprising of 1813."

2 A monk named Hui-yuan founded a White Lotus Society in the fourth century. In 1133 Mao Tzu-yuan borrowed this name for the religious society that he established, and most studies of the "White Lotus Society" begin with the twelfth century. See Daniel L. Overmyer, "Folk-Buddhist Religion: Creation and Eschatology in Medieval China," *History of Religions* 12, no. 1 (1972): 46ff., and his *Folk Buddhist Religion: Dissenting Sects in Late Traditional China*, forthcoming. See also Chan Hok-lam, "The White Lotus–Maitreya Doctrine and Popular Uprisings in Ming and Ch'ing China," *Sinologica* 10, no. 4 (1969); and Richard Yung-deh Chu, "An Introductory Study of the White Lotus Sect in Chinese History."

3 Overmyer, "Folk-Buddhist Religion," pp. 53–57, and his *Folk Buddhist Religion*, chap. 7. Chao-lien, *Hsiao-t'ing tsa-lu* [Miscellaneous notes from the

Hsiao pavilion], 2: 55–56. For date of books, see also PHHP, "Introduction," and CSL 281.19–21, 18/12/24 Edict.

4 See the following for some examples of apparent sect foundings: A Hung-yang (Red Sun) and a Hun-yuan (Chaotic Origin) sect each claimed they were founded by P'iao Kao in 1594. See Chao Wei-pang, "Secret Religious Societies in North China in the Ming Dynasty," *Folklore Studies* 7 (1948): 96–97; Overmyer, "Folk-Buddhist Religion," p. 56; James Inglis, "The Hun Yuen Men," *Chinese Recorder* 39 (1908): 270; Samuel Couling, *Encyclopedia Sinica*, p. 246. Hsien-t'ien (Former Heaven), Lung-hua (Dragon Flower), and Wu-wei (Effortless Action) sects claimed Patriarch Lo Ch'ing of the Wan-li reign (1573–1619) as their founder. See Couling, *Encyclopedia*, pp. 241, 609, 610; Joseph Edkins, *Chinese Buddhism*, pp. 371–77; J. J. M. de Groot, *Sectarianism and Religious Persecution in China*, pp. 181–84; Overmyer, *Folk Buddhist Religion*, chap. 6. A Tsai-li (Believer) sect was founded by Yang Ts'un-jen at the end of the Ming. See Wing-tsit Chan, *Religious Trends in Modern China*, p. 156, or Chao Tung-shu, *Li chiao shih-hua* [An illustrated history of the Li sect]. A Huang-t'ien (Yellow Heaven) sect was founded in the mid–sixteenth century. See C. K. Yang, *Religion in Chinese Society*, p. 215. A Lung (Dragon) school sect was taught in Chihli province in the Wan-li reign by a Mrs. Liu. See NYC 41.28–31, 21/3/3.

The following, culled from a variety of dissimilar and not always reliable secondary sources, may refer to the activities of White Lotus groups. **1528**: Li Fu-ta in Shansi province. See T'ao Hsi-sheng, "Ming-tai Mi-le Pai-lien-chiao chi ch'i-t'a 'yao-tsei' " [Maitreya and White Lotus sect members and other 'religious rebels' of the Ming period] in *Ming-tai tsung-chiao* [Religion in the Ming period], pp. 9–12 (citing *Ming shih* 206). **1545**: Lo T'ing-yü in Anhwei. See T'ao Hsi-sheng, "Pai-lien chiao," p. 13 (citing *Ming shih* 117). **1551**: Hsiao Ch'in in Shansi. See Li Shou-k'ung, "Ming-tai Pai-lien-chiao k'ao-lueh" [A brief study of the White Lotus sect in the Ming period] in *Ming-tai tsung-chiao*, p. 42 (citing *Ming shih* 327). **1547**: Yang Hui in Shantung. See Richard Chu, "White Lotus Sect," pp. 116–17. **1557**: Yen Hao in Chahar. See T'ao Hsi-sheng, "Pai-lien chiao," pp. 13–14 (citing *Ming shih* 209). Ma Tsu-shih in Chekiang. See Li Shou-k'ung, "Ming-tai Pai-lien chiao," p. 43. **1565**: Chang Ch'ao-yung in Chihli. See Li Shou-k'ung, "Ming-tai Pai-lien chiao," p. 43. **1566**: Sect in Szechwan. See T'ao Hsi-sheng, "Pai-lien chiao," p. 12 (citing *Ming shih* 206). **1591**: Liu T'ien-chu in Peking. See Li Shou-k'ung, "Ming-tai Pai-lien chiao," p. 44 (citing *Ming shih* 221). **1600**: Chao I-p'ing in Anhwei. See Li Shou-k'ung, "Ming-tai Pai-lien chiao," pp. 44–45 (citing *Ming shih* 232). **1621–27**: Twenty sect-led uprisings. See Richard Chu, "White Lotus Sect," pp. 109, 258.

5 The people whose confessions provide information about Chia-ch'ing period sects fall into three categories: (1) individuals who belonged to one of the sects around Peking which later joined Lin Ch'ing's K'an Trigram and were part of the Eight Trigrams rebellion—approximately 600 people, 215 of whom were arrested and gave detailed testimony; (2) individuals who participated in the Eight Trigrams uprising or in the planning for that uprising and who came from a variety of other districts in Honan, Chihli, and Shantung—1,090 people named in the sources for 140 of whom there are confessions; and (3)

individuals who joined White Lotus sects in north China which established no connections with the Eight Trigrams—several hundred people and only several dozen confessions. (Much more information in this third category is available, particularly in the Palace Museum archives in Taiwan.)

Information about sect literature is preserved in the PHHP. Its author Huang Yü-p'ien 黄育楩 was made magistrate of Chü-lu district in central Chihli province in 1833. While prosecuting members of sects in that district he confiscated nearly seventy different religious books belonging to these groups. In order to discredit the beliefs of this religion, Huang wrote three essays in which he first quoted extensively from the confiscated scriptures and then presented his own arguments against the ideas contained in those passages. His book *P'o-hsieh hsiang-pien* [A detailed refutation of heterodoxy] (1883) is therefore an excellent source for religious documents that have not survived. (See PHHP, "Introduction.") Many of the passages Huang quoted have been translated and discussed by Western scholars. See Overmyer, *Folk Buddhist Religion*, chap. 3, and Chao Wei-pang, "Secret Religious Societies," pp. 95–115. There are also numerous articles in Chinese and Japanese based on Huang's work.

Huang Yü-p'ien's investigations took place only twenty years after the 1813 rebellion in a district where there had long been followers of White Lotus sects, some of whom joined the Eight Trigrams. See index entries for Yang Yü-shan and the Ta-sheng sect in Chü-lu.

6 See Paul Pelliot, "Les Bronzes de la Collection Eumorfopoulos publiés par M. W. P. Yetts (I et II)," *T'oung Pao* 27 (1930): 392; H. H. Dubs, "An Ancient Chinese Mystery Cult," *Harvard Theological Review* 35 (1942): 223; PHHP 4.5; Henri Maspero, "The Mythology of Modern China," in *Asiatic Mythology*, ed. Hackin, p. 382. Dubs's fascinating article is about a mass movement in the year 3 B.C. in which people believed that the end of the world was coming and that *Hsi-wang-mu* would save them. In that year there had been a great drought, and during the early spring a mass panic began among the common people who were convinced that a great disaster was imminent. They "frightened each other" and "became excited and ran [from place to place] each holding a stalk of straw or hemp which they carried and passed on to others, saying, 'I am transporting the wand [of the goddess's edict].' " Thousands took to the roads, letting down their hair, walking barefoot or riding chariots or horses, "galloping fast and making themselves post-messengers to transmit and transport the wands." By that summer the frenzy had increased. People gathered in the imperial capital: they "met in the wards, lanes and footpaths, making sacrifices and setting out utensils, singing and dancing, sacrificing to *Hsi-wang-mu*." These believers also transmitted to one another a charm which read, "The Mother informs her people that those who wear this writing will not die." People built fires on top of buildings at night as beacons, and waited, beating drums and calling out, "exciting and frightening one another." It was said that "people with vertical/slanting eyes will come." By the fall, however, when no visitation had occurred, "the frenzy stopped." (This paragraph has been taken from *chüan* 11, 26, and 27 of the *History of the Former Han Dynasty*, trans. H. H. Dubs [Baltimore: Waverly Press, 1938–55] and from Dubs, "Cult," p. 235.)

For *Hsi-wang-mu*'s metamorphosis into the queen of a western paradise, see passages from the *Shan-hai ching* 山海經 quoted in Dubs, "Cult," p. 231, and Lewis Hodous, "Chinese Conceptions of Paradise," *Chinese Recorder* 45 (1914): 362. For her famous peaches of immortality, see Dubs's article, portions of the Ming novel *Hsi-yu chi* 西遊記 translated by Arthur Waley under the title of *Monkey* (New York: Grove Press, 1958) pp. 54–55; and Maspero, "Mythology," p. 383.

7   The evidence indicates that *wu-sheng lao-mu*, *wu-sheng fo-mu*, and *wu-sheng fu-mu* are grammatically parallel phrases; in the PHHP the terms *wu-sheng mu* or simply *wu-sheng* are often used. Because of this and because of the persistent character of this deity as a mother, I have preferred to translate *fu-mu* with the singular term "progenitor" rather than its normal plural meaning of "parents" or "father and mother." It may well be that the weight of ordinary usage was so great that anyone who spoke this phrase frequently (as did all sect members in their daily recitation of the eight-character mantra of which *wu-sheng fu-mu* was a part) gradually substituted the idea of "parents." For *fo-mu*, see KCT 18322, Yung-cheng 2/6/12.

8   Daniel L. Overmyer, "The Tz'u-hui t'ang: A Contemporary Religious Sect on Taiwan," paper presented at the annual meeting of the Canadian Society for Asian Studies, June 1974, University of Toronto, p. 1; Marjorie Topley, "The Great Way of Former Heaven," *Bulletin of the School of Oriental and African Studies* 26, no. 2 (1963): 370. Both articles describe quite respectable sects active today in Taiwan and Singapore. I am most grateful to Professor Overmyer for introducing me to the Tz'u-hui t'ang and for allowing me to accompany him on one of his visits with them in the summer of 1973.

9   Overmyer, "Folk-Buddhist Religion," pp. 59–60; Chao Wei-pang, "Secret Religious Societies," p. 102; PHHP 1.1–2.

10 White Lotus scriptures drew heavily on Buddhist sutras and Chinese popular religion in general for their language and imagery. For this quote see Overmyer, "Folk-Buddhist Religion," p. 61. For another telling of this story, see a scripture quoted by Hsiao Kung-chuan on pp. 232–33 in his *Rural China: Imperial Control in the Nineteenth Century.*

11 Overmyer, "Folk-Buddhist Religion," pp. 60–62, citing four different scriptures.

12 See Edkins, *Chinese Buddhism*, pp. 221–22, or William E. Soothill and Lewis Hodous, *A Dictionary of Chinese Buddhist Terms*, pp. 57, 232.

13 According to Buddhist sutras, when Maitreya Buddha comes to be born on earth, he will find enlightenment sitting under the dragon-flower tree—so called because its branches resemble a dragon or a dragon's head. There the Buddha would hold three meetings or assemblies where he would speak about the Law and save mankind. See *Dai Kan-Wa jiten* [Dictionary of Chinese], ed. Morohashi Tetsuji, ♯48818.141, quoting the *Mi-le hsia sheng ching* [Sutra on Maitreya coming into the world]; also Topley, "Great Way Sects," p. 373. White Lotus sects adopted this prediction but altered it so that the Mother herself would hold three assemblies, one at the end of each kalpa.

14 KCT 018945, 20/6/13 Sun Chia-wang. The character *yang* used as a sect name is generally given as 陽, though sometimes as 洋 and less often as 羊. The *P'o-hsieh hsiang-pien* cites texts seen by the author and uses the first char-

acter *yang* 陽, and I have done likewise. I have tentatively translated this character as "sun," but the meaning of *yang*, the complement of *yin* 陰, one of the two fundamental polar forces in the universe, is far more extensive. *Yang* 陽 refers to this light, bright, strong, positive force. As we shall see, sect members paid tribute to the sun (called *t'ai-yang* 太陽) as a manifestation and symbol of this force. Other authors have relied on the second form *yang* 洋 and translated it as "ocean." See Overmyer, "Folk-Buddhist Religion," p. 56. For "ocean" see de Groot, *Sectarianism*, p. 443.

15   PHHP 4.24–25; Chao Wei-pang, "Secret Religious Societies," p. 105.

16   During the Ch'ing dynasty the day was divided into twelve *shih* 時, intervals of two hours. I have translated *shih* as "hour-period."

17   Such a scheme is described in a scripture entitled *P'u-ming ju-lai wu-wei liao-i pao-chüan* 普明如來無爲了義寶卷, for which see Overmyer, "Folk-Buddhist Religion," p. 65, Richard Chu, "White Lotus Sect," pp. 70–71, or Chao Wei-pang, "Secret Religious Societies," pp. 105–06; all are based on the text located at PHHP 2.10. An identical scheme was described in 1815 by an arrested sect member named Wang T'ien-i, who recounted "what his grand-mother had told him." See SYT 333–36, 20/12/25. In 1815 a believer named Fang Jung-sheng made up a calendar in which there were eighteen months in each year. NYC 42.13–22, 20/12/14 Memorial; NYC 42.32–33, 20/12/16 Edict. See also the text cited by Overmyer on p. 66 and portions of an unnamed text quoted in PHHP 3.10 (and translated by Overmyer on pp. 66–67).

18   KCT 018945, 20/6/13 Sun Chia-wang.

19   Topley, "Great Way Sects," p. 372.

20   Ibid.

21   The first quotation is from Overmyer, "Folk-Buddhist Religion," p. 66. The second is from Chao Wei-pang, "Secret Religious Societies," p. 103.

22   For "epidemic" see KCT 018960, 20/6/20 Memorial. For "wind of destruc-tion" see C. K. Yang, *Religion in Chinese Society*, p. 235, where he describes a Huang-t'ien sect in Manchuria in the late nineteenth century.

23   CPT 209–221, 1/9/25 Chang Cheng-mo. For the Eight Trigrams, see *Chi-ning district gazetteer*, 4.20–29 Liu Ning.

24   Quotations are from SYT 81–83, 22/11/8 Ch'en Sheng-r, and SYT 419–22, 22/9/27 Ch'iu Tzu-liang. See also C. K. Yang, *Religion in Chinese Society*, pp. 234–35. Richard Wilhelm in *The Soul of China*, p. 297, quotes a prophecy printed up and distributed in Shansi in 1923 that despite some possible Christian influence appears to speak about these same ideas of salvation and the millennium:

> The 23rd day of the 10th month will be a day of misery, and wild animals will appear upon the earth to oppress men. [But] when the new year arrives, all men will laugh and when they are asked why they laugh, they will say, "The True Lord is here and we go to meet him." Then will come the great period of salvation and the faithful will live to see it. The unfaithful, however, and those who do evil, will know great misery. He who does good will save his life.

25   In the late nineteenth and early twentieth centuries some sects asserted that

the third period had already arrived and they were waiting for its imminent end. See de Groot, *Sectarianism*, pp. 179–80. Topley ("Great Way Sects," p. 372) describes a sect in Singapore in the 1950s whose members believed that "unless there is a change in spiritual outlook, the world will end with the Wind Catastrophe in the form of a hydrogen bomb." See also Chao Wei-pang, "Secret Religious Societies," p. 115.

26 Overmyer, "Folk-Buddhist Religion, p. 57; Topley, "Great Way Sects," p. 372.

27 *Chi-ning district gazetteer* 4.20–29 Li Ching-hsiu. This appears to be a romanticized description of the north China plain area that in the middle Ch'ing was the heartland for these White Lotus sects. Believers interviewed by Topley in Singapore retained this vision of a Cloud City where they could go by means of paper charms and incantations to avoid the kalpa calamities. See her "Great Way Sects," p. 372.

28 Topley, "Great Way Sects," p. 370; PHHP 2.10; Overmyer, *Folk Buddhist Religion*, chap. 7, n. 103. Behind this millennial vision we can see a rather typical Chinese faith in the social and cosmic consequences of correct moral behavior, what Jerome Grieder has called "a common [Chinese] conviction that men's minds must be made over before the conditions of their lives can change." See his *Hu Shih and the Chinese Renaissance* (Cambridge: Harvard University Press, 1970), p. 327.

29 SYT 317–25, 22/9/24 Wang Jui.

30 In 1796 a White Lotus rebel said that their leader had on his hands the characters for "sun" and "moon" (which together make up the character *ming* 明, as in the Ming dynasty). CPT 209–21, 1/9/25 Chang Cheng-mo.

31 For Li as a favored surname for White Lotus groups, see SYT 93–94, 19/11/7 Ch'in Li; CFCL 29.1–6, 18/12/26 Niu Liang-ch'en; NYC 41.28–31, 21/3/3 Mrs. Liu Kung; CPT 209–21, 1/9/25 Chang Cheng-mo. For the belief in Lao-tzu as a messiah figure, see Anna Seidel, *La Divinization de Lao Tseu dans le Taoisme des Han*, and her "Image of the Perfect Ruler in Early Taoist Messianism: Lao-tzu and Li Hung," *History of Religions* 9 (1969–70): 216–47. See also the discussion about this article in Holmes Welch, "The Bellagio Conference on Taoist Studies," *History of Religions* 9 (1969–70): 113ff.

32 For Liu, see NYC 41.28–31, 21/3/3 Mrs. Liu Kung; SYT 93–94, 19/11/7 Ch'in Li; CFCL 3.9–13, 18/9/18 Lin Ch'ing. For the family of sect teachers named Liu from Shan district in Shantung, see CSL 309.42–44, CL 13/2/30 [1748]; CSL 908.7–8, CL 37/5/7 [1772]; CSL 1261.18–21, CL 51/7*/21 [1786]; and n. 81 in Part Two.

33 CFCL 24.21–26, 18/12/11 Feng K'e-shan. For Feng's ideas about Chu Yen-shuang, see Part Two, n. 137. For Chu and Niu-pa in other White Lotus sects, see de Groot, *Sectarianism*, pp. 351, 353, 367.

34 SYT 93–94, 19/11/17 Ch'in Li; KCT 018960, 20/6/20 Memorial; PHHP 1.2–3 citing a scripture about Patriarch Kung-chang. For Chang T'ien-shih, see C. K. Yang, *Religion in Chinese Society*, pp. 113–14, 191.

35 SYT 333–36, 20/12/25 Wang T'ien-kuei; SYT 343–45, 20/12/25 Wang K'e-chin; SYT 337–38, 20/12/25 Wang Heng-chung; C. K. Yang, *Religion in Chinese Society*, p. 234. See also pp. 21–22 above.

36 NYC 41.28–31, 21/3/3 Mrs. Liu Kung.

37 PHHP 1.9–10.

38 KCT 015861, 19/6/20 Edict.

39 CFCL 29.6–8, 18/12/26 Composite confession.

40 For *chia-tzu* day, see CFCL 1.29–32, 18/9/15 Chang Chien-mu. For 8/15, see above pp. 63, 65. Also *Chi-ning district gazetteer* 4.20–29 Chou T'ing-lin; CFCL 29.1–6, 18/12/26 Hsu An-kuo; CFCL 4.5–9, 18/9/19 Lin Ch'ing; Richard Chu, "White Lotus Sects," p. 121.

41 SYT 49, 21/3/3 Tu Lo-chang.

42 SYT 51–52, 22/9/5 Wang Jui.

43 For *chiu-kung*, see *Dai Kan-Wa jiten*, ed. Morohashi Tetsuji, ♯167.128. For the use of the eight trigrams for a rebel organization (in addition to the rebellion of 1813), see de Groot, *Sectarianism*, pp. 336–38 and Part Two, n. 4, for the Eight Trigram uprising of 1786. Also for a Chin-tan pa-kua 金丹八卦 (Golden Elixir Eight Trigrams) sect in 1812, see CSL 257.18–20, 17/5/17 Edict.

44 By the twentieth century at the latest, it was a well-established practice in some sects for this communication to take place through "spirit seances" where the Eternal Mother spoke either through a medium or in writing with a sand planchette. See the articles on the I-kuan tao 一貫道 (Way of Undivided Unity) in north China and Manchuria by Willem Grootaers listed in the bibliography. There is no mention of a seance of any kind in material dealing with the Eight Trigrams of 1813.

45 PHHP 2.3; Overmyer, "Folk-Buddhist Religion," p. 56. The story of another sect founder, Patriarch Lo, has been told in English in several places. See Edkins, *Chinese Buddhism*, pp. 371–77, and de Groot, *Sectarianism*, pp. 179–83 for two versions.

46 Condensed from PHHP 1.3–20.

47 Chao Wei-pang, "Secret Religious Societies," p. 109. More than a dozen of these stories are summarized by Huang Yü-p'ien in PHHP 4.3–8, and 4.16–17. Chao Wei-pang has summarized these on pp. 109–10.

48 KCT 011671, 13/8/1 Composite confession.

49 Chao Wei-pang, "Secret Religious Societies," pp. 111–12.

50 For examples, see KCT 016424, 19/9/6 Teng Lo-san; CFCL 42.31–34, 21/6/3 Liu Yü-lung; CFCL 25.7–10, 18/12/12 Memorial. Pictures of *fu* used by Red Spear assemblies (*hung-ch'iang hui* 紅槍會)—twentieth-century groups that grew at least in part out of the White Lotus tradition—can be seen on pp. 121–24 of Tai Hsuan-chih, *Hung-ch'iang hui (1916–1949)* [The Red Spear Society, 1916–1949].

51 CFCL 38.2–6, 19/2*/4 Composite confession.

52 For date of books, see n. 3. For whether books were printed or copied, see SYT 211, 22/12/21 Edict, and SSTC, 19/6/1 Edict to Hsien-fu. Huang Yü-p'ien says that the scriptures he confiscated were printed (PHHP, "Introduction," p. 1). Of the books mentioned in documents I have seen for the years 1810–25, five were specifically described as handwritten, while the rest—several dozen—were printed. See NYC 39.31–37, 19/7/30 Ch'i Wen-chang; SYT 165, 22/6/17 Edict; SSTC, 19/5/20 Memorial from Hsien-fu; NYC 41.35–42, 21/5/8 Memorial. Of an additional group of sixteen books seized in 1817, twelve were handwritten and four printed. See SYT 217–22, 22/12/

21 Memorial. If this sample is at all typical, books were printed and written out longhand in about equal proportions.

53 KCT 017254, 19/1/17 Memorial.

54 See KCT 017254, 19/1/17 for the search for Lin Ch'ing's book. For an example of a sect member's getting rid of his own copies, see SYT 103–04, 21/1/18 Ying Ling-hsiao.

55 It is difficult to estimate how many books or how many different books were in circulation at any one time. During the years 1813 to 1817 the Ch'ing government recovered and eliminated at least seventy-five—not necessarily all different—White Lotus scriptures. The references below indicate a minimum of how many were reported as confiscated. CFCL 22.17, 18/11/25 one or more; CPT 189–90, 18/12/10 one; CFCL 25.7–10, 18/12/12 five; CPT 435, 18/12/21 nineteen; KCT 017254, 19/1/17 one; CFCL 36.6–8, 19/2/14 two or more; CFCL 38.2–6, 19/2*/4 one or more; SSTC, 19/5/20 three; KCT 015625, 19/6/7 one; KCT 015815, 19/6/28 one or more; NYC 39.31–37, 19/7/30 one; KCT 016424, 19/9/6 two; KCT 018834, 20/6/1 one; KCT 018945, 20/6/13 two; NYC 40.10–12, 20/7/6 eight; SYT 273–75, 21/2/25 one; NYC 41.28–31, 21/3/3 one; NYC 41.35–42, 21/5/8 five or more; SYT 17–18, 21/12/5 one or more; SYT 165, 22/6/17 one; SYT 217–22, 22/12/21 sixteen.

56 PHHP, "Introduction," pp. 1–2. Also, see the list at SYT 217–22, 22/12/21 Memorial from the Grand Council. Of these sixteen books, twelve consisted of one volume, three of two volumes, and one of three volumes. The books used by some sects on Taiwan look either like Buddhist sutras (with large type characters and pleated pages in the style of Ch'ing memorials) or like the "moral books" (*shan-shu* 善書) distributed by other temples on the island (that is, they are ordinary printed books which usually have pictures of various deities including the Eternal Mother at the front). There are photographs of the *P'iao-kao lin-fan ching* 飄高臨凡經 in Sawada Mizuho, "Koyo-kyō no shi-tan" [Preliminary remarks on the Hung-yang sect], *Tenri daigaku gakuho* 24 (1957): 78–79. *Pao-chüan tsung-lu* [A comprehensive bibliography of sacred scrolls], ed. Li Shih-yü, has photographs of several religious books including the *Hun-yuan hung-yang ju-lai wu-chi P'iao-kao-tsu lin-fan pao-chüan* 混元弘陽如來無極飄高臨凡寶卷.

57 Frederic H. Balfour, *Taoist Texts*, p. 73.

58 For example, see CFCL 1.29–32, 18/9/15 Chang Chien-mu; KKCK 202.1, 18/9/19 Lin Ch'ing.

59 For the Ming dynasty rebellion, see de Groot, *Sectarianism*, pp. 166–68. For the prophecies about Maitreya being born as a member of this family, see nn. 17 and 35 above. See also Chao Wei-pang, "Secret Religious Societies," pp. 101–02. For the extent of this family's network during the Chia-ch'ing reign, see as samples CSL 311.25–26, 20/10/29 Edict; SYT 241–42, 21/2/21 Edict; SYT 343–45, 20/12/25 Wang K'e-chin. For its survival into at least Tao-kuang times, see Hsiao Kung-chuan, *Rural China*, pp. 232–33, 635. I have begun a detailed investigation of this family and their history.

60 NYC 41.28–31, 21/3/3 Mrs. Liu Kung.

61 CPT 435, 18/12/12 Memorial from the Grand Council.

62 KCT 018945, 20/6/13 Sun Chia-wang.

63 See Part Two, n. 107, for Lin Ch'ing's book. SYT 343–45, 20/12/25 Wang K'e-chin, and C. K. Yang, *Religion in Chinese Society*, p. 234; both cite passages making it possible to identify Lin Ch'ing's book with these others.

64 NYC 38.27–31, 19/8/2 Wo Lo-yun; KCT 015625, 19/6/7 Composite confession.

65 KCT 015815, 19/6/28 Memorial and Wang Ying-chieh.

66 CFCL 33.16–19, 19/1/27 Chang Chiu-ch'eng; CSL 257.27–29, 17/5/25 Memorial; de Groot, *Sectarianism*, pp. 409–10.

67 These registers were also called *hao-pu* 號簿 or *pu-chi* 簿籍 or *ti-pu* 底簿. For name lists made up by Eight Trigram groups, see Part Two, n. 149, and CFCL 29.1–6, 18/12/26 Hsu An-kuo; CFCL 35.21–25, 19/2/10 Yang Yü-shan; KCT 017303, 19/11/19 Ch'ü Fu-r; KCT 017077, 19/11/3 Ch'in Li; CFCL 25.7–10, 18/12/12 Liu Tsung-lin; SYT 317–25, 22/9/24 Wang Jui; SYT 203–09, 22/11/18 Tung Kuo-t'ai.

   For name lists made up by other sects, see CPT 361–62, 18/11/22 Kuo Jui-fu; CSL 257.27–29, 17/5/25 Edict; CSL 257.18–20, 17/5/17 Edict. This last mentioned source states that books belonging to a Luan district (Chihli) sect (possibly the Wang family) listed more than five thousand people who had joined in the preceding forty years, an average of over one hundred people a year.

68 The chronological relationship between the phrases *fu-mu* and *lao-mu* is not clear. The sect scriptures quoted by Huang Yü-p'ien use *lao-mu*. Temples destroyed by the government in northern Honan in the late 1830s also commemorated *Wu-sheng lao-mu* (see de Groot, *Sectarianism*, pp. 22, 529). Yet every sect member interrogated during the Chia-ch'ing period I have studied (approximately 1810–20) who quoted the eight-character chant said *fu-mu*. De Groot cites two other sects (in 1823 and 1833) who also preferred *fu-mu* (*Sectarianism*, pp. 492, 512). A sect in 1724 said *fo-mu* 佛母 (KCT 18322, Yung-cheng 2/6/12). These chants were believed to have great power, and clearly believers searched for exactly the right formula.

   In Chia-ch'ing period materials, I did encounter two other mantras (one six and one eight characters), each mentioned only once, both similar to each other and neither far removed from the standard *fu-mu* formula. See NYC 38.67–72, 20/9/6 Chang Feng, and KCT 018834, 20/6/1 Hsing Shih-k'uei.

69 NYC 40.3–6, 20/5/27 Kuo Lo-yun; KCT 018960, 20/6/20 Chang Lo-chiao. Another long chant was: "Eternal Progenitor in Our Original Home in the World of True Emptiness, Past, Present and Maitreya-to-come." SYT 93–96, 21/3/4 Chang Po-ch'ing. None of these longer chants was taught in a sect that became part of the Eight Trigrams.

70 KKCK 223.1–3, 18/10/17 Memorial from the Grand Council and Board of Punishments.

71 See Kenneth K. S. Ch'en, *Buddhism in China*, pp. 326–28.

72 *Chi-ning district gazetteer* 4.20–29 Liu Ning; CFCL 1.22–27, 18/9/15 Ts'ui Shih-chün. An observer described the procedure of one twentieth-century sect as follows: "In the morning at sunrise, they are kneeling down and folding their hands, facing the sun until it has risen high into the sky. In the evening at sunset, they have to do the same thing until the sun has disap-

peared behind the mountains" (Paul Serruys, "Folklore Contributions in *Sino-Mongolica*," *Folklore Studies* 6, no. 2 [1947]: 26). The description comes from an article written by a Dutchman in 1925 (and translated by Serruys) about a Chin-tan (Golden Elixir) sect. For another description see Wilhelm, *The Soul of China*, p. 300 for the Hung-wan (Red Swastika) sect in Peking in the 1920s.

73 See n. 14 for more on *yang* 陽 in sect ideology. For another chant referring to the sun, see KCT 016869, 19/11/18 Chao Fei-i. Liu Ts'un-yan suggests an association between efficacious exercises and the position of the sun was to be found in "popular Taoism": "The Taoist priests of ancient times had invested a theory of inhaling air or *ch'i* 氣 (facing either the sun in the morning or the full moon at night) so that they could benefit from the essences emitted from the heavenly bodies." See his "Taoist Self-Cultivation in Ming Thought," in *Self and Society in Ming Thought*, ed. William Theodore de Bary, pp. 303–04. A scripture that may have belonged to a White Lotus sect stated that springtime (when life was new), dawn and dusk each day, and the 1st and 15th of each month (the days of the new and full moon) were times when the air was especially full of the "cosmic breath" (*ch'i*). See the *I-chin ching* described in Clarence G. Vichert, "Fundamental Principles in Chinese Boxing," *Journal of the West China Border Research Society* 7 (1935): 44–45. For a description of a nineteenth-century sect that more explicitly paid tribute to the power of the sun, see F. H. James, "North China Sects," *Chinese Recorder* 30 (1899): 74–75.

Many scholars have seen a Manichean influence on the ideas of these White Lotus sects in the form of this emphasis on light (as opposed to darkness). Kenneth Ch'en discusses this problem briefly on pp. 15–16 in his *Buddhism in China*. For Manicheism, see Abraham Jackson, *Researches in Manicheism*, and his "Sketch of the Manichean Doctrine Concerning the Future Life," *Journal of the American Oriental Society* 50 (1930): 177–98.

74 The most common terms for "recite" were *nien* 念, *nien-sung* 念誦, or *mo-sung* 默誦. For these terms and for simplified recitation, see KKCK 211.1, 18/9/29 Li Yü-lung; CFCL 16.30–35, 18/11/5 Ts'ao Lun; KKCK 225.1, 18/10/18 Liu Chin-ts'ai; CFA 59, 20/2/27 Keng Shih-an; KKCK 214.2, 18/10/9 Kao Wu; SYT 161–63, 21/12/26 Shao Chün; CFCL 34.16–19, 19/2/2 Liu K'un. For the use of incense, see NYC 38.7–10, 19/3/14 Wang Chin-tao.

75 First quotation: CFCL 16.30–35 18/11/5 Ts'ao Lun. Second quotation: KKCK 222.1–2, 18/10/16 Kuo Ch'ao-chün; see also SYT 85–86, 19/12/3 Meng Ta-t'ou.

76 First quotation: KKCK 203.1, 18/9/19 Kung Shu. Second quotation: CFCL 16.30–35, 18/11/5 Ts'ao Lun.

77 NYC 41.42–47, 21/6/26 P'ei Ching-i.

78 KCT 016869, 19/11/18 Chao Fei-i; NYC 41.42–47, 21/6/26 P'ei Ching-i.

79 For privacy, see NYC 41.42–47, 21/6/26 P'ei Ching-i. For group meditation, see, for example, KKCK 206.1, 18/9/22 Kao Ta, and Part One, "Money and Meetings." Arthur Smith describes a sect in Shantung in the 1880s where members were known to sit all night in meditation. ("Sketches of a Country Parish," *Chinese Recorder* 12 (1882): 322.)

80 The judicial commissioner conducting this interrogation thereupon ordered

smoke from burning coal and paper to be blown into this criminal's nose (while he was in trance). "Once this was done, he was unable to circulate his breath and began to confess. . . . [A few days later] Hsing Shih-k'uei died in prison as a result of the smoke inhalation" (KCT 018834, 20/6/1 Memorial).

Joseph Edkins visited members of a Wu-wei sect in Shantung in the 1870s and observed one man go into a trance. "Once I asked a believer . . . how he performed his religious duties. . . . He then took his seat on a stool in a cross-legged attitude. At first he sat tranquil, with eyes closed; but gradually he became extremely excited, though without speaking. His chest heaved, his breathing became extremely violent, his eyes shot fire—he seemed to be the subject of a demoniacal possession. . . . After remaining in this excited mood for some minutes, he suddenly brought it to a termination, left the stool on which he had been sitting, and resumed conversation as rationally as before. The bystanders said that this man was able to cause his soul to go out of his body and return when he pleased" (*Religion in China*, p. 187). For another description by an observer of a Chihli sect in the 1870s, see Prosper Leboucq, *Associations de la Chine*, p. 25.

81 PHHP 1.21. See also Chao Wei-pang, "Secret Religious Societies," p. 100.

82 CFA 12, 19/3/16 Liu Ta-lu and Jen T'ien-te.

83 Topley, "Great Way Sects," pp. 375–76. When Lin Ch'ing initiated Niu Liang-ch'en into his sect, "he used his hand to indicate the place between my eyebrows, and said that my nature (*hsing* 性) was there" (CFCL 29.1–6, 18/12/26 Niu Liang-ch'en).

84 NYC 40.3–6, 20/5/27 Kuo Lo-yun.

85 For these phrases, see KCT 011671, 13/8/1 Sung Chin-hui; SYT 227–34, 22/11/20 Ch'ü Ming-r; and SYT 17–18, 21/12/5 Composite confession, respectively.

86 SYT 45–46, 21/3/3 Liu Wen-t'ung. For T'ang Ssu-chiu, see KCT 018583, 20/5/9 Yeh Fu-ming.

87 In the parlance of sixteenth-century followers of Wang Yang-ming, *kung-fu* meant an active effort at cultivation of the mind. See William Theodore de Bary's Introduction to his *Self and Society in Ming Thought*, p. 20. White Lotus sects used the term to refer to physical and mental self-cultivation. *Kung-fu* was sometimes written 功夫.

88 NYC 40.21–29, 20/12/19 Chang Lo-chiao; SYT 131–35, 22/10/18 Wang Pao and Kao Chu.

89 NYC 39.3–8, 19/4/1 Lu Lao.

90 SYT 131–35, 22/10/18 Wang Pao and Kao Chu. I have combined these two confessions.

91 One reference states that a patient was given tea leaves as a cure. SYT 191–212, 22/9/14 Grand Council list.

Ailments cured included: five instances of leg ulcers (SYT 301–03, 20/2/28 Chu Mo-r; SYT 41–42, 22/9/3 Hai-k'ang; SYT 467–69, 19/12/18 Mrs. Chu Hsing; SYT 257–59, 20/9/21 Sung Erh; SYT 173–75, 21/11/21 Wang Chen); pain in the leg (NYC 40.53–57, 21/5/27 Yü Ch'eng-r); broken leg (SYT 191–212, 22/9/14 Grand Council list); eye injury (SYT 83–84, 19/12/3 Ch'en Wu); eye infection (KCT 017262, 19/12/17 Jen San); stomach pain

(SYT 177–78, 22/8/19 Ts'ui Wu); "not feeling too well" (SYT 131–32, 22/10/ 18 Wang Pao); contagious disease (SYT 233–42, 22/6/20 Hu Ch'eng-te).

Of the eighty-three sect teachers in the Peking area (i.e., people who took pupils), seventeen (or 20 percent) were healers and converted pupils by healing them. (There were probably more teachers than this, since it was definitely in a criminal's interest to assert that he had no pupils.) A total of forty-six people confessed that they had been cured prior to joining a sect. This is 7 percent of the six hundred people who joined a sect in the Peking area.

92 Alexander Williamson, a missionary in north China in the mid–nineteenth century, relates: "We are often mistaken for doctors: a poor fellow would come up holding his jaw, and asking for a cure for toothache; another had something wrong with his eyes, and a third poked a sick child in our faces" (*Journeys in North China, Manchuria, and Eastern Mongolia*, pp. 269–70).

93 For examples, see SYT 171–90, 22/9/14 Grand Council list. Healers might be brought into a sect (if they were not already in one) by their patients. For example, when Chang Tzu-sheng used acupuncture to cure Li Lao's son, Li Lao invited Chang to become his pupil and join his sect. KKCK 220.1–2, 18/10/15 Chang Tzu-sheng.

94 KCT 018960, 20/6/20 Chang Lo-chiao. KKCK 221.1–3, 18/10/16 Tung Kuo-t'ai. The members of the early twentieth-century sect called the I-ho-ch'üan 義和拳—better known as the Boxers—carried this one step further and claimed to be invulnerable to bullets.

95 CFCL 42.31–34, 21/6/3 Liu Yü-lung.

96 SYT 47–48, 21/3/3 Liu Ming-t'ang.

97 KCT 018960, 20/6/20 Chang Lo-chiao.

98 Pa-kua boxing: SYT 233–42: 22/6/20 Hu Ch'eng-te; CFCL 24.21–26, 18/12/ 11 Feng K'e-shan. Yin-yang boxing: KCT 016303, 19/8/16 Liu Yuan. Mei-hua boxing: KCT 016647-E, 19/10/30 Tung Wen-ming. Pa-fan boxing: NYC 40.3–6, 20/5/27 Kuo Lo-yun. I-ho boxing: KCT 016647-E, 19/10/30 Lu Fu.

99 SYT 85–86, 19/12/3 Meng Ta-t'ou.

100 SYT 195–96, 22/8/23 Hai-k'ang.

101 CFCL 24.21–26, 18/12/11 Feng K'e-shan.

102 KCT 017623, 20/1/26 Pien Erh. CFA 37, 19/11/2 Su Chien-te.

103 SYT 161–63, 21/12/26 Shao Chün. The word of a prisoner on his "true" motives for joining a sect cannot be taken at face value, and this is one subject on which government-elicited confessions are unreliable. It was in the interest of captured sect members to minimize their religious commitment and to emphasize the "lures" used to "trick" them into joining a sect. In this particular case (the statement by Shao Chün), the narrator might have been genuinely converted and then as an added benefit allowed to take a cut of his teacher's business, or it could have been the promise of such benefits that induced him to join. There is simply no way to be sure. The people who joined White Lotus sects were, as will become clear, definitely interested in "good benefits" (*hao-ch'u* 好處) of all sorts.

For some, sect membership definitely meant economic security. Tu Yu-r, for example, was a beggar. He had lost his parents, been adopted, and then sent out to make his own living. He was crippled by injuries received during an interrogation at the district yamen which were compounded by an accident several years later, and he walked with difficulty. Since that accident, he had lived by "running" errands, begging, and helping out at funerals and weddings in his village. At night he slept in the temple in the village. Tu was then invited by a sect teacher from his village to join his group and assist in small ways. Tu explained, "He promised to give me food and clothing for the rest of my life; this was something I wanted very much." Thereafter, Tu helped his teacher by delivering messages within the vicinity, buying and preparing food for big dinners at sect meetings, and opening the gate for visitors. See Chang Lao-liu's confession for a similar story. Chang's teacher told him that "being in the assembly and thus being fed was a lot better than going about begging." Both these men rightly considered themselves lucky to be part of this group whose members were comparatively affluent and economically secure. The sect gave them employment, a household to belong to, prestige and protection, as well as food, drink, comrades, and excitement. NYC 38.67–72, 20/9/6 Tu Yu-r; SYT 381–88, 23/4/29 Chang Lao-liu.

For the value of 10 cash, see Appendix 2.

104 KKCK 211.1, 18/9/29 Li Yü-lung.

105 For incense: CFCL 1.22–27, 18/9/15 Ts'ui Shih-chün, and SYT 85–86, 22/11/8 Mrs. Ch'en Li. For buddha: KCT 011671, 13/8/1 Sung Chin-hui.

106 KCT 018945, 20/6/13 Composite confession. For other examples, see NYC 40.3–6, 20/5/27 Kuo Lo-yun; SYT 85–86, 22/11/8 Mrs. Ch'en Li.

107 SYT 255–57, 20/1/25 Mrs. Chang Liu.

108 KCT 018960, 20/6/20 Chang Lo-chiao.

109 Chao Wei-pang, "Secret Religious Societies," p. 104; KKCK 218.1–2, 18/10/12 Yü Chi-ch'ing.

110 CFCL 17.4–7, 18/11/6 Tung Kuo-t'ai. Lin Ch'ing was perhaps emulating the Ch'ing practice of having officials kotow before an imperial edict.

111 Quotation from KCT 018960, 20/6/20 Chang Lo-chiao. For other references to this practice, see CFCL 12.27–31, 18/10/20 Li Chih-mao; KCT 019556, 20/8/13 Chang Wei-han; NYC 38.7–10, 19/3/14 Wang Chin-tao. Moxa consisted of small flammable cones of dried powdered wormwood or mugwort leaves that were burned as counterirritants, often in conjunction with acupuncture treatments.

112 Sources for the quotations are, in order, KCT 018960, 20/6/20 Chang Lo-chiao; CFCL 12.27–31, 18/10/20 Li Chih-mao; CFCL 1.22–27, 18/9/15 Ts'ui Shih-chün. The Tsai-li sect in the late Ch'ing and Republican period used such secret signs. See Wing-tsit Chan, *Religious Trends in Modern China*, p. 157.

113 For an example of a sect that did distribute seals to the membership, see CFCL 28.11–13, 18/12/24 Liu Tsung-lin.

114 KCT 011671, 13/8/1 Composite confession. One believer described his departure as follows: "I left the sect and was no longer part of the assembly" (出教不在會中) (KCT 017488, 20/1/9 Sung Ts'ai).

115 Joseph Edkins, "Books of the Modern Religious Sects in North China," *Chinese Recorder* 19 (1888): 266.

116 SYT 203–09, 22/11/18 Wang T'ien-ts'ai.
117 CPT 35–36, 19/1/6 Edict.
118 CSL 257.27–29, 17/5/25 Edict. See also KKCK 222.1, 18/10/16 Ma Sheng-chang.
119 NYC 40.21–29, 20/12/19 Chang Lo-chiao.
120 KKCK 221.1, 18/10/16 Ma Sheng-chang. Arthur Smith was very interested in these White Lotus sects, especially as they related to the problems of the Western missionary in China. He identified such seekers as "doctrine lovers" —people who would easily, perhaps too easily, be converted to any belief, including Christianity. ("Sketches of a Country Parish," pp. 250, 255.) In describing a millenarian sect of Korean origin in the United States in the early 1960s, John Lofland, *Doomsday Cult*, pp. 166–67, notes the presence of these same types whom he calls "veteran seekers." "Rarely committed to any religion, they instead carve out a career of studying each religious fad that arises. They are the first to listen and perhaps lend support to new religious movements and the first to move on to even newer ones. . . . Veteran seekers are afflicted with metaphysical lusting for such proper food as 'higher understanding' and 'deeper knowledge'. . . . [The sect that Lofland studied] disparagingly referred to veteran seekers as 'religious bums' who were neither coming from nor going to any place in particular."
121 See NYC 33.13–14, 18/12/23 Liu Tsung-lin. For more information on the average age of those who participated in the palace attack, see Part Three, n. 48. All "statistics" that are presented are drawn from information on members of sects in the area of Peking which were associated with the Eight Trigrams. I have the names of 600 such believers, 215 of whom were arrested and gave testimony. See n. 5.
122 Evidently, women were not normally prosecuted as principals in criminal cases involving heretical sects. For several sample cases in which women were not to be arrested, see CFCL 7.30–32, 18/9/30 Memorial (this is the case involving Ts'ui Shih-chün's sect in Chin-hsiang district, which is discussed in some detail in Part Three); KCT 011671, 13/8/1 Memorial (this is the 1808 case of the Jung-hua Assembly, which is discussed in detail in Part Two); NYC 39.3–8, 19/4/1 Memorial (a Fo 佛 [Buddha] school sect was here judged to be heretical, but the women, if they repented, were allowed to go free); NYC 33.13–14, 18/12/23 Edict (here the emperor stated that women who had had their names listed as contributors to a sect that joined the Eight Trigrams should not be prosecuted unless they had actively joined the rebellion).

   Women did not participate in the attack on the Forbidden City in Peking in 1813—one phase of the Eight Trigrams uprising—and were treated in the subsequent investigations (which provide the basis for most of the source material I have used) as dependents. Even if they belonged to a sect, if a man in their family had been a rebel, the women were sentenced as his relatives. According to the law this meant being made slaves in the households of "meritorious officials" and, according to a new substatute promulgated in the fall of 1813, sent to officials in the provinces of Kwangtung, Fukien, Szechwan, and Kansu. (See KKCK 211.1–2, 18/9/30 Memorial from Grand

Council and Board of Punishments; KKCK 217.1–2, 18/10/12 Memorial; CFCL 22.25, 18/11/27 Memorial). The statutes are cited in *Manuel du Code Chinois*, trans. Guy Boulais, ♯1024 and 1025.

Only 6 percent of the 600 sect members in the Peking area whose names I have found in the sources (see nn. 5, 121) were women. If we assume that 108 known wives of sect members were themselves believers (as was usual but not universal practice), this figure is increased to 20 percent. The names of wives and daughters are generally not listed in memorials or edicts, and from the materials I have used it is almost impossible to determine how many women members there were.

123 I have information about 225 different occupations for sect members (out of the same pool of 600 believers in the Peking area). Those nine individuals with rank (the 4 percent) were at least four and perhaps five members of the imperial clan, Manchus; one fifth-rank Manchu official; one sixth-rank Manchu military official; one third-rank Manchu bodyguard in the household of a prince; and one fourth-rank military official, a Chinese bannerman. For the latter, see CFCL 16.30–35, 18/11/5 Ts'ao Lun. For all the others, see Part Two, n. 17.

There is also information about the class or occupational background of (1) some participants in the 1813 rebellion from areas other than Peking, and (2) individuals who practiced other White Lotus sects elsewhere in north China during the 1810s. (See n. 5). This information tells us nothing about percentages but only that there were people of such-and-such a background in a sect. The Ch'ing government was particularly concerned about people with degrees, ranks, or official position who joined rebel or heretical groups. Those who are recorded as having joined White Lotus sects included a *chien-sheng*, see CPT 189–90, 18/12/10 Hung Kuang-han; a sixth-rank sergeant by purchase, see CFCL 26.1–2, 18/12/14 Ch'en Hsiang; and three military *sheng-yuan* who belonged to one of the Eight Trigram sects and participated in the rebellion, see CFCL 28.1–4, 18/12/21 Li Sheng-te; CFCL 25.15–17, 18/12/12 Memorial; CFCL 34.19, 19/2/4 Memorial; CSL 280. 2–4, 18/12/2 Edict; SYT 215, 21/11/26 Edict. Two other military *sheng-yuan* joined the rebellion as leaders and may have been in a sect previously, see CFCL 25.15–17, 18/12/12 Chu Ch'eng-chih; NYC 32.16–25, 18/12/3 List. The quota for military *sheng-yuan* for the three provinces of Chihli, Shantung, and Honan was over five thousand. See Chang Chung-li, *The Chinese Gentry*, pp. 94, 134, and Table 20 for more on military *sheng-yuan*. For these and other examination degrees, see *The Chinese Gentry* or H. S. Brunnert and V. V. Hagelstrom, *Present Day Political Organization of China*, ♯954–64.

124 This group of thirty-two people included: Sixteen eunuchs (see Part Two, particularly nn. 15 and 87. There are two other bits of information about eunuchs in SSTC, 19/5/16 Edict; and CSL 276.7, 18/10/2 Edict). Four grain measurers (SYT 131–32, 22/10/18 Wang Pao; KKCK 211.2, 18/10/2 Li Chiu). One former errand boy in a government granary office (KKCK 226.1, 18/10/19 Chu Liu-t'ao). Four headmen responsible for certain village areas near Peking (see Part Three, "Discovery," for Sung Chin-jung, Chu Jui, and Liu Chin-pao; and SYT 103–05, 20/1/10 Sung Ts'ai). One copyist in an office of the metropolitan bureaucracy (see Part Two n. 17). Two district constables

(CFCL 17.4–7, 18/11/6 Ts'ao Lun. *N.B.* Here as throughout, the name that follows the source citation is the person making the confession, and not in this instance the name of the person holding the position in question). One Manchu soldier (Brunnert and Hagelstrom, #732, KKCK 223.1–3, 18/10/17 Memorial). Two bondservants who worked for the households of Manchu princes (see Part Two, n. 17). One former clerk who was also a former permanent attendant for two provincial officials (KKCK 221.1–3, 18/10/16 Tung Kuo-t'ai).

The class of yamen underlings was better represented by members of the Eight Trigram sects and rebellion outside the Peking area (no. 2 described in n. 5). There were six yamen runners (called *tsao-i* 皂役, *k'uai-i* 快役, or *chuang-t'ou* 壯頭) from Honan and Shantung who were in one of these sects and in the rebellion. See NYC 32.12–16, 18/12/3 Ch'in Li; CFCL 41.3–4, 19/7/6 Huang P'an-kung; NYC 38.73–75, 20/9/6 Ke Li-yeh; SYT 423–24, 20/11/28 Ma Shih; CFCL 26.15–16, 18/12/15 Ts'ai K'e-chia; CFA 64, 20/3/20 Ts'ai Wu-k'uei. Niu Liang-ch'en, a principal organizer of the Eight Trigrams, had worked as a treasury clerk in Honan, and a sect member named Li Chih-kuo had worked with him. See CFA 25, 19/7/24 Li Chih-kuo; NYC 31.18–21, 18/12/16 Niu Liang-ch'en.

125 For more on hired laborers see Part Three, n. 50, plus the following sources. The Peking sects included forty-three men who did hired agricultural work at least part-time. Some of these men worked in the fields during peak seasons and at other times did a variety of other things. See n. 128. SYT 147–49, 19/12/5 Sung Erh; SYT 381–88, 23/4/29 Chang Lao-liu; SYT 389–91, 21/6/30 Chang Ch'i-hua; SYT 55–57, 19/10/8 Chang Ta-ts'ui; SYT 83–84, 19/12/3 Ch'ai Hsi; CFA 68, 20/3/29 Chu Erh-t'u-tzu; SYT 375–77, 19/12/14 Chu Lung; KKCK 228.1–2, 18/10/22 Chu Yü; KKCK 229.1–2, 18/10/23 Han Ta-tzu; KCT 017330, 19/2*/21 Han Ts'un-lin; SYT 303–05, 19/12/10 Kao Liu; KKCK 229.1, 18/10/22 Li Feng-yin; KCT 017162, 18/12/10 Li Shih-kung; CFA 40, 19/11/3 Liu Ch'i-shih-r; SYT 251–54, 20/9/21 Liu Ch'i-wu; KKCK 236.1, 18/10/27 Liu San; SYT 119–23, 22/10/17 Liu Hsi-r; KCT 017623, 20/1/26 Pien Erh; KCT 017094 19/12/2 Sung Kuang-pi; KKCK 219.1–2, 18/10/14 Sung Wei-yin; SYT 63–64, 21/10/12 Sung Yü-tzu; SYT 213–14, 20/2/20 Tung Kuo-t'ai; SYT 113–15, 21/11/15 Wang Chin-fu; SYT 189–90, 19/12/6 Wang Lu; SYT 383, 19/7/26 Wang Ta-ming; SYT 247–49, 20/9/21 Wu Chin-ts'ai; CFA 55, 20/2/9 Mao Lien-teng.

126 Many peasants combined agriculture with other sources of income. See sections entitled "Labor" in Ramon H. Myers, *The Chinese Peasant Economy: Agricultural Development in Hopei and Shantung, 1890–1949.* For an introduction to the problem of peasant societies and economic relations in those societies, see Sidney W. Mintz, "A Note on the Definition of Peasantries," *The Journal of Peasant Studies* 1, no. 1 (1973): 91–106; and Eric R. Wolf, *Peasants* (Englewood Cliffs, N.J.: Prentice Hall, 1966), esp. chap. 2.

Sixteen men stated explicitly that they worked the land. Some of the terms they most commonly used were *chung ti* 種地, *chuang nung* 莊農, or *wu nung* 務農. See KKCK 224.3, 18/10/18 Chu Lin; SYT 223–24, 19/4/12 Han Ch'eng-chang; KCT 017262, 19/12/17 Jen San; SYT 219–21, 19/4/12 Ho

Shih-k'uei; SYT 259–61, 19/11/20 Ch'ü Fu-r; SYT 83–84, 19/12/3 Ch'en Hsi; SYT 95–98, 20/1/10 Chang Hsi and Kan Niu-tzu; SYT 133–35, 20/1/12 Ma Wen-liang; SYT 93–94, 20/10/14 Jen Tzu-k'uei; SYT 223–25, 21/11/26 Li T'ing-yung; SYT 161–63 21/12/26 Shao Chün.

Among others who derived income from agriculture were: Twenty men who hired others as agricultural laborers and can therefore be assumed to have owned (or rented) land (see n. 125). Two men who stated that they rented land—*tsu-chung* 租種 (SYT 59–61, 21/10/12 Chang Ch'i; SYT 173–75, 21/11/21 Wang Chen). Two men who owned land (SYT 245–48, 22/11/21 Ch'ü Ming-r, who owned about 50 or 60 *mou*; KCT 011671, 13/8/1 Ch'en Mao-lin, whose father had owned but mortgaged 150 *mou*, later sold). Three men who described working in the fields and did not indicate that anyone had hired them to do so (SYT 259–60, 20/1/25 Chang Liu; SYT 325–26, 20/2/30 Pai Yü).

127   There were seventy-one men arrested in months just during and after the rebellion who made confessions but in those confessions stated no occupation. Given the fact that all others arrested during this same period did specify a particular craft or trade (see below) and that no one said "I work the land" (all those specific first-person statements cited in the first part of n. 126 come from a later period), I believe that these seventy-one men—all of whom were from villages—very probably derived their income from the "normal" source, the land.

128   Sources for these jobs are as follows:
    Peddlers: SYT 151–52, 19/12/5 Niu Shih; SYT 157–59, 20/2/17 Chang Te-fa; CFA 55, 20/2/9 Mao Lien-teng. All three peddlers also worked part of the year as hired laborers. *Stone masons*: CFA 37, 19/11/2 Su Chien-te; NYC 38.67–72, 20/9/6 Chang Feng. *Seller of ducks and chickens*: SYT 301–03, 20/2/28 Chu Mo-r. *Seller of beancurd*: CFA 24, 19/5/18 Chia Wan-chin; KKCK 204.1, 18/9/19 Liu Chin-t'ing. *Collected and sold firewood*: SYT 301–03, 20/2/28 Chu Mo-r. *Seller of paper*: KKCK 204.1, 18/9/19 Fan Ts'ai. *Brick factory worker*: SYT 205–08, 20/7/11 Hao Pa. *Had a fruit stand in Peking*: KKCK 203.1, 18/9/19 Hsiung Chin-ts'ai. *Theater owner*: KKCK 212.1, 18/10/3 Liu Ch'ao-tung. *Cook*: CFA 13, 19/3/14 Liu Erh-ch'u-tzu. *Waiter*: KKCK 224.3, 18/10/18 Chu Lin. *Household servants*: SYT 171–90, 22/9/14 Ning Liu; KKCK 232.1–3, 18/10/26 Wang Wu. *Hauler*: SYT 63–64, 21/10/12 Sung Yü-tzu. *Cart driver*: KCT 015579, 19/2*/16 Tai Wu; SYT 183–84, 20/1/18 Ts'ao Hei-tzu. *Bow maker* (a Manchu): KKCK 223.1–3, 18/10/17 Memorial. *Seller of windowpanes*: SYT 203–09, 22/11/18 Tung Kuo-t'ai. *Teashop proprietor* (he also worked his own and other people's lands): SYT 247–49, 20/9/1 Wu Chin-ts'ai. *Seller of vegetables*: SYT 137–45, 20/10/16 List. *Bower of cotton* (*t'an mien* 彈綿): SYT 251–54, 20/9/21 Liu Ch'i-wu. *Weavers*: SYT 161–63, 21/12/26 Shao Chün; NYC 40.53–57, 21/5/27 Yü Ch'eng-r. There is more information on weavers in SYT 221–22, 19/11/18 Mrs. Ts'ao Sun; SYT 109–11, 21/11/15 Li Yü; SYT 39–41, 22/12/4 Mrs. Chang Lu. Most of these household weavers were from Ku-an and Hsin-ch'eng districts southwest of Peking. *Acupuncturist*: KKCK 220.1–2, 18/10/15 Chang Tzu-sheng.
    Information on other Eight Trigram rebels (not from Peking) indicates that sect members also included among their members the following occupations:

Butchers: KCT 016813, 19/11/15 Ch'en Ch'en; KCT 016995, 19/11/25 Ho Chin-piao. *Cattle herder*: KCT 016813, 19/11/15 Ch'en Ch'en. *Buddhist monks*: *Chi-ning district gazetteer* 4.20–29 Ch'ing-fang; CFCL 21.28–32, 18/11/24 Hsu-ch'ien and Tsung-yin; CFCL 5.33–34, 18/9/23 Memorial. *Fortune-tellers*: KCT 018945, 20/6/13 Sun Chia-wang; CFCL 33.16–19, 19/1/27 Chang Chiu-ch'eng.

129 KKCK 204.1, 18/9/19 Liu Chin-t'ing; KCT 011671, 13/8/1 Composite confession.

130 Li Wen-ch'eng was in one instance called the "Overall Manager" (*tsung tang-chia* 總當家), perhaps in contrast with Lin Ch'ing's "Overall Patriarch" (*tsung tsu-shih* 總祖師) and "Overall Sect Head" (*tsung chiao-t'ou* 總教頭). If these were complementary titles, paralleling the relationship of ruler on the one hand and sage on the other, then *tang-chia* might have implied an organizer as opposed to a religious expert. For Li and Lin titles see Part Two, n. 81; and CFCL 7.10–12, 18/9/28 Ma Ch'ao-tung. For other uses of the term *tang-chia*, see CFCL 8.13–15, 18/10/1 Memorial; KCT 016167, 19/8/2 Wo Lo-yun; KKCK 204.1, 18/9/19 Tung Kuo-t'ai; KCT 018651, 20/5/16 Wang San; SYT 271–72, 20/4/24 Tung Kuo-t'ai; NYC 38.58–60, 20/3/25 Chao Te; SYT 301–03, 20/2/28 Chu Mo-r; NYC 40.63–67, 21/6/18 Ts'ai Ming-shan; KCT 016869, 19/11/18 Chao Fei-i.

131 In the late nineteenth and early twentieth centuries, more elaborate hierarchies with more unusual titles were created by White Lotus sects, and sects began to erect more temples and public halls. It appears that this change was due to a decrease in government scrutiny and prosecution. For sects with more extensive offices and titles, see de Groot, *Sectarianism*, p. 190; Topley, "Great Way Sects," p. 374; Serruys, "Folklore Contributions," pp. 20–21, 26; and George Miles, "Vegetarian Sects," *Chinese Recorder* 33 (1902): 1–10.

132 CFCL 1.29–32, 18/9/15 Chang Chien-mu.

133 KCT 018834, 20/6/1 Hsing Shih-k'uei. SYT 171–90, 22/9/14 Composite confession.

134 For information on Triad societies, see Leon F. Comber, *A Chinese Secret Society in Malaya: A Survey of the Triad Society, 1800–1900* (Locust Valley, N.Y.: J. J. Austin Inc., 1959), his bibliography, and the bibliography in *Popular Movements and Secret Societies in China, 1840–1950*, ed. Jean Chesneaux.

135 Sixteen percent represented 24 out of 151 cases.

136 The figures for teachers of women are based on twenty-one cases. The figures for pupils of female teachers are based on ten cases.

137 NYC 41.28–31, 21/3/3 Mrs. Liu Kung.

138 NYC 33.4–5, 18/12/20 Memorial from Na-yen-ch'eng. In the documents relating to the Eight Trigrams uprising, there is only one reference to a woman's being active in battle, an incident that is described below on pp. 261–62.

139 CFCL 36.6–8, 19/2/14 Composite confession.

140 For example, see the discussion in Richard Chu, "White Lotus Sect," pp. 126–31.

141 De Groot stated that sects in Amoy in the 1880s regarded each other as "sister communities" rather than as rivals (*Sectarianism*, p. 191).

142 "老君門離卦教. . . [also called] 義和門." KCT 018583, 20/5/9 Yeh Fu-ming.

143 "東方震卦. . . . 龍華會教." KCT 018243, 20/4/13 Fang Ying-ch'eng.

144 The leader Lin Ch'ing described these changes with somewhat less clarity: "My sect's original name was the San-yang (Three Suns) sect, which was divided into groups named for the three colors, Azure (*ch'ing*), Red (*hung*) and White (*pai*). It also had the name Lung-hua (Dragon Flower) Assembly. Because [later] it was divided into eight trigrams, it also had the name Pa-kua (Eight Trigrams) Assembly. Later they changed the name to T'ien-li (Heavenly Doctrine) Assembly" (NYC 31.18-21, 18/12/16 Niu Liang-ch'en quoting what Lin Ch'ing had told him).

145 For example, after a Ta-sheng sect was investigated and its leaders arrested in 1811, members ceased to meet together and referred to their group as a "dispersed assembly" (*san-hui* 散會). Their leaders (called *san-hui-shou* 散會首, "heads of the dispersed assembly") finally decided to revive and reestablish their sect (keeping the old name) by bringing their members together once more. NYC 38.67-72, 20/9/6 Chang Feng; CFCL 33.16-19, 19/1/27 Chang Chiu-ch'eng.

146 CFA 12, 19/3/16 Jen T'ien-te.

147 This term was used as follows: "When I got married, I didn't know that my husband's family were all *tsai-li*" (KCT 017364, 19/2/26 Mrs. Chu Hsing). Later in the nineteenth century Tsai-li became the name of other sects in Chihli and Manchuria. For Chia-ch'ing period Tsai-li, see SYT 291-97, 19/3/15 Chu Hai-ch'ing; NYC 40.3-6, 20/5/27 Kuo Lo-yun. For late Ch'ing Tsai-li, see L. C. Arlington and William Lewisohn, *In Search of Old Peking*, p. 216; Wing-tsit Chan, *Religious Trends in Modern China*, pp. 156-57; Jerome Ch'en, "Origin of the Boxers," in *Studies in the Social History of China and Southeast Asia*, ed. Jerome Ch'en and Nicholas Tarling (Cambridge: Cambridge University Press, 1970), p. 69; Jean Chesneaux, "Secret Societies in China's Historical Evolution," p. 9; Samuel Couling, *Encyclopedia*, p. 573; James Gilmore, "Tobacco, Whisky and Opium," *Chinese Recorder* 19 (1888): 164; Prosper Leboucq, *Associations de la Chine*, p. 47; and S. Evan Meech, "The Northern Rebellion," *Chinese Recorder* 23 (1892): 135-36.

148 CFCL 26.1-2, 18/12/14 Ch'en Hsiang; CFCL 38.2-6, 19/2*/4 Ch'en Heng-i, Wang Shih-ch'ing and Ch'en Wen-ch'ing; CPT 435, 18/12/21 Memorial; CFCL 22.17, 18/11/25 Wang Shih-ch'ing; CPT 449-54, 18/11/26 Kao Te-ming.

149 The main organizers of the rebellion are not known to have been vegetarians, but some of the groups incorporated into the Eight Trigrams did practice moderate dietary regimens. KCT 011671, 13/8/1 Sung Chin-hui; KKCK 218.1-2, 18/10/12 Yü Chi-ch'ing.

150 Examples are the Hsien-t'ien (Former Heaven) sect in Amoy in the 1880s (see de Groot, *Sectarianism*, p. 190); the Yao-ch'ih (Jade Pool) sect in Hankow around 1900 (see Miles, "Vegetarian Sects," passim); the Hsien-t'ien sect in Singapore in the 1950s (see Topley, "Great Way Sects," p. 375); the Hun-yuan (Chaotic Origin) sect in Manchuria in the 1890s (see Inglis, "Hun Yuen Men," p. 370); and the Chin-tan (Golden Elixir) sect in Jehol in the 1920s (see Serruys, "Folklore Contributions," pp. 23-24).

De Groot relates an extreme case in which members of two families, following the instructions of their teacher, stopped eating altogether in the hope of "ascending to heaven in broad daylight." They all died of starvation and were cremated. The teacher was arrested and sentenced according to the statute on criminals who kill (or drive to suicide) three or more people in one household (*Sectarianism*, pp. 160–61).

151 A group in Shantung in 1813 did not eat garlic or scallions and would not even allow them to be brought into their village (CPT 423–24, 18/10/29 Edict). Some followers of a group that became part of the Eight Trigrams allowed all meat except beef or horse (SYT 171–90, 22/9/14 Ch'ing-feng and others). A late nineteenth century Tsai-li (Believer) sect forbid its members to eat pork (Leboucq, *Associations de la chine*, p. 47).

152 For vegetarian meals only on the 15th of the month, see KCT 018945, 20/6/13 Sun Chia-wang. For vegetarian meals at sect meetings, see NYC 41.42–47, 21/6/26 P'ei Ching-i.

153 NYC 38.2–4, 19/2/15 Memorial; CPT 35–36, 19/1/6 Edict.

154 KKCK 218.1–2, 18/10/12 Yü Chi-ch'ing.

155 KCT 011671, 13/8/1 Composite confession.

156 See Serruys, "Folklore Contributions," p. 24, for the Chin-tan sect in Jehol in the 1920s.

157 KKCK 221.1–3, 18/10/16 Tung Kuo-t'ai; KKCK 234.1, 18/10/27 Tung Kuo-t'ai.

158 For helping out others, see KCT 011671, 13/8/1 Sung Chin-hui and CSL 244.9–10, 16/6/7 Edict. For diligence and thrift, see Wing-tsit Chan, *Religious Trends in Modern China*, p. 157, describing the Tsai-li sect of the late nineteenth and twentieth centuries.

159 "Benevolent, righteous . . . "—see NYC 41.42–47, 21/6/26 P'ei Ching-i. "Respect heaven . . ."—CFA 64, 20/3/20 Ts'ai Wu-k'uei.

160 See Henri Maspero, "Procédés de 'nourir le principe vital' dans la religion Taoiste ancienne," *Journal Asiatique* 229 (1937): 177–252, 353–430. There is one scripture quoted by Huang Yü-p'ien (PHHP 2.9) and translated by Chao Wei-pang ("Secret Religious Societies," p. 101) that includes the line, "If a male or female could absorb the various kinds of energy (*ch'i*) of the other through sexual intercourse, he or she could become immortal."

161 KCT 017364, 19/2/26 Mrs. Chu Hsing (the daughter-in-law).

162 SYT 117–19, 22/11/10 Mrs. Li Hsuan; SYT 355–56, 22/9/24 Wu Hsien-ta.

163 KCT 018834, 20/6/1 Hsing Shih-k'uei.

164 SYT 343–45, 20/12/25 Wang K'e-chin; SYT 333–36, 20/12/25 Wang Tien-kuei; *Chi-ning district gazetteer* 4.20–29 Liu Ning and others; KCT 018945, 20/6/13 Sun Chia-wang; CFCL 1.22–27, 18/9/15 Ts'ui Shih-chün.

165 Large and small gifts: NYC 40.3–6, 20/5/27 Kuo Lo-yun. Installment money: CFCL 1.22–27, 18/9/15 Ts'ui Shih-chün.

166 Vegetarian offerings: NYC 41.42–47, 20/6/26 P'ei Ching-i. Semiannual meetings: KCT 018945, 20/6/13 Sun Chia-wang; SYT 331–33, 22/9/24 Wang Liang; SYT 355–56, 22/9/24 Wu Hsien-ta; SYT 349–51, 22/9/24 Wang Pi. Leader's birthday: KCT 015816, 19/6/26 Li T'ien-hsiang.

167 NYC 33.13, 18/12/25 Ch'in Li.

168 Arthur Smith, describing sects in the 1880s ("Sketches of a Country Parish," p. 248) suggests the following division of the spoils: "[At sect meetings] every member comes with his assessed contribution. . . . The leader provides the

bread-cakes offered and then eaten, and takes care to keep the expenses down to help with the gross-receipts. At certain times, he reports to his next higher master, gives him a portion—say half—of his receipts, and appropriates the rest unto himself."

169 NYC 39.31–37, 19/7/30 Memorial; SYT 165, 22/6/17 Edict; PHHP 4.2.

170 KKCK 221.1–3, 18/10/16 Tung Kuo-t'ai.

171 CFCL 25.7–10, 18/12/12 Liu Tsung-lin.

172 NYC 38.73–75, 20/9/6 Ke Li-yeh.

173 See Part Two, n. 90.

174 SYT 331–33, 22/9/24 Wang Liang.

175 SYT 209–11, 20/7/11 Liu Chin-pao.

176 KKCK 211.2, 18/10/2 Li Chiu.

177 SYT 381–88, 23/4/29 Chang Lao-liu; NYC 38.67–72, 20/9/6 Tu Yu-r. See n. 103.

178 Cloth: SYT 173–74, 21/1/25 Tung Kuo-t'ai. Donkey, mules, silver: KKCK 211.1–3, 18/10/16 Tung Kuo-t'ai. Five hundred taels and other silver: NYC 32.12–16, 18/12/3 Ch'in Li; SYT 611–13, 19/12/25 Tung Kuo-t'ai; NYC 31.18–21, 18/12/16 Niu Liang-ch'en.

179 For Yuan Mei, see Arthur Waley, *Yuan Mei, Eighteenth Century Poet* (New York: Macmillan Co., 1956), pp. 47, 108. Liang-huai salt merchants made twelve gifts of money to the Ch'ing government between the 5th month of 1810 and the 4th month of 1814. These gifts ranged from 100,000 to 4 million taels, and averaged about 1.2 million taels per gift. (See SYT 159–64, 24/10/16 Memorial from the Grand Council.) All gifts were for the purpose of river repair except for the paltry 100,000 taels given for military expenses in the fall of 1813. For gentry income, see Chang Chung-li, *The Income of the Chinese Gentry*, p. 328.

180 CSL 244.9–10, 16/6/7 Memorial; CFCL 1.6–9, 18/9/13 Memorial; CFA 17, 19/4/15 Li Erh.

181 KCT 018945, 20/6/13 Sun Chia-wang; KKCK 206.1–2, 18/9/22 Yang Chin-chung; CPT 381–84, 18/11/23 Edict; NYC 41.42–47, 21/6/26 P'ei Ching-i. See also Topley, "Great Way Sects," p. 274; Smith, "Sketches of a Country Parish," p. 248; Serruys, "Folklore Contributions," p. 23; Edkins, *Chinese Buddhism*, p. 378.

182 CFCL 36.6–8, 19/2/14 Memorial.

183 KCT 018945, 20/6/13 Sun Chia-wang; KCT 015580, 19/2*/21 Li Wu; NYC 41.42–47, 21/6/26 P'ei Ching-i. See also Smith, "Sketches of a Country Parish," pp. 247–48; Serruys, "Folklore Contributions," p. 23; Inglis, "Hun Yuen Men," p. 270; de Groot, *Sectarianism*, p. 200.

During the late nineteenth and twentieth centuries some sects met in "vegetarian halls" or in temples. See de Groot, *Sectarianism*, p. 200, and Topley, "Great Way Sects," p. 383 for examples of this.

184 NYC 41.42–47, 21/6/26 P'ei Ching-i. For other descriptions of meetings, see KCT 011671, 13/8/1 Composite confession; CPT 381–84, 18/11/23 Edict.

185 Quotation is from de Groot, *Sectarianism*, p. 190. See also CSL 244.9–10, 16/6/7 Memorial.

186 C. K. Yang, *Religion in Chinese Society*, p. 298.

187 The Eight Trigrams spoke of their rebellion as "making known the Way" (*ming-tao* 明道). See Part Two, n. 136.

Topley ("Great Way Sects," p. 378) describes the way in which Hsien-t'ien sects in Singapore divided their activities into *yin* types and *yang* types, each with its own names, and she attempts to correlate this division with the different sect names used by this group. Lev Deliusin states that the I-kuan tao in north China at the end of the Ch'ing was divided into secret (*an-hsien* 暗線, "dark thread") and open (*ming-hsien* 明線, "bright thread") structures, according to familiarity with sect secrets. See his "I-kuan Tao Society," in *Popular Movements and Secret Societies in China*, ed., Chesneaux, pp. 230–31.

188 CFCL 32.36–38, 19/1/24 Kao Chi-yuan; CFCL 7.30–32, 18/9/30 Edict; CFCL 1.22–27, 18/9/15 Ts'ui Shih-chün.

189 KCT 016167, 19/8/2 Wu Lo-yun; KCT 015625, 19/6/7 Wang Ta-chih and Yang Chien; SYT 141-42, 21/10/24 Edict; CSL 68.4–5, 5/5/21 Edict; CSL 258.9–11, 17/6/12 Edict.

190 CSL 244.9–10, 16/6/7 Wang Pang-yen and edict; KCT 016487, 19/9/24 Memorial; KCT 016167, 19/8/2 Wu Lo-yun; KCT 017105, 19/12/7 Memorial; CSL 258.14–16, 17/6/16 Edict; KCT 016958-E, 19/11/25 Memorial; CSL 257.12–13, 17/5/8 Edict; SYT 107–11, 17/6/9 Li Ching-fu; NYC 40.7–10, 20/6/24 Lu Lao-pin; CSL 257.27–29, 17/5/25 Sun P'eng.

191 For the effect of these prosecutions on a small branch of this sect in Hsiung district (in Chihli), see SYT 209–11, 20/7/11 Liu Chin-pao, and NYC 38.67–72, 20/9/6 Chang Feng.

192 CFCL 33.16–19, 19/1/27 Chang Chiu-ch'eng; CSL 257.12–13, 17/5/8 Edict; KCT 015625, 19/6/7 Memorial.

193 See Derk Bodde and Clarence Morris, *Law in Imperial China*, pp. 77–78 for levels of punishments.

194 CFCL 29.6–8, 18/12/26 T'ien K'e-ch'i and others; CSL 258.14–16, 17/6/16 Edict; CFCL 22.29–30, 18/11/28 Edict; CFCL 26.31–34, 18/12/16 Edict; CFCL 29.6–8, 18/12/26 Memorial. For *ling-ch'ih*, the so-called lingering death, see Bodde and Morris, *Law in Imperial China*, pp. 93–95.

195 CFCL 29.9–10, 18/12/26 Yang Yü-shan; CFCL 35.21–25, 19/2/10 Yang Yü-shan; CFCL 31.10–11, 19/1/13 Kao T'an-chao; KKCK 227.1–2, 18/10/21 Tung Kuo-t'ai.

PART TWO

1 Chan Hok-lam, "The White Lotus–Maitreya Doctrine and Popular Uprisings in Ming and Ch'ing China," *Sinologica* 10, no. 4 (1969): 217–18; J. J. M. de Groot, *Sectarianism and Religious Persecution in China*, pp. 166–68. There were probably other sects that generated rebellious activity during the collapse of the Ming dynasty. For a few hints of this, see James B. Parsons, *The Peasant Rebellions of the Late Ming Dynasty* (Tucson: University of Arizona Press, 1970), pp. 189, 220.

2 De Groot, *Sectarianism*, p. 293; Richard Yung-deh Chu, "An Introductory Study of the White Lotus Sect in Chinese History," p. 142.

3 De Groot, *Sectarianism*, pp. 297–304; Arthur W. Hummel, ed., *Eminent Chinese of the Ch'ing Period*, p. 660; Richard L. K. Jung, "The Rebellion of Wang Lun in Shantung, 1774," in "The Ch'ien-lung Emperor and His Military Leaders:

Rebellion and the Decline of the Ch'ing Dynasty, 1774–1788" (Ph. D. diss in progress, Harvard University).

4 De Groot, *Sectarianism*, pp. 336–38; CSL 1261.15–18, CL 51/7*/20 Edict; CSL 1261.18–21, CL 51/7*/21 Edict; CSL 1261.33–36, CL 51/7*/26 Edict; CSL 1261.45–46, CL 51/7*/28 Edict; CSL 1262.8–10, CL 51/8/2 Edict.

5 De Groot, *Sectarianism*, pp. 354–75; Ho Ping-ti, *Studies on the Population of China, 1368–1953*, pp. 149–53; Philip A. Kuhn, *Rebellion and Its Enemies in Late Imperial China: Militarization and Social Structure, 1796–1864*, pp. 39–40.

6 In 1746 (CL 11) assembly heads of the Hung-yang 宏陽 sect from Ta-hsing and Wan-p'ing districts were arrested. Their sect had allegedly been transmitted for over one hundred years. See CSL 271.1–2, CL 11/7/16 Edict.

7 CSL 1261.18–21, CL 51/7*/21 Edict; CSL 1262.3–4, CL 51/8/1 Edict; SYT 215–16, CC 22/8/26 Edict; SYT 317–25, CC 22/9/24 Wang Jui; de Groot, *Sectarianism*, pp. 336–38.

8 SYT 317–25, 22/9/24 Wang Jui. This group was uncovered in 1817 (CC 22) when at least twenty of their members were arrested and interrogated. See pp. 97–99 for their refusal to join Lin Ch'ing.

9 KCT 018919, 20/6/10 Liu Chin-t'ing; NYC 38.67–72, 20/9/6 Tu Yu-r.

10 SYT 161–63, 21/12/26 Shao Chün; SYT 103–11, 23/11/9 Memorial; KKCK 221.1–3, 18/10/16 Tung Kuo-t'ai.

11 In addition to its literal meaning of "flourishing," the name Jung-hua is very close in sound to the name Lung-hua 龍華 (Dragon Flower). According to sect teachings the Eternal Mother would hold three Lung-hua Assemblies for her followers. These two names are occasionally used interchangeably with reference to this group, and it seems likely that Jung-hua was an equally auspicious modification of the earlier name. Jung-hua is sometimes written 榮花.

12 KKCK 227.1–2, 18/10/21 Tung Kuo-t'ai; SYT 355–56, 22/9/24 Wu Hsien-ta.

13 KKCK 235.1–2, 18/10/27 Wang Lao; SYT 309–17, 20/7/17 Memorial; KCT 017742, 20/2/1 Liu Ta; KKCK 225.1, 18/10/18 Liu Chin-ts'ai; KKCK 209.1–2, 18/9/28 Li Lao.

14 CFA 17, 19/4/15 Li Ch'ao-yu.

15 KKCK 206.1–2, 18/9/22 Kao Ta and Yang Chin-chung; KCT 015580, 19/2*/21 Liu Wu and Li Ta; KCT 015571, 18/10/2 Liu Te-shan; CFA 17, 19/4/15 Li Ch'ao-yu. The Fruit Office was part of the Department of Ceremonial within the Imperial Household and was responsible for supplying the fruit used in sacrifices and ceremonies. See H. S. Brunnert and V. V. Hagelstrom, *Present Day Political Organization of China*, ♯79A.

16 It is possible that the link between Liu Hsing-li and these brothers was the Manchus' household servant and graveyard keeper, a man named Ning Liu. Ning Liu had taken Li Ch'ao-tso as his teacher. He could have introduced his Manchu employers to his teacher's teacher (Liu Hsing-li) when they were ill, or conversely could have been introduced to the sect by them. SYT 171–90, 22/9/14 Ning Liu, Ch'ing-feng, and Hai-k'ang.

17 Hai-k'ang's pupils included his two grandsons (or great-grandsons), also members of the imperial clan; a fifth-rank administrator for the Imperial Clan Court (Brunnert and Hagelstrom, ♯67); a eunuch who worked for the household of the Yü 裕 Prince; a former copyist in the Hui-tien office; two plain-blue banner bondservants; a sixth-rank lieutenant in the Guards'

Division (Brunnert and Hagelstrom, ♯734.3); and a bordered-white Manchu bannerman who was a third-rank bodyguard in the household of the Hsiao 蕭 Prince. SYT 171–212, 22/9/14 Composite confession and Grand Council list. For other possible pupils under Liu Hsing-li, see KKCK 223.1–3, 18/10/17 Memorial.

It was even asserted that the *bei-tzu* (a Prince of the Blood of the fourth degree [Brunnert and Hagelstrom, ♯19]) named I-ch'ün had asked Hai-k'ang to cure an ulcer on his leg in 1805, and afterward had kotowed to Hai-k'ang. Since I-ch'ün had died by the time this fact was uncovered, the Chia-ch'ing Emperor chose not to probe into this potentially embarrassing matter. SYT 41–42, 22/9/3 Hai-k'ang. See also Hummel, *Eminent Chinese*, p. 374.

The involvement of a few of these Manchus in a heretical sect was first uncovered in 1813 during the intensive search for sect members carried out at that time. Hai-k'ang (who was both pupil and teacher in a sect) was arrested, stripped of his status as a member of the imperial clan, made a commoner, and sent to Sheng-ching (Manchuria) to be imprisoned for life. Four years later, in 1817, it was learned that Hai-k'ang had actually known in advance about the attack on the palace, had contributed money to the sect for such an attack, and had waited at home on the day of the uprising in anticipation of its success. His case was reopened, investigated at the highest levels, and his sentence changed to death by slicing; this was reduced by the emperor to immediate strangulation. CSL 276.21–22, 18/10/11 Edict; SYT 109–11, 22/9/10 Edict.

18 SYT 93–94, 20/10/14 Jen Tzu-kuei; KKCK 208.1, 18/9/24 Ch'ü Ssu (this and other confessions by Ch'ü Ssu may be found in their entirety in Appendix 1); SYT 55–56, 13/4/7 Edict; KCT 011671, 13/8/1 Composite confession. It was this memorial from the governor-general of Chihli that summarized the case against the Jung-hua Assembly members in this year. See figure 1 (p. 40) for a diagram of this sect's organization. There were probably more than seventy believers. There were wives of many of the sect members who probably belonged, but only three of them are here counted for sure. The government investigation in 1808 did not probe deeply and only sixteen men were arrested and interrogated. There is some evidence to indicate a group of followers under a man called Ku Chung-te (who might have been Ku Liang's relative), at least a dozen men, may have been part of this original Jung-hua Assembly as well. CFA 52, 20/2/6 Ku Chung-te.

19 Some years before, the father of these two men had inherited a piece of already mortgaged land. In 1797, the two brothers had "divided the stove," that is, split into two economically separate households; the mortgaged and still unredeemed land was not formally divided between them. Ch'en Mao-lin, who was the elder brother, nevertheless sold half that land and then used the proceeds of this sale to redeem the rest of the property. This transaction left him richer by 75 *mou* and 200 taels, yet he gave nothing to his younger brother, who was understandably upset. Later Ch'en Mao-lin joined the Jung-hua Assembly; when Ku Liang died, it was Ch'en's own teacher who took over as sect head, and Ch'en's place within the sect improved accordingly. Several months after this the younger brother, Ch'en Mao-kung, seeing a way to get revenge, reported the group to the government. He simulta-

neously filed a complaint against a revenue clerk with whom he had a grievance, and ironically was himself sentenced to a beating when the clerk was found to be innocent of the charge. See KCT 011671, 13/8/1 Composite confession and memorial.

20 Not such an empty act as one might think; dead criminals (or their relatives) were often dug up and their corpses cut into small pieces. For example, see Part Four, n. 190.

21 See CSL 206.2–5, 14/1/1 Edict. All criminals sentenced to penal servitude were to have their punishment reduced one degree. See Derk Bodde and Clarence Morris, *Law in Imperial China*, pp. 77–78, for degrees of punishments. KKCK 221.1–3, 18/10/16 Tung Kuo-t'ai; KKCK 222.1, 18/10/16 Sung Chin-yao.

22 The officials for whom Mr. Lin worked were the subdistrict deputy-magistrate for Wan-p'ing *hsien*, and then the subprefect for the southern-district of the capital area. These posts are described in Brunnert and Hagelstrom, ♯857.3 and ♯795B, respectively. For the position of clerk, see Ch'u T'ung-tsu, *Local Government in China under the Ch'ing*, chap. 2.

23 SYT 91–92, 19/12/3 Tung Kuo-t'ai; SYT 87–90, 19/12/3 Wang Shao-hsiang. The primary source for Lin Ch'ing's life is his nephew's testimony, n. 26.

24 See Robert H. G. Lee, *The Manchurian Frontier in Ch'ing History*, esp. chap. 5.

25 This official is described in Brunnert and Hagelstrom, ♯836.2. For the position of personal attendant see Ch'u T'ung-tsu, *Local Government*, chap. 5.

26 This account is based almost entirely on the testimony of Lin Ch'ing's nephew Tung Kuo-t'ai 董幗太, and he readily acknowledged that his knowledge of his uncle's past was based on what his grandmother, Lin Ch'ing's mother, had told him. His matter-of-fact recitation of failure and irresponsibility probably reflect the elderly woman's disgust and dissatisfaction with her son and may not place the events of Lin Ch'ing's life in the best light. Lin's mother did not live to see him succeed as a sect leader. Tung Kuo-t'ai's long narrative about his uncle's life is located in KKCK 221.1–3, 18/10/16. This was filled out by other statements by Tung, primarily: CFCL 20.33–34, 18/11/21; SYT 169–73, 19/11/14; SYT 209–10, 20/6/19; SYT 91–92, 19/12/3. See Part Three, n. 116 for more on Tung Kuo-t'ai. Other relevant information on Lin Ch'ing comes from SYT 87–90, 19/12/3 Wang Shao-hsiang; CFCL 16.30–35, 18/11/5 Ts'ao Lun; CFCL 3.9–13, 18/9/18 Lin Ch'ing.

27 KKCK 221.1–3, 18/10/16 Tung Kuo-t'ai.

28 SYT 39–49, 19/12/2. This description comes from an official who was instructing a prisoner to describe and claim (falsely) that he knew Lin Ch'ing. Chao-lien, a contemporary observer whose account of the Eight Trigrams rebellion is very unreliable, describes Lin Ch'ing as "tall, with a dark sallow complexion, and lots of whiskers" (*Hsiao-t'ing tsa-lu*, 4.44–45).

29 See n. 26.

30 KKCK 221.1–3, 18/10/16 Tung Kuo-t'ai; SYT 213–14, 20/2/20 Tung Kuo-t'ai; CFCL 3.9–13, 18/9/18 Lin Ch'ing.

31 NYC 31.18–21, 18/12/16 Niu Liang-ch'en; CFCL 29.1–6, 18/12/26 Niu Liang-ch'en; KKCK 221.1–3, 18/10/16 Tung Kuo-t'ai.

32 NYC 31.18–21, 18/12/16 Niu Liang-ch'en.

33 KCT 016027, 19/7/24 Li Hsing-pang.

34 This was reduced to forty blows. For routine reduction of beatings, see Bodde and Morris, *Law in Imperial China*, p. 77.

35 NYC 31.18–21, 18/12/16 Niu Liang-ch'en; CFCL 29.1–6, 18/12/26 Niu Liang-ch'en; KKCK 221.1–3, 18/10/16 Tung Kuo-t'ai; SYT 209–10, 20/6/19 Tung Kuo-t'ai.

36 KKCK 222.1–2, 18/10/16 Kuo Ch'ao-chün; CFCL 3.9–13, 18/9/18 Lin Ch'ing; KKCK 205.1, 18/9/18 Lin Ch'ing; SYT 203–09, 22/11/18 Wang T'ien-ts'ai; KKCK 221.1–3, 18/10/16 Tung Kuo-t'ai.

37 SYT 169–73, 19/11/14 Tung Kuo-t'ai; see also n. 28.

38 KKCK 204.1, 18/9/19 Liu Chin-t'ing; KKCK 221.1–3, 18/10/16 Tung Kuo-t'ai.

39 KKCK, 221.1–3, 18/10/16 Tung Kuo-t'ai.

40 KKCK 204.1, 18/9/19 Tung Kuo-t'ai.

41 KKCK 221.1–3, 18/10/16 Tung Kuo-t'ai; SYT 169–73, 19/11/14 Tung Kuo-t'ai.

42 Ts'ao Lun was a member of the plain-yellow banner. His grandfather's elder brother had risen to the second rank as vice-president of the Board of Works. Ts'ao Lun's grandfather had held official positions, and his father had been a subprefect (fifth rank) in southwestern China. In 1797 during an attack on his city by rebellious Miao tribesmen, T'sao Lun's father had died and his wives had killed themselves. Ts'ao Lun himself was not fully able to take advantage of this relatively illustrious ancestry. His own mother was only a concubine, and he was the third of three sons. In 1793, by which time he had a wife and three sons of his own to support, Ts'ao had received an appointment as a controller, sixth rank, in the Imperial Equipage Department in Peking; in 1801 he was promoted to the fifth rank. (For these positions and Ts'ao's rank as captain, see Brunnert and Hagelstrom, #125, and #726.)

Most of our information about Ts'ao Lun's poverty comes from Ts'ao's own testimony and is therefore not entirely reliable. Desperate actions motivated by deprivation were viewed more sympathetically by the government than voluntary association with rebels, and Ts'ao Lun justified his association with Lin Ch'ing on the grounds that poverty forced him to take assistance from such a man. On trial and faced with probable execution, it was very much in Ts'ao's interest to overstate his own impoverishment and hope for leniency. In 1813 Ts'ao's brother and three sons all had employment of some sort. Nevertheless, the fact that Lin Ch'ing did to some extent assist him should not be disputed. The sources for this account of Ts'ao Lun are CFCL 16.30–35, 18/11/5 Ts'ao Lun; KKCK 227.3 and 228.1, 18/10/21 Ts'ao Fu-ch'ang (his son); KKCK 221.1–3, 18/10/16 Tung Kuo-t'ai; KKCK 225.1, 18/10/18 Tung Kuo-t'ai.

43 Lin Ch'ing had sworn brotherhood with four other men in 1793, and it was one of these sworn brothers (who was also a sect member later) who now swore brotherhood with Ts'ao. KCT 017503, 20/1/14 Ts'ui Wu.

44 For Dodo and this title see Hummel, *Eminent Chinese*, p. 215.

45 They hunted wildcats (*yeh-mao* 野貓). KKCK 221.1–3, 18/10/16 Tung Kuo-t'ai; KKCK 204.1, 18/9/19 Ch'en Shuang.

46 KKCK 221.1–3, 18/10/16 Tung Kuo-t'ai.

47 On the other hand, Lin did not indiscriminately take in every potential

follower. There was a young man named Wang Shao-hsiang whose grandfather had been Lin Ch'ing's tutor and whose father had been Lin Ch'ing's
friend many years before. At birth the boy had been "given" to Lin Ch'ing
as an adopted son. His father later died and the boy and his mother were
quite poor; neither could hold a regular job and the boy generally picked
pockets or stole for a living. They often came and tried to borrow money from
Lin Ch'ing. Lin had always made a minimal effort to fulfill his obligations as
an adopted father, giving the boy money or clothing to pawn when he came
asking for help. But after he joined the sect, Lin Ch'ing became less patient
with the young man (then in his twenties) and did not bother with Wang
after that, saying that he was "poor and good for nothing." SYT 91–92,
19/12/2 Tung Kuo-t'ai; SYT 87–90, 19/12/3 Wang Shao-hsiang.

48 SYT 349–51, 22/9/24 Wang Pi; SYT 331–33, 22/9/24 Wang Liang; SYT
355–56, 22/9/24 Wu Hsien-ta.

49 SYT 97–99, 19/7/7 Li T'ien-shou.

50 KKCK 204.1, 18/9/19 Tung Kuo-t'ai.

51 KKCK 221.1–3, 18/10/16 Tung Kuo-t'ai.

52 Ibid. Quotation is from KKCK 206.1, 18/9/21 Lin Ch'ing.

53 There are problems involved in assessing the relationship between Li Wen-
ch'eng and Lin Ch'ing, particularly in determining which was the "chief
evil-doer." All the evidence suggests that as far as planning and inspiring the
rebellion, the initiative and leadership came more from Lin Ch'ing. Nevertheless, it should be remembered that not only Lin himself and all his followers but also the Ch'ing government (proud of its success in quickly
seizing Lin) had an interest in building up his role. Two texts for Lin Ch'ing's
second confession indicate that Ch'ing historians slightly altered the evidence
to do just that. (See KKCK 202.1, 18/9/19 for the original, and CFCL 4.5–9,
18/9/19 for the modified version.) On the other hand, it was Li Wen-ch'eng
who was to rule after the new kalpa era had arrived. The account that I give,
crediting Lin with much of the initiative and placing him at the top of the
Eight Trigrams pyramid, is borne out overwhelmingly by all the evidence,
but it surely oversimplifies a complicated and competitive relationship.

54 In 1808 Liang Chien-chung was sixty-six years old; he had inherited management of the Chiu-kung sect from his father, who had in turn learned it from
another resident of their district. This Liang family was probably related to
those Liangs who participated in the 1786 uprising. Li Wen-ch'eng's adopted
son (from the same area and also a sect member) was an acquaintance of one
of those men arrested during that uprising and actually came to visit him at
the Board of Punishments prison in Peking. NYC 32.12–16, 18/12/3 Ch'in
Li; CSL 1264.15–18, CL 51/9/7 Hao Jun-ch'eng; CFCL 25.1–2, 18/12/12
Feng K'e-shan; CFCL 28.11–13, 18/12/24 Liang Chien-chung.

55 NYC 33.13, 18/12/15 Ch'in Li; CFCL 28.11–13, 18/12/24 Liang Chien-
chung; CFCL 25.7–10, 18/12/2 Liu Tsung-lin.

56 CFCL 29.1–6, 18/12/26 Hsu An-kuo; SYT 97–98, 22/9/9 Mrs. Su Huang.

57 Hsu's conversion of a man named Hu Erh-fa can serve as an illustration of
how he propagated the sect, which he called the Chen Trigram. In 1811 when
he was thirty-five years old, Hu Erh-fa became ill with a contagious disease.
His uncle, who lived in a village in Ts'ao district in Shantung, told him that
there was a person called Hsu An-kuo from Chihli who had come to their

area to cure people. Hu's relatives and some acquaintances arranged to invite Hsu An-kuo to come to Hu's house (probably paying his way) to effect a cure. When he arrived, "Hsu An-kuo lit a stick of incense, offered wine in sacrifice, selected a formula, and recited a spell. He told me [Hu Erh-fa] to drink the sacrificed wine." The cure worked, and Hu Erh-fa, in gratitude, became Hsu An-kuo's pupil. Hsu gave him a new name—Ch'eng-te 成德 (Completed Virtue)—and taught him how to select the right formulas for curing illness and how to recite the eight-character chant. He also told his new pupil to contribute 30 cash, explaining that this would buy him an enfeoffment in the Chen Trigram (i.e., Chiu-kung) sect. He urged Hu to study boxing techniques and promised that "in the future there would be benefits."

Hu Ch'eng-te was from Hu-chia village in Ts'ao district. During the great famine of 1786 (CL 51) when he was a boy, he and his father had left home and gone to southern Honan to find work. Hu had grown up there and lived working the land and selling beancurd. His father had taught him to do a Pa-kua (Eight Trigrams) form of boxing, but neither had belonged formally to a sect. In 1810 Hu had returned to Shantung to his native village where he stayed with and worked for his relatives there. After being ill and then cured, Hu Ch'eng-te again left Shantung to return to his family south of the Yellow River. He did not come back to Ts'ao until the summer of 1813. SYT 233–42, 22/6/20 Hu Ch'eng-te; SYT 325–30, 22/6/30 Hu Ch'eng-te; CFCL 29.1–2, 18/12/26 Hsu An-kuo.

58 Li Wen-ch'eng lived in Hsieh-chia village, less than ten miles from Hua city. His grandfather was buried in this area and the Li lineage in the village was not small—at least six adult male cousins or second cousins. SYT 91–93, 19/7/7 Tung Kuo-t'ai; NYC 32.12–16, 18/12/3 Ch'in Li; CFCL 20.18–20, 18/11/21 Memorial; KCT 016426, 19/9/7 Li Kuo-fu; SYT 309–12, 19/10/22 Li Kuo-fu; KCT 018099, 20/3/24 Li Kuo-fu; CFCL 1.6–9, 18/9/13 Li San-lung and others; NYC 29.33–35, 18/11/11 Composite confession.

59 NYC 33.13, 18/12/25 Ch'in Li.

60 Quotation comes from NYC 33.33–34, 18/12/25 Feng K'e-kung and others. Other information on Feng located in CFCL 22.5–7, 18/11/25 Sung Yueh-lung; CFCL 29.1–6, 18/12/26 Feng K'e-shan.

61 For Feng's friends and this milieu, see SYT 403–05, 19/9/22 Chiang Tao-hsueh; SYT 305–12, 19/10/22 Chang Lo-feng and Li Kuo-fu. Hsiao Kung-chuan, *Rural China: Imperial Control in the Nineteenth Century*, pp. 454–58 has colorful descriptions of some of these "weed people."

62 For example, there was an incident in which two men from Hua district pitted their birds against one another for sport and got into a quarrel. One of the men came to the magistrate's yamen to file a complaint but instead asked Feng K'e-shan and another man (a former yamen runner) to try first to mediate the dispute. Feng decided how much money was owed, extracted half of it right away, and arranged for the rest to be paid later. After a month, when the debt still had not been paid in full, Feng went himself to the defaulter to demand payment. (He was not successful, but later got even by falsely naming the defaulter as a rebel leader.) NYC 33.21, 19/1/4 Chang Te-shui.

63 NYC 32.39–40, 18/12/16 T'ang Hu-tzu; CFCL 24.21–26, 18/21/11 Feng K'e-shan.

64 CFCL 24.21–26, 18/12/11 Feng K'e-shan.

65 Quotation: NYC 33.13, 18/12/25 Ch'in Li. For Li's takeover see also KKCK 221.1–3, 18/10/16 Tung Kuo-t'ai; CFCL 24.9–11, 18/12/9 Feng K'e-shan; and KKCK 233.1–3 and 234.1, 18/10/27 Tung Kuo-t'ai.

66 CFCL 25.7–10, 18/12/12 Liu Tsung-lin; CFCL 29.1–6, 18/12/26 Niu Liang-ch'en; KKCK 204.1, 18/9/19 Tung Kuo-t'ai.

67 Contemporary references to this comet may be found in Chao-lien, *Hsiao-t'ing tsa-lu* [Miscellaneous notes from the Hsiao pavilion], 4.44–59; *Shantung province gazetteer* (1911), 11.17; Yao Yuan-chih (1773–1852), *Chu-yeh-t'ing tsa-chi* [Miscellaneous jottings from the Chu-yeh pavilion] (1893), 7.1; Chiang Hsiang-nan, *Ch'i-ching-lou wen-ch'ao* [Writings from the Ch'i-ching tower] (1837), 5.45.

These accounts have been confirmed by Western observations, and this comet, called a Great Comet because it was visible to the naked eye, is described in Brian Marsden, *Catalogue of Cometary Orbits* (Cambridge, Mass.: Smithsonian Astrophysical Observatory, 1972), pp. 7, 15, and 32. According to the Chinese calendar, it appeared on the 2d day of the 3d month of CC 16 (1811), was closest to the earth on 16/7/24, and remained visible with diminishing brightness until the fall of the following year (17/7/11). Yao Yuan-chih stated that it was visible for one hundred days beginning in the 7th lunar month of 1811. Chiang Hsiang-nan said it was visible for half a year.

According to Yao Yuan-chih, the Board of Astronomy cited a comet during the T'ang dynasty and another during the K'ang-hsi reign in order to demonstrate that comets coming from that section of the heavens and appearing for this long a period were not, as some maintained, signs of war or flood, but indicators of glory for the ruler. Yao went on to note, however, that in 1813 there were both floods and war. Chiang Hsiang-nan imagined a conversation between Lin Ch'ing and Li Wen-ch'eng as they met to talk about rebellion and observed this bright comet in the sky: Li Wen-ch'eng remarked that it was surely a good omen, and "with such a heavenly portent, heaven must assist our enterprise."

68 KKCK 202.1, 18/9/19 Lin Ch'ing; CFCL 16.30–35, 18/11/5 Ts'ao Lun.

69 Of all the districts on the north China plain where the rebellion eventually took place, only Hua and Chün in Honan experienced economic difficulties in 1811. As it turned out, Lin and Li had gambled wisely, and the next two years brought with them spreading agricultural disaster. CSL 242.10, 248.7, 248.17, 248.22 in CC 16/4 and 17/9. See Part Four, nn. 27 and 28.

70 KKCK 221.1–3, 18/10/16 Tung Kuo-t'ai.

71 CFCL 1.22–27, 18/9/15 Ts'ui Shih-chün.

72 KKCK 202.1, 18/9/18 Lin Ch'ing; NYC 32.12–16, 18/12/3 Ch'in Li; CFCL 4.5–9, 18/9/19 Lin Ch'ing; KKCK 232.1–3, 18/10/26 Wang Wu; KKCK 227.3 and 228.1, 18/10/21 Ts'ao Fu-ch'ang.

73 CFCL 25.7–10, 18/12/12 Liu Tsung-lin. See also CFCL 28.11–13, 18/12/24 Liang Chien-chung.

74 NYC 33.13, 18/12/25 Ch'in Li; CFCL 25.7–10, 18/12/12 Liu Tsung-lin; NYC 33.13–14, 18/12/23 Liu Tsung-lin.

75 KKCK 202.1, 18/9/19 Lin Ch'ing; KKCK 221.1–3, 18/10/16 Tung Kuo-t'ai.

76 CFCL 29.1–6, 18/12/26 Niu Liang-ch'en; KKCK 202.1, 18/9/19 Lin Ch'ing. The translation of *p'an* 盤 as "controller" is tentative. Sect usage of this term

is obscure. In this instance the term *t'ien-p'an* is meant to be a title or position, grammatically comparable to *t'ien-wang* ("king of heaven," "heavenly king"). In other instances *t'ien-pan* stands alone and appears to mean something along the lines of "the heavenly ordained occupation," for it is used to refer to the time when the Maitreya takes charge of the sect. See SYT 333–38, 20/12/25 Wang Tien-k'uei and Wang Heng-chung. It was probably not necessary for sect members to know precisely what such terms meant anyway; it was more important for the terms to be unusual and impressive than to be clear and exact.

77 KKCK 221.1–3, 18/10/16 Tung Kuo-t'ai; KKCK 202.1, 18/9/19 Lin Ch'ing.
78 See Anna K. Seidel, "The Image of the Perfect Ruler in Early Taoist Messianism: Lao-tzu and Li Hung," *History of Religions* 9 (1969–70): 216–47.
79 Chan Hok-lam, "White Lotus–Maitreya Doctrine," p. 218. For a discussion of these two roles, see also Harold L. Kahn, *Monarchy in the Emperor's Eyes: Image and Reality in the Ch'ien-lung Reign* (Cambridge: Harvard University Press, 1971), p. 74.
80 CFCL 1.29–32, 18/9/15 Chang Chien-mu; NYC 32.12–16, 18/12/3 Ch'in Li; NYC 30.22–25, 18/11/25 Memorial.
81 NYC 32.12–16, 18/12/3 Ch'in Li; CFCL 1.29–32, 18/9/15 Chang Chien-mu; CFCL 3.9–13, 18/9/18 Lin Ch'ing; NYC 31.18–21, 18/12/16 Niu Liang-ch'en.
     Other of Lin's appellations in his role as sect leader were Overall Sect Head of the Eight Trigrams (*pa-kua tsung chiao-t'ou* 八卦總教頭) or Overall Patriarch (*tsung tsu-shih* 總祖師). Lin Ch'ing's name and title of Patriarch of Latter Heaven were written on the first page of registers which contained the names of all Eight Trigrams sect members. Liu Lin had been known as the Sect Master of Former Heaven (*hsien-t'ien chiao-chu* 先天教主) and so it is possible that Lin Ch'ing was also known as the Sect Master of Latter Heaven. See NYC 32.12–16, 18/12/3 Ch'in Li; CFCL 6.5–6, 18/9/26 Ts'ai Ch'eng-kung and memorial; CFCL 7.10–12, 18/9/28 Ma Ch'ao-tung.
     In this role as the reincarnation of Liu Lin, Lin Ch'ing was known (at least among sect members in the Shantung–Honan region where this Liu Lin figure may have been better known) by a variety of disguised and symbolic names: Liu Shuang-mu 劉雙木, Liu Hsiang-mu 劉霜木, Liu Feng-t'ien 劉奉天, Liu Chen-k'ung 劉真空, Liu Hsing-kuo 劉興幗, or Venerable Master Liu 老劉爺. See sources cited above, plus CFCL 3.9–13, 18/9/18 Memorial; *Chi-ning district gazetteer* 4.20–29 Chou T'ing-lin; CFCL 1.22–27, 18/9/15 Ts'ui Shih-chün; CFCL 42.31–34, 21/6/3 Liu Yü-lung.
82 CFCL 1.29/32, 18/9/15 Chang Chien-mu. In one religious book confiscated in 1772 there was the phrase "pacifying the barbarians will only be done by someone from the Chou or Liu families" (平胡不出周劉戶) (CSL 906.23–24, CL 37/4/13 Edict). Another (NYC 42.32–33, CC 20/12/16 Edict) contained the passage:

> As soon as the Ch'ing dynasty is finished
> Ssu-cheng-wen Buddha
> will come down to earth in the Wang school.
> The barbarians are finished.
> What man will ascend the throne?

The sun and moon [i.e., the Ming] will return,
[the throne] will belong to the Niu-pa [i.e., person
surnamed Chu] of the Great Ming.

清朝以盡
四正文佛
洛在王門
胡人盡
何人登基
日月復來
屬大明牛八

In both these instances, the Manchus were referred to as *hu* 胡, the traditional term for barbarian tribes from the north.

83 KKCK 202.1, 18/9/19 Lin Ch'ing.

84 KKCK 221.1–3, 18/10/16 Tung Kuo-t'ai. The box of ingots was one foot long, six inches wide, and four inches high.

85 CFCL 16.30–35, 18/11/5 Ts'ao Lun; KKCK 232.1–3, 18/10/26 Wang Wu; KKCK 227.3 and 228.1, 18/10/21 Ts'ao Fu-ch'ang.

86 CFCL 3.9–13, 18/9/18 Liu Te-ts'ai; SYT 381, 19/12/14 Tung Kuo-t'ai and Liu Pei-r; KKCK 235.1, 18/10/27 Liu Chin-te; KKCK 214.1, 18/10/9 Pien Fu-kuei. Liu Te-ts'ai was not the only one of Lin Ch'ing's followers who was adopted. Of the 175 people in that sect who were arrested and for whom confessions are available, 32 (or 18 percent) were adopted. Of these only 2 were eunuchs; 7 worked as hired agricultural laborers.

87 Liu Te-ts'ai worked in the Chi-hua Gate. The others were Kao Kuang-fu (Chung-ts'ui building), Chang T'ai (Yueh-hua Gate), Liu Chin (T'ien-ch'iung building), Wang Fu-lu (Yü-sha room), Yü Chi-ch'ing (Chi-shen office), Yen Chin-hsi (K'un-ning palace), and Ku Chin-lu (it is not known where he worked). CFCL 3.2–4, 18/9/18 Memorial; KKCK 218.1–2, 18/10/12 Yü Chi-ch'ing; CFCL 3.9–13, 18/9/18 Liu Te-ts'ai.

88 KKCK 218.1–2, 18/10/12 Yü Chi-ch'ing.

89 This was Yen Chin-hsi; his father ran a household goods store in Peking and his mother came from a village southwest of Peking near Sung-chia where Lin Ch'ing lived. Yen had originally been converted by one of his maternal uncles. When Liu Te-ts'ai came to tell him about the sect, Yen told him that he already belonged but had forgotten the eight-character chant. Liu refreshed his memory but never considered Yen his pupil. KKCK 203.1, 18/9/19 T'ien Ma-r; CFCL 3.9–13, 18/9/18 Liu Te-ts'ai.

90 The amount given was 600 cash (by one account), 1,000 or 2,000 cash or even 2 taels (by another account). This is a large but not enormous amount of money per man, though undoubtedly a nice supplement to their salary. The total cost to Lin Ch'ing was more substantial. To have supported six eunuchs with 1 tael a month for two years would have cost about 150 taels. For monthly salaries, see Appendix 3. KKCK 218.1–2, 18/10/12 Yü Chi-ch'ing and Yen Chin-hsi; KKCK 218.2, 18/10/13 Yü Chi-ch'ing; KKCK 221.1–3, 18/10/16 Tung Kuo-t'ai.

This pattern of gifts to the eunuchs was reversed in the summer of 1813 when Lin's eunuch pupils presented him with a small silver ingot and a cart. KKCK 221.1–3, 18/10/16 Tung Kuo-t'ai; NYC 32.12–16, 18/12/3 Ch'in Li.

91 Liu Ti-wu, then in his forties, was one of four sons in the Chu family, plain-

blue banner bondservants from Sang-fa village. When he was young he had been given to the Liu family as an adopted son as part of an exchange of sons extending over two generations. Liu Ti-wu and his real brothers (whose surnames were Chu) all belonged to Ku Liang's Jung-hua Assembly. As a young man, Liu Ti-wu had worked in villages to the east of his home, and when he finally moved to Yang-hsiu village he became acquainted with Li Lao (who lived there) and his Pai-yang sect. After Ku Liang died and the sect was investigated by the government, Liu Ti-wu changed and took Li Lao as his new teacher. His brothers, on the other hand, remained in the Jung-hua Assembly and became pupils of Lin Ch'ing. In 1812 Liu Ti-wu learned of Lin Ch'ing's preparations for rebellion and brought Li Lao to meet him in hope of combining the two groups. For Liu's family see SYT 217, 20/2/20 Liu Pei-r.

92 SYT 205–08, 20/7/11 Hao Pa; SYT 91–93, 19/7/7 Tung Kuo-t'ai; KKCK 209.1–2, 18/9/28 Li Lao; KKCK 211.1, 18/9/29 Li Yü-lung.

93 KKCK 208.1, 18/9/24 Ch'ü Ssu.

94 SYT 317–25, 22/9/24 Wang Jui; SYT 155–56, 22/8/17 Mrs. Ts'ui Shih.

95 KKCK 222.1–2, 18/10/16 Kuo Ch'ao-chün.

96 KKCK 212.1, 18/10/3 Liu Ch'ao-tung.

97 KKCK 209.1–2, 18/9/28 Li Lao. See also SYT 359–62, 20/9/26 Wu Hsi.

98 There were many general promises. For examples see KKCK 207.1, 18/9/24 Liu Hsing-li; KKCK 216.1–2, 18/10/11 Li Liu; KKCK 204.1, 18/9/19 Liu Chin-t'ing. For examples of more specific posts see KCT 017330, 19/2*/21 Han Ts'un-lin; CFCL 17.4–7, 18/11/6 Ts'ao Lun; KKCK 215.1, 18/10/9 Liu Kou-r. Two eunuchs (one a pupil under Ch'en Shuang, one under Liu Hsing-li) were in fact both promised the post of chief eunuch in return for their cooperation in the palace attack. KKCK 206.1–2, 18/9/22 Yang Chin-chung; CFCL 3.9–13, 18/9/18 Liu Te-ts'ai.

99 KCT 017262, 19/12/17 Jen San; KKCK 220.1–2, 18/10/15 Chang Tzu-sheng; KKCK 214.1, 18/10/9 Chin Hei.

100 Specifically Ku-an district: nine villages; Ta-hsing district: eight villages; Tung-an district: one village; Hsin-ch'eng district: four villages; T'ung district: eleven villages and the city; Hsiung district: eight villages; Wan-p'ing district: fifteen villages; and the city of Peking. These figures, based on all available reliable information, represent a minimum. See Part Three, n. 46 for comments on these "statistics."

101 Although sect membership was applied by extension to the nuclear family of a believer, his extended family (in-laws, cousins, etc.) was not automatically included. There are several examples from among Lin Ch'ing's pupils of sect membership becoming a source of contention within a family, and one believer, out of anger, deliberately excluded his nephew, with whom he had had difficult relations for several years, from both the sect and the rebellion. On the other hand, there are far more instances of brothers who brought one another and their other relatives by blood and by marriage into the sect after them. For bad relations see SYT 171–212, 22/9/14 Composite confession; KCT 011671, 13/8/1 Composite confession; SYT 103–05, 20/1/10 Sung Ts'ai.

102 KKCK 221.1–3, 18/10/16 Tung Kuo-t'ai; CFCL 17.4–7, 18/11/6 Ts'ao Lun and Tung Kuo-t'ai.

103 The godsons were T'ien Ch'i-chin, Ho Ch'i-yun, and Chu Ping-jen. Those

who helped Lin Ch'ing were Chih Chin-ts'ai, Liu Fu-shou, and Liu Ch'eng-hsiang (who had his own room). There is also a government reference to a "concubine" (*ch'ieh* 妾), a Miss Ch'en, who cannot be identified (see CFCL 27.24, 18/12/20 Edict). KKCK 221.1–3, 18/10/16 Tung Kuo-t'ai; SYT 39–40, 20/2/3 Sung Ch'eng-ch'uan; CPT 127–31, 18/12/7 Wanted list; SYT 93–94, 20/10/14 Jen Tzu-kuei; KKCK 219.1, 18/10/14 Liu Fu-shou; SYT 271–72, 20/4/24 Tung Kuo-t'ai.

104 One of these men was Li Wen-ch'eng's adopted son Liu Ch'eng-chang; another was a man called Ch'in Li who was an assistant of Li's; the third was a sect leader from Tz'u district in southern Chihli and a friend of Liu Ch'eng-chang called Chao Te-i. The three did not stay long in Sung-chia, just long enough to deliver both money and messages, and in the case of Chao Te-i, to be introduced to Lin Ch'ing.

Ch'in Li was in his early thirties, a former runner in the Chün district yamen, whose father and grandfather had both practiced a White Lotus sect. Ch'in had joined Li Wen-ch'eng's group, and being bright and able to read and write, he helped Li manage sect business. He was captured after the battle in which Li Wen-ch'eng died, and his testimony is an important source of information about Li and his sect. SYT 611–13, 19/12/25 Tung Kuo-t'ai; NYC 32.12–16, 18/12/3 Ch'in Li; SYT 191–93, 20/6/18 Tung Kuo-t'ai; KKCK 227.1–2, 18/10/21 Tung Kuo-t'ai; SYT 379, 19/7/26 Tung Kuo-t'ai; SYT 15–17, 22/9/2 Su Kuang-tsu; SYT 93–94, 19/11/7 Sheng T'ai.

105 These men were Wei Chen-tsung (from Chün city where his father had a teashop) and Feng Hsueh-li. KCT 017586, 20/2/2 Memorial; NYC 33.19–20, 18/12/25 Feng K'e-shan; SYT 611–13, 19/12/25 Tung Kuo-t'ai: CFCL 29.1–6, 18/12/26 Niu Liang-ch'en.

106 It is possible that at about this time two lesser sect leaders from Honan, An Huai-p'u and Kuo Ming-ju, also came to pay their respects to Lin Ch'ing. CFCL 23.33–34, 18/12/5 Tung Kuo-t'ai; CFCL 28.11–13, 18/12/24 Liang Chien-chung; NYC 31.18–21, 18/12/16 Niu Liang-ch'en.

107 For the government recovery of this book, see KCT 017254, 19/1/17 Memorial. A book with very nearly the same title—*San-chiao* 教 *ying-chieh tsung* 總-*kuan t'ung-shu*—was owned by the Wang family of Shih-fo-k'ou. In 1815 a member of this family quoted a passage from this book about the three Buddhas and added a phrase stating that Maitreya would come and be born to that Wang family. SYT 343–45, 20/12/25 Wang K'e-ch'in. See Part One n. 63; C. K. Yang, *Religion in Chinese Society*, p. 234; and Yano Jinichi, "Kuan-yü Pai-lien-chiao chih luan" [On the White Lotus sect rebellion], *Jen-wen yueh-k'an* 6 (1935): 7–8.

108 This slogan is reminiscent of that used by the rebel band at Liang-shan-p'o in the famous popular novel *Shui-hu chuan*. Their slogan, which had a similar meaning, was *t'i-t'ien hsing-tao* 替天行道. Ogawa Tamaki, "The Author of the Shui-hu Chuan," *Monumenta Serica* 17 (1958): 321.

109 CFCL 5.14–16, 18/9/22 Chu Ch'eng-chen; CFCL 29.1–6, 18/12/26 Hsu An-kuo.

110 KCT 016869, 19/11/18 Chao Fei-i; CFCL 15.20–23, 18/11/1 Jung Hsing-t'ai.

111 CFCL 15.1–2, 18/10/29 Liu Ching-t'ang; CFCL 42.26–27, 21/4/2 Chou Wen-sheng; CFCL 42.28–29, 21/5/10 Li Fa-yen.

112 By 1813 Ch'eng Pai-yueh was sending his grandson to Peking monthly to deliver messages (and perhaps money) to Lin Ch'ing. CFCL 29.1–6, 18/12/26 Hsu An-kuo; CFCL 5.14–16, 18/9/22 Chu Ch'eng-chen; CFCL 21.28–32, 18/11/24 Hsu-ch'ien; CFCL 23.35–39, 18/12/6 Liu Lin.

113 Ts'ui Shih-chün 崔士俊 was originally a member of the Li Trigram sect taught by the family of sect masters from Honan named Kao. Ts'ui had joined that sect in 1804, but nine years later he was introduced to Hsu An-kuo and was persuaded that Hsu's sect was superior. Ts'ui did not find the new sect very different as far as daily sect practices were concerned, but he was interested in what his new teacher could tell him about regularizing and recording contributions and about the imminent arrival of the new kalpa. Ts'ui had a large following of his own, and all of them became part of the Eight Trigrams when he did. For the Kao family Li Trigram sect, see Part One. It was actually a member of the Kao family who introduced Ts'ui to Hsu An-kuo. CFCL 1.22–27, 18/9/15 Ts'ui Shih-chün; CFCL 32.36–38, 19/1/24 Kao Chi-yuan; *Chi-ning district gazetteer* 4.20–29 Liu Ning.

114 These pupils were Ts'ui Shih-chün (from Chin-hsiang), his pupil Chang Chien-mu (from Ch'eng-wu), and Chu Ch'eng-fang and his cousin Chu Ch'eng-kuei (both from Ts'ao district). CFCL 1.22–27, 18/9/15 Ts'ui Shih-chün; CFCL 1.29–32, 18/9/15 Chang Chien-mu; CFCL 5.14–16, 18/9/22 Chu Ch'eng-chen; *Chi-ning district gazetteer* 4.20–29 Liu Ning.

115 Ibid. Li Wen-ch'eng's speech about endless blessings (能造萬刧之苦 · · · 也能修萬刧之福) is quoted by Chang Chien-mu.

116 CFCL 24.21–26, 18/12/11 Feng K'e-shan.

117 KKCK 221.1–3, 18/10/16 Tung Kuo-t'ai.

118 義和門 or 義和拳. NYC 38.73–75, 20/9/6 Ke Li-yeh; SYT 363–65, 20/9/26 Ke Li-yeh; KCT 016303, 19/8/16 Liu Yuan; SYT 423–24, 20/11/28 Ma Shih.

119 Huo Ying-fang had moved to Ku-ch'eng district (Chihli) from Hua. In 1810 his cousin Huo Ying-pi (who belonged to a Pa-kua sect) came to visit and taught the sect to his cousin and several neighbors. Huo Ying-fang subsequently took at least ten pupils of his own and transmitted the sect through three subsequent generations to at least thirty-four-men. CFCL 26.31–34, 18/12/16 Huo Ying-fang; CFCL 34.16–19, 19/2/2 Liu K'un and others.

120 KCT 016303, 19/8/16 Liu Yuan; SYT 423–24, 20/11/28 Ma Shih; CFCL 26.31–34, 18/12/16 Huo Ying-fang; CFCL 24.21–26, 18/12/11 Feng K'e-shan.

121 CFCL 28.1–4, 18/12/21 Li Sheng-te; KCT 015815, 19/6/28 Wang Ying-chieh.

122 In the first month of 1813 Huo Ying-fang had come to visit his cousin, and together with three of his pupils was taken to be introduced to Li Wen-ch'eng. In the 4th month, Huo arranged for a gift of four rolls of pale blue cloth to be sent to Lin Ch'ing. CFCL 26.31–34, 18/12/16 Huo Ying-fang; CFCL 34.16–19, 19/2/2 Composite confession; SYT 173–74, 21/1/25 Tung Kuo-t'ai.

123 CFCL 28.1–4, 18/12/21 Sung Yü-lin; CFCL 35.25–27, 19/2/10 Ma Lao-t'ai; CFCL 24.21–26, 18/12/11 Feng K'e-shan; KKCK 221.1–3, 18/10/16 Tung Kuo-t'ai.

124 CFCL 24.21–26, 18/12/11 Feng K'e-shan; KCT 015815, 19/6/28 Wang Ying-

chieh; KCT 016437, 19/9/4 Li Hui-i. For Sung's following see NYC 38.73–75,
20/9/6 Ke Li-yeh; SYT 363–65, 20/9/26 Ke Li-yeh; SYT 423–24, 20/11/28
Ma Shih; KCT 016303, 19/8/16 Liu Yuan; CFCL 23.6–7, 18/12/2 Sung Shu-
te; CFCL 28.1–4, 18/12/21 Li Sheng-te and Sung Yü-lin; CFCL 21.20–22,
18/11/24 Kuo Wei-chen; CFCL 23.26–27, 18/12/3 Sung Shu-te; CFA 19,
19/4/14 Sung Ch'ang-sheng; KCT 016647-E, 19/10/30 Li Fu; CFCL 36.1–2,
19/2/12 Feng Shih-ch'i; KCT 016437, 19/9/4 Li Hui-i and others; KCT
015815, 19/6/28 Liu Chan-k'uei. For the names of the members of this group,
see my dissertation, "The Eight Trigrams Uprising of 1813," Part Two, n. 124.

125 Liu Yü-lung was not tall, had a beard, a round face, ruddy cheeks, and had
lost his two front teeth. In his early fifties, he was a stone mason by trade, but
he had a variety of other talents and was known especially for his ability to
paint lifelike pictures of tigers and for his skill at fighting. In 1803 Liu learned
the Chin-chung-chao (Armor of the Golden Bell) technique of fighting from
a chance acquaintance (they met in a teashop at a fair in Shantung). A few
years later Liu borrowed a book containing the various talismans and chants of
the Golden Bell system, which he studied and used to cure illnesses. In 1808
and 1809, Liu Yü-lung was involved in a civil legal proceeding that eventually necessitated that he go to the provincial capital of Pao-ting. While
there, Liu became acquainted with one member of the Jung-hua Assembly,
Ch'en Mao-lin. It was at this time that Ch'en (together with Lin Ch'ing and
others) were on trial for their sect activities, and Liu's meeting with Ch'en
was rather like Lin Ch'ing's meeting with Niu Liang-ch'en (which was taking
place at this time). Liu Yü-lung was converted by Ch'en Mao-lin to that sect,
became his pupil, and that winter went to visit his new teacher near Peking.
Liu met Niu Liang-ch'en who was then beginning work as a tutor in that
village, and may also have met Lin Ch'ing. Liu's new teacher had taught him
the Jung-hua Assembly's system of yogic meditation, and combining these
techniques with his skills in various forms of fighting and his ability to make
charms that could cure illness, Liu Yü-lung began to make a reputation for
himself. He combined the martial with the meditational aspects of the White
Lotus tradition and, returning to central Chihli, began to take disciples. The
size of his following is not known, but it is clear that Liu did not neglect his
finances. He told new pupils that they would be expected to send their teacher
a "small gift" (of 30 cash) every month, and a "large gift" (about 200 cash)
four times a year. KCT 016763–E, 19/10/20 Wanted list; CFCL 42.31–34,
21/6/3 Liu Yü-lung; KCT 018752, 20/5/27 Kuo Lo-yun; NYC 40.30–33,
21/2/10 Memorial; SYT 47–48, 21/3/3 Liu Ming-t'ang.

126 Yang later went to Hua district to meet Li Wen-ch'eng and to deliver messages among different trigram groups in Honan, Shantung, and Chihli. When
he finally returned home in the 7th month of 1813 he had traveled at least six
hundred miles in three months and had met with all the top trigram leaders.
As Yü K'e-ching's pupil, Yang took orders from Li Wen-ch'eng for purposes
of the uprising. CFCL 35.21–25, 19/2/10 Yang Yü-shan; KKCK 227.1–2,
18/10/21 Tung Kuo-t'ai; CFCL 3.9–13, 18/9/18 Lin Ch'ing; CFCL 33.
14–16, 19/1/27 Li Fu-yuan; CFCL 29.9–10, 18/12/26 Yang Yü-shan.

127 KKCK 227.1–2, 18/10/21 Tung Kuo-t'ai; SYT 91–93, 19/7/7 Tung Kuo-

t'ai; KCT 016863, 19/11/12 Ch'in Li; NYC 32.12–16, 18/12/3 Ch'in Li; KCT 017077, 19/11/3 Ch'in Li; CFCL 3.9–13, 18/9/18 Lin Ch'ing.

128 KKCK 221.1–3, 18/10/16 Tung Kuo-t'ai.

129 CPT 581–86, 18/12/29 Ma Lao-t'ai; CFCL 35.25–27, 19/2/10 Ma Lao-t'ai.

130 CFCL 29.1–6, 18/12/26 Niu Liang-ch'en and Hsu An-kuo; CFCL 24.21–26, 18/12/11 Feng K'e-shan; SYT 91–93, 19/7/7 Tung Kuo-t'ai; NYC 31.18–21, 18/12/16 Niu Liang-ch'en; CFCL 5.14–16, 18/9/22 Chu Ch'eng-chen; CFCL 35.21–25, 19/2/10 Yang Yü-shan.

131 Chi-ning district gazetteer 4.20–29 Chou T'ing-lin and others; CFCL 29.1–6, 18/12/26 Hsu An-kuo; CFCL 1.29–32, 18/9/15 Chang Chien-mu.

132 CSL 267.22–23, 18/3/28 Edict.

133 Sung Hsiang (1756–1826), Hung-hsing shan-fang i-kao [Posthumous works from the Hung-hsing study], p. 96, "Five Stanzas Recording My Feelings on the Road through Honan."

134 Awards of relief and tax assistance to these areas in 1813 may be found in the Ch'ing shih-lu at CSL 265.2, 266.14, 266.27, 266.28, 268.5, 268.14, 268.23, 269.8–9, 269.17, 270.21, 272.26, 275.17. See also Hua district gazetteer 12.1; Tung-ming district gazetteer 2.21–22; K'ai district gazetteer 1.59; Ta-ming prefecture gazetteer 4.93–94; Chin-hsiang district gazetteer 11.19–20; Chü-yeh district gazetteer 2.27; Ch'eng-wu district gazetteer 9.31; Shantung province gazetteer 11.17; CSL 273.3–4, 18/9/4 Edict; SYT 25–26, 18/9/4 Edict; CFCL 24.11–12, 18/12/9 Memorial; CSL 274.15, 18/9/18 Edict.

135 The drought in the Peking area had been relieved by rain late in the 6th month. See SYT 205, 18/4/23 and SYT 5, 18/7/1. For Lin Ch'ing's rhyme, see KKCK 226.1–3, 18/10/21 Statement by the deputy-magistrate. When authorizing funds for wages of soldiers who were being sent from northern Chihli to take part in the suppression, the emperor noted that "the price of grain has risen in the northern and southern prefectures of Chihli province," and he authorized an increase in the soldiers' pay to the amount of 150 cash per day. CSL 274.15, 18/9/18 Edict.

136 CFCL 29.1–6, 18/12/26 Niu Liang-ch'en; SYT 233–42, 22/6/20 Hu Ch'eng-te. For other references to this phrase ming-tao, see SYT 49, 21/3/3 Tu Lo-shang; NYC 31.18–21, 18/12/16 Niu Liang-ch'en.

137 CFCL 4.5–9, 18/9/19 Lin Ch'ing. The text for the quotation is:

八月中秋
中秋八月
黄花滿地開放

Feng K'e-shan quoted another popular saying that he said was current: "If you want red flowers to bloom, Yen-shuang must come." Yen-shuang, he explained, stood for Chu Yen-shuang 朱鹽霜 and Li Wen-ch'eng had taken Yen-shuang as his nickname in order to associate himself with this surname of the Ming royal family. CFCL 24.21–26, 18/12/11 Feng K'e-shan.

It is unlikely that there was a real possibility of there being an intercalary month that year. During the Chia-ch'ing reign intercalary months fell regularly (with only one exception) at intervals of 34 or 35 months. The last one had been a intercalary 3d month in 1811 (CC 16), and thus the logical succeeding one would have been early in 1814 (CC 19), and indeed there was a second 2d month that year. Lin Ch'ing probably knew that an intercalary month was due sometime in the winter of that year, but it seems unlikely he could have counted on it for the 8th month. By the time the CC 18 calendar and almanacs were available he would have known. Chao-lien (*Hsiao-t'ing tsa-lu* 4.44–59) states that the Board of Astronomy had in fact scheduled an intercalary month as a second 8th month but had changed its mind when they saw the comet of 1811. This seems unconvincingly dramatic and too neat. If we consider the overall "policy" of the Board of Astronomy on intercalary months as deduced from the actual calendar, the likelihood of there being an intercalary 8th month appears even more remote. During the entire dynasty intercalary months fell regularly between the 2d and 7th months of the year: all but five (of sixty-five) had been one of those months. There had been intercalary 8th months in 1680 and 1718 but none since. (Calendar information derived from Cheng Ho-sheng, *Chin-shih chung-hsi shih jih tui-chao piao* [An equivalency chart for dates in Chinese and Western history in the modern period].

138 See the beginning of Part Two above: Wang Hao-hsien in 1622, and the other Eight Trigrams in 1786 (they selected the intercalary 7th month that year as the fulfillment of the prophecy). For a prophecy about an intercalary 8th month in the year of the Boxers, see "Editorial Commentary," *Chinese Recorder* 31 (August 1900): 426. For another bit of prophecy about 8/15, three rulers, red light (*hung-yang?*), etc., see Ida Pruitt, *A Daughter of Han: Autobiography of a Chinese Working Woman* (New Haven: Yale University Press, 1945), p. 244.

139 In general, see Ramon H. Myers, *The Chinese Peasant Economy: Agricultural Development in Hopei and Shantung, 1890–1949*, pp. 41–42, 70, 89–90, 106, 153–55.

140 There are references to harvesting in the Peking area being completed during the 9th month though not by the 15th day. Various individuals testified that on that day they were working on the land, in the buckwheat fields, harvesting buckwheat, harvesting the beans, doing their beans, bringing in the millet stalks, at work husking (the millet), winnowing grain, or that they had finished harvesting, piled up their sorghum in the courtyard, or put their black beans out to dry in the courtyard. Hired laborers began work in the 7th month that year and worked through the 9th month. SYT 325–26, 20/2/30 Pai Yü; SYT 419–21, 20/11/28 Sung Wen-ch'ao; SYT 65, 21/10/12 Yang Te; SYT 83–85, 19/12/3 Ch'en Wu; SYT 299–301, 19/12/10 Liu Ch'i-shih-r; SYT 103–05, 20/1/10 Sung Ts'ai; SYT 81–83, 22/11/8 Ch'en Sheng-r; SYT 203–09, 22/11/18 Wang T'ien-ts'ai; CFA 58, 20/2/12 Sung Chin-pao; SYT 533, 19/3/23 Pa-lan-t'ai; KKCK 225.1, 18/10/18 Liu Chin-ts'ai; KKCK 219.1, 18/10/14 Liu Fu-shou; KCT 017094, 19/12/2 Sung Erh; KKCK 236.1, 18/10/27 Liu San.

The only reference to the planting of winter wheat is a negative one. A local official touring Wan-p'ing district in the early 9th month noticed that the people in the southern part of the district (where Lin Ch'ing lived) were not planting their wheat. They were agitated and would only tell him that they were afraid to plant (KKCK 226.1–3, 18/10/21 Ch'en Shao-jung). The implication is that they knew of the impending Eight Trigrams uprising. The observation also suggests, however, that elsewhere the winter wheat was already being planted in the early 9th month.

On 9/21 of that year the governor of Shantung traveled through the area of western Shantung along the Chihli border just north and east of where there were active rebels and commented that the "late-planted crop of sorghum had not yet been harvested" (CFCL 6.8–9, 18/9/26 Memorial). Ten days later he reported that the harvesting of the summer crop of sorghum had begun (SSTC, 18/10/6 Memorial from T'ung-hsing).

141 For the emperor's 1812 trip see CSL 259.21 through 261.17, CC 17/7, 17/8, 17/9 passim. For the 1813 trip see CSL 271.28 through 273.22, CC 18/7, 18/8, 18/9 passim. Also CFCL 1.3–4, 19/3/29 Edict.

142 Red turbans had been worn during Wang Hao-hsien's uprising in 1622 and in an abortive uprising in 1768 (see above pp. 63–65). White had similarly been used for centuries as a color for rebellion and is said by some to be associated with Manichean strains in popular Chinese religion. For example, see Richard Chu, "White Lotus Sect," pp. 26–33.

143 For example, see NYC 40.37–41, 21/6/3 Wang Yuan.

144 For example, see CFCL 26.31–34, 18/12/16 Huo Ying-fang; KKCK 211.1, 18/9/29 Li Yü-lung; KKCK 216.1, 18/10/11 Li San.

145 CFCL 24.21–26, 18/12/11 Feng K'e-shan.

146 Sung Yüeh-lung later arranged merely to fortify his own village and wait for Li Wen-ch'eng (rather than attacking the district offices). Ma Lao-t'ai and his men were told to set fires outside Pao-ting city as a signal and to open the city gates for the men from Honan when they arrived. CFCL 28.1–4, 18/12/21 Li Sheng-te; CPT 581–86, 18/12/29 Ma Lao-t'ai. For the rest: CFCL 29.1–6, 18/12/26 Niu Liang-ch'en; CFCL 37.21–22, 19/2/24 Wang Chin-tao; CFCL 35.21–25, 19/2/10 Yang Yü-shan; CFCL 10.17–20, 18/10/10 Wang Ch'i-shan; KKCK 227.1–2, 18/10/21 Tung Kuo-t'ai; KKCK 204.1, 18/9/19 Tung Kuo-t'ai; CFCL 26.31–34, 18/12/16 Huo Ying-fang.

147 NYC 32.12–16, 18/12/3 Ch'in Li; CFCL 24.21–26, 18/12/11 Feng K'e-shan; NYC 31.18–21, 18/12/16 Niu Liang-ch'en. It had originally been planned that there would be a Civil Trigram Master (*wen kua-chu* 文卦主) and a Military Trigram Master (*wu kua-chu* 武卦主), namely Li Wen-ch'eng and Wang Hsiang (who was Feng K'e-shan's boxing teacher). When Wang Hsiang died in the 4th month of 1813, this set of titles was apparently dropped and Lin Ch'ing and Feng K'e-shan became instead the Sage of Learning and Sage of Military Ability. Similarly, the titles *t'ien-wang, ti-wang, jen-wang* had originally been designated for Lin, Li, and Feng. By this meeting it had been decided to let those three keep the higher title of Controller, and to use these titles for Li and those two who were to help him rule.

148 NYC 32.12–16, 18/12/3 Ch'in Li; CFCL 24.21–26, 18/12/11 Feng K'e-shan. There was an abundance of other titles actually employed by the Eight Trigrams during their rebellion, but it is not clear which of these were planned in advance and which were created to meet the needs of a changed situation; they are discussed on pp. 217–19.

149 CFCL 19.4–9, 18/11/14 Memorial; *Chi-ning district gazetteer* 4.20–29 Chin-

hsiang leader arrested with list of names; CFCL 35.21–25, 19/2/10 Yang Yü-shan, Yang asked his followers to make up a list; SYT 419–22, 22/9/27 Ch'iu Tzu-liang, Ku-an sect made up a list of all its members.

150 CFCL 1.29–31, 18/9/15 Chang Chien-mu.

位列上中下
才分天地人
五行生父子
八卦定君臣

151 My information on this name is extremely limited. One reference to the T'ien-li Assembly came in a confession by a sect member called Chiang Fu-hsing; this remark was repeated in the first memorials to reach the emperor about the rebellion, and for this reason it was recorded in the *Ch'ing shih-lu* and later given wide currency. The name was never used by the sect members except to refer to the group in the act of rebellion. See CFCL 1.6–9, 18/9/13 Chiang Fu-hsing; CFCL 2.23–24, 18/9/16 Sung Shang-chung; CFCL 1.1–2, 18/9/12 Memorial; CFCL 4.24–25, 18/9/20 Edict.

152 *Tung-ming district gazetteer* 2.21–22, heavy rain for forty days beginning in the 8th month; *Hua district gazetteer* 11.13, a big rain began falling on 8/7; *Ts'ao district gazetteer* 18.10, 8th month, incessant rain for over forty days; *Chi-ning district gazetteer* 4.20–29, rain began on 9/1 and fell for ten days.

153 For some descriptions of how gentry and other rather different sorts of rebels in the sub-Yangtze region mobilized and organized themselves on the local, regional, and national level, see Kuhn, *Rebellion and Its Enemies*, pp. 165–75. The case of the Eight Trigrams indicates that White Lotus sects used very distinctive links to build their organizations, and one does not see "the same kinds of linkages and the same levels of organization . . . within both the orthodox, gentry-dominated Confucian culture and the various hetero-dox, secret-society dominated sectarian subcultures" (p. 165). Organiza-tionally, the Eight Trigrams were not a mirror image of their rivals.

PART THREE

1 For this paragraph, see *Chin-hsiang district gazetteer* 9.14, and CFCL 38.23–24, 19/2*14. The Chia-ch'ing Emperor later suggested that Governor T'ung-hsing's response to word of possible trouble in Chin-hsiang may not have been as swift as Wu Chieh described it. The emperor stated that at first the gover-nor had been unwilling to believe the report, thinking it false and generated by factional feuding within the provincial bureaucracy, and the director of education had had to argue strenuously to persuade him that this was not the case. See CSL 280.2–4, 18/12/2 Edict.

My account of what happened in Chin-hsiang is drawn largely from a detailed description of these events by the acting Chin-hsiang magistrate Wu Chieh himself. This narrative is located in the *Chi-ning district gazetteer* (Chi-ning being the higher administrative unit of which Chin-hsiang was a part) (1840) 4.20–35 and is entitled simply "An account by the Chin-hsiang district magistrate Wu Chieh." Although these events certainly redounded to Mag-istrate Wu's credit and place his actions in a most favorable light, the account is relatively modest and unassuming and full of detail only hinted at in other gazetteers.

2 *Chi-ning district gazetteer* 4.20–29 Magistrate Wu's account; CFCL 1.22–27, 18/9/15 Memorial; Sheng Ta-shih, *Ching-ni chi* [Account of the suppression of the rebels] (1820) 2.1–6. Sheng Ta-shih's account of events in Chin-hsiang is quite similar to Wu Chieh's narrative and adds some details. Sheng said (in his preface) that he talked with people involved in suppressing these rebels; he seems to have talked with Wu or perhaps saw a copy of the account which later appeared in the gazetteer.

3 KKCK 223.1–3, 18/10/17 Memorial from the Grand Council.

4 SSTC and CFCL 1.22–27, 18/9/15 Memorial from T'ung-hsing.

5 CFCL 28.1–4, 18/12/21 Sung Yü-lin and Li Sheng-te; NYC 38.73–75, 20/9/6 Ke Li-yeh; CFA 19, 19/4/14 Sung Ch'ang-sheng; CFCL 24. 21–26, 18/12/11 Feng K'e-shan; SYT 363–65, 20/9/26 Ke Li-yeh; SYT 423–24, 20/11/28 Ma Shih; KCT 016437, 19/9/4 Li Hui-i and others.

6 CFCL 26.31–34, 18/12/16 Huo Ying-fang; CFCL 21.5–8, 18/11/23 Composite confession.

7 NYC 40.37–41, 21/6/3 Wang Yuan.

8 NYC 40.37–41, 20/6/3 Wang Yuan and others.

9 CFCL 35.21–25, 19/2/10 Yang Yü-shan; CFCL 33.14–16, 19/1/27 Li Fu-yuan.

10 CFCL 35.21–25, 19/2/10 Yang Yü-shan; CFCL 29.9–10, 18/12/26 Memorial; CFCL 31.10–11, 19/1/13 Kao T'an-chao.

11 CFCL 26.31–34, 18/12/26 Huo Ying-fang; CFCL 28.1–4, 18/12/21 Sung Yü-lin; CFA 19, 19/4/14 Sung Ch'ang-sheng; NYC 38.73–75, 20/9/6 Ke Li-yeh; NYC 40.37–41, 21/6/3 Composite confession.

12 CFCL 33.14–16, 19/1/27 Li Fu-yuan. Yang Yü-shan's situation was further complicated by competition within his own district. It was at this time that the former Ta-sheng sect head Li Ching (who was then in prison) began to reorganize his followers for a rebellion which he predicted would begin during the intercalary 2d month of 1814. Li Ching sent out word to his pupils. trying to inspire them to believe in his predictions and telling them to make up yellow banners as their symbol. There was at least one pupil of Yang Yü-shan's who received white banners from Yang and, at the same time, yellow banners from Li Ching. It is indicative of the general psychology of sect members in such a position that he kept them both until he saw that first one and then the other would not succeed, then he burned both banners. (See Part One, pp. 59–60.)

13 CFCL 28.1–4, 18/12/21 Sung Yü-lin.

14 This was a ninth-rank position; see H.S. Brunnert and V.V. Hagelstrom, *Present Day Political Organization of China*, #857.3.

15 CFCL 23.27–28, 18/12/3 Memorial; NYC 31.18–21, 18/12/16 Niu Liang-ch'en; NYC 32.12–16, 18/12/3 Ch'in Li; *Hua district gazetteer* 8.82, 8.87.

    Unfortunately, we have no information about how it was that Deputy-Magistrate Liu obtained Li Wen-ch'eng's name. There were many sect members from Lao-an, and it is likely that most of them had heard of Li Wen-ch'eng.

16 NYC 30.22–25, 18/11/25 Memorial; CFCL 23.27–28, 18/12/3 Memorial;

NYC 32.12–16, 18/12/3 Ch'in Li; Yang Fang, *Kung-ch'uan [Yang] Kuo-yung-hou tzu-pien nien-p'u* [Autobiography of Yang Fang], 3.19–33.

17   Here as elsewhere Feng K'e-shan's own testimony is not reliable. He stated that his cousins had reported him to the district authorities in the middle of the 8th month. These men themselves stated (supported by all other evidence) that they had not gone to the authorities until after Li Wen-ch'eng had been arrested and Feng K'e-shan's name had been mentioned by Niu Liang-ch'en in his confession; they had not gone previously because "we were afraid that if we informed sooner, they [the Eight Trigrams] would have harmed us." NYC 33.33–34, 18/12/25 Feng K'e-k'uan and others; NYC 33.35, 19/1/9 Feng K'e-kung and others; CFCL 24.21–26, 18/12/11 Feng K'e-shan.

18   CFCL 18.19–23, 18/11/13 Chang Tao-lun; CFCL 1.32–33, 18/9/15 Memorial.

19   A number of sect members had worked at the Hua district yamen. Niu Liang-ch'en, who now found himself in jail there, had been a treasury clerk prior to 1806; it is not known if he worked there again after 1811 when he returned to Honan. Li Chih-kuo, another rebel, was serving as a treasury clerk, and two runners, Huang P'an-kung and Hsu Chan-k'uei, both joined the rebels. KCT 017220, 19/12/22 Hsu Chan-k'uei; CFA 25, 19/7/24 Li Chih-kuo; CFCL 41.3–4, 19/7/6 Huang P'an-kung; CFCL 1.1–2, 18/9/12 Memorial; NYC 31.18–21, 18/12/16 Niu Liang-ch'en.

20   NYC 32.12–16, 18/12/3 Ch'in Li; NYC 30.36–38, 18/12/12 Huang Hsing-tsai; NYC 31.18–21, 18/12/16 Niu Liang-ch'en.

21   KCT 018146, 20/3/25 Chao Te.

22   It is difficult to determine the size of the group that attacked the yamen and occupied the city. Huang Hsing-tsai, a participant, says he brought eight or nine hundred men from Lao-an market alone. Hua and adjacent Chün district were areas of maximum sect strength and the participation in the attack by many high-ranking sect leaders probably meant that each brought a considerable following. I have the names of only twenty-seven individuals who attacked the district yamen, many of whom were leaders, and testimony from six of them. KCT 018146, 20/3/25 Chao Te; NYC 38.7–10, 19/3/14 Wang Chin-tao; KCT 016703, 19/11/2 Wang Hsueh-tao; NYC 30.36–38, 18/12/12 Huang Hsing-tsai; KCT 015774, 19/6/20 Liu Ta-shun; CFCL 41.1–2, 19/5/22 Wang Chung.

      Other accounts of the attack on the yamen are NYC 31.18–21, 18/12/16 Niu Liang-ch'en; CFCL 29.1–6, 18/12/26 Niu Liang-ch'en; NYC 32.12–16, 18/12/3 Ch'in Li; CFCL 3.22–23, 18/9/18 Sung Hsing and others; CFCL 28.11–13, 18/12/24 Liu Tsung-lin; *Hua district gazetteer* 8.81–85.

      There were actually eighteen other prisoners in jail at that time. Information about the subsequent behavior of these and other prisoners freed by the Eight Trigrams may be found in Randle Edwards, Chang Wejen, and Chang Ch'en Fu-mei (trans.), "Voluntary Surrender: Cases and Materials," item 21. I am grateful to Randle Edwards for this information.

23   Those killed included six secretaries (*mu-yu* 幕友) to the magistrate; two children and one concubine of those secretaries; three relatives of the magistrate, including his daughter-in-law; the constable; another *mu-yu*; twenty-one of the magistrate's household servants; a visiting relative of the director of schools; the director of schools' wife, daughter-in-law, two daughters, and two grandsons; other of his relatives by marriage, and household servants (eleven

people); the Green Standard army sergeant; the subdistrict deputy-magistrate. The subdirector of schools (who was over seventy years old) was not killed. The director of schools survived his jump into the well (presumably an attempted suicide) with only a broken shoulder. For these and other facts about the attack on Hua city see CFCL 32.29–30, 19/3/12 Memorial; CFCL 40.17–18, 19/4/26 Memorial; NYC 34.23–25, 18/12/16 Memorial; CFCL 1.32–33, 18/9/15 Memorial; *Hua district gazetteer* 12.1–4.

24 CFCL 1.3–4, 18/9/12 Memorial; CFCL 1.6–9, 18/9/13 Memorial; CFCL 1.13–16, 18/9/14 Memorial; NYC 32.25–26, 18/12/8 Ch'in Li.

25 CFCL 1.6–9, 18/9/13 Memorial; *Tung-ming district gazetteer* 1.18–19, 2.2–3; CFCL 1.13–16, 18/9/14 Memorial (this report exaggerates the seriousness of the situation at Tung-ming).

26 CFCL 29.1–6, 18/12/26 Hsu An-kuo; CFCL 5.14–16, 18/9/22 Chu Ch'eng-chen.

27 CFCL 29.1–6, 18/12/26 Hsu An-kuo; CFCL 5.14–16, 18/9/22 Chu Ch'eng-chen; *Chi-ning district gazetteer* 4.20–29; SYT 233–42, 22/6/20 Hu Ch'eng-te; CFCL 19.33–36, 18/11/18 Memorial.

28 SYT 233–42, 22/6/20 Hu Ch'eng-te; SYT 325–30, 22/6/30 Hu Ch'eng-te. Hu had spent his years in Honan supporting himself by growing wheat, driving a cart, carrying water, bowing cotton, doing everyday chores and, when there was no work, begging.

29 I have the names of twenty-three. CFCL 2.24–26, 18/9/16 Memorial; SYT 233–42, 22/6/20 Hu Ch'eng-te; CFA 64, 20/3/20 Ts'ai Wu-k'uei; KCT 016750, 19/11/13 Li Ch'eng; KCT 016869, 19/11/18 Chao Fei-i and Chao Fei-jen; CFCL 26.15–16, 18/12/15 Ts'ai K'e-chia; CFCL 28.35–36, 18/12/25 Fang T'ing-yü and Liu Chu; CFCL 26.43–44, 18/12/16 Liu Kuei; CFCL 29.12–13, 18/12/26 P'ang Erh-ma and others; CFCL 7.10–12, 18/9/28 Ma Ch'ao-tung.

30 KCT 016750, 19/11/13 Li Ch'eng.

31 CFCL 26.15–16, 18/12/15 Ts'ai K'e-chia; CFA 64, 20/3/20 Ts'ai Wu-k'uei.

32 CFCL 19.33–36, 18/11/18 Memorial; CFCL 2.24–26, 18/9/16 Memorial; KCT 016869, 19/11/18 Chao Fei-jen; KCT 016750, 19/11/13 Li Ch'eng. For prisoners see Randle Edwards et al., "Voluntary Surrender," item 21.

33 SYT 233–42, 22/6/20 Hu Ch'eng-te; CFCL 4.14–16, 18/9/19 Memorial; KCT 016869, 19/11/18 Chao Fei-jen.

34 I know the names of twenty-eight participants. KCT 019320, 20/7/18 Chao Chen-wu; CFCL 42.28–29, 21/5/10 Li Fa-yen; KCT 016869, 19/11/18 Chao Fei-i; CFCL 42.26–27, 21/4/2 Chou Wen-sheng; SYT 215, 21/11/26 Li Hsing-tien; SYT 9–10, 24/5/3 Ho Ch'ing-k'uei; SYT 131–32, 22/1/29 Ts'ao Hsing-ssu; CFCL 29.12–13, 18/12/26 Hsu Feng-yun; CFCL 21.28–32, 18/11/24 Tsung-yin and Chang Chih; CFCL 12.5–7, 18/10/17 Ts'ao Kuang-hui; NYC 32.36, 18/12/17 Memorial.

35 KCT 018902, 20/6/16 Chao Chen-wu; KCT 019320, 20/7/18 Chao Chen-wu.

36 KCT 019320, 20/7/18 Chao Chen-wu; CFCL 19.33–36, 18/11/18 Memorial; Randle Edwards et al., "Voluntary Surrender," item 21. The magistrate had been transferred and there was only an acting magistrate (without his family) in residence. This situation may have contributed to the lack of leadership in this district.

37 *Chi-ning district gazetteer* 4.20–29; *Chin-hsiang district gazetteer* 9.14; Sheng Ta-

shih, *Ching-ni chi,* 2.1–6 (this account has details about preventive measures taken by Magistrate Wu, as does the *Chi-ning district gazetteer* 4.30–35).

38   CFCL 4.14–16, 18/9/19 Memorial; CFCL 5.14–16, 18/9/22 Memorial.

39   These were members of the Hung-ch'üan 紅拳 (Red Boxing) Assembly, led by Chang Ching-wen. Chang had been in this sect for many years and had learned from his father and grandfather the system of boxing which gave his group its name. CFCL 23.39–41, 18/12/6 Chang Lin-chih and Chang Ching-wen; CFCL 15.1–2, 18/10/29 Liu Ching-t'ang.

40   CFCL 15.18–20, 18/11/1 Liu Ch'eng; NYC 33.22–32, 18/12/20 Wanted list.

41   KKCK 235.1, 18/10/27 Liu Chin-te; KKCK 221.1–3, 18/10/16 Tung Kuo-tai.

42   They intended to kill the *kuan min* 官民, officials and ordinary citizens, of Peking. KKCK 235.1, 18/10/27 Liu Chin-te; CFCL 17.4–7, 18/11/6 Ch'ü Ssu; KKCK 202.1, 18/9/19 Lin Ch'ing; KKCK 229.1–2, 18/10/23 Sun Fa and Han Ta-tzu; CSL 281.21–24, 18/12/24 Edict.

43   KKCK 227.3, 18/10/21 Ch'ü Ssu; KKCK 207.1, 18/9/24 Liu Hsing-li; KKCK 208.1, 18/9/24 Ch'ü Ssu; CFCL 17.4–7, 18/11/6 Ch'ü Ssu. See Appendix 1 for the texts of Ch'ü Ssu's testimony.

There are several terms used by the rebels themselves to describe the violent acts that would constitute their rebellion. *Nao-shih* 鬧事, meaning "to cause trouble, make an uproar, be involved in activities which are out of control," is the most common phrase. Another common term is *tsao-fan* 造反, "to rise up against, to make a rebellion." Rebels also sometimes said *ch'i-shih* 起事, "to start the affair, to rise up in rebellion." The single character *fan* 反 is used occasionally to refer simply to the state of being in rebellion against the government. All these terms are relatively neutral or positive in their connotations, and (with the exception of *fan*) were not used by the Ch'ing government. The government used terms such as *luan* 亂, "chaos or disorder," *ni* 逆, "rebellion aimed at the heart of the dynasty," or *mou-fan* 謀反, a general term for plotting rebellion. The government called the rebels *tsei-fei* 賊匪, "violent bandits," or *chiao-fei* 教匪, "sect bandits." For more on this subject see my article "Die Chinesische Terminologie für Rebellen," *Saeculum* 23:4 (1972): 374–96.

44   CFCL 3.9–13, 18/9/18 Liu Te-ts'ai; KKCK 207.1, 18/9/23 Liu Chin; KKCK 221.1–3, 18/10/16 Tung Kuo-t'ai; KKCK 235.1, 18/10/27 Liu Chin-te; KKCK 205.1, 18/9/18 Lin Ch'ing; CSL 282.22, 19/1/15 Edict.

Nowhere in the confessions do the rebels discuss why they chose the noon hour, nor is there any mention of their intent to go directly to the Great Interior. The emperor speculated about their choice of the noon hour-period. I have read back from what happened to suggest what they intended. The gates were poorly guarded and they did go directly to the Great Interior.

45   CFCL 42.31–34, 21/6/3 Liu Yü-lung; SYT 157–59, 21/2/13 Tung Kuo-t'ai.

46   These generalizations are based on data available for 126 of the 239 known participants in the palace attack (i.e., 52 percent). These and subsequent figures on the number of participants in the palace attack are entirely my own. No list of participants as such is available in the source material. Government figures are very approximate (e.g., "there were about two hundred rebels in all"). Lin Ch'ing himself gave various estimates ranging from 100 to 140, and Tung Kuo-t'ai said there were "about a hundred." (KKCK 205.1,

18/9/18 Lin Ch'ing; CFCL 4.5–9, 18/9/19 Lin Ch'ing; KKCK 204.1, 18/9/19 Tung Kuo-t'ai.) The actual figure was much higher. I made up my lists on the basis of all those arrested over a five year period and those named in their confessions. My figures should be taken as a minimum, for there were surely some who avoided government discovery and I have included no one for whom there was not reasonable evidence.

I divided these participants into two categories: those who actually left home and started for Peking, and those who knew that the rebellion would occur but stayed at home on 9/15. In cases where there is no more evidence than the person's word that he did or did not leave home that day, I have followed the conclusions drawn by the Board of Punishments—they had access to much more information and made a careful effort to distinguish between those who went and those who did not (in order to assign the proper punishment).

My totals for those involved in the palace attack are, therefore, as follows: for the Tung-hua Gate, 107 actually went and 27 knew but remained at home; for the Hsi-hua Gate, 132 went and 68 knew but did not go. A total of 239 men left home that day, 103 (including 8 not associated with either gate) remained behind; 342 in all. Subsequent generalizations and "statistics" will be based on information available about these men. Other generalizations have been made on the basis of information about all those who lived in the Peking area and belonged to one of the component groups of Lin Ch'ing's K'an Trigram at one time or another, some of whom may not have been involved in the rebellion. (See Part One, n. 5.)

47 Even including the people who did not go into the city, the two groups numbered 134 (for the east) and 200 (for the west). This partially reflects the larger number of sect members living in villages to the west and south of Peking. It is possible that the rebels knew that the empress's quarters were located on the western side of the Great Interior and planned accordingly. For the empress see CFCL 2.7–12, 18/9/16 Memorial from Mien-ning and Mien-k'ai. For banners and groups of ten, see KKCK 205.1, 18/9/18 Lin Ch'ing.

48 I have information as to the ages of 167 of the 239 who actually left home to participate in the palace attack.

Age	No. of men	%
under 19	6	4
in 20s	28	17
in 30s	57	34
in 40s	47	28
in 50s	17	10
in 60s	8	5
over 70	4	2

49 The actual figure for those with relatives involved must be assumed to be greater than this. For many people there is no information on family one way or the other, and flat denials ("I have no brothers," "my father knew nothing about it") must be taken as possible lies. I have assumed a brother or cousin

relationship for men from the same village whose surname and first character of their proper name were the same (e.g., Sung Chin-yao and Sung Chin-hui). At least 180 (of the total 342)had either a father, son, brother, or cousin in the sect. Of these, 113 had brothers or cousins, 112 had fathers or sons, and at least 45 had both a brother or cousin and a father or son in the sect.

50 There were 44 known hired laborers in the entire K'an Trigram group; of these, 37 participated in (30) or knew about (7) the rebellion. We know the dates when 26 of these 37 joined the sect. Nearly all of them (23) joined during 1812 and 1813, and nearly half (12 of those 26) joined in the last two months prior to the uprising. Of the 37 involved in the plans for rebellion, 21 (57 percent) were recruited to the sect by someone for whom they had done hired labor (but not all at the last minute). The overall pattern is not conclusive, but if we look at several of the sect leaders, it becomes clear that hired agricultural workers were brought into the sect as pupils like other members of a teacher's household. Li Lao and his family had eight hired laborers whom they converted, Ch'ü Ssu brought in six, Chu Hsien five. It was obviously safer, particularly at the last minute, to have these men as insiders rather than outsiders. For Li Lao see KCT 017742, 20/2/1 Liu Ta; KCT 017966, 20/2/28 Liu Ta; KKCK 225.1, 18/10/18 Liu Chin-ts'ai; KKCK 220.1–2, 18/10/15 Chang Tzu-sheng; KKCK 235.1–2, 18/10/27 Wang Lao; SYT 133–36, 19/8/9 Liang Chuang-r; SYT 113–15, 21/11/15 Wang Chin-fu; SYT 359–62, 20/9/26 Wu Hsi. For Ch'ü Ssu see KKCK 226.1, 18/10/19 Chu Liu-t'ao-r; CFA 16, 19/4/12 Chang Ch'i; KKCK 214.2, 18/10/9 Kao Wu; KKCK 215.1, 18/10/9 Liu Kou-r; KCT 015579, 19/2*/16 Tai Wu. See Appendix 1 for some of these confessions. For Chu Hsien see SYT 41–42, 20/2/3 Hu Ming-chu; SYT 41–42, 20/5/4 Liu P'ang-hsiao-tzu; SYT 213–14, 20/2/20 Tung Kuo-t'ai; KKCK 223.1–3, 18/10/17 Memorial; SYT 273–74, 20/4/24 Liu Hsi-r; CFA 2, 19/2/26 Mrs. Chu Hsing.

51 For descriptions of the cloth, see KCT 017330, 19/2*/21 Han Ts'un-lin and KCT 017262, 19/12/17 Jen San. Chang Ta-ts'ui bought five feet of cloth for 500 cash (KCT 016531, 19/10/7 Chang Ta-ts'ui). For Lin Ch'ing's cloth purchases see KKCK 221.1–3, 18/10/16 Tung Kuo-t'ai. Lin could have purchased three feet of cloth for about 170–200 people. A Chinese foot was somewhat smaller than our twelve inches.

52 KKCK 208.1, 18/9/24 Ch'ü Ssu; CFCL 2.4–7, 18/9/16 Memorial.

53 CFCL 2.12–14, 18/9/16 Memorial. The Chinese text reads:

同心合我
永不分離
四季平安

54 For iron bars see KKCK 229.1–2, 18/10/23 Han Ta-tzu; KKCK 214.1–2, 18/10/9 Li Yuan-lung; KKCK 225.3, 18/10/19 Pien Wen-liang. For Li Ch'ao-tso see KKCK 212.1, 18/10/3 Li Lan. For refusal to make more than three see KKCK 209.1–2, 18/9/28 Li Lao. For Li Wu see KKCK 197.1, 18/11/4 Edict and Chang T'ien-sheng. One of the eunuchs used a double-bladed sword two feet long (and one inch wide) with his name on it. CFCL 3.4–5, 18/9/18 Memorial.

55 KKCK 209.1–2, 18/9/28 Li Lao; SYT 91–93, 20/1/10 Ma Wen-t'ung; SYT

135–36, 19/8/9 Liang Chuang-r; SYT 395–97, 19/11/24 Wang San; KKCK 211.1, 18/9/29 Li Yü-lung; KKCK 210.1, 18/9/29 Li Shih-hung; KKCK 225.1, 18/10/18 Liu Chin-ts'ai; KKCK 220.1–2, 18/10/15 Chang Tzu-sheng; KKCK 235.1–2, 18/10/27 Wang Lao; SYT 359–62, 20/9/26 Wu Hsi; KKCK 224.3, 18/10/18 Kao Ch'eng; KKCK 211.1, 18/9/29 Chang Lao; KCT 017623, 20/1/26 Pien Erh; KCT 017262, 19/12/17 Jên San; SYT 471–73, 19/12/18 Jen San; KCT 017189, 19/12/13 Tung Erh; SYT 301–03, 20/2/28 Chu Mo-r; KKCK 213.1, 18/10/8 Han Fu; SYT 205–08, 20/7/11 Hao Pa; SYT 59–61, 21/10/12 Chang Ch'i; SYT 303–05, 19/12/10 Kao Liu; SYT 85–86, 19/12/3 Meng Ta-t'ou; SYT 257–59, 20/9/21 Sung Erh.

56 One man was given 400 cash. Each member of Li Wu's group was given 200 cash by Lin Ch'ing the night before. KKCK 229.1–2, 18/10/23 Han Ta-tzu; KKCK 213.1, 18/10/3 Li Ming. Knives cost 350 or 500 cash. KKCK 211.1, 18/9/29 Li Yü-lung; SYT 91–93, 20/1/10 Ma Wen-t'ung.

The cost of outfitting and feeding all the participants in the palace attack can be roughly estimated at between 200,000 and 300,000 cash, or 120–175 taels—assuming about 300 for cloth, 400 for a knife, and 200 for a meal, for between 200 and 300 people. Most of this expense was borne by sect leaders, especially (at least half) by Lin Ch'ing. The gifts Lin received from his pupils in the south alone were more than sufficient to cover these costs.

57 SYT 93–94, 20/10/14 Jen Tzu-kuei.

58 See KKCK 229.1, 18/10/23 Sun Fa; SYT 251–54, 20/9/21 Liu Ch'i-wu; KCT 017623, 20/1/26 Pien Erh; SYT 131–32, 22/10/18 Wang Pao; SYT 81–83, 22/11/8 Ch'en Sheng; SYT 117–19, 22/11/10 Wei Hsien-chieh; SYT 351–53, 22/11/29 Wang Ch'eng; KKCK 221.1–3, 18/10/16 Tung Kuo-t'ai.

59 SYT 171–90, 22/9/14 Hai-k'ang, Ch'ing-yao, and Ch'ing-feng.

60 CFCL 16.30–35, 18/11/5 Ts'ao Lun; KKCK 227.3, 18/10/21 Ts'ao Fu-ch'ang; KKCK 231.1, 18/10/26 Ts'ao Fu-ch'ang.

Ts'ao Lun maintained that he had not proselytized among his army unit and had no followers at Tu-shih Pass. A government investigation confirmed this. Nevertheless, Ts'ao had been told to convert followers among his soldiers as early as 1811 and might have done so. His explanation that "they wanted me to bring new people into the assembly, and although I said at the time that I would, later on the more I thought about it, the more afraid I got, and so in the end I recruited no one" is not entirely convincing. It is likely that Lin Ch'ing considered Ts'ao Lun a good advertisement for his cause even if Ts'ao had no pupils—Lin did brag to a potential rebel that he had not only eunuchs but an officer in the Ch'ing military establishment as part of his group. After all, Ts'ao Lun might have brought his unit over to the rebel side had the palace attack been a success. See CFCL 16.30–35, 18/11/5 Ts'ao Lun; CFCL 22.37–38, 18/11/30 Memorial; CFCL 35.21–25, 19/2/10 Yang Yü-shan.

61 KKCK 227.3, 18/10/21 Ts'ao Fu-ch'ang. See Brunnert and Hagelstrom, ♯731 for this post.

62 KKCK 227.3 and 228.1, 18/10/21 Ts'ao Fu-ch'ang.

63 An-shun did not return to Peking until after the palace attack. When he finally located his mother and the rest of his household, he found Wang Wu and started to question him about his connections with Lin Ch'ing. Wang told him that he had been to Lin Ch'ing's house only once and perhaps his

name hadn't been written down on their lists, he didn't know. An-shun "wanted to turn him in but I realized that my family was a rather prominent one and that to have such a man associated with us would not look good. I couldn't make up my mind, so I didn't turn him in immediately." In fact, An-shun helped Wang plan his flight, but before Wang could leave, his name was mentioned in another confession and he was arrested. KKCK 231.1–3, 18/10/26 An-shun; KKCK 232.1–3, 18/10/26 Wang Wu.

64 Quote is from KKCK 221.1–3, 18/10/16 Tung Kuo-t'ai. See also KKCK 219.1–2, 18/10/14 Liu Fu-shou, Sung Wei-yin, and Tung Po-ying.

65 Most districts were divided into zones (usually called *hsiang* 鄉), for each of which the magistrate appointed a resident to serve as *ti-pao*, a kind of local constable or resident agent of the magistrate. Ch'u T'ung-tsu describes his responsibilities as follows: "The *ti-pao* served as the messenger to the magistrate, whose orders he passed on to the villagers or ward residents. It was also his duty to keep an eye on suspicious persons and to report cases of robbery, homicide, salt smuggling, fire, etc. He could report minor disputes . . . but he was not authorized to settle them." Ch'u goes on to point out that "a *ti-pao* was merely a man rendering service to the yamen, and as such he had a very inferior social status. He was often beaten by the magistrate for failing to report or carry out assignments promptly" (*Local Government in China under the Ch'ing*, p. 4). From the point of view of those engaged in illegal activity, the *ti-pao* was in essence a resident informer for the government. Several instances in which these quasi-officials became sources of information for the government about the Eight Trigrams are described in Part Three, "Discovery."

66 CPT 439–40, 18/10/30 Edict; SYT 419–22, 22/9/27 Ch'iu Tzu-liang. The government ultimately investigated this charge late in the 10th month of 1813, but did not probe into it. Ch'iu Tzu-liang did not mention his services to the rebels at this time, and only did so when he was arrested and questioned in the fall of 1817.

67 For Chu Hsien and family, see CPT 447–48, 18/11/25 Li Lu-tzu; KCT 016304, 19/8/16 Tung Kuo-t'ai; KCT 016763-E, 19/10/20 Wanted list; KCT 017364, 19/2/26 Mrs. Chu Hsing; SYT 375–77, 19/12/14 Chu Lung.

It was Chu's second wife, Miss Lung, who brought the family into the Jung-hua Assembly. She and her brothers were pupils of Sung Chin-hui and, after marrying Chu Hsien, Miss Lung converted first his mother and then the other members of the household. See KCT 017364, 19/2/26 Mrs. Chu Hsing; CFA 50, 20/2/3 Mrs. Chu Hsing.

For *ling-ts'ui*, see Robert H. G. Lee, *The Manchurian Frontier in Ch'ing History*, pp. 25–29.

Chu Hsien had studied boxing with Lin Ch'ing's associate from Honan, Feng K'e-shan, but his temperament appears to have been more pacific. His daughter-in-law related that "a few years before, Chu Hsien and his mother had gone to the T'an-che temple to burn incense. When they returned Chu Hsien had said, 'It is so secluded and quiet in the mountains. If one could just live there and cultivate oneself, it would be easy to be happy' " (KCT 017364, 19/2/26 Mrs. Chu Hsing; CFCL 29.1–6, 18/12/26 Niu Liang-ch'en).

For Chinese bondservants in general, see Jonathan D. Spence, *Ts'ao Yin and the K'ang-hsi Emperor: Bondservant and Master* (New Haven: Yale University Press, 1966). For more on banner lands around Peking, see Muramatsu Yuji, "Banner Estates and Banner Lands in 18th Century China—Evidence from Two New Sources," *Hitotsubashi Journal of Economics* 12, no. 2 (1972): 1–13.

68 This is his brother-in-law, Chao Han-ch'en's, version, which is clearly self-serving. In fact it is likely that Chao already knew that Chu Jui was in the sect and he was probably a member himself. It was Chao's sister, Chu Jui's wife, who herself had taught the sect to her adopted grandson the previous year. Sources for this account are SYT 291–97, 19/3/15 Chu Hai-ch'ing; CFCL 39.40–42, 19/3/16 Chu Hai-ch'ing; CFCL 39.37–39, 19/3/14 Shan-kuei and Chu Kuei-shan; SYT 463–65, 19/12/18 Chao Han-ch'en; KCT 017259, 19/12/17 Chao Han-ch'en; SYT 467–69, 19/12/18 Mrs. Chu Hsing; SYT 299–316, 19/3/15 Statements by various members of the Yü Prince's staff.

69 CSL 288.7–10, 19/3/21 Edict; CFCL 39.45–47, 19/3/18 Edict. The normal punishment for knowing of a rebellion in advance and not reporting it was 100 blows and exile at a distance of 3,000 li. For a member of the imperial clan this was normally converted to deprivation of two years' salary. Because Yü-feng had already had his title taken away, it was decided that he should continue to receive his salary, but be made to pay up all back fines and remain under house arrest. This decision was made by a joint recommendation of the Imperial Clan Court, the Grand Council, and the presidents of the Six Boards. Yü-feng had been interrogated by the Grand Council and Imperial Clan Court before sentencing, but transcripts of his statements were not included with the normal Grand Council records. CFCL 39.40–42, 19/3/16 Memorial; CFA 10, 19/3/16 Memorial; CFCL 39.45–47, 19/3/18 Edict.

70 Brunnert and Hagelstrom, #795B. This official was under the authority of the prefect of Shun-t'ien prefecture and was one of four such subprefects responsible for the area around Peking.

71 KKCK 226.1, 18/10/21 Chang Pu-kao; CFCL 15.11–13, 18/10/30 Memorial from the Grand Council.

72 This official was a subordinate of the magistrate of Wan-p'ing (the district directly to the west and south of Peking). See Brunnert and Hagelstrom, #857.3. Sources for the following account are KKCK 226.1–3, 18/10/21 Ch'en Shao-jung; KKCK 227.1, 18/10/21 Sung Chin-jung; KKCK 230.1–3, 18/10/25 Ch'en Chü-chou.

73 Governor-General Wen Ch'eng-hui was at that moment involved in preparations for procuring the men and material needed for the campaign against Li Wen-ch'eng in the south. For quote about cheaper flour, see Part, Two, n. 135.

74 Ch'en Shao-jung continued to make arrests in the Sung-chia area. On 9/22, when he was passing through one village, the *ti-pao* there informed him that a young woman who was the wife of a rebel had turned herself in. Ch'en took this woman (Mrs. Chu Hsing, Chu Hsien's daughter-in-law) to his yamen and then kept her there, refusing either to try her case or to release her. Late in the 9th month, when responsible officials were being investigated

and punished for allowing Lin Ch'ing to plot rebellion, Ch'en, hoping to reduce his punishment, pointed out that he had learned about Lin Ch'ing in advance. He was dismissed from his post nevertheless, and kept Mrs. Chu Hsing with his household when they moved from the yamen. In the 11th month of that year, after he was interrogated and his case settled, Ch'en was released and returned home. He kept the young woman as his concubine, and later, when he found employment as a tutor for a family in the capital, he brought her along with him. Finally, in the 2d month of 1814 Mrs. Chu Hsing's identity and connections with the rebel leadership were discovered, she was arrested, and Ch'en was punished. SSTC, 18/9/29 Memorial from the Censorate; KCT 017364, 19/2/26 Mrs. Chu Hsing; SSTC, 19/2*/7 Memorial from the Grand Council and Board of Punishments.

75 Yet another example of these quasi-official government agents failing to do their duty can be cited. Liu Chin-pao had been a member of Yang Pao's Ta-sheng sect until 1811, when the sect was investigated. His son, brother, and nephew continued in the sect and were among those under Yang Pao who acknowledged Lin Ch'ing's leadership and became part of his K'an Trigram. In 1813, however, Liu was serving as a *hsiang-yueh* 鄉約, a head of a rural zone, similar to a *ti-pao*. He was busy helping prepare soldiers to be sent on campaign in Honan and made no effort to report the planned Peking uprising to the local magistrate. Nonetheless, it is unlikely that Liu Chin-pao was unaware of his friends', relatives', and fellow-villagers' part in organizing the palace attack. For *hsiang-yueh*, see Ch'u T'ung-tsu, *Local Government*, p. 204. For Liu, See SYT 209–11, 20/7/11 Liu Chin-pao.

76 CFCL 2.27–29, 18/9/17 Edict.

77 There are twenty-two known members of this group who left home for Peking, and four others who remained at home. For their names see my "Eight Trigrams Uprising of 1813," Part Three, n. 77.

   Those name lists represented my efforts to bring some kind of order to documentary material that is considerably less clear. Furthermore, almost every sect member or rebel was known by more than one name. Government interrogators asked prisoners to give alternative names for people they mentioned, but in many cases I have had to assume probable identity between people based only on strong circumstantial evidence. I chose often arbitrarily between nicknames in order to assign one "real name" to each person. (For some alternate names, see index.) From those name lists and the accompanying sources, an interested reader would be able to recreate the original pool of information from which I drew my conclusions. Sources for the movements of this group are KKCK 204.1, 18/9/19 Liu Chin-t'ing; KCT 018919, 20/6/10 Liu Erh-ch'eng; SYT 267–68, 20/6/23 Liu Erh-ch'eng and Han Ta-tzu; SYT 209–11, 20/7/11 Liu Chin-pao; KKCK 204.1, 18/9/19 Fan Ts'ai; KKCK 229.1–2, 18/10/23 Han Ta-tzu; NYC 38.67–72, 20/9/6 Chang Feng and Tu Yu-r; KCT 019599, 20/8/20 Lu Ta-shui; SSTC, 18/11/18 Memorial from the Grand Council; KCT 016763-E, 19/10/20 Wanted list.

78 Forty-five men left for Peking. Twenty-six others knew about the plans but remained at home for one reason or another. For their names see my "Eight Trigrams Uprising of 1813," Part Three, n. 78. Sources for Li Wu's group

are: KKCK 205.1, 18/9/20 Memorial; SYT 419–22, 22/9/27 Ch'iu Tzu-liang; KKCK 221.1–3, 18/10/16 Tung Kuo-t'ai; SYT 121–24, 22/11/10 Tung Kuo-t'ai; SYT 423–24, 22/9/27 Mrs. Hsin Wang; SYT 117–19, 22/11/10 Mrs. Li Hsuan; SYT 85–86, 22/11/8 Mrs. Ch'en Li; CFA 53, 20/2/9 Pai Lai-tzu; SYT 253–54, 20/1/25 Memorial; KCT 016763-E, 19/10/20 Wanted list; SYT 137–54, 20/10/16 Wanted list; SYT 103–17, 23/11/9 Wanted list; CFCL 4.5–9, 18/9/19 Memorial; SYT 389–91, 21/6/30 Chang Ch'i-hua; KKCK 230.1, 18/10/24 Chang K'un; SYT 381–88, 23/4/29 Chang Lao-liu; SYT 259–60, 20/1/25 Chang Liu; KKCK 197.1, 18/11/4 Chang T'ien-sheng; SYT 81–83, 22/11/8 Ch'en Sheng; KCT 017330, 19/2*/21 Han Ts'un-lin; SYT 133–35, 22/10/18 Kao Chu; SYT 97–99, 19/7/7 Li T'ien-shou; KCT 015816, 19/6/26 Li T'ien-hsiang; CFA 45, 20/1/24 Mrs. Chang Liu and Chang Liu; SYT 255–57, 20/1/25 Mrs. Chang Liu; SYT 261, 20/1/25 Liu Hsing-t'ing; CFCL 2.2–4, 18/9/16 Sung Shang-chung; CFCL 2.40–43, 18/9/17 Sung Shang-chung; NYC 40.63–67, 21/6/18 Ts'ai Ming-shan; SYT 383–87, 21/6/30 Ts'ai Ming-shan; SYT 351–53, 22/11/29 Wang Ch'eng; SYT 317–25, 22/9/24 Wang Jui; SYT 349–51, 22/9/24 Wang Pi; SYT 131–32, 22/10/18 Wang Pao; SYT 117–19, 22/11/10 Wei Hsien-chieh; SYT 331–33, 22/9/24 Wang Liang; SYT 355–56, 22/9/24 Wu Hsien-ta; NYC 40.53–57, 21/5/27 Yü Ch'eng-r.

79 SYT 97–99, 19/7/7 Li T'ien-shou. For feast, SYT 381–88, 23/4/29 Chang Lao-liu.

80 NYC 40.63–67, 21/6/18 Ts'ai Ming-shan; SYT 383–87, 21/6/30 Ts'ai Ming-shan. I have combined these two confessions.

81 See n. 78; information on the palace attack itself may be found in the confessions of Chang Ch'i-hua, Mrs. Chang Liu, Chang K'un, Chang Lao-liu, Chang T'ien-sheng, Ch'en Sheng, Han Ts'un-lin, Liu Hsing-t'ing, Sung Shang-chung, Ts'ai Ming-shan, Wang Ch'eng, Wang Jui, Wang Pao, Wu Hsien-ta, and Yü Ch'eng-r.

82 Six members of this group went into Peking, seven did not. For their names see my "Eight Trigrams Uprising of 1813," Part Three, n. 82. KCT 017966, 20/2/28 Chang Erh-ch'iao and Liu Ta; CFA 59, 20/2/27 Keng Shih-an, Shih Kuei, and Shih San; SYT 337–39, 20/2/30 Keng Shih-an; SYT 109–11, 20/12/9 Wang Erh-tao; CFCL 27.41–43, 18/12/20 Memorial.

83 For information on this inn where many sect members spent the night see KCT 016531, 19/10/7 Chang Ta-ts'ui; SYT 301–03, 20/2/28 Chu Mo-r; CFA 59, 20/2/27 Keng Shih-an; SYT 337–39, 20/2/30 Keng Shih-an; CFA 68, 20/3/29 Chu Ch'iu; KKCK 211.1, 18/9/29 Chang Lao; SYT 359–62, 20/9/26 Wu Hsi.

84 For the names of these men see my "Eight Trigrams Uprising of 1813," Part Three, n. 84. SYT 147, 20/8/10 Ch'en Ssu; KKCK 216.1–2, 18/10/11 Li Liu; KKCK 229.1, 18/10/23 Sun Fa; SYT 203–09, 22/11/18 Tung Kuo-t'ai; KKCK 203.1, 18/9/19 T'ien Ma-r; SYT 251–54, 20/9/21 Liu Ch'i-wu; SYT 383, 19/7/26 Wang Ta-ming; CFA 37, 19/11/2 Mrs. Ho Su; CFA 53, 20/2/9 Mrs. Li Pei and Mrs. Hsueh Wang; CFCL 3.13–15, 18/9/18 Memorial; CFA 46, 20/1/25 Memorial; SYT 137–45, 20/10/16 Wanted list; KKCK 223.1–3, 18/10/17 Memorial; SYT 17–18, 20/3/3 Memorial; KCT 016763-E, 19/10/20 Wanted list.

85 For the names of the Ma-chü-ch'iao group see my "Eight Trigrams Uprising of 1813," Part Three, n. 85. KKCK 206.1–2, 18/9/22 Yang Chin-chung; KKCK 212.1, 18/10/3 Li Lan; KKCK 208.1, 18/9/25 Li Ch'ao-tso and Chao Mi; KKCK 209.1, 18/9/26 Kao Lao; KKCK 207.1, 18/9/24 Chao Tseng and Liu Hsing-li; CFCL 15.10, 18/10/29 Memorial; SYT 171–212, 22/9/14 Ch'ing-feng, Ch'ing-yao, and Hai-k'ang; SYT 43–44, 22/8/6 Ch'ing-yao; SYT 41–42, 22/9/3 Hai-k'ang; CFA 22, 19/5/9 Li Ch'ao-yu; CFA 17, 19/4/15 Li Ch'ao-yu; KKCK 211.2, 18/10/2 Li Chiu.

86 For the names of this group see my "Eight Trigrams Uprising of 1813," Part Three n. 86. Sources for those who came from Sung-chia village: KKCK 219.2, 18/10/14 Tung Po-ying; SYT 225–26, 19/4/12 Tung Kuo-t'ai; SYT 107, 20/1/20 Tung Kuo-t'ai; KKCK 235.1, 18/10/27 Chi Te-ch'uan; CFA 39, 19/11/2 Ho Shih-ch'eng; SYT 219–21, 19/4/12 Ho Shih-kuei; SYT 93–94, 20/10/14 Jen Tzu-kuei; SYT 17–18, 20/3/3 Sun Pa; KKCK 219.1–2, 18/10/14 Sung Wei-yin; SYT 419–21, 20/11/28 Sung Wen-ch'ao; KKCK 229.3, 18/10/23 Sung Wen-teng; CFCL 3.9–13, 18/9/18 Lin Ch'ing; SYT 251–54, 20/9/21 Liu Ch'i-wu; KKCK 222.1–2, 18/10/16 Kuo Ch'ao-chün; CFA 24, 19/5/18 Chia Wan-chin; KCT 019414, 20/8/4 Mrs. Lu Wang; CFCL 2.4–7, 18/9/16 Memorial; KCT 016763-E, 19/10/20 Wanted list; KKCK 203.1, 18/9/19 Hsiung Chin-ts'ai; KKCK 219.1, 18/10/14 Liu Fu-shou; CFCL 21.12–14, 18/11/23 T'ien Ch'i-lu; SYT 109, 20/1/10 Liu Pei-r.

    Sources for those from small adjacent villages: KKCK 214.1, 18/10/9 Chin Hei; KKCK 216.1–2, 18/10/11 Li Tai-jung and Li Liu; KKCK 205.1, 18/9/20 Memorial; SYT 133–45, 20/10/16 Wanted list; KKCK 203.1, 18/9/19 T'ien Ma-r and Liu San; CFCL 3.9–13, 18/9/18 Liu Te-ts'ai; plus the wanted list and confessions (above) of Liu Fu-shou, Hsiung Chin-ts'ai, and Tien Ch'i-lu.

87 For this dinner, see KKCK 213.1, 18/10/3 Chu Lin; KCT 017162, 18/12/10 Li Shih-kung; SYT 191–93, 20/6/18 Tung Kuo-t'ai.

88 KKCK 214.1, 18/10/9 Chin Hei.

89 For the names of those who went see my "Eight Trigrams Uprising of 1813," Part Three, n. 89. KKCK 204.1, 18/9/19 Ch'en Shuang; CFCL 3.9–13, 18/9/18 Liu Te-ts'ai; KKCK 207.1, 18/9/23 Liu Chin; KKCK 203.1, 18/9/19 Kung Shu; KKCK 213.1, 18/10/3 Chu Lin and Li Ming; KKCK 228.1–2, 18/10/22 Chu Yü; KKCK 220.1, 18/10/15 Li Feng-ch'uan; KCT 017094, 19/12/2 Sung Kuang-pi; SYT 121–24, 19/12/4 Sung Kuang-pi; KKCK 220.1, 18/10/15 Ch'ung Yung-an; KKCK 225.3, 18/10/19 Pien Wen-liang; KKCK 214.1, 18/10/9 Pien Fu-kuei; KKCK 214.1, 18/10/8 Ho Wan-chin; KKCK 229.1, 18/10/22 Li Feng-yin; SYT 375–77, 19/12/14 Chu Lung; KKCK 222.1, 18/10/16 Ma Sheng-chang; KCT 017199, 19/12/13 Chu Lung; KKCK 219.1, 18/10/14 Liu Fu-shou; SYT 247–49, 20/9/21 Wu Chin-ts'ai; SYT 113–36, 20/10/16 Wanted list; KKCK 205.1, 18/9/20 Memorial; SYT 103–17, 23/11/9 Wanted list; KKCK 212.1, 18/10/3 Liu Ch'ao-tung; KKCK 235.1, 18/10/27 Liu Chin-te; KCT 017364, 19/2/26 Mrs. Chu Hsing; KCT 017259, 19/12/17 Mrs. Chu Hsing; SYT 467–69, 19/12/18 Mrs. Chu Hsing; KKCK 215.1, 18/10/9 Ch'en Liang; SYT 463–65, 19/12/17 Chao Han-ch'en; SYT 291–97, 19/3/15 Chu Hai-ch'ing.

90 KCT 017364, 19/2/26 Mrs. Chu Hsing. See also SYT 291–97, 19/3/15 Chu

Hai-ch'ing. Chu Hsien did not enter the palace, escaped from Peking, and was never arrested; his relatives were all seized and punished. See Conclusion, n. 1.

91 KKCK 212.1, 18/10/3 Liu Ch'ao-tung.

92 For names see my "Eight Trigrams Uprising of 1813," Part Three n. 92. Sources for those from Yang-hsiu village are the confessions (see n. 55 above) of Li Lao, Li Shih-hung, Li Yü-lung, Wang Lao, Liang Chuang-r, Wu Hsi, Han Fu, Kao Ch'eng, Liu Chin-ts'ai and Pien Erh. Also KCT 016531, 19/10/7 Chang Ta-ts'ui; SYT 433–34, 19/7/29 Liu Pei-r; SYT 109, 20/1/10 Liu Pei-r; KKCK 213.1–2, 18/10/8 Wang Yu-yin; SYT 103–11, 23/11/9 Wanted list; SYT 113–32, 20/10/16 Wanted list.

Sources for those from T'i-shang, Chou-chia, and Ma-chü-ch'iao villages: SYT 133–38, 20/1/12 Ma Wen-liang and Ma Wen-ming; SYT 97–99, 20/1/10 Kan Niu-tzu, Chang Hsi, and Mrs. Ma Chang; SYT 325–26, 20/3/30 Pai Yü; SYT 81, 19/12/3 Wang Wu; CFA 68, 20/3/29 Chu Ch'iu; and the confessions (see n. 55 above) of Tung Erh, Ma Wen-t'ung, Jen San, Chang Ch'i, Kao Liu, Meng Ta-t'ou, Sung Erh, Wang San, Chu Mo-r, and Hao Pa.

93 KCT 017189, 19/12/13 Tung Erh.

94 KKCK 213.1, 18/10/8 An Kuo-t'ai. The case of An Kuo-t'ai is a good illustration of some of the difficulties that arise in evaluating rebel confessions. An maintained that he was not a sect member and had merely been asked by Ch'ü Ssu to join the rebellion. A fellow villager stated that An was at the meeting at Ch'ü Ssu's house on 9/10. Ch'ü Ssu and An Kuo-t'ai himself stated that An refused to participate in the palace attack and did not go into Peking on the 15th. On the other hand, another member of this group claimed that he saw An in Peking that day. In this case, the evidence is particularly contradictory, though somewhat greater in favor of An's not having gone. The Board of Punishments decided that he was simply a criminal who knew about the rebellion but did not participate in it. See An Kuo-t'ai confession above; KKCK 208.1, 18/9/24 Ch'ü Ssu; KKCK 211.2, 18/10/2 Chang Yung-jui; KKCK 214.1–2, 18/10/9 Li Yuan-lung; KKCK 223.1–3, 18/10/17 Memorial.

95 "Death if you went" quotation: SYT 245–48, 22/11/21 Ch'ü Ming-r. Ch'ü's instructions to men at Flower Market: SYT 227–34, 22/11/20 Ch'ü Ming-r.

96 KKCK 207.1, 18/9/23 Liu Chin; KKCK 203.1, 18/9/19 Kung Shu; CFCL 3.9–13, 18/9/18 Liu Te-ts'ai; KKCK 222.1, 18/10/16 Ma Sheng-chang; KKCK 204.1, 18/9/19 Ch'en Shuang; KKCK 220.1–2, 18/10/15 Chang Tzu-sheng; CFCL 7.32–34, 18/9/30 Edict; CFCL 1.2–17, 19/3/29 Edict; CFCL 22.22–23, 18/11/27 Edict; CFCL 2.2–4, 18/9/16 Memorial.

The government chose to minimize the rebel actions at this gate by not always including the eunuchs in the count and variously reporting the number of rebels who successfully entered as five, six, or seven. I know the names of six. They were Liu Te-ts'ai and Liu Chin, Ch'en Shuang, Kung Shu, Liu Chin-yü, and Chu Chen. The last was either Wang Shih-yu or Liu Ti-wu.

97 KKCK 236.1, 18/10/27 Liu San.

98 "They're rebelling!" (反了反了): SYT 395–97, 19/11/24 Wang San. For the scene at the gate see also KKCK 222.1, 18/10/16 Ma Sheng-chang; KKCK 214.2, 18/10/9 Kao Wu; KKCK 236.1, 18/10/27 Cheng Han-kuei.

For throwing away knives and cloth, see KCT 017303, 19/11/19 Ch'ü Fu-r; SYT 257–59, 20/9/21 Sung Erh; CFA 68, 20/3/29 Chu Ch'iu; KKCK 213.1, 18/10/3 Chu Ch'iu; SYT 91–93, 20/1/10 Ma Wen-t'ung; SYT 301–03, 20/2/28 Chu Mo-r; KCT 017262, 19/12/17 Jen San.

99 Sources for description of Tung-hua Gate group inside the palace: KKCK 203.1, 18/9/19 Kung Shu; KKCK 207.1, 18/9/23 Liu Chin; CFCL 3.9–13, 18/9/18 Liu Te-ts'ai; KKCK 204.1, 18/9/19 Ch'en Shuang; CPT 277, 18/9/23 Memorial from the Grand Council; CFCL 7.32–34, 18/9/30 Edict; CFCL 19.23–25, 18/11/18 Edict; CSL 277.24–25, 18/10/26 Edict; KKCK 230.3, 18/10/26 Memorial from the Grand Council; CFCL 2.7–12, 18/9/16 Memorial from Mien-ning and Mien-k'ai.

100 KKCK 203.1, 18/9/19 T'ien Ma-r; KKCK 212.1, 18/10/3 Li Lan; KKCK 216.1–2, 18/10/11 Li Liu; KKCK 214.1, 18/10/9 Chin Hei; KKCK 208.1, 18/9/25 Li Ch'ao-tso; KKCK 203.1, 18/9/19 Hsiung Chin-ts'ai; KKCK 204.1, 18/9/19 Fan Ts'ai; KCT 017330, 19/2*/21 Han Ts'un-lin; CFCL 21.12–14, 18/11/23 T'ien Ch'i-lu; CFCL 7.32–34, 18/9/30 Edict.

101 Sources for the Hsi-hua Gate group inside the palace are the confessions (see n. 100 above) of T'ien Ma-r, T'ien Ch'i-lu, Fan Ts'ai, and Hsiung Chin-ts'ai; KKCK 204.1, 18/9/19 Liu Chin-t'ing; KKCK 208.1, 18/9/25 Chao Mi; KKCK 206.1–2, 18/9/22 Kao Ta and Yang Chin-chung; KKCK 203.1, 18/9/19 Liu San; CFCL 2.40–43, 18/9/17 Sung Shang-chung; CFCL 2.1–2, 18/9/16 Memorial from the princes and ministers in Peking; CFCL 2.2–4, 18/9/16 Memorial from the Gendarmerie and Sung Shang-chung; CFCL 2.12–14, 18/9/16 Memorial from the Imperial Household; CPT 89–90, 18/9/16 Memorial from the Grand Council; CFCL 1.2–17, 19/3/29 Edict; SYT 239–40, 19/9/16 Memorial from the Grand Council; CFCL 2.7–12, 18/9/16 Memorial from Mien-ning and Mien-k'ai; CFCL 7.4–6, 18/9/27 Memorial from the Grand Council; CFCL 2.35–37, 18/9/17 Edict; CFCL 12.1–3, 18/10/17 Memorial from the Gendarmerie; CFCL 2.30–33, 18/9/17 Memorial.

102 Two months later, the Chia-ch'ing Emperor described an incident that supposedly occurred on the night of the 15th and that, he maintained, was described in rebel confessions. There is no mention of it in any rebel statements I have seen, and this appears a rather obvious example of Ch'ing tampering with the historical record in a minor way in order to make a point. According to the emperor:

> In the middle of the night, while government soldiers were making searches and arrests, there was a sudden rain and a peal of thunder. Two rebels were struck [by lightning] and fell into the canal, while many other rebels jumped into the water in fear. . . . All later confessed that during the peal of thunder they had seen the figure of the god Kuan-ti, and this had made them lose heart.

The figure of Kuan-ti, explained the emperor, had appeared in the distance amid the confusion of this moment of rain and thunder and, seeing him standing on the Wu Gate, the rebels had been terrified and lost their nerve. See CFCL 1.2–17, 19/3/29 Edict (in this edict the emperor described the

so-called ten miracles that protected the dynasty); CFCL 2.20–21, 18/9/16
Editorial commentary; CFCL 17.1–2, 18/11/6 Edict.

See Part Four, n. 184 for another example of the creation of an incident
to prove that the gods were on the side of the dynasty. The cult of Kuan-ti
關帝 (also known as Kuan-kung 關公 or Kuan Yü 關羽) was encouraged by
the Ch'ing government because he symbolized what C. K. Yang calls "the
civic values of loyalty, righteousness, and devoted support for the legitimate
political power" (*Religion in Chinese Society*, pp. 160–61).

103 KKCK 204.1, 18/9/19 Fan Ts'ai.
104 CFCL 21.12–14, 18/11/23 T'ien Ch'i-lu.
105 CFCL 2.33–34, 18/9/17 Memorial; CFCL 4.5–9, 18/9/19 Memorial; CFCL
7.4–6, 18/9/27 Memorial; CSL 277.22–23, 18/10/24 Edict; CSL 276.20–21,
18/10/11 Edict.
106 CPT 89–90, 18/9/16 Memorial from the Grand Council; KKCK 199.1–2,
18/9/16 Memorial.
107 His sons memorialized the following day describing their role in the fighting
and concluding, "Our mother the empress, the concubines of the second
rank and below, as well as we your sons and the nine imperial princesses
have been protected by our imperial father's might and good fortune and are
therefore all safe. We beg you to be comforted" (KKCK 201.1–2, 18/9/16
Memorial).

The Chia-ch'ing Emperor was effusive in his praise of his second son
Mien-ning. This was the son whom he had already (in 1799) chosen secretly
as his successor and who would rule from 1821 to 1850 as the Tao-kuang
Emperor. He was consequently delighted to see his judgment (which was
not public knowledge) confirmed and was surely proud to find that the
Manchu skills of the hunt and of battle had not been entirely lost in the
family. As a reward, Mien-ning was enfeoffed as the Chih 智 Prince and
had his salary doubled. Later historians have sometimes stated inaccurately
that Mien-ning was made heir-apparent because of his role in defending the
palace.

The participation of the future Tao-kuang Emperor in the Eight Trigrams
rebellion, although often inaccurately reported, has been one of the primary
reasons why this uprising achieved some distinction with historians. Western
visitors in Peking in the early twentieth century reported that in the Chung-
ho hall (which is not where the fighting took place) there was once an arrow
that could be seen embedded in the roof and that was allegedly shot by Tao-
kuang in his defense of the palace. I have been told by a recent visitor to
Peking that a plaque has been placed (more accurately) at the Lung-tsung
Gate to indicate where this arrow supposedly struck. In reality, Mien-ning
used a musket.

For the emperor's interlinear comments on his sons' memorial see SSTC,
18/9/16 Memorial from Mien-ning and Mien-k'ai. For Mien-ning's rewards
see CFCL 2.14–15, 18/9/16 Edict. For the selection of Mien-ning as heir, see
Arthur Hummel, *Eminent Chinese of the Ch'ing Period*, p. 574 (Fang Chao-ying's
biography of the Tao-kuang Emperor). For the arrow see L. C. Arlington
and William Lewisohn, *In Search of Old Peking*, pp. 37–39.

108 CFCL 1.29–32, 18/9/15 Chang Chien-mu.

109 KKCK 221.1–3, 18/10/16 Tung Kuo-t'ai; SYT 225–26, 19/4/12 Tung Kuo-t'ai; KKCK 219.1, 18/10/14 Liu Fu-shou; SYT 219–21, 19/4/12 Ho Shih-k'uei.

110 KKCK 219.1–2, 18/10/14 Sung Wei-yin, Liu Fu-shou, and Tung Po-ying; KKCK 228.1–2, 18/10/22 Chu Yü; KKCK 214.1, 18/10/9 Pien Fu-kuei; KKCK 214.1, 18/10/8 Ho Wan-chin; KKCK 213.1, 18/10/3 Chu Lin and Li Ming; KKCK 220.1, 18/10/15 Li Feng-ch'uan and Ch'ung Yung-an.

111 KKCK 221.1–3, 18/10/16 Tung Kuo-t'ai; SYT 271–72, 20/4/24 Tung Kuo-t'ai; SYT 331–33, 22/9/24 Wang Liang; KKCK 227.1–2, 18/10/21 Tung Kuo-t'ai; SYT 173–74, 21/1/25 Tung Kuo-t'ai; CFCL 3.9–13, 18/9/18 Lin Ch'ing. Those who arrested Lin Ch'ing included a sublieutenant (Brunnert and Hagelstrom, #752F) and men from the Imperial Household (Brunnert and Hagelstrom, #81).

112 KKCK 221.1–3, 18/10/16 Tung Kuo-t'ai; KKCK 219.1, 18/10/14 Liu Fu-shou and Sung Wei-yin; KKCK 228.1–2, 18/10/22 Chu Yü; KKCK 227.1, 18/10/21 Sung Chin-jung; CFCL 7.14–17, 18/9/28 Edict; CFCL 3.5–6, 18/9/18 Memorial; CFA 58, 20/2/12 Sung Chin-pao.

113 CFCL 3.5–6, 18/9/18 Memorial.

114 SSTC, 18/9/19 Memorial forwarded from the Shun-t'ien prefects; KKCK 226.1–3, 18/10/21 Ch'en Shao-jung.

115 CFCL 3.5–6, 18/9/18 Memorial.

116 Lin Ch'ing's confessions may be found in CFCL 3.9–13, 18/9/18 (alternate and more accurate text in KKCK 205.1); CFCL 4.5–9, 18/9/19 (alternate text in KKCK 202.1); KKCK 206.1, 18/9/21.

   Tung Kuo-t'ai was finally executed, by strangulation, in 1822 (SYT 407, Tao-kuang 2/10/28). His major statements about the Eight Trigrams are KKCK 204.1, 18/9/19; KKCK 219.2–3, 18/10/15; KKCK 221.1–3, 18/10/16; KKCK 224.1–2, 18/10/18; KKCK 225.1, 18/10/18; KKCK 227.1–2, 18/10/21; KKCK 229.3, 18/10/24; KKCK 233.1–3 and 234.1, 18/10/27; CFCL 17.4–7, 18/11/6; CFCL 20.33–34, 18/11/21; SYT 225–26, 19/4/12; SYT 91–93, 19/7/7; SYT 379, 19/7/26; SYT 431–32, 19/7/29; SYT 123–24, 19/11/9; SYT 169–73, 19/11/14; SYT 611–12, 19/12/25; SYT 107, 20/1/20; SYT 213–14, 20/2/20; SYT 271–72, 20/4/24; SYT 191–93, 20/6/18; SYT 209–10, 20/6/19; SYT 171–74, 21/1/25; SYT 121–24, 22/11/10; SYT 203–09, 22/11/18; SYT 371–73, 24/6/29.

117 KKCK 206.1, 18/9/21 Lin Ch'ing.

118 CFCL 5.24, 18/9/23 Edict.

119 See CFCL 2.40–43, 18/9/17 for the execution of those involved in the palace attack. As of the 6th month of 1816, 285 rebels had been executed (either by slicing, beheading, or strangulation), and 577 others who were sect members, relatives, or otherwise involved to a lesser degree had been sentenced with some form of banishment. CFCL 42.31–34, 21/6/3. Those banished were sent variously (under different statutes) to Sinkiang, Heilungkiang, or, in the case of women, Kwangtung, Fukien, Szechwan, or Kansu, usually to be the slaves of meritorious officials, government soldiers, or "barbarian" tribes. Considering the large number of sect members and their relatives who were sent to these areas, it seems more than possible that White Lotus teachings

were consequently disseminated in these places. For samples of these sentences see CFCL 22.25, 18/11/27 Memorial; SSTC, 18/11/27 Instructions to military-governors; CFCL 27.41–43, 18/12/20 Memorial; KKCK 223.1–3, 18/10/17 Memorial; CSL 281.5, 18/12/17 Memorial and edict.

120 Examples of this policy are too numerous to cite in full. The government was being pragmatic as well as merciful: "Ignorant people who practice these sects are very numerous, how could we kill or execute them all?" (NYC 28.23–26, 18/10/9 Edict). See also for some samples CFCL 14.8–11, 18/10/27 Edict; CFCL 1.17–18, 18/9/14 Edict; NYC 28.19–23, 18/10/1 Memorial from Na-yen-ch'eng; CFCL 19.9–13, 18/11/14 Edict; NYC 33.18–19, 19/1/4 Edict.

121 The list of proposed changes generated by this rebellion is very long and many of these proposals can be found in the *Ch'ing shih-lu*. Some of the more significant changes were increased supervision by local civil officials of Chinese bondservants and bannermen who lived in the countryside (for example, see CSL 277.29, 18/10/27 Edict; CFCL 24.1, 18/12/7 Edict; CSL 280.25, 18/12/15 Edict); closer supervision of eunuchs (SSTC, 19/5/16 Edict to the Grand Secretariat; CSL 276.7, 18/10/2 Edict); and improvement of weapons used by palace guards (CSL 275.28–29, 18/9/30 Edict; CSL 277.8, 18/10/19 Edict). Three months before the rebellion, some of the imperial bodyguards were found to be smoking opium (SYT 69, 18/6/14 Edict), but this was nowhere mentioned as a factor in the palace attack.

Part Four

1 I have the names of 1,090 people (almost all men) who belonged to an Eight Trigrams sect or to their rebellion but were not part of Lin Ch'ing's group (see Part One, n. 5). Of these, 133 came from districts in central Chihli and did not take part in the uprising. (Those from Ching and Ku-ch'eng numbered 99; those from Yung-nien 19, others 14.) Of those whose residence is known and who definitely belonged to a sect before the uprising took place, 123 came from Hua or Chün districts, 226 from Shantung.

Most of those known to be from Shantung came from Chin-hsiang district for it was there that massive arrests took place prior to the rebellion. The sect network there included at least 183 persons, all pupils of Ts'ui Shih-chün. If there were comparable networks in Ts'ao and Ting-t'ao districts, then the size of the sect in all of southwestern Shantung was probably at least 600 persons. This figure is corroborated by Hsu An-kuo, the teacher of these believers, who stated that he had "600 to 700 pupils" in Shantung (CFCL 29.1–6, 18/12/26).

Our information about Hua and Chün sect members is inadequate. Huang Hsing-tsai stated that his contingent alone for the initial attack on Hua consisted of 800–900 people (NYC 30.36–38, 18/12/12); the total size of this attacking group was probably several thousand (see Part Three, n. 22). There were extensive rebel networks in Hua and Chün and a prerebellion group of one or two thousand seems a good guess.

2 What follows is a summary of figures for all rebels killed, captured, or surrendered during the rebellion in the southern plain. Here, as throughout this

section, figures on the number of rebels killed are based on the reports of Ch'ing military commanders to the emperor. These estimates are usually given in round numbers, i.e., two to three hundred, six to eight thousand, and were not intended to be more precise. There is no way to check most of these figures, and I use them, with reservations, because there is nothing else.

(a) Shantung. Total of 4,400 killed and 2,800 captured alive. See CFCL 1.1–2, 18/9/12 Memorial; CFCL 3.19–21, 18/9/18 Memorial; CFCL 6.23, 18/9/26 Edict; CFCL 7.9–10, 18/9/28 Memorial; CFCL 9.5–6, 18/10/3 Memorial. One official estimated that 5,000 rebels had been eliminated in Shantung and 6,000 to 7,000 had fled to the west: CFCL 19.14–16, 18/11/16 Memorial from T'o-chin.

(b) In Hua and Chün districts during the 9th and 10th months 12,300 to 13,100 were killed and 1,500 captured. See CFCL 1.32–33, 18/9/15 Memorial; CFCL 3.22–23, 18/9/18 Memorial; CFCL 5.11–14, 18/9/22 Memorial; CFCL 8.1–3, 18/10/1 Memorial; CFCL 6.5–8, 18/9/26 Memorial; CFCL 11.1–4, 18/10/13 Memorial; NYC 28.32–35, 18/10/13 Memorial; CFCL 1.1–2, 18/9/12 Memorial; CFCL 9.22–25, 18/10/7 Memorial; NYC 34.13–14, 18/11/11 Memorial; NYC 29.10–11, 18/10/28 Memorial; NYC 29.1–3, 18/10/22 Memorial; NYC 29.5–6, 18/10/24 Memorial; NYC 29.22–23, 18/11/3 Memorial.

(c) In the battle of Tao-k'ou 9,000 to 10,000 were killed, 8,400 to 9,400 captured alive. See NYC 29.14–16, 18/11/1 Memorial.

(d) Battles in the vicinity of Hua city and mopping up in villages during the 10th, 11th, and 12th months (but not included above): 4,100 were killed, 800 were captured, and 1,650 surrendered as "refugees." See NYC 29.26–28, 18/11/6 Memorial; CFCL 24.3–7, 18/12/8 Memorial; NYC 30.36–38, 18/12/12 Memorial; CFCL 25.7–10, 18/12/12 Memorial; CFCL 18.23–25, 18/11/13 Memorial; CFCL 19.30–32, 18/11/18 Memorial; NYC 30.1–4, 18/11/14 Memorial; NYC 29.33–35, 18/11/11 Memorial; NYC 29.29–32, 18/11/11 Memorial; NYC 29.10–11, 18/10/28 Memorial; NYC 34.13–14, 18/11/11 Memorial; CFCL 19.4–9, 18/11/14 Memorial; CFCL 16.35–38, 18/11/5 Memorial.

(e) Retaking of Hua city: 36,000 to 38,000 were killed, 2,000 were captured, and 20,000 were "refugees." See NYC 31.1–4, 18/12/12 Memorial; NYC 33.4–5, 18/12/20 Memorial; NYC 35.16–17, 19/1/4 Memorial; NYC 31.8–12, 18/12/15 Memorial; Yang Fang, Nien-p'u, 3.33; CFCL 28.8–10, 18/12/23 Memorial; NYC 32.28–31, 18/12/25 Memorial.

(f) Li Wen-ch'eng's band in flight: 4,800 to 5,400 killed, 200 captured. See NYC 30.1–4, 18/11/14 Memorial; CFCL 21.16–20, 18/11/24 Memorial; NYC 30.22–25, 18/11/25 Memorial; NYC 31.25–27, 18/12/20 Memorial; CFCL 16.35–38, 18/11/5 Memorial; CFCL 19.4–9, 18/11/14 Memorial; CFCL 18.9–10, 18/11/11 Memorial.

These figures total 70,600 to 75,000 killed, and 37,350 to 38,350 captured or surrendered. The total of all those involved voluntarily or involuntarily was somewhere between 108,000 and 113,000 people. Those who died or were captured in the retaking of Tao-k'ou and Hua city totaled 75,000 to 79,000. Those who lost their lives or were seized in battles in the countryside numbered 32,600 to 34,100. Those involved in Honan and southern Chihli (as opposed to Shantung) totaled between 95,000 and 101,000. (For an estimate of the original size of the Hua city population see n. 15.)

3 KCT 016810, 19/11/15 Memorial.

4 NYC 34.23–25, 18/12/16 Chao Hsin-chieh statement. For the director and subdirector of schools see Brunnert and Hagelstrom, *Present Day Political Organization of China*, #857.5 and 857.6.

5 In Hua, Ts'ao, and Ting-t'ao, 18, 41, and 15 prisoners respectively were freed from jail by the rebels. Of these 74 men, 10 (all in Ts'ao) refused to take their freedom, 29 voluntarily surrendered to the government at a later date (having first enjoyed their liberty), 6 were re-arrested, and the other 29 escaped permanently, perhaps joining and dying with the Eight Trigrams. See Randle Edwards et al., "Voluntary Surrender," item 21. For freeing of prisoners see also KCT 016750, 19/11/13 Li Ch'eng.

6 SYT 143–46, 19/10/14 Wei Ping-ch'ün; SYT 177–78, 19/7/14 Wei Hsiu-te (his son).

7 CFCL 41.3–4, 19/7/6 Huang P'an-kung. For the testimony of children whose parents were killed for refusing to cooperate with the rebels, see SYT 153, 19/3/10 Ch'in Chu-r; SYT 159, 19/3/10 Chang Hei-hsiao-r; SYT 305–06, 19/4/18 List of children.

During the campaign against the Eight Trigrams, families were uprooted and many children were orphaned. Ch'ing soldiers took possession of some of these children, either buying or simply "adopting" them, and brought the children back with them to their posts when the campaign was over. This practice was contrary to army regulations, and when the Chia-ch'ing Emperor learned of it (three months after military operations were over), he ordered an investigation. Those children who were relatives of rebels or whose parents had been killed by the rebels were singled out (the former for punishment, the latter for rewards). Those who had living relatives were returned to them; those without family were allowed to remain with the soldiers who had brought them away. A minimum of one thousand children were involved. Although this practice was technically against the rules, these children were apparently considered legitimate booty, and even Grand Councillor T'o-chin allowed nearly sixty members of his staff to bring back children. The emperor censured the soldiers and commanders but did not punish them, saying instead that it was his own fault for not having explicitly forbidden this (i.e., reminded people of the regulations) and that he realized that "the campaign was concluded rather quickly." See CFCL 39.16–20, 19/3/10 Edict; SYT 137–66, 19/3/10 Memorial from the Grand Council; SSTC, 19/3/18 Memorial from T'o-chin; CFCL 39.8–9, 19/3/4 Memorial; SYT 413–15, 19/3/20 Memorial from the Grand Council; KCT 015669, 19/6/16 Memorial; KCT 015818, 19/6/26 Memorial.

As a result of these investigations, the testimony of several hundred children (detailed in several dozen cases) became part of the historical record. The following is typical and can serve as a sample; it is the statement of a girl named Ch'in Chu-r:

> I live in the north gate area of Hua district in Honan. Age fourteen. My grandparents died previously of illness. My father's name was Ch'in

Fu-kuei. In the 9th month of CC 18 White Lotus sect people were in the [Hua] city; they tried to force my father to join them, but he would not and so they killed him. My mother was Miss Kao. When she saw my father killed by the rebels, she jumped in the well and killed herself. My younger brother Man-k'un-r ran off somewhere. I wanted to run away. [After Hua city was retaken] the Lieutenant [so-and-so] of the Light Division told me he would take me to the capital [SYT 153, 19/3/10 Ch'in Chu-r].

8 SYT 177–78, 19/7/14 Wei Hsiu-te.

9 For some samples see SYT 489–90, 19/3/22 Pai-te; KCT 019478, 20/8/1 Sang Te; KCT 017805, 20/2/16 Li Yang-r; SYT 163, 19/3/10 Li Ching-r (child); KCT 017220, 19/12/22 Hsu Chan-kuei; SYT 443–44, 19/3/21 Yin Chin-te; SYT 307–16, 19/4/18 Grand Council list of children; SYT 321–22, 19/4/18 Grand Council list.

10 KCT 019478, 20/8/1 Sang Te.

11 KCT 015951, 19/7/7 Liu Ch'un-nü (child); KCT 016027, 19/7/24 Li Hsing-pang.

12 SYT 209–12, 19/9/14 Yang Chu-r.

13 SYT 157, 19/3/10 Chu Ch'un-niu (child); SYT 209–12, 19/9/14 Yang Chu-r (child); SYT 155, 19/3/10 Ch'en Hei (child); SYT 161, 19/3/10 Yang Yun-r (child).

14 SYT 177–78, 19/7/14 Wei Hsiu-te; SYT 155, 19/3/10 Ch'en Hei (child); SYT 157, 19/3/10 Chu Ch'un-niu (child); SYT 163, 19/3/10 Li Ching-r (child); KCT 015951, 19/7/7 Liu Ch'un-nü (child); NYC 34.23–25, 18/12/16 Chao Hsin-chieh.

15 In 1814 an official noted that in Hua city at market time there were at least 10,000 people (KCT 016527, 19/10/9 Memorial); the population prior to the rebellion was probably at least this size. In 1867 there were about 10,000 ting 丁 (male adults liable for labor services) in the city. If the same ratio of ting to "mouths" (口, individuals) existed for the city as for the countryside in that year, the city population was about 13,500 (*Hua district gazetteer* 5.32–33). For more on *ting*, households, "mouths," and population statistics, see Ho Ping-ti, *Studies on the Population of China, 1368–1953*, esp. part 1. For those killed or seized after the battle of Hua in the 12th month, see n. 2.

16 SYT 151–52, 19/3/10 Li Hsi-r (child); KCT 018635, 20/5/18 Memorial.

17 NYC 38.76–78, 20/9/10 Liu Chih-kao; CFCL 41.3–4, 19/7/6 Chao Ping-jang; CFCL 42.23, 21/3/27 Wang Erh-k'e-chia; CFCL 24.3–7, 18/12/8 Memorial; NYC 30.36–38, 18/12/12 Huang Hsing-tsai; KCT 017220, 19/12/22 Ch'eng Hua-t'ing.

18 NYC 29.29–32, 18/11/11 Memorial; CFCL 21.1–3, 18/11/23 Memorial; NYC 28.37–39, 18/10/17 Edict.

19 For the incident involving the K'ung family see CFCL 34.19, 19/2/4 Memorial. For Wang Liang-tao see CFCL 42.24–25, 21/3/28 Chu Ch'eng.

20 KCT 019320, 20/7/18 Chao Chen-wu.

21 CFCL 29.1–6, 18/12/26 Hsu An-kuo.

22 CFCL 42.24–25, 21/3/28 Tsung Yuan-te.

23 CFCL 28.23–24, 19/2*/14 Memorial; *Chi-ning district gazetteer* 4.20–29; *Chin-hsiang district gazetteer* 9.14.

24 SYT 305–06, 19/4/18 Wang Kuei-ni.

25 SYT 151–52, 19/3/10 Liu Hsi-r.

26 CFA 65, 20/3/24 T'ien Lien-yuan.

27 Hua and Chün had had floods and droughts in 1803, 1804, 1805, and 1806; after a five-year respite the cycle had begun again in 1811. Drought set in and by the fall government assistance was necessary because of further damage caused by hailstones and flooding. In the spring of 1813 the drought began once more. For government relief (in the form of tax exemptions and extension of food supplies) prior to 1811 see CSL 118.2, 122.8, 125.3, 132.13, 147.19, 150.38, 152.23, 159.1, 165.6. For information and sources for disasters in 1811–13 see Part Two, nn. 69 and 134.

28 Six of the districts in southwestern Shantung where the Eight Trigrams had organized had experienced economic difficulties in 1803–4 and again in 1812–13; on the other hand, the districts of Ting-t'ao and Ts'ao where the rebellion was most successful had needed no relief of any kind in the past decade until the drought of 1813. For Yü-t'ai, Shan, Chü-yeh, Ch'eng-wu, Ke-tse, and Chin-hsiang prior to 1813 see CSL 118.37, 122.15, 123.1, 125.3, 127.23, 133.41, 243.13, 248.5, 253.5, 255.4, 257.17, 260.29–30, 263.24, 265.2. Also *Chin-hsiang district gazetteer* 11.19–20; *Chü-yeh district gazetteer* 2.27. For all of southwestern Shantung in 1813 see Part Two, n. 134.

The last decade had not been unusually difficult for the three southernmost districts of Chihli province—Tung-ming, Ch'ang-yuan, and K'ai—but in 1812 and 1813 they had seen flood, drought, and hailstorms, followed by drought again and the accompanying famine. The other districts to the north, which were not involved in the rebellion, had been much harder hit by the 1813 famine. For the 1813 situation, see Part Two, n. 134. For the years before 1813 see CSL 122.4–5, 122.10, 125.3, 261.10, 265.2, and *K'ai district gazetteer* 1.59; *Ta-ming prefecture gazetteer* 4.93–94.

29 For the rain, see above Part Two, n. 152.

30 For Liu Chü's rank, see Brunnert and Hagelstrom, ♯412A.7. For the rest, see CFCL 18.23–25, 18/11/13 Memorial; CFCL 23.9, 18/12/2 Memorial and Liu Chü.

31 KCT 018401, 20/4/19 Composite confession of members of the Pi family; NYC 38.20–21, 21/6/29 Pi Fu-li.

32 CFCL 4.14–16, 18/9/19 Memorial from the governor of Shantung (who was not at that time on the scene and whose source for this statement is not given).

33 KCT 018651, 20/5/16 Wang Sen; NYC 38.80–85, 20/11/11 Wang Sen. For a list of villages in Hua district occupied for varying periods of time, see n. 91.

34 KCT 018401, 20/4/19 Pi family; NYC 38.20–21, 21/6/29 Pi Fu-li.

35 For Liu Kao-yü see NYC 38.21–22, 19/4/20 Liu Kao-wang. For Chao Te see KCT 018146, 20/3/25 Chao Te. For the division of Lin Ch'ing's men into groups of ten, see p. 149.

36 NYC 29.1–3, 18/10/22 Memorial; CFCL 42.26–27, 21/4/2 Chou Wen-sheng; KCT 018651, 20/5/16 Memorial; SYT 233–42, 22/6/20 Hu Ch'eng-te; CFCL 10.24–28, 18/10/12 Memorial.

37 For this practice and sources, see Part One, n. 111. One man, who by his own account was forced to join the rebels, stated in a straightforward but uninformative confession that the hair of his queue was cut off (割去). KCT 015602, 19/6/3 Kuo P'ei-shang. There is no other reference to queue cutting.

38 KCT 019556, 20/8/13 Chang Wei-han.

39 This phrase *ma ch'ien tao* (written as either 馬前到 or 馬前刀) literally meant "those who get there before the horses" or "those knives who are ahead of the horses." For this phrase see NYC 32.12–16, 18/12/3 Ch'in Li; CFCL 10.10–15, 18/10/9 Memorial; SYT 315–18, 19/5/25 An Hei; NYC 29.35–37, 18/11/11 Wang Ch'i-chih and others.

40 SYT 233–42, 22/6/20 Hu Ch'eng-te; KCT 016995, 19/11/25 Ho Chin-piao; KCT 019478, 20/8/1 Ho Shu; KCT 017805, 20/2/16 Li Yang; KCT 015972, 19/7/12 Liu San-kang; KCT 019478, 20/8/1 Sang Te; SYT 243–45, 22/6/20 Wang K'e-chün; CFCL 42.15–16, 20/12/14 Wang Ping-yuan; CFA 65, 20/3/24 Chao Te-yuan.

41 KCT 016813, 19/11/15 Ch'en Ch'en and others.

42 KCT 016995, 19/11/25 Ho Chin-piao; KCT 019478, 20/8/1 Ho Shu.

43 KCT 017220, 19/12/22 Wang Wen-cho.

44 NYC 32.32–34, 18/12/12 Ch'eng Chin-shui.

45 One of ten districts in Wei-hui prefecture, Hua alone had 40 percent of the prefectural population. The *Wei-hui prefecture gazetteer* (1788) gives the population of Hua district as 76,000 households and 674,000 people. In 1812 the population of the entire prefecture was somewhat less than in 1788, but no figures for individual districts are available. By 1867 there were 92,000 households in Hua district—which at a similar ratio would mean a population of over 800,000. The total Wei-hui prefectural population in 1788 was 1,733,000. The population of Chün district in 1788 was 218,000, 12 percent of the prefecture. See *Wei-hui prefecture gazetteer* 18.5, *Hua district gazetteer* 5.32–33, and *Chia-ch'ing ch'ung-hsiu i-t'ung-chih* [A gazetteer for the nation revised during the Chia-ch'ing reign] (1812) 196.7.

   By Hsiao Kung-chuan's average for district populations—100,000 in 1749 and 250,000 in 1819—the population of Hua was very large (see *Rural China*, p. 5). There were 710,000 *mou* of agricultural land in Hua district in 1788, which means a ratio of about one *mou* per person. See *Wei-hui prefecture gazetteer* 17.6, 18.5.

46 If from the total number of people involved in the rebellion, we subtract (1) an estimate of the original population of Hua city, (2) those rebels who came from Shantung, and (3) those who joined Li Wen-ch'eng in his flight—for all of which see nn. 2 and 15—we are left with between 80,000 and 90,000 people who joined the rebels and could have come from Hua district. (This figure definitely includes people from southern Chihli and from Chün who moved into Hua and became indistinguishable from the others.) This is a maximum of 10 to 13 percent of the 700,000 or 800,000 residents of Hua district.

   Two other equally rough estimates of the rebel impact suggest a similar proportion. In all available documentation about this rebellion, only between 90 and 100 villages are mentioned by name, either as residences of rebels or as places where they came to camp or plunder. In 1867 there were 1,200 villages in Hua district, and the figure for the earlier period was probably not much different. Thus only 7 percent of the villages were "involved" (*Hua district gazetteer* 18.5). After the rebellion, Ch'ing authorities reported that they had confiscated nearly 40,000 *mou* of land, land that was ostensibly rebel property but that included all property abandoned during the uprising. This figure represents only about 6 percent of the 710,000 *mou* that was the registered acreage for the district in 1788. See KCT 016810, 19/11/15 Memorial; *Wei-hui prefecture gazetteer* 17.6. While all these figures are admittedly crude, they do suggest that approximately 10 percent of the district residents became directly involved in the rebellion.

47 For one example of a man in this category who later testified to the government, see KCT 015602, 19/6/3 Chang Erh-hsiao.

48 See CSL 113.8, 118.22, 122.8, 125.3, 132.13, 147.19, 150.38, 152.23, 242.10, 248.7, 248.17, 248.22, 253.4, 261.11, 268.5, 268.23, 269.17, 272.26.

49 Government figures indicate that a total of between 5,000 and 5,600 rebels were killed in the course of Li's flight (see n. 2(f)). Of these, 2,000 had been killed even before the rebel band entered the districts here in question, and at this point Li's following numbered about 1,700 to 1,800 men. Therefore only about 1,500 to 1,600 people joined them in flight through western Honan.

50 KCT 016703, 19/11/2 Wang Hsueh-tao. The Chia-ch'ing Emperor, when he read Wang Hsueh-tao's testimony, commented, "How fortunate that they did not take Wang Hsueh-tao's advice. They might have spread in all directions; this way we quickly eliminated them" (CFCL 41.30, 19/11/2 Edict).

51 NYC 35.9–12, 18/12/25 Memorial; CFCL 11.1–4, 18/10/13 Memorial. For a little more on Tao-k'ou see Madrolle's Guide Books, *Northern China and Korea* (London: Hachette, 1912), p. 201. For an interesting description of Chün city and particularly of the "religious fairs" held on the low hills outside the city—including the temple of "the chief attraction . . . the idol-goddess 'Lao Nai Nai' (The Old Grandmother)"—see W. H. Grant, "Hsun-hsien Fair, Honan," *China Mission Yearbook* (1914), pp. 138–39.

52 CFCL 6.5–8, 18/9/26 Memorial and Ts'ai Ch'eng-kung; CFCL 3.19–21, 18/9/18 Memorial; CFCL 5.2–4, 18/9/21 Memorial.

53 CFCL 15.20–23, 18/11/1 Jung Hsing-t'ai.

54 The trigram king was Wang Hsiu-chih; Li's adopted son was Liu Ch'eng-chang. See CFCL 4.5–9, 18/9/19 Lin Ch'ing; KCT 015951, 19/7/7 Liu Ch'un-nü. For those other Trigram leaders who were from Chün district see NYC 33.37–42, 19/1/16 Memorial; NYC 33.22–32, 18/12/20 Memorial; NYC 33.14–18, 19/1/14 Memorial; CFCL 25.7–10, 18/12/12 Memorial; CFCL 6.5–8, 18/9/26 Ts'ai Ch'eng-kung; KCT 017220, 19/12/22 Ch'eng Hua-t'ing; CPT 127–31, 18/12/7 Memorial from the Grand Council.

55 CFCL 1.16–17, 18/9/14 Memorial; KCT 017340, 19/12/25 Ts'ai Shih-kuei.

56 CFCL 1.16–17, 18/9/14 Memorial; CFCL 42.24–25, 21/3/28 Chu Ch'eng; KCT 017340, 19/12/25 Ts'ai Shih-kuei; KCT 019556, 20/8/13 Chang Wei-han; CFCL 5.11–14, 18/9/22 Memorial; CFCL 5.2–4, 18/9/21 Memorial.

57 CFCL 5.11–14, 18/9/22 Memorial; CFCL 3.22–23, 18/9/18 Memorial; CFCL 4.18, 18/9/19 Edict.

58 CFCL 8.1–3, 18/10/1 Memorial; CFCL 7.21, 18/9/29 Memorial.

59 Sources for rebels killed outside Chün city: CFCL 1.32–33, 18/9/15 Memorial; CFCL 3.22–23, 18/9/18 Memorial; CFCL 5.11–14, 18/9/22 Memorial;
CFCL 6.5–8, 18/9/26 Memorial; CFCL 8.1–3, 18/10/1 Memorial.

60 CFCL 3.22–23, 18/9/18 Memorial and Sung Hsing; NYC 32.12–16, 18/
12/3 Ch'in Li.

61 CFCL 12.27–31, 18/10/20 Li Chih-mao; CFCL 15.23–25, 18/11/1 Memorial.

62 CFCL 11.1–4, 18/10/13 Confession.

63 The sources indicate only that Liu suddenly disappeared. I am simply
guessing that this was a logical mission and Liu a likely person to undertake
it. He had been to Lin Ch'ing's house at least twice before. SYT 15–17,
22/9/2 Su Kuang-tsu; KCT 015774, 19/6/20 Liu Ta-shun; NYC 32.12–16,
18/12/3 Ch'in Li.

64 NYC 32.16–25, 18/12/3 List; NYC 32.12–16, 18/12/3 Ch'in Li. NYC 31.18–
21, 18/12/16 Niu Liang-ch'en.

65 CFCL 24.21–26, 18/12/11 Feng K'e-shan.

66 In his first confession Feng stated that he had left Shantung and come to Hua
at the end of the 8th month. (This much is plausible because we know he had
gone to Shantung to accompany Lin Ch'ing part way back to Peking after
the Tao-k'ou meeting.) Then, he said, his name was mentioned to the
authorities and he fled and returned only after Hua had been occupied. For
Feng's conflicting testimony and his role in the attack on Hua city, see Part
Three, nn. 17 and 22. Also NYC 33.35, 18/12/20 Memorial; NYC 33.33–34,
18/12/25 Memorial.

67 CFCL 18.19–23, 18/11/13 Ch'e Te-hsin. See below n. 151.

68 NYC 32.12–16, 18/12/3 Ch'in Li.

69 *T'ien-shun* was the era-name selected by the Ming Emperor Ying-tsung
(reigned 1436–49 and again 1457–64) when he was reinstalled as emperor in
1457 after having been the captive of the Mongols for seven years. NYC
32.12–16, 18/12/3 Ch'in Li.

70 The eight trigram kings were Wang Tao-lung (Li Trigram); Liu Tsung-shun
(Ken); Sung K'e-chün (Chen); Shou Kuang-te (Ch'ien); Feng Hsiang-lin
(K'un); Wang Hsiu-chih (Sun); Liu Kuo-ming (Tui); and Yin Lao-te,
succeeded by his son Yin Chen-ch'ung (K'an). NYC 32.12–16, 18/12/3
Ch'in Li. There are references (some not very reliable) to sixty-eight men
called trigram lords, about eight for each trigram. It was not uncommon for
several captured rebels to agree that so-and-so was a trigram lord but to
differ as to which trigram he belonged to.

71 The term *chiu-kung* referred to nine astrological divisions of the sky, somewhat
similar to the signs of the zodiac, which were used in fortune-telling. (See
Part One, n. 43.) These White Lotus sects linked the nine mansions with the
eight trigrams and used both as names for their groups. For example, the head
of the Nine Mansions sect to which Li Wen-ch'eng had originally belonged
was referred to as "a Nine Mansions Trigram head in the Eight Trigram
Assembly" (NYC 33.13, 18/12/25 Ch'in Li).

72 NYC 32.12–16, 18/12/3 Ch'in Li; NYC 30.36–38, 18/12/12 Huang Hsing-
tsai; CFCL 16.1–6, 18/12/26 Hsu An-kuo.

73 There are many examples of this. When Chen Mansion King Sung K'e-chün
enfeoffed him, the rebel Wang Fa-wen changed his name to Chin-tao 進道

(Entering the Way) and made up a banner for himself that read, "Chen Mansion Lord Wang Chin-tao, Entrusted by Heaven to Prepare the Way." NYC 38.7–10, 19/3/14 Wang Chin-tao.

74 KCT 019367, 20/7/19 Tung T'ien-chu; NYC 38.7–10, 19/3/14 Wang Chin-tao; CFCL 41.3–4, 19/7/6 Chao Ping-jang; CFCL 23.9–11, 18/12/3 Shen Wen-hsien.

75 CFCL 41.3–4, 19/7/6 Huang P'an-kung; KCT 019556, 20/8/13 Chang Wei-han; CFCL 26.7–9, 18/12/14 Chang Yuan-lu; NYC 38.7–10, 19/3/14 Wang Chin-tao.

76 The sources for these titles are as follows: Chief Minister through Adjutants: NYC 32.12–16, 18/12/3 Ch'in Li; NYC 33.22–32, 18/12/20 List; NYC 32.16–25, 18/12/3 List; CFCL 23.1–2, 18/12/1 Memorial; CFCL 37.21–22, 19/2/24 Wang Chin-tao; NYC 33.36, 19/1/4 Sung San-ni; Brunnert and Hagelstrom, ♯751B, 752A, 752C.

Advance Officer through Assistant Superintendant: NYC 32.16–25, 18/12/3 List; NYC 33.22–32, 18/12/20 List; CFCL 41.1–2, 19/5/22 Wang Chung; KCT 017162, 18/12/10 Li Shih-kung.

Promised posts: KCT 019556, 20/8/13 Chang Wei-han; *Chi-ning district gazetteer* 4.20–29 Li Ching-hsiu; KKCK 206.1–2, 18/9/22 Yang Chin-chung; CFCL 3.9–13, 18/9/18 Liu Te-ts'ai; CFCL 23.1–2, 18/12/1 Memorial; NYC 38.78–79, 20/9/23 Li To; CFCL 42.26–27, 21/4/2 Chou Wen-sheng; Brunnert and Hagelstrom, ♯50, 848, 856.

The title "Great Commander Who Summons Men and Horses . . ." (see Li Ching-hsiu confession above) was exactly the title taken by Wu San-kuei (the Ming general who served the Manchus) when he rebelled against the Ch'ing and set up his own dynasty in 1673. See Arthur W. Hummel, ed., *Eminent Chinese of the Ch'ing Period*, p. 879. See also n. 83. Had Wu become a popular rebel hero?

77 CFCL 12.5–7, 18/10/17 Hu Erh-pang-tzu and Ts'ao Kuang-hui; CFCL 24.21–26, 18/12/11 Feng K'e-shan.

78 Sung was a *hua-chiang* 畫匠 or *hua-kung* 畫工. For more on him see NYC 32.12–16, 18/12/3 Ch'in Li; KCT 017586, 20/2/2 Memorial; NYC 31.18–21, 18/12/16 Niu Liang-ch'en; SYT 611–13, 19/12/25 Tung Kuo-t'ai; NYC 30.36–38, 18/12/12 Huang Hsing-tsai. For Niu and Sung being in charge see NYC 30.36–38, 18/12/12 Huang Hsing-tsai; NYC 31.18–21, 18/12/16 Niu Liang-ch'en; CFCL 41.3–4, 19/7/6 Huang P'an-kung.

79 For Niu Liang-ch'en's activities as a rebel, see n. 81 and NYC 34.23–25, 18/12/16 Memorial; CFCL 24.21–26, 18/12/11 Feng K'e-shan; CFCL 15.18–20, 18/11/1 Liu Ch'eng; CFCL 3.22–23, 18/9/18 Sung Hsing; KCT 016027, 19/7/24 Li Hsing-pang; KCT 016750, 19/11/13 Li Ch'eng; NYC 38.76–78, 20/9/10 Wu Ch'eng-ni; KCT 019367, 20/7/19 Tung T'ien-chu; KCT 015774, 19/6/20 Liu Ta-shun; CFCL 41.3–4, 19/7/6 Chao Ping-jang.

80 CFCL 29.1–6, 18/12/26 Niu Liang-ch'en; NYC 31.8–12, 18/12/15 Memorial.

81 For Niu's confessions, see NYC 31.18–21, 18/12/16 and CFCL 29.1–6, 18/12/26.

82 CFCL 25.5–7, 18/12/12 Memorial; KCT 017162, 18/12/10 Li Shih-kung; CFCL 42.26–27, 21/4/2 Chou Wen-sheng; NYC 33.22–32, 18/12/20 List.

83 SYT 233–42, 22/6/20 Hu Ch'eng-te; CFCL 26.43–44, 18/12/16 Hou Wen-

chih. Wu San-kuei had also been known as the Lord (and then Great Commander) Who Pacifies the West—*p'ing-hsi po* 平西伯 and *p'ing-hsi ta-chiang-chün*. These were titles granted to Wu by the newly established Ch'ing dynasty. See Hummel, *Eminent Chinese*, p. 878.

84 CFCL 9.16–20, 18/10/6 Memorial; CFCL 6.5–8, 19/8/26 Ts'ai Ch'eng-kung.

85 For the monk see CFCL 21.28–32, 18/11/24 Tsung-yin. For clothing see SYT 233–42, 22/6/20 Hu Ch'eng-te; for a rebel who was killed wearing a blue ceremonial gown (*mang-p'ao* 蟒袍) see NYC 29.14–16, 18/11/1 Memorial; CFCL 15.18–20, 18/11/1 Liu Ch'eng. T'ien Jih-tseng called himself an imperial son-in-law (*fu-ma* 駙馬) because his father-in-law was a mansion king. KCT 017340, 19/12/25 Memorial; Brunnert and Hagelstrom, #15. (This was a pre-Ch'ing term for imperial son-in-law.)

86 CFCL 28.11–13, 18/12/24 Liu Tsung-lin; CFCL 29.1–6, 18/12/26 Hsu An-kuo and Niu Liang-chen; CFCL 19.25–28, 18/11/18 Wei Te-chung; CFCL 16.35–38, 18/11/5 Liu Pao-i; KCT 018651, 20/5/16 Han Chin-pang; CFCL 18.9–10, 18/11/11 Yang T'ing-kang; CFCL 19.4–9, 18/11/14 Memorial and Kuo Ming-shan; KCT 015972, 19/7/12 Liu San-kang; KCT 016763-E, 19/10/20 Wanted list; CFCL 23.9–11, 18/12/3 Memorial; NYC 30.36–38, 18/12/12 Huang Hsing-tsai.

87 For the Shen brothers see KCT 017586, 20/2/2 Memorial; KCT 016763-E, 19/10/20 Wanted list. For the Huang brothers see NYC 30.36–38, 18/12/12 Huang Hsing-tsai; NYC 29.14–16, 18/11/1 Composite confession. For the Chu brothers see CFCL 29.1–6, 18/12/26 Hsu An-kuo; NYC 32.12–16, 18/12/3 Ch'in Li; CFCL 5.14–16, 18/9/22 Chu Ch'eng-chen; NYC 33.22–32, 18/12/20 List; CFCL 10.17–20, 18/10/10 Wang Ch'i-shan.

88 NYC 33.14–18, 19/1/4 Ch'in Li.

89 CFCL 41.3–4, 19/7/6 Huang P'an-kung.

90 NYC 38.76–78, 20/9/10 Liu Chih-kao; CFCL 41.3–4, 19/7/6 Chao Ping-jang; CFCL 42.23, 21/3/27 Wang Erh-k'e-chia; CFCL 24.3–7, 18/12/8 Memorial; NYC 30.36–38, 18/12/12 Huang Hsing-tsai; KCT 017220, 19/12/22 Ch'eng Hua-t'ing.

91 After Hua city was seized on 9/6, rebels also occupied the market town of Lao-an in southeastern Hua district, killing the resident subprefect and his family; they dug trenches around the town and told the residents to join the Eight Trigrams or be killed. Similarly, Chen Trigram King Sung K'e-chün took his followers and made camp in the village of T'ao-yuan located to the northeast of the district city. In subsequent days and weeks, the rebels occupied for varying lengths of time Pai-mao village, Ssu-chien-fang (the home of Sun Trigram King Wang Hsiu-chih), Hsieh-chia village (Li Wen-ch'eng's home), Shen-chia village, and P'an-chang village—all located to the north and east of Hua city. To the east and south (adjacent to southern Chihli) they also occupied Pa-li-ying, Liu-ku, Ts'ao-ch'i-ying, Nan-hu (the camp of Tui Trigram King Liu Kuo-ming), Wang-chia-tao-k'ou, and Ting-luan market.

For Lao-an: NYC 30.36-38, 18/12/12 Huang Hsing-tsai; NYC 34.23–25, 18/12/16 Memorial; CFCL 1.1–2, 18/9/12 Memorial; SYT 159, 19/3/10 Chang Hei-hsiao-r; SYT 303–22, 19/4/18 Memorial from the Grand Council: lists and confessions of children from rebel areas. (See n.7.)

For T'ao-yuan: NYC 32.12–16, 18/12/3 Ch'in Li; NYC 38.7–10, 19/3/14

Wang Chin-tao; CFCL 37.21–22, 19/2/24 Wang Chin-tao; CFCL 18.9–10, 18/11/11 Yang T'ing-kang.

For Pai-mao: KCT 019478, 20/8/1 Ho Shu; KCT 016995, 19/11/25 Li Ta-jung; NYC 29.33–35, 18/11/11 Memorial.

For Ssu-chien-fang: CFCL 15.18–20, 18/11/1 Liu Ch'eng; NYC 32.12–16, 18/12/3 Ch'in Li; CFCL 16.35–38, 18/11/5 Liu Pao-i.

For Hsieh-chia: CFCL 12.5–7, 18/10/17 Ts'ao Kuang-hui; CFCL 24.21–26, 18/12/11 Feng K'e-shan.

For Shen-chia: *K'ai district gazetteer* 6.42–43.

For P'an-chang: NYC 32.12–16, 18/12/3 Ch'in Li; KCT 015972, 19/7/12 Liu San-kang; CFCL 14.12–15, 18/10/27 Memorial.

For Pa-li-ying and Liu-ku: NYC 29.29–32, 18/11/11 Memorial; NYC 32.12–16, 18/12/3 Ch'in Li; NYC 29.10–11, 18/10/28 Memorial; NYC 34.13–14, 18/11/11 Memorial; CFCL 18.19–23, 18/11/13 Memorial; CFCL 9.22–25, 18/10/7 Memorial; CFCL 37.21–22, 19/2/24 Wang Chin-tao; NYC 38.7–10, 19/3/14 Wang Chin-tao; SYT 239–40, 21/5/29 Shih K'uei.

For Ts'ao-ch'i-ying: KCT 017220, 19/12/22 Wang Wen-ch'ao; NYC 29.1–3, 18/10/22 Memorial.

For Nan-hu: NYC 32.12–16, 18/12/3 Ch'in Li; CFCL 19.25–28, 18/11/18 Wei Te-chung; CFCL 9.22–25, 18/10/7 Memorial.

For Wang-chia-tao-k'ou: CFA 65, 20/3/24 Chao Te-yuan; NYC 38.56–58, 20/3/4 Chao Te-yuan; NYC 32.12–16, 18/12/3 Ch'in Li; NYC 29.29–32, 18/11/11 Memorial.

For Ting-luan: NYC 29.1–3, 18/10/22 Memorial; NYC 34.4–6, 18/11/3 Memorial; NYC 32.32–34, 18/12/12 Ch'eng Chin-shui; NYC 34.13–14, 18/11/11 Memorial.

92 First quotation: CFCL 5.14–16, 18/9/22 Memorial. Second quotation: *Chi-ning district gazetteer* 4.20–29 Magistrate's account.

93 An investigation in the 1930s reported that nearly 60 percent of the items normally pawned were articles of clothing, nearly 40 percent were "personal ornaments," and the rest were agricultural implements. Presumably the rebels helped themselves to the clothing and ornaments. As the weather was becoming colder—the 9th month in 1813 corresponded to October by the Western calendar—warm clothing would have been particularly desirable. For pawnshop contents, see Lo Kuo-hsien, "Chinese Rural Finance and the Pawnshops" (1937), translated and published in *Agrarian China: Selected Source Materials from Chinese Authors*, ed. Institute of Pacific Relations, p. 190.

94 SYT 233–42, 22/6/20 Hu Ch'eng-te.

95 For food, valuables, and clothing see CFCL 4.14–16, 18/9/19 Memorial; KCT 018401, 20/4/19 Pi family; CFCL 5.14–16, 18/9/22 Memorial; KCT 015970, 19/7/10 Li Ti-ssu; KCT 018651, 20/5/16 Wang Sen.

For the rest see CFCL 10.24–28, 18/10/12 Memorial; CFCL 13.13–16, 18/10/22 Memorial; *Chi-ning district gazetteer* 4.20–29 Magistrate's account; NYC 29.17, 18/11/1 Memorial.

96 CFCL 19.33–36, 18/11/18 Memorial; KCT 016869, 19/11/18 Chao Fei-i; CFCL 22.7–8, 18/11/25 Memorial; KCT 015970, 19/7/10 Li Ti-ssu; KCT 019320, 20/7/18 Chao Chen-wu; SYT 233–42, 22/6/20 Hu Ch'eng-te.

97 CFCL 10.10–15, 18/10/9 Memorial. For more on scouts see CFCL 5.14–16,

18/9/22 Memorial; CFCL 4.14–16, 18/9/19 Memorial; CFCL 6.8–9, 18/9/ 26 Memorial.

98   CFCL 26.1–6, 18/12/26 Hsu An-kuo; CFCL 42.26–27, 21/4/2 Chou Wen-sheng; KCT 016750, 19/11/13 Li Ch'eng; KCT 018651, 20/5/16 Wang Sen; NYC 38.80–85, 20/11/11 Wang Sen; SYT 233–42, 22/6/20 Hu Ch'eng-te.

99   SYT 233–42, 22/6/20 Hu Ch'eng-te.

100 CFCL 13.13–16, 18/10/22 Memorial.

101 CFCL 9.16–20, 18/10/6 Memorial.

102 For An-ling: CFCL 9.16–20, 18/10/6 Memorial. For Hu-chia: CFCL 8.20–22, 18/10/2 Memorial; CFCL 10.17–20, 18/10/10 Memorial and Wang Ch'i-shan.

103 CFCL 10.17–20, 18/10/10 Memorial and Wang Ch'i-shan.

104 For the Manchu see CFCL 5.1–2, 18/9/21 Edict, and Brunnert and Hagel-strom, ♯99.1 and 951. More than 600 rebels were killed, more than 200 captured; 60-odd mules and horses, 23 carts and more than 300 banners were recovered. CFCL 10.24–28, 18/10/12 Memorial; KCT 018401, 20/4/19 Pi family; CFCL 9.16–20, 18/10/6 Memorial.

105 Hu Ch'eng-te, for example, went back to central Honan where his family was. Once he had crossed the Yellow River, he had no problem avoiding arrest. He lived quietly there for five years; then he made the mistake of returning once more to his native village. There Wang K'e-chün—whom Hu had forced to drive his cart while a rebel—recognized and reported him. Hu's comment: "I didn't realize that Wang was acting as a spotter for the government. He tricked me and got me arrested and I hate him" (SYT 233–42, 22/6/20 Hu Ch'eng-te; SYT 243–45, 22/6/20 Wang K'e-chün).

106 "Timid will flee": CFCL 6.16–18, 18/9/26 Edict. See also NYC 28.23–26, 18/10/9 Edict; NYC 28.43–44, 18/10/11 Edict; NYC 28.19–23, 18/10/1 Memorial; CFCL 8.29–32, 18/10/2 Edict.

107 CFCL 5.21, 18/9/22 Edict; CFCL 5.21–22, 18/9/22 Editorial commentary.

108 In Chin-hsiang district (Shantung) contributions were expected to parallel landholdings: those with more than 100 *mou* were to provide one man for the defense of the city and to contribute 5 taels for the repair of the city wall, plus food supplies, weapons and torches; those with between 50 and 100 *mou* were to supply one man for the defense of the city but nothing else; those with between 30 and 50 *mou* were to provide one man for every two households. In reality, there were many large cash contributions (exactions might be a better word) of which those of 100 taels or more (the largest being 600 taels) were listed in the local gazetteer. *Chi-ning district gazetteer* 4.30–35; Sheng Ta-shih, *Ching-ni chi*, 2.6.

     Beginning in the middle of the 11th month of 1813 and continuing into the first few months of 1814, rewards were authorized by the emperor for militia and local gentry for their assistance in the suppression. See CFCL and NYC (particularly *chüan* 35). For a sample see CFCL 32.1–5, 19/1/19 Memorial and edict.

109 See CFCL 14.22–23, 18/10/28 Memorial.

110 *Ch'eng-wu district gazetteer* 6.37–39.

111 *Chi-ning district gazetteer* 4.20–29; CFCL 42.16, 21/1/28 Chieh San; SYT 239–40, 21/5/29 Shih K'uei.

112 CFCL 6.23, 18/9/26 Memorial. For the battle on the 13th at K'ung-lien-keng, see n. 96.

113 CFCL 1.13–16, 18/9/14 Memorial.

114 CFCL 1.13–16, 18/9/14 Memorial; *K'ai district gazetteer* 1.69, 6.42–43.

115 CFCL 5.21, 18/9/22 Edict; CFCL 1.13–16, 18/9/14 Memorial; CFCL 1.6–9, 18/9/13 Memorial; CFCL 5.2–4, 18/9/21 Memorial.

116 The editors of the CFCL (published 1818) summarized this experience: "Previously when we employed soldiers in Szechwan, Hupei, and Shensi, we often hastily called up and hired militia (*hsiang-yung* 鄉勇) to go on military campaigns [with the regular army]. Those who were enrolled on our lists numbered no less than several hundred thousand men. They were people without fixed occupations who violated our prohibition on further fighting. Their comings and goings were irregular, and they were arrogant, proud, and intractable. After a victory they were hard to discipline but, not surprisingly, it was even harder to deal with them when it came time to pull back. When they were disbanded or dismissed, they turned into vagrants. If disciplinary measures were taken against them they became fierce, and they were difficult to control if we kept them on as soldiers. The example of the Ning-Shan Brigade soldiers [former militia who rioted in the fall of 1806] is clear. This time [i.e., in the campaign against the Eight Trigrams], on the other hand, our policy called for strengthening the walls and clearing the countryside and orders were given to organize and train militia solely for the defense of one's own countryside. They were not permitted to go with the army into battle" (CFCL 5.12–22, 18/9/22 Editorial commentary). For Ning-Shan riot see CSL 164.22–24, 11/7/16 Edict. The Hua district militia was the only one permitted to go "on campaign with the army."

The organization of what Philip Kuhn calls higher-level militia was permitted, but these men were locally funded and fought only locally. See, for example, the military *chü-jen* from Ke-tse district who had "linked together" (聯絡) more than one thousand militiamen from over a dozen villages. CFCL 6.23, 18/9/26 Memorial. For more on the Ch'ing policy toward militia, see Kuhn, *Rebellion and Its Enemies in Late Imperial China*, particularly Part Two.

117 SYT 235–42, 19/10/19 Statement by Meng Ch'i-chan; NYC 34.6–7, 18/11/3 Memorial.

118 NYC 34.13–14, 18/11/11 Memorial.

119 NYC 29.1–3, 18/10/22 Memorial. This contrasts with the common view of Chia-ch'ing period armies as corrupt and ineffective.

120 See NYC 34.13–14, 18/11/11 Memorial; NYC 29.10–11, 18/10/28 Memorial.

121 Having served as Hua magistrate for less than a year, Meng Ch'i-chan was dismissed when a censor's charges and subsequent investigations revealed certain improprieties in his administration. For his appointment to the post see NYC 34.6–7, 18/11/3 Memorial. For the censor's charges and Meng's defense see CSL 297.28–30, 19/9/26; SYT 235–42, 19/10/19 Meng Ch'i-chan. For his punishment and eventual release from banishment see SYT 285–96, 19/10/22 Memorial from the Grand Council; SYT 65–66, 23/9/4 Edict.

122 For the disposition of soldiers in the north China plain area see *Ch'in-ting*

Ta Ch'ing hui-tien shih-li [Imperial Ch'ing statutes and precedents] 1818, *chüan* 470 and 471.

123 CFCL 1.20–21, 18/9/14 Edict; NYC 28.19–23, 18/10/1 Memorial; NYC 28.23–26, 18/10/9 Edict.

124 CFCL 1.11–12, 18/9/13 Memorial; SSTC, 18/9/13 Memorial from the director of the Yellow River Administration.

125 CFCL 21.4–5, 18/11/23 Memorial; CFCL 8.3–5, 18/10/1 Memorial; CFCL 8.8–9, 18/10/1 Edict.

126 CFCL 8.20–22, 18/10/2 Memorial.

127 CFCL 10.28–29, 18/10/12 Chu Te-san.

128 This was the Hsu-chou Brigade-General Shen-hung. CFCL 1.38, 18/9/15 Edict; CFCL 6.9–13, 18/9/26 Memorial.

129 Hummel, *Eminent Chinese*, p. 446; Chiang Hsiang-nan, *Ch'i-ching lou wen-ch'ao*, 5.1–9, "A biography of Liu Ch'ing." Liu's position as salt commissioner is in Brunnert and Hagelstrom, # 835.2.

130 These soldiers included 100 Manchus from the Banner garrison at Te; the rest were provincial Green Standard forces. CFCL 4.14–16, 18/9/19 Memorial; CFCL 8.17–20, 18/10/2 Memorial.

131 For these battles see CFCL 8.17–20, 18/10/2 Memorial, and sources cited in n. 2(a).

132 CFCL 13.26–28, 18/10/23 Memorial.

133 CFCL 1.1–2, 18/9/12 Memorial; CSL 273.16, 18/9/12 Edict.

134 CFCL 9.22–25, 18/10/7 Memorial; CFCL 2.39, 18/9/17 Edict; CFCL 3.19–21, 18/9/18 Memorial; CFCL 9.5–6, 18/10/3 Memorial.

135 CFCL 11. 9–10, 18/10/13 Edict.

136 For the rebels in southern Chihli during this period see CFCL 11.4–5, 18/10/13 Memorial; CFCL 13.32–34, 18/10/24 Memorial; CFCL 14.12–15, 18/10/27 Memorial; CFCL 13.1–3, 18/10/21 Memorial; CFCL 12.7–8, 18/10/17 Memorial; CFCL 14.22–23, 18/10/28 Memorial; NYC 34.4–6, 18/11/3 Memorial; CFCL 8.3–5, 18/10/1 Memorial; CFCL 9.5–6, 18/10/3 Memorial; CFCL 11.9–10, 18/10/13 Edict; CFCL 13.26–28, 18/10/23 Memorial.

137 CFCL 14.12–15, 18/10/27 Memorial; CFCL 14.16–17, 18/10/27 Edict; KCT 015972, 19/7/12 Liu San-kang.

138 CFCL 16.35–38, 18/11/5 Memorial.

139 CFCL 13.38–40, 18/10/24 Edict; CFCL 16.24–26, 18/11/4 Memorial.

140 CFCL 1.5, 18/9/12 Edict; CFCL 1.20–21, 18/9/14 Edict; and n. 57.

141 CFCL 11.1–4, 18/10/13 Memorial.

142 Hummel, *Eminent Chinese*, pp. 896–97; CFCL 1.4, 18/9/12 Edict; NYC 28.1–2, 18/9/22 Memorial; NYC 28.4–7, 18/9/25 Memorial.

143 CFCL 11.1–4, 18/10/13 Memorial.

144 NYC 28.5, 18/9/17 Edict; NYC 28.29–30, 18/10/13 Edict. For Na-yen-ch'eng see Hummel, *Eminent Chinese*, pp. 584–87.

145 For Na-yen-ch'eng's journey to Chün see NYC 28.31–32, 18/10/13 Memorial; NYC 28.19–23, 18/10/1 Memorial; NYC 29.1–3, 18/10/22 Memorial. Na-yen-ch'eng's troops consisted of 1,000 men from the Manchu garrison at Sian, 1,000 Manchu cavalry from Sian, 500 Manchus from the Outer Artillery and Musketry Division in Peking and 500 Manchus from the Light Division in Peking (Brunnert and Hagelstrom, # 737 and 738

respectively), and 500 Green Standard soldiers from his own (the governor-general of Shen-Kan) command at Lan-chou. See CFCL 2.39, 18/9/17 Edict; NYC 28.4–7, 18/9/25 Memorial; CFCL 7.20, 18/9/29 Edict; CFCL 7.22, 18/9/29 Edict; NYC 28.11–12, 18/10/4 Memorial; CFCL 11.12, 18/10/13 Memorial; NYC 28.44–46, 18/10/18 Memorial.

Kao-ch'i's soldiers were 500 Green Standard from, the Ho-pei garrison, 1,200 Green Standard from his own (the governor of Honan) command and from the Ho-nan garrison, and 1,300 Green Standard from the Ching-tzu-kuan (in Honan) regiment. See CFCL 1.20–21, 18/9/14 Edict; CFCL 1.32–33, 18/9/15 Memorial; CFCL 6.5–8, 18/9/26 Memorial; NYC 28.44–46, 18/10/18 Memorial.

Wen Ch'eng-hui led 2,000 men from the commands of the governor-general and military-governor of Chihli, all Green Standard. See NYC 28.32–35, 18/10/13 Memorial; CFCL 1.1–2, 18/9/12 Memorial; CFCL 9.22–25, 18/10/7 Memorial.

146 NYC 29.5–6, 18/10/24 Memorial.

147 NYC 29.10–11, 18/10/28 Memorial; NYC 29.1–3, 18/10/22 Memorial.

148 For the battle, see n. 2(c), and NYC 34.13–14, 18/11/11 Memorial.

149 NYC 29.22–23, 18/11/3 Memorial; NYC 28.44–46, 18/10/18 Memorial.

150 For Liu's and Sung's battles see CFCL 19.25–28, 18/11/18 Wei Te-chung. For Li Wen-ch'eng's changing residences see NYC 32.12–16, 18/12/3 Ch'in Li; CFCL 19.28–30, 18/11/18 Ssu Yü-k'uei; NYC 29.33–35, 18/11/11 Confession.

151 See nn. 65 and 66. Sung Yueh-lung described Feng's appearance when he departed:

> Feng K'e-shan is thirty-two years old. He has a round face, normal-colored complexion and is slightly pockmarked. He is heavily built. Feng was wearing a blue corded riding jacket made from fox skin, and a sheepskin covered with a layer of blue cloth as an outer wrap. On his head he wore a felt cap; his shoes were made of brown cloth. He carried a cotton sack inside of which he carried some purple flowered cloth. He was dressed as a seller of medicines.

Interrogated by the arresting magistrate, Feng claimed that his name was Liu Ming-te, "but his words and manner were uneasy and he had the accent of someone from Hua district in Honan. We compared his age and description with those on the wanted list and they matched those of Feng K'e-shan." Feng was transferred to the provincial capital of Chihli, interrogated there by the governor-general, and having made a preliminary confession, placed in chains in a wooden cage and sent under substantial guard to the Board of Punishments in Peking. He was later examined by the Grand Council and finally by the emperor in a court interrogation (together with his former colleagues now also arrested, Hsu An-kuo and Niu Liang-ch'en) and executed by slow slicing on the 12th day of the 1st month in 1814.

For Sung Yueh-lung see CFCL 22.5–7, 18/11/25 Sung Yueh-lung. For other information about Feng's flight and arrest see CFCL 28.1–4, 18/12/21 Sung Yü-lin; CFCL 24.21–26, 18/12/11 Feng K'e-shan; CFCL 24.9–11, 18/12/9 Memorial; CFCL 31.3–4, 19/1/12 Memorial.

152 For Hua city, see *Hua district gazetteer* maps and *Chia-ch'ing ch'ung-hsiu i-t'ung-*

chih 196.7. For rebel measures to protect the city see CFCL 13.19–20, 18/10/ 22 Edict.

A rebel scout arrested early in the 10th month, reported in an otherwise not entirely reliable confession that rebel morale had fallen considerably— "all were crying and regretting that it was too late" (NYC 28.44–46, 18/10/8 Chang Te).

For more on initiating and resisting a siege, see Herbert Franke, "Siege and Defense of Towns in Medieval China," pp. 151–201 in Frank A. Kierman, Jr., ed., *Chinese Ways in Warfare* (Cambridge: Harvard University Press, 1974).

153 NYC 29.26–28, 18/11/6 Memorial; CFCL 24.3–7, 18/12/8 Memorial.
154 CFCL 19.25–28, 18/11/18 Wei Te-chung; NYC 31.18–21, 18/12/16 Niu Liang-ch'en; CFCL 16.10–12, 18/11/3 Liu Erh-fan-ts'ao and others.
155 CFCL 19.25–28, 18/11/18 Wei Te-chung; NYC 31.18–21, 18/12/16 Niu Liang-ch'en; CFCL 20.16–17, 18/11/21 Sung Kuo-hsing; NYC 32.12–16, 18/12/3 Ch'in Li; CFCL 20.25–27, 18/11/21 Edict.
156 CFCL 13.10, 18/10/21 Edict; CFCL 13.38–40, 18/10/24 Edict; CFCL 16.16–18, 18/11/3 Edict; CFCL 16.24–26, 18/11/4 Memorial.

T'o-chin was a Manchu from the bordered-yellow banner; see Hummel, *Eminent Chinese*, p. 177. He was called back to Peking from Manchuria (where he was conducting an investigation) to help handle the palace attack and was then sent south to supervise military operations. T'o-chin's actions as a commander were not a success; he did little and what he did often brought criticism from the emperor. In the end, T'o never led his men in battle, was sent to Hua city after it was retaken to discuss reconstruction, stayed there two days, and then returned to the capital. See CFCL 2.4, 18/9/16 Edict; CFCL 13.10, 18/10/21 Edict; CFCL 19.14–16, 18/11/16 Memorial; CFCL 17.27–28, 18/11/10 Memorial; CFCL 17.30–33, 18/11/10 Edict; CFCL 20.1–2, 18/11/19 Memorial; CFCL 20.4–8, 18/11/19 Edict; CFCL 20.27–28, 18/11/21 Edict; SSTC, 18/11/25 Memorial from T'o-chin; CFCL 24.15–17, 18/12/9 Edict; NYC 35.1–2, 18/12/17 Memorial.

157 For the 11/1 battle see CFCL 16.35–38, 18/11/5 Memorial and Liu Pao-i. For the rest see CFCL 16.10–12, 18/11/3 Liu Erh-fan-ts'ao; CFCL 19.28–30, 18/11/18 Ssu Yü-k'uei.
158 CFCL 19.4–9, 18/11/14 Memorial and K'ung Ch'uan-wen.
159 CFCL 19.28–30, 18/11/18 Ssu Yü-k'uei; CFCL 20.16–17, 18/11/21 Sung Kuo-hsin; NYC 32.12–16, 18/12/3 Ch'in Li.

Those who accompanied Li Wen-ch'eng and lost their lives with him included: Liu Kuo-ming (Tui Trigram king), Lu Chün-t'ai (K'un Trigram lord), Wang Hsueh-i (Tui Trigram lord), Lo Kuo-wang (Ch'ien Trigram Lord), Wang Chin-tao (brigade-general), and Sung K'e-chün (Chen Trigram king). See Sung Kuo-hsin confession above.

160 CFCL 18.9–10, 18/11/11 Memorial; CFCL 18.23–25, 18/11/13 Memorial; *Tung-ming district gazetteer* 2.2–3; NYC 29.33–35, 18/11/11 Memorial; CFCL 18.19–23, 18/11/13 Memorial.

For the band that joined Li en route see NYC 29.10–11, 18/10/28 Memorial; NYC 29.35–37, 18/11/11 Memorial and Wang Ch'i-chih; NYC 34.13–14, 18/11/11 Memorial.

161 See CFCL 18.23–25, 18/11/13 Memorial; NYC 32.12–16, 18/12/3 Ch'in Li.

162 E.g., the battle in Yang-wu district: NYC 29.33–35, 18/11/11 Memorial; CFCL 18.19–23, 18/11/13 Memorial; NYC 30.1–4, 18/11/14 Memorial.

163 NYC 30.1–4, 18/11/14 Memorial. Yang Fang had been in mourning, having previously served as Sian brigade-general. Then forty-three years old, Yang was a veteran of the campaigns against the White Lotus rebels a decade earlier and was a protégé of Yang Yü-ch'un. See Hummel, *Eminent Chinese*, pp. 884–85 for Fang Chao-ying's biography of Yang, and also Yang's autobiography *Kung-ch'uan [Yang] Kuo-yung-hou tzu-pien nien-p'u* (1840). For the soldiers Yang led see n. 170.

164 CFCL 18.19–23, 18/11/13 Memorial; CFCL 20.22–23, 18/11/21 Memorial.

165 CFCL 18.19–23, 18/11/13 Memorial; CFCL 20.22–23, 18/11/21 Memorial; NYC 30.1–4, 18/11/14 Memorial; CFCL 20.16–17, 18/11/21 Sung Kuo-hsin.

166 It may be that none remained behind but rather that local disturbances of some sort caused by the rebels continued after they had departed and then died out quietly. CFCL 20.15–16, 18/11/21 Memorial; NYC 32.12–16, 18/12/3 Ch'in Li; CFCL 19.28–30, 18/11/18 Memorial; NYC 30.16–19, 18/11/24 Memorial.

167 For the number of supporters rallied, see nn. 2(f) and 49.

168 CFCL 20.15–16, 18/11/21 Memorial; NYC 32.12–16, 18/12/3 Ch'in Li; CFCL 19.28–30, 18/11/18 Memorial; NYC 30.8–10, 18/11/23 Memorial; NYC 30.16–19, 18/11/24 Memorial; CFCL 21.16–20, 18/11/24 Memorial.

169 CFCL 21.1–3, 18/11/23 Memorial; CFCL 21.16–20, 18/11/21 Memorial.

170 Yang Fang, *Nien-p'u*, 3.19–33, and Chiang Hsiang-nan, *Ch'i-ching-lou wen-ch'ao* 5.45–53. According to the report of Yang Fang and his subordinates to Special Imperial Commissioner Na-yen-ch'eng, those soldiers who refused to advance were Green Standard soldiers from garrisons in Honan province, Manchu soldiers from Banner regiments at Sian, and Manchu soldiers from the Light Division in Peking (NYC 34.15–16, 18/12/3 Memorial). Other soldiers who took part in these Ssu-ch'ai battles were cavalry from Kirin and Heilungkiang, Green Standard soldiers from the command of the governor-general of Shen-Kan, and Green Standard cavalry from the command of the military-governor of Shen-Kan. See also CFCL 21.16–20, 18/11/24 Memorial; NYC 30.16–19, 18/11/24 Memorial.

171 NYC 32.12–16, 18/12/3 Ch'in Li; NYC 30.22–25, 18/11/25 Memorial.

172 NYC 32.12–16, 18/12/3 Ch'in Li; NYC 30.22–25, 18/11/25 Memorial.

173 Yang Fang, *Nien-p'u*, 3.30. Also NYC 30.22–25, 18/11/25 Memorial; NYC 34.17–18, 18/12/3 Memorial; CFCL 23.30–33, 18/12/5 Memorial and Niu Shih-wang.

174 NYC 29.29–37, 18/11/11 Memorials; NYC 30.1–4, 18/11/14 Memorial; NYC 30.8–10, 18/11/23 Memorial.

175 NYC 29.29–32, 18/11/11/ Memorial; CFCL 17.27–28, 18/11/10 Memorial; CFCL 19.28–30, 18/11/18 Memorial.

176 NYC 29.29–32, 18/11/11 Memorial; NYC 29.35–37, 18/11/11 Memorial.

177 NYC 30.8–10, 18/11/23 Memorial.

178 CFCL 24.3–7, 18/12/8 Memorial. For list see NYC 32.16–25, 18/12/3.

179 CFCL 24.3–7, 18/12/8 Memorial; NYC 30.36–38, 18/12/12 Huang Hsing-tsai.

180 CFCL 24.3–7, 18/12/8 Memorial.

181 For example: "It is getting near the end of the year. The tributaries from
Outer Mongolia have all come to the capital and I have already personally
told them that Na-yen-ch'eng and the others are now besieging Hua city, and
that the city would be taken very shortly and the campaign brought to an
end. They were delighted. How can you now allow any more delays?"
(CFCL 25.15–17, 18/12/9 Edict).

The emperor's pleasure at the retaking of Hua on 12/10 was somewhat
diluted by news of the outbreak of another separate uprising in the mountains
of Shensi. Late in the 11th month, a group of lumbermen turned to looting
after they had been put out of work. This small incident grew, gaining
strength in an area where the price of grain had risen and where there was
evident famine. Although these rebels used banners of different colors to
organize themselves, their rising had no connection either with the Eight
Trigrams or with any White Lotus sect. (Could Li Wen-ch'eng and his band
have reached an area where there was such discontent, might they—like the
White Lotus rebels a decade before—have found new strength for their
rebellion?) The soldiers already on campaign in Honan were sent to suppress
these rebels after Hua was retaken. For this reason, documentary material
about this Nan-shan (南山 Southern Mountains) uprising is included in the
CFCL and makes up the bulk of the last third of this work. The first reference
to this uprising is located in CFCL 25.17–21, 18/12/12 Memorial. Com-
menting on this uprising (which was suppressed with very little difficulty),
the editors of the CFCL noted: "The bandits from the San-ts'ai gorge of
Shensi went and plundered grain because they were starving. That is why
they rebelled. Certainly this is not like the behavior of the sect-rebels (chiao-
fei) who mulled over their plotted rebellion for a long time. It has not been so
long since the Southern Mountains were pacified [following the White Lotus
rebellion] and the people there were still unsettled. They may also have been
taking advantage of the fact that Shensi province troops had been transferred
out of the area [to suppress the Eight Trigrams]" (CFCL 25.27–28, 18/12/12
Commentary).

182 NYC 30.36–38, 18/12/12 Memorial and Huang Hsing-tsai.
183 NYC 31.1–4, 18/12/12 Memorial.
184 NYC 33.4–5, 18/12/20 Memorial; NYC 35.16–17, 19/1/4 Memorial; NYC
31.8–12, 18/12/15 Memorial; Yang Fang, Nien-p'u, 3.33.

The "history" of this night battle is interesting. In his memorial sent 12/12
Na-yen-ch'eng stated that his soldiers had, on his orders, rested for only a few
hours and then attacked again. In another memorial (sent 12/29, received
1/4) he gave another, different, corroborated and more credible account—
one that I have followed in my description of these events. But in this memorial Na also stated that during the battle that night "a temple next to the
city wall suddenly caught fire, and by the light of the fire our men could see
as clear as day." Na went on to say—less convincingly—that the front hall of
that temple had been dedicated to Kuan-ti, and although the entire temple
had burned down the image of Kuan-ti had remained intact. (The rear hall
of the temple was said to be dedicated to San-chiao fo 三教佛 Buddha of the
Three Religions.) The emperor, pleased at this second testimony to Kuan-
ti's supernatural protection of his dynasty, made much of this "unusual" fire

and listed it as one of the ten acts of Heaven's mercy that permitted the suppression of the Eight Trigrams. For Kuan-ti's alleged participation in the palace attack see Part Three, n. 102. For the ten acts of mercy see CFCL 1.2–17, 19/3/29 Proclamation.

185 NYC 33.22–32, 18/12/20 Memorial; Yang Fang, *Nien-p'u*, 3.19–33; CFCL 28.8–10, 18/12/23 Memorial; NYC 33.37–42, 19/1/16 Memorial; NYC 35.16–17, 19/1/4 Memorial.

186 NYC 31.1–4, 18/12/12 Memorial; CFCL 28.8–10, 18/12/23 Memorial; NYC 32.28–31, 18/12/25 Memorial; NYC 31.8–12, 18/12/15 Memorial. See also n. 2(e).

187 NYC 33.4–5, 18/12/20 Memorial; NYC 31.8–12, 18/12/15 Memorial.

188 NYC 33.7–9, 19/1/19 Memorial; NYC 33.7, 19/1/10 Edict.

189 SYT 439–41, 19/3/21 Memorial; CFCL 29.1–6, 18/12/26 Hsu An-kuo.

190 The emperor ordered that "if on the way it looks like Hsu An-kuo will not survive the journey to Peking, pick a populated area and execute him by cutting him into ten thousand pieces" (SSTC, 18/12/16 Edict to Kuang-hou). See also KCT 017302, 18/12/22 Memorial, and CFCL 26.42, 18/12/16 Memorial.

Hsu's family (like the families of other rebel leaders) was completely eliminated. Even before Hua had been retaken, Ch'ing officials had located the graves of his parents and grandparents in Ch'ang-yuan district and dug up the remains. The governor of Shantung memorialized about this in gruesome detail: "My men immediately dug up the graves and identified the skeletons of that rebel's great-great-grandfather and great-great-grandmother, which were a green color and those of his great-grandfather and great-grand-mother, which were a purple color. The corpse of that rebel's grandfather, Hsu Liu-ch'ing, was wrapped in vines, and that of his grandmother, Miss Huo, had white hair as long as her body. That rebel's father, Hsu Ch'eng-ch'un, and mother, Miss Chang, and his wife, Miss Li, were all buried [in another place] northeast of that village. My men then located this place and dug up their bodies. All the corpses were subsequently burned. There was fluid which oozed out from the brain of Miss Huo [Hsu's grandmother]. The ashes were then scattered on the main road where they were trampled by the carts and horses" (CFCL 20.18–20, 18/11/21 Memorial).

191 KCT 017302, 18/12/22 Memorial; CFCL 26.42, 18/12/16 Memorial.

192 CFCL 31.3–4, 19/1/12 Memorial.

193 NYC 33.22–32, 18/12/20 Memorial.

194 The financial dimension of the suppression of the Eight Trigrams is not fully documented in the available source material. Nowhere did the Chia-ch'ing Emperor or any of his officials comment on the total cost. I have built up my estimate of the total cost on the basis of a variety of not always altogether clear or complete statements about partial expenses. Despite their illusion of precision, these figures must be taken as approximations only.

Between the 9th and the 12th months of 1813, at least 3,993,000 taels were spent for military expenses and special relief connected with the suppression of the Eight Trigrams. Broken down by province, this total included 517,000 for Kiangsu (13 percent), 1,030,000 for Chihli (26 percent), 850,000 for Shantung (21 percent), and 1,596,000 for Honan (40 percent). The high expenses for Kiangsu (where there was no fighting but where soldiers were transferred to the borders to defend this rich and important region) are worth remarking, but over a third of this money was contributed by Liang-huai salt merchants and the rest came from the Salt Commission and provincial treasuries. The Chihli province expenses, originally paid for out of the provincial and Ch'ang-lu Salt Commission treasuries, were eventually paid for by the former officials of that province (those who held office between 1806 and 1812), who were made to contribute their *yang-lien* 養廉 money as a punishment for allowing the rebellion (the palace attack particularly) to occur. Shantung took 400,000 taels from its provincial treasury, 80,000 from the Lin-ch'ing toll station treasury, 300,000 from the Salt Commission treasury, and 70,000 was donated by salt merchants from that province. Honan took 226,000 taels from its provincial treasury, 70,000 from its delinquent officials, and 1,300,000 from the Liang-huai Salt Commission treasury.

In sum, officials from these provinces supplied 970,000 taels (26 percent), provincial treasuries 793,000 (19 percent), and the rest (55 percent) came from Ch'ing taxes on commerce—the treasuries of salt commissions and transit tolls and donations from merchants. Of the nearly four million taels spent, over 80 percent was spent on military actions as opposed to relief.

The cost to the Ch'ing government itself was relatively small, but it is not clear to me whether the reliance on merchant sources was a sign of Ch'ing strength or weakness. Ch'ien-lung period campaigns had generally been more expensive, but they also lasted longer than the mere three months needed to suppress the Eight Trigrams. The first campaign against the Chin-ch'uan minority people in Szechwan in 1747–48 had cost nearly eight million taels; the second campaign against them in 1771–77 cost nearly seventy million; the Burma campaign in 1766–69 cost nine million taels; and the suppression of the T'ien-ti-hui rebellion in Taiwan in 1787–88 cost eight million.

See Chao I, *Yen-p'u tsa-chi* [Miscellaneous notes] (1877), 2.43–44. I am grateful to Beatrice S. Bartlett for this reference. See also Hummel, *Eminent Chinese*, pp. 7–8, 370.

To put these costs further in context, we might compare them with the annual income from the land tax. In 1753 (a year for which figures are available) the land tax revenue for the entire country was over 54 million taels; for Chihli province it was more than 3 million taels, for Shantung more than 5 million, for Honan nearly 5 million, and for Kiangsu about 8.5 million. (See Yeh-chien Wang, *An Estimate of the Land-Tax Collection in China, 1753 and 1908*, Harvard East Asian Monographs 52 [Cambridge: Harvard University, East Asian Research Center, 1973], table 27.) Between the 5th month of 1810 and the 4th month of 1814, Liang-huai salt merchants gave 12,400,000 taels to the government, almost all for river repair. (SYT 159–64, 24/10/16 Memorial from the Grand Council; see also Part One, n. 179.)

Sources for Kiangsu expenses: CFCL 6.9–13, 18/9/26 Memorial; SSTC, 18/10/14 Edict to T'ung-hsing; SSTC, 18/10/14 Memorial from Heng-ling; CFCL 29.17–19, 18/12/26 Edict; CFCL 38.35–38, 19/2*/22 Memorial.

Sources for Shantung expenses: CFCL 6.8–9, 18/9/26 Memorial; CFCL 18.23–25, 18/11/13 Memorial; CFCL 19.32–33, 18/11/18 Memorial; CFCL 30.24–26, 19/1/8 Memorial and edict; CFCL 24.31–32, 18/12/11 Memorial.

Sources for Honan expenses: CFCL 12.8–10, 18/10/17 Memorial; CFCL 13.16–17, 18/10/22 Memorial; CFCL 13.19–20, 18/10/22 Edict; CFCL 24.18–19, 18/12/9 Memorial; CFCL 35.8–9, 19/2/8 Memorial.

Sources for Chihli expenses: CFCL 4.25–26, 18/9/20 Memorial; CFCL 7.27–28, 18/9/29 Memorial; SSTC, 18/10/20 Memorial from Kuang-hui; CFCL 18.23–25, 18/11/13 Memorial; NYC 35.8, 18/12/27 Memorial; CFCL 31.30–31, 19/1/16 Memorial; NYC 37.20–21, 19/4/12 Memorial; NYC 37.23–25, 19/12/14 Memorial.

195 NYC 32.12–16, 18/12/3 Ch'in Li.

CONCLUSION

1 On 12/7 in 1813 the Board of Punishments issued the first of at least four wanted lists that were to be used to search for and identify sect leaders and other known Eight Trigram rebels; a censor had memorialized proposing the creation of such lists and the emperor had agreed. (See CSL 280.11–13, 18/12/7.) These lists were divided into the two categories of most wanted and second-most wanted; the four lists I have seen contained between forty and seventy names. Each name was followed by a description and a brief statement about the man's role in the rebellion; the degree of detail depended on the availability of information from captured colleagues. Lin Ch'ing's nephew Tung Kuo-t'ai, who remained in prison at the Board of Punishments for years, supplied much of the information about Peking area sect members, and most of the wanted criminals were followers of Lin Ch'ing. Many of these criminals were never caught, despite repeated (at least one a month for several years) and vehement edicts from the emperor promising rewards for the arrest of any of these men. (For example, see CSL 296.31–32, 19/9/15 Edict.) In many cases, these exhortations bred the arrests of innocent men. For a few months officials at Shan-hai-kuan (a pass between China proper and Manchuria) were particularly shameless about forcing innocent men to make false confessions about participation in this rebellion. These confessions were very unconvincing, however, and the emperor quickly ordered an investigation. See CFCL 27.13–15, 18/12/18 Memorial; CFCL 31.8, 19/1/12 Memorial, for more on this.

A copy of one wanted list that was sent as an enclosure to an edict to a governor in south China is preserved in KCT 016763-E, 19/10/20 in the Palace Museum. It is handwritten none too legibly on paper about half the size of the standard memorial or edict. For the Chinese bondservant and associate of Lin Ch'ing, Chu Hsien, it has the following entry:

> Chu Hsien 祝現 or Chu Hsien 祝顯. Age forty-six. Long face. Ordinary colored complexion. Brown mustaches. Very tall and heavily built. From Sang-fa village in Wan-p'ing district. According to Tung Kuo-t'ai's testimony, this criminal was the overall leader from Sang-fa; Lin Ch'ing appointed him to lead men in through the Hsi-hua Gate to stir up trouble.

2 See Part Four, n. 170 for one incident in which government soldiers did not obey orders to attack under relatively unfavorable circumstances. Com-

menting on the performance of the soldiers involved in these campaigns, the Chia-ch'ing Emperor noted that "for zealousness, the Kirin and Heilung-kiang soldiers rank first, the Light Division and Artillery and Musketry Division [from Peking] rank second, and the Green Standard soldiers rank third" (CFCL 39.16–20, 19/3/10 Edict). The same ranking was true as far as the orderliness of the soldiers' behavior while on campaign. (CFCL 26.40–42, 18/12/16 Edict.) The government lost only 1,913 soldiers in the course of the campaign, 253 Manchu and 1,660 (Chinese) Green Standard soldiers—representing 4.9 and 8.6 percent of the Manchu and Chinese soldiers involved in the fighting (see below). (NYC 35.19–22, 19/1/9 Memorial from Na-yen-ch'eng.)

For other scattered comments on the state of the military establishment in 1813 see NYC 28.23–26, 18/10/9 Edict; CFCL 9.16–20, 18/10/6 Memorial; NYC 28.4–7, 18/9/25 Memorial; NYC 29.19, 18/11/1 Edict; NYC 35.1–2, 18/12/17 Memorial; CFCL 9.7–9, 18/10/4 Edict; and CSL 287.1–2, 19/3/1 Edict. The last edict was a response to a censor's memorial that stated in strong language that outside the capital area the provincial garrison posts were undermanned and in serious disrepair.

In a memorial, Special Imperial Commissioner Na-yen-ch'eng stated that fifteen to sixteen thousand soldiers had taken part in the seige of Hua (NYC 34.26–27, 18/12/17). By my count, in all 24,600 soldiers were transferred from their posts and involved in the fighting in some way. Of these, 19,500 (including 1,200 cavalry) were Green Standard soldiers, and 5,100 (including 1,000 cavalry) were Manchus. By province, the units involved were as follows:

Kiangsu: 1,000 Green Standard from Hsu-chou. See CFCL 1.38, 18/9/15 Edict; CFCL 6.9–13, 18/9/26 Memorial. (Primarily used for mopping-up.)

Shansi: 1,000 Green Standard from Ta-t'ung. See CFCL 18.19–23, 18/11/13 Memorial; CFCL 20.22–23, 18/11/21 Memorial. (Primarily used for mopping-up.)

Peking: 500 Banner soldiers from the Outer Artillery and Musketry Division (Brunnert and Hagelstrom, # 737); and 500 Banner soldiers from the Light Division (Brunnert and Hagelstrom, # 738). See CFCL 7.20, 18/9/29 Edict. *Total 1,000.*

Manchuria: 1,000 Banner soldiers from Kirin and 1,000 from Heilung-kiang. See NYC 34.13–14, 18/11/11 Memorial. *Total 2,000.*

Shantung: 100 Banner soldiers from Te; 300 Green Standard including 100 cavalry from Chi-nan (Shantung governor's command); 1,000 Green Standard from Teng-chou; 100 Green Standard cavalry from Yen-chou. See CFCL 4.14–16, 18/9/19 Memorial; CFCL 8.17–20, 18/10/2 Memorial; CFCL 1.27–29, 18/9/15 Memorial; CFCL 7.10–12, 18/9/28 Memorial; CFCL 14.12–15, 18/10/27 Memorial. *Total 1,500.*

Honan: 1,000 Green Standard from Ho-pei brigade at Huai-ch'ing; 1,200 Green Standard from K'ai-feng (Ho-nan brigade and governor's command); 1,300 Green Standard from the Ching-tzu-kuan regiment. See CFCL 1.32–33, 18/9/15 Memorial; CFCL 1.38–39, 18/9/15 Edict; CFCL 1.20–21, 18/9/14 Edict; CFCL 6.5–8, 18/9/26 Memorial; NYC 28.44–46, 18/10/18 Memorial; CFCL 5.11–14, 18/9/22 Memorial. *Total 3,500.*

Chihli: 100 Green Standard from Pao-ting (governor-general's command);

1,600 Green Standard from Ku-pei-k'ou (military-governor's command); 2,500 Green Standard from Hsuan-hua; 2,000 Green Standard from Cheng-ting. See CFCL 1.1–2, 18/9/12 Memorial; CFCL 3.19–21, 18/9/18 Memorial; CFCL 9.5–6, 18/10/3 Memorial; NYC 35.19–22, 19/1/9 Memorial. *Total 7,100.*

Shensi & Kansu: 500 Green Standard from Lan-chou (governor-general's command); 2,000 Green Standard, including 1,000 cavalry, from Ku-yuan (military-governor's command); 2,000 Green Standard from Ching-ning and Ching-yuan; 1,000 Green Standard from Ho-chou and Lan-chou; 1,000 Manchu cavalry from Sian; 1,000 Banner soldiers from Sian. See NYC 28.44–46, 18/10/18 Memorial; CFCL 2.39, 18/9/17 Edict; NYC 28.4–7, 18/9/25 Memorial; CFCL 7.22, 18/9/29 Edict; CFCL 11.12, 18/10/13 Memorial; NYC 28.11–12, 18/10/4 Memorial; CFCL 11.1–4, 18/10/13 Memorial; CFCL 14.30–31, 18/10/28 Memorial; NYC 35.19–22, 19/1/9 Memorial. *Total 7,500.*

3 See Frederic Wakeman, Jr., "The Secret Societies of Kwangtung, 1800–1856," pp. 29–47 in Jean Chesneaux, ed., *Popular Movements and Secret Societies in China, 1840–1950.*

4 For the Taiping rebellion, see Jen Yu-wen, *The Taiping Revolutionary Movement* (New Haven: Yale University Press, 1973) or Franz Michael, *The Taiping Rebellion: History and Documents,* 3 vols. (Seattle: University of Washington Press, 1966–71).

5 A variety of White Lotus sects have been banned in both Chinas since 1949. For one example, see the 7 June 1953 radio broadcast by the deputy mayor of Shanghai entitled "Why Must We Prohibit the Reactionary Taoist Cults?" (pp. 177–182 in Donald E. MacInnis, ed., *Religious Policy and Practice in Communist China: A Documentary History* [New York: Macmillan, 1972]). The deputy mayor maintained that "the backbone members of the higher ranks in the reactionary Taoist cults have been deceiving the masses under the cover of the burning of joss sticks, kowtowing before their shrines, living on vegetarian diets, and saying Buddhist prayers while in effect their organizations were actually secretly involved in counter-revolutionary activities. . . . We can say definitely that reactionary cults like the Yi Kuan Tao are absolutely not religious organizations, but counter-revolutionary organizations" (p. 178). When members of an I-kuan-tao sect were arrested in Taipei in 1971 the government there took a similar position and maintained that "it is not really a religion. . . . Yikuan Tao adherents . . . try to deceive the people with boasts of magical powers and to frighten them with warnings that they can survive the imminent destruction of the world only by joining the sect" ("Taiwan Raids Secret Rituals in a Move to Curb an Outlawed Religious Group," *New York Times,* 25 April 1971).

6 The study of non-Western millenarianism has concentrated on the island cultures of the South Pacific, African tribes, and North and South American Indians. Some basic works on millenarian movements are Sylvia L. Thrupp, ed., *Millennial Dreams in Action: Studies in Revolutionary Religious Movements* (New York: Schocken Books, 1970); Yonina Talmon, "Millenarism," *International Encyclopedia of the Social Sciences* (New York: Macmillan, 1968) 10:349–62; Anthony F. C. Wallace, "Revitalization Movements," *American*

Anthropologist 58 (1956); 264–81; Eric J. Hobsbawm, *Primitive Rebels: Studies in Archaic Forms of Social Movements*, 2d ed. (New York: W. W. Norton, 1965), chaps. 4, 5, and 6; Kenelm Burridge, *New Heaven New Earth: A Study of Millenarian Activities* (New York: Schocken Books, 1969); Weston La Barre, "Materials for a History of Crisis Cults," *Current Anthropology* 12 (1971): 3–44; and Bryan Wilson, *Magic and the Millennium: A Sociological Study of Religious Movements of Protest Among Tribal and Third-world People* (New York: Harper and Row, 1973).

7 A classic work on medieval Christian sects is Norman Cohn, *The Pursuit of the Millennium: Revolutionary Millenarists and Mystical Anarchists of the Middle Ages*, rev. and expanded ed. (New York: Oxford University Press, 1970). For the Mahdist movement in the Sudan, see Richard H. Dekmejian and Margaret J. Wyszomirski, "Charismatic Leadership in Islam: The Mahdi of the Sudan," *Comparative Studies in Society and History* 14 (1972): 193–214; or Peter M. Holt, *The Mahdist State in the Sudan, 1881–1898: A Study of Its Origins, Development and Overthrow* (Oxford: Clarendon, 1958). There are some striking similarities in organization and practice between White Lotus sects and the Sufi orders of Islam. See Michael Gilsenan, *Saint and Sufi in Modern Egypt: An Essay in the Sociology of Religion* (Oxford: Clarendon, 1973), for example, or for Sufi sects in central Asia: Joseph Fletcher, "China's Northwest at the Time of the Ming-Ch'ing Transition" (Paper prepared for the conference "From Ming to Ch'ing: State, Region and Individual in a Period of Conquest," Palm Springs, Calif., 27 November–1 December, 1974). For India and Southeast Asia, see Justus M. Van Der Kroef, "Javanese Messianic Expectations: Their Origin and Cultural Context," *Comparative Studies in Society and History* 1 (1959): 299–323 or his "Messianic Movements in the Celebes, Sumatra and Borneo," pp. 80–121 in Sylvia L. Thrupp, ed., *Millennial Dreams in Action*; Stephen Fuchs, *Rebellious Prophets: A Study of Messianic Movements in Indian Religions* (New York: Asia Publishing House, 1965); Kitsiri Malalgoda, "Millennialism in Relation to Buddhism," *Comparative Studies in Society and History* 12 (1970): 424–41; and Sheldon Shapiro, "Patterns of Religious Reformations," *Comparative Studies in Society and History* 15 (1973): 143–57.

APPENDIX 2

1 KKCK 204.1, 18/9/19 Fan Ts'ai; KCT 018945, 20/6/13 Composite confession; CFA 59, 20/2/27 Keng Shih-an; CFCL 1.22–27, 18/9/15 Ts'ui Shih-chün.

2 SYT 349–51, 22/9/24 Wang Pi.

3 NYC 40.3–6, 20/5/27 Kuo Lo-yun.

4 SYT 355–56, 22/9/24 Wu Hsien-ta; SYT 209–11, 20/7/11 Liu Chin-pao; SYT 331–33, 22/9/24 Wang Liang; KCT 015816, 19/6/26 Li T'ien-hsiang; SYT 97–99, 19/7/7 Li T'ien-shou; KKCK 209.1–2, 18/9/28 Li Lao.

5 CFCL 28.11–13, 18/12/24 Liang Chien-chung; SYT 15–17, 19/10/3 Chung Yu-i; SYT 171–90, 22/9/14 Composite confession; KKCK 211.2, 18/10/2 Li Chiu; KKCK 209.1–2, 18/9/28 Li Lao; KKCK 222.1–2, 18/10/16 Kuo Ch'ao-chün; SYT 97–99, 19/7/7 Li T'ien-shou.

6 SYT 331–33, 22/9/24 Wang Liang; KCT 017364, 19/2/26 Mrs. Chu Hsing.

7 KKCK 232.1–3, 18/10/26 Wang Wu. See also Frank H. H. King, *Money and*

Monetary Policy in China, 1845–1895, or P'eng Hsin-wei, *Chung-kuo huo-pi shih* [A History of Chinese currency].

In 1870 a Western missionary in Fukien attempted to survey the "typical" expenditures by Chinese for religious festivals and observances during the year. The ten people he sampled spent an average of nearly 20,000 cash each year for these activities. See the anonymous article "On Native Contributions" *Chinese Recorder* 2 (1870): 211–15.

APPENDIX 3

1 Northern Chihli: KCT 011671, 13/8/1 Ch'en Mao-lin; NYC 36.18–20, 19/12/14 Memorial from Na-yen-ch'eng. Southern Chihli: NYC 37.25–27, 19/9/8 Memorial from Na-yen-ch'eng.
2 KCT 011671, 13/8/1 Ch'en Mao-lin.
3 Temple land: NYC 41.32–35, 21/4/18 Memorial from Na-yen-ch'eng. Rest: KCT 016810, 19/11/15 Memorial from the governor of Honan.
4 SYT 291–97, 19/3/15 Composite confession.
5 SYT 593, 19/9/29 Han Chih.
6 Ibid.
7 SYT 369–71, 19/12/14 Tung Erh.
8 KKCK 221.1–3, 18/10/16 Tung Kuo-t'ai.
9 NYC 35.28–30, 19/1/16 Memorial from Na-yen-ch'eng.
10 KKCK 221.1–3, 18/10/16 Tung Kuo-t'ai. This seems quite high.
11 Room rents: SYT 163, 20/2/17 Chiang K'uan; SYT 169, 20/2/17 Wang Ssu; SYT 121–24, 19/12/4 Sung Kuang-pi. Food for militia: *Chi-ning district gazetteer* 4.30–35. Other food: KKCK 229.1–2, 18/10/23 Han Ta-tzu; CFCL 3.26, 18/9/18 Edict.
12 Knife: KKCK 211.1, 18/9/29 Li Yü-lung. Cloth: KCT 016531, 19/10/7 Chang San. People: KCT 017829, 20/2/13 Li Ta-wang; KKCK 230.1, 18/10/24 Chang K'un. For similar lists of prices in Peking in the 1790s as noted by a Western visitor, see J. L. Cranmer-Byng, ed., *An Embassy to China . . .* , p. 244.

Selected Bibliography

Arlington, L. C., and Lewisohn, William. *In Search of Old Peking*. Peking: Henri Vetch, 1935.

Balfour, Frederic H. *Taoist Texts*. Shanghai: Kelly and Walsh, ca. 1884.

Bodde, Derk, and Morris, Clarence. *Law in Imperial China*. Cambridge: Harvard University Press, 1967.

Boulais, Guy, trans. *Manuel du Code Chinois*. Variétés sinologiques series no. 55. Shanghai, 1924; reprint ed., Taipei, 1966.

Brunnert, H. S., and Hagelstrom, V. V. *Present Day Political Organization of China*. Trans. A. Beltchenko and E. E. Moran. Shanghai, 1912.

CFA. See Abbreviations Used in Notes.

CFCL. See Abbreviations Used in Notes.

Chan Hok-lam. "The White Lotus–Maitreya Doctrine and Popular Uprisings in Ming and Ch'ing China." *Sinologica* 10 (1969): 211–33.

Chan, Wing-tsit. *Religious Trends in Modern China*. New York: Columbia University Press, 1953.

Chang Chung-li. *The Chinese Gentry*. Seattle: University of Washington Press, 1955.

———. *The Income of the Chinese Gentry*. Seattle: University of Washington Press, 1962.

Chang I-ch'un 張一純. "Kuan-yü T'ien-li-chiao ch'i-i erh-san shih" 關於天理教起義二三事 [A few things about the T'ien-li sect uprising]. *Li-shih chiao-hsueh* 歷史教學 1 (1962): 23–25.

Chao I 趙翼. *Yen-p'u tsa-chi* 簷曝雜記 [Miscellaneous notes]. 1877.

Chao-lien 昭槤. *Hsiao-t'ing tsa-lu* 嘯亭雜錄 [Miscellaneous notes from the Hsiao pavilion]. Completed ca. 1814–15; Shanghai, 1880.

Chao Tung-shu 趙東書. *Li-chiao shih-hua* 理教史畫 [An illustrated history of the Li sect]. Taipei, 1956.

Chao Wei-pang. "Secret Religious Societies in North China in the Ming Dynasty." *Folklore Studies* 7 (1948): 95–115.

Ch'en, Jerome. "Secret Societies." *Ch'ing-shih wen-t'i* 青史問題 1, no. 3 (1966): 13–16.

Ch'en, Kenneth K. S. *Buddhism in China*. Princeton: Princeton University Press, 1964.

Cheng Ho-sheng 鄭鶴聲. *Chin-shih chung-hsi shih jih tui-chao piao* 近世中西史日對照表 [An equivalency chart for dates in Chinese and Western history for the modern period]. Reprint ed., Taipei: Commercial Press, 1966.

Ch'eng-wu district gazetteer (Shantung): *Ch'eng-wu hsien-chih* 城武縣志. 1830.

Chesneaux, Jean. "Secret Societies in China's Historical Evolution." In *Popular Movements and Secret Societies in China, 1840–1950*, pp. 1–22. Edited by Jean Chesneaux. Stanford: Stanford University Press, 1972.

Chi-ning district gazetteer (Shantung): *Chi-ning chih-li chou-chih* 濟寧直隸州志. 1840.

Chia-ch'ing ch'ung-hsiu i-t'ung-chih 嘉慶重修一通志 [A gazetteer for the nation revised during the Chia-ch'ing reign]. 1812; reprint ed., 1934.

Chiang Hsiang-nan 蔣湘南. *Ch'i-ching-lou wen-ch'ao* 七經樓文鈔 [Writings from the Ch'i-ching tower]. 1837.

Chihli province gazetteer: *Chi-fu t'ung-chih* 畿輔通志. 1884.

Chin-hsiang district gazetteer (Shantung): *Chin-hsiang hsien-chih* 金鄉縣志. 1860.

Ch'in-ting Ta-Ch'ing hui-tien shih-li 欽定大清會典事例 [Imperial Ch'ing statutes and precedents], 1818.

Chü-yeh district gazetteer (Shantung): *Chü-yeh hsien-chih* 鉅野縣志. 1840.

Chu, Richard Yung-teh. "An Introductory Study of the White Lotus Sect in Chinese History." Ph.D. dissertation, Columbia University, 1967.

Ch'u T'ung-tsu. *Local Government in China under the Ch'ing*. Cambridge: Harvard University Press, 1962.

Couling, Samuel. *Encyclopedia Sinica*. Shanghai: Kelly and Walsh, 1917.

CPT. See Abbreviations Used in Notes.

Cranmer-Byng, J. L., ed. *An Embassy to China, Being the journal kept by Lord Macartney during his embassy to the Emperor Ch'ien-lung 1793–1794*. Hamden, Conn.: Archon Books, 1963.

CSL. See Abbreviations Used in Notes.

De Bary, William Theodore. "Introduction." In *Self and Society in Ming Thought*, pp. 1–27. Edited by W. T. de Bary. New York: Columbia University Press, 1970.

de Groot. *See* Groot.

Deliusin, Lev. "The I-kuan Tao Society." In *Popular Movements and Secret Societies in China, 1840–1950*, pp. 225–33. Edited by Jean Chesneaux. Stanford: Stanford University Press, 1972.

Dubs, Homer H. "An Ancient Chinese Mystery Cult." *Harvard Theological Review* 35 (1942): 221–40.

Edkins, Joseph. "Books of the Modern Religious Sects in North China." *Chinese Recorder* 19 (1888): 261–68, 302–10.

———. *Chinese Buddhism: A volume of sketches, historical, descriptive and critical*. London, 1880.

———. *Religion in China*. 2d ed. Boston, 1878.

Edwards, Randle; Chang Wejen; and Chang Ch'en Fu-mei, trans. "Voluntary Surrender: Cases and Materials." Paper prepared for the East Asian Legal Studies Program, Harvard University.

Groot, J. J. M. de. *Sectarianism and Religious Persecution in China*. Amsterdam, 1903–04; reprint ed., 2 vols in 1, Taipei, 1969.

Grootaers, Willem. "Une séance de spiritism dans une religion secrète à Péking en 1948." *Mélanges chinois et bouddhiques* 9 (1948–51): 92–98.

———. "Une societé secrete moderne, 一貫道 I-Kuan-Tao, Bibliographie annotée." *Folklore Studies* 5 (1946): 316–52.

Ho Ping-ti. *Studies on the Population of China, 1368–1953*. Cambridge: Harvard University Press, 1959.

Hodous, Lewis. "Chinese Conceptions of Paradise." *Chinese Recorder* 45 (1914): 358–71.

Hsiang Chueh-ming 向覺明. "Ming-Ch'ing chih-chi chih pao-chüan wen-hsueh yü Pai-lien-chiao." 明清之際之寶卷文學與白蓮教 [The White Lotus sect and the sacred scroll literature of the Ming-Ch'ing transition period]. *Wen-hsueh* 文學 2, no. 6 (1934): 1218–25.

Hsiao Kung-chuan. *Rural China: Imperial Control in the Nineteenth Century*. Seattle: University of Washington Press, 1960.

Hsiao Yü-min 蕭育民. "Ch'ing Chia-ch'ing T'ien-li-chiao ch'i-i" 清嘉慶天理教起義 [The T'ien-li sect rebellion in the Chia-ch'ing reign of the Ch'ing dynasty]. In *Chung-kuo nung-min ch'i-i lun-chi* 中國農民起義論集 [Discussions on peasant uprisings in China]. Edited by Li-shih chiao-hsueh yueh-k'an she 歷史教學月刊社. 2d edition. Peking, 1958.

Hsiung Te-chi 熊德基. "Chung-kuo nung-min chan-cheng yü tsung-chiao chi ch'i hsiang-kuan chu wen-t'i" 中國農民戰爭與宗教及其相關諸問題 [Several questions on the relationship between peasant wars and religion in China]. *Li-shih lun-ts'ung* 歷史論叢 1 (1964): 79–102.

Hua district gazetteer (Honan): *Hua hsien chih* 滑縣志. 1867.

Huang Yü-p'ien 黃育楩. *P'o-hsieh hsiang-pien* 破邪詳辯 [A detailed refutation of heterodoxy]. 1883. (Abbreviated PHHP.)

Hummel, Arthur W., ed. *Eminent Chinese of the Ch'ing Period*. Washington D.C.: Government Printing Office, 1943–44.

Inglis, James. "The Hun Yuen Men 混元門." *Chinese Recorder* 39 (1908): 270–71.

Institute of Pacific Relations. *Agrarian China: Selected Source Materials from Chinese Authors*. London: George Allen & Unwin, 1939.

Jackson, Abraham V. W. *Researches in Manicheism*. New York, 1932.

———. "A Sketch of the Manichean Doctrine Concerning the Future Life." *Journal of the American Oriental Society* 50 (1930): 177–98.

James, F. H. "North China Sects." *Chinese Recorder* 30 (1899): 74–76.

K'ai district gazetteer (Chihli): *K'ai chou chih* 開州志. 1882.

Kates, George N. *The Years That Were Fat: Peking 1933–1940*. New York: Harper & Bros., 1952.

KCT. See Abbreviations Used in Notes.

King, Frank H. H. *Money and Monetary Policy in China, 1845–1895*. Cambridge: Harvard University Press, 1965.

KKCK. See Abbreviations Used in Notes.

Kuhn, Philip A. *Rebellion and Its Enemies in Late Imperial China: Militariza-*

tion and Social Structure, 1796–1864. Cambridge: Harvard University Press, 1970.

Lan-i wai-shih. *See* Sheng Ta-shih.

Leboucq, Prosper. *Associations de la Chine: Lettres du P. Leboucq, missionaire au Tche-ly sud-est*. Paris, 1880.

Lee, Robert H. G. *The Manchurian Frontier in Ch'ing History*. Cambridge: Harvard University Press, 1970.

Li Shih-yü 李世瑜, ed. *Pao-chüan tsung-lu* 寶卷綜錄 [A comprehensive bibliography of sacred scrolls]. Peking, 1961.

Li Shou-k'ung 李守孔. "Ming-tai Pai-lien-chiao k'ao-lueh" 明代白蓮教考略 [A brief study of the White Lotus sect in the Ming period], pp. 17–47 in *Ming-tai tsung-chiao* 明代宗教 [Religion during the Ming], vol. 10 of *Ming-shih lun-ts'ung* 明史論叢 [Collected essays on Ming history]. Edited by Pao Tsun-p'eng 包遵彭. Taipei: Student Bookstore, 1968.

Liu Ts'un-yan. "Taoist Self-Cultivation in Ming Thought." In *Self and Society in Ming Thought*, pp. 291–330. Edited by W. T. de Bary. New York: Columbia University Press, 1970.

Lofland, John. *Doomsday Cult: A Study of Conversion, Proselytization, and Maintenance of Faith*. Englewood Cliffs, N.J.: Prentice-Hall, 1966.

Maspero, Henri. "The Mythology of Modern China." In *Asiatic Mythology*, pp. 252–84. Edited by J. Hackin et al. London, 1932.

————. "Procédés de 'nourir le principe vital' dans la religion Taoiste ancienne." *Journal Asiatique* 229 (1937): 177–252, 353–430.

Meech, S. Evan. "The Northern Rebellion." Letter to the Editor in *Chinese Recorder* 23 (1892): 135–36.

Miles, George. "Vegetarian Sects." *Chinese Recorder* 33 (1902): 1–10.

Morohashi Tetsuji 諸橋轍次, ed. *Dai Kan-Wa jiten* 大漢和辭典 [Dictionary of Chinese]. Tokyo, 1960.

Myers, Ramon H. *The Chinese Peasant Economy: Agricultural Development in Hopei and Shantung, 1890–1949*. Cambridge: Harvard University Press, 1970.

Naquin, Susan. "Millenarian Rebellion in China: The Eight Trigrams Uprising of 1813." Ph.D. dissertation, Yale University, 1974.

NYC. See Abbreviations Used in Notes.

Onoda Sayoko 小野田サヨ子. "Kakei jūhachinen no tenrikyōdo no ran ni tsuite" 嘉慶十八年の天理教徒の亂について [A study of the rebellion by the T'ien-li sect in the year Chia-ch'ing 18]. *Shisō* 史草 7, no. 10 (1966): 44–58.

Overmyer, Daniel L. "Folk-Buddhist Religion: Creation and Eschatology in Medieval China." *History of Religions* 12, no. 1 (1972): 42–69.

————. *Folk Buddhist Religion: Dissenting Sects in Late Traditional China*. Cambridge: Harvard University Press, forthcoming.

————. "The Tz'u-hui t'ang: A Contemporary Religious Sect on Taiwan." Paper presented at the annual meeting of the Canadian Society for Asian Studies, June 1974, University of Toronto.

P'eng Hsin-wei 彭信威. *Chung-kuo huo-pi shih* 中國貨幣史 [A history of Chinese currency]. Shanghai, 1954.

PHHP. See Abbreviations Used in Notes.

Porter, Henry D. "A Modern Shantung Prophet." *Chinese Recorder* 18 (1887): 12–21.

Sawada Mizuho 澤田瑞穂. "Koyo-kyō no shi-tan" 弘陽教の試探 [Preliminary remarks on the Hung-yang sect]. *Tenri daigaku gakuho* 天理大學學報 24 (1957): 63–85.

Seidel, Anna K. *La Divinization de Lao Tseu dans le Taoisme des Han.* Paris: École Francaise d'Extreme Orient, 1969.

———. "The Image of the Perfect Ruler in Early Taoist Messianism: Lao-Tzu and Li Hung." *History of Religions* 9 (1969–70): 216–47.

Serruys, Paul. "Folklore Contributions in *Sino-Mongolica*: Notes on Customs, Legends, Proverbs, and Riddles of the Province of Jehol, Introduction and Translations." *Folklore Studies* 6 (1947): 1–128.

Shantung province gazetteer: Shan-tung t'ung-chih 山東通志. 1911.

Sheng Ta-shih 盛大士 [Lan-i wai-shih 蘭蕟外史]. *Ching-ni chi* 靖逆記 [Account of the suppression of the rebels]. 1820.

Smith, Arthur H. "Sketches of a Country Parish." *Chinese Recorder* 12 (1882): 245–66, 317–44; 13 (1882): 280–99.

Soothill, William E., and Hodous, Lewis. *A Dictionary of Chinese Buddhist Terms.* London, 1937.

Spence, Jonathan D. *Ts'ao Yin and the K'ang-hsi Emperor: Bondservant and Master.* New Haven: Yale University Press, 1966.

SSTC. See Abbreviations Used in Notes.

Sung Hsiang 宋湘. *Hung-hsing shan-fang i-kao* 紅杏山房遺簾 [Posthumous works from the Hung-hsing study]. Ca. 1826; reprint ed., Taipei, 1971.

SYT. See Abbreviations Used in Notes.

Ta-ming prefecture gazetteer (Chihli): *Ta-ming fu-chih* 大名府志 1853.

Tai Hsuan-chih 戴玄之. *Hung-ch'iang hui* 紅槍會 *(1916–1949)* [The Red Spear Society, 1916–1949]. Taipei, 1973.

T'ao Ch'eng-chang 陶成章. *Chiao-hui yuan-liu k'ao* 教會源流考 [A Study of the origins of sects and societies]. Canton, 1910. Reprinted in *Chin-tai mi-mi she-hui shih-liao* 近代秘密社會史料 [Historical materials on modern secret societies]. Edited by Hsiao I-shan 蕭一山. 2d edition, Taipei, 1965.

T'ao Hsi-sheng 陶希聖. "Ming-tai Mi-le Pai-lien-chiao chi ch'i-t'a'yao-tsei" ' 明代彌勒白蓮教及其他'妖賊' [Maitreya and White Lotus sect members and other religious rebels of the Ming period]. pp. 5–16 in *Ming-tai tsung-chiao* 明代宗教 [Religion during the Ming], vol. 10 of *Ming-shih lun-ts'ung* 明史論叢 [Collected essays on Ming history]. Edited by Pao Tsun-p.eng 包遵彭. Taipei: Student Bookstore, 1968.

Topley, Marjorie. "The Great Way of Former Heaven: A Group of Chinese Secret Religious Sects." *Bulletin of the School of Oriental and African Studies* 26 (1963): 362–92.

Tung-ming district gazetteer (Chihli): *Tung-ming hsien-chih hsu* 東明縣志續. 1911.

Vichert, Clarence G. "Fundamental Principles in Chinese Boxing." *Journal of the West China Border Research Society* 7 (1935): 43–46.

Wei-hui prefecture gazetteer (Honan): *Wei-hui fu-chih* 衛輝府志. 1788.

Wei Yuan 魏源. *Sheng-wu chi* 聖武記 [Record of imperial campaigns] 1842.

Welch, Holmes H. "The Bellagio Conference on Taoist Studies." *History of Religions* 9 (1969–70): 107–36.

Wilhelm, Richard. *The Soul of China*. New York: Harcourt Brace, 1928.

Williamson, Alexander. *Journeys in North China, Manchuria, and Eastern Mongolia*. London, 1870.

Yang, C. K. *Religion in Chinese Society*. Berkeley: University of California Press, 1961.

Yang Fang 楊芳. *Kung-ch'uan [Yang] Kuo-yung-hou tzu-pien nien-p'u* 宮傅[楊] 果勇候自編年譜 [Autobiography of Yang Fang]. 1840.

Yano Jinichi 矢野仁一. "Kuan-yü Pai-lien-chiao chih luan" 關於白蓮教之 亂 [On the White Lotus sect rebellion]. Translated from the Japanese by Yang T'ieh-fu. *Jen-wen yueh-k'an* 人文月刊 6, nos. 1 and 2 (February and March 1935): 1–8 and 9–20.

Yao Yuan-chih 姚元之. *Chu-yeh-t'ing tsa-chi* 竹葉亭雜記 [Miscellaneous jottings from the Chu-yeh pavilion]. 1893; reprint ed., Taipei, 1969.

Glossary-Index